R. Murray Schafer

R. Murray Schafer

A Creative Life

L. Brett Scott

ROWMAN & LITTLEFIELD
Lanham • Boulder • New York • London

Published by Rowman & Littlefield
An imprint of The Rowman & Littlefield Publishing Group, Inc.
4501 Forbes Boulevard, Suite 200, Lanham, Maryland 20706
www.rowman.com

6 Tinworth Street, London SE11 5AL, United Kingdom

Copyright © 2019 by L. Brett Scott

All rights reserved. No part of this book may be reproduced in any form or by any electronic or mechanical means, including information storage and retrieval systems, without written permission from the publisher, except by a reviewer who may quote passages in a review.

British Library Cataloguing in Publication Information Available

Library of Congress Cataloging-in-Publication Data

Names: Scott, Brett (L. Brett) author.
Title: R. Murray Schafer : a creative life / L. Brett Scott.
Description: Lanham : Rowman & Littlefield, [2019] | Includes bibliographical references, discography, and index.
Identifiers: LCCN 2018041967 (print) | LCCN 2018042861 (ebook) | ISBN 9780810888265 (Electronic) | ISBN 9780810888258 (cloth) | ISBN 9781538158234 (pbk) Subjects: LCSH: Schafer, R. Murray. | Composers—Canada—Biography. | Schafer, R. Murray—Criticism and interpretation.
Classification: LCC ML410.S228 (ebook) | LCC ML410.S228 S26 2019 (print) | DDC 780.92 [B]—dc23
LC record available at https://lccn.loc.gov/2018041967

Contents

Acknowledgments	vii
Part I: The Biography	**1**
1 Childhood and Early Adulthood	3
2 Uncertainty, the Temporal Muse, and Wanderlust	19
3 Homecoming and Education from the Other Side	37
4 Academia, Notoriety, and New Endeavors	49
5 Country Life, Renewed Creativity, and Change	67
6 Two Loves, Financial Concerns, and the *Patria* Cycle	83
7 Loneliness, Reconciliation, Happiness, and New Challenges	103
Part II: The Writings	**119**
8 The Educational Writings	121
9 Soundscape Publications	139
10 Scholarly Writing and Nonfiction	157
11 Works of Fiction	175
Part III: The Theatrical Works	**185**
12 *Loving* and the Non-*Patria* Theatrical Works	187
13 The *Patria* Cycle	205
Part IV: The Compositions	**239**
14 Early and Transitional Compositions	241
15 The Compositions for Choir	259

16	The Compositions for Voice	279
17	The Concerti and Other Orchestral Works	293
18	The Chamber, Solo, and Electronic Compositions	315

Appendix A: Chronological List of Compositions — 333

Appendix B: Select Discography — 345

Notes — 347

Bibliography — 365

Index — 369

About the Author — 379

Acknowledgments

Although numerous people helped along the way, the book would not have happened at all were it not for three special individuals. The first is the subject of this book, R. Murray Schafer, who responded warmly in 2001 to a doctoral student that wished to write about his choral music. The second is his wife, Eleanor James. The two of them opened their lives and home to me over many years, helping to fashion the relationship that is the foundation of this book.

The third is my wife, Krista. She was the one who first suggested and then insisted that this book should be written. She was my companion throughout this process, encouraging, copyediting, and questioning when needed. She is as much a part of this book as she is a part of my life. This is for you, Amor.

Part I

The Biography

Chapter One

Childhood and Early Adulthood

FAMILY BACKGROUND

Raymond Murray Schafer was born on the eighteenth of July 1933 in Sarnia, Ontario, Canada. Shortly before his birth his parents had moved there from the western province of Manitoba. His mother, born Belle Anderson Rose, grew up near Souris, Manitoba, in the small rural community of Bunelody.[1] Her family was originally from Warsaw, Ontario, but like many entrepreneurial residents of eastern Canada they had traveled west in the late 1800s to take advantage of the cheap farmland offered by the Canadian government to encourage settlement of the country's vast western territories. Murray's father Harold Schafer was born in Erie, Illinois, but his family immigrated to Manitoba in the early twentieth century. Joe Schafer, Murray's paternal grandfather, first settled in Moline but later moved to the town of McConnell, where he built a combination hotel and boarding house and operated it with the family until 1922. That year he sold the business and relocated his family to the larger community of Hamiota, there to take over the proprietorship of the boarding house and hotel next to the railroad. As in many rural Manitoba towns of the early twentieth century, the railway was the main transportation hub and lifeline of the community,[2] connecting it directly to the provincial capital of Winnipeg. Crew members that came out on the trains from Winnipeg to load up grain cars from the local elevator would stay overnight at the Schafers' hotel. Although Hamiota remains a vibrant town, both Moline and McConnell have gone the way of many small prairie communities: a name on a sign, with no buildings.

After the move to Hamiota, Harold served as an overnight guard in the town bank, sleeping in the building with a loaded revolver. In the winter his morning routine would include shoveling out the snow that had drifted under the door overnight and preparing tea for the bank employees when they arrived shivering in the morning cold.[3] In 1924 Harold was hired as a stock clerk for the Imperial Oil Company with an initial posting in Brandon, the largest city in western Manitoba. As he moved up the company's ranks he was transferred to Ontario, first to Sarnia in 1932 then to Toronto in 1934. He continued to have success in his career, achieving the rank of western accounting supervisor in 1943. This position required extensive traveling and often extended stays of weeks or even months at the various regional offices that he oversaw. Harold retired in 1965 and passed away in 1980.[4] Belle followed him in 1994.

CHILDHOOD — AN ARTIST IN SPITE OF HIMSELF

A year after the transfer to Sarnia, Raymond Murray Schafer was born, weighing eight pounds and twelve ounces at birth. His brother David Paul Schafer joined the family on January 26, 1937.[5] Paul was also destined to pursue a career in the arts, but primarily as an arts administrator, serving for a while as assistant director of the Ontario Arts Council and helping to establish York University's Arts Administration Program.[6] In recounting their childhood, Paul recalls that Murray, being four years older, would often bully his younger brother. Paul would exact his revenge by beating him at cards or at hockey, which would drive Murray to distraction. The thrashings at the hands of his older brother ended when Paul was fifteen and finally able to physically turn the tables on his sibling. This led to a rebalancing of the relationship, and the two brothers have maintained a close connection through their adult life.[7]

After the Schafers' relocation to Ontario, Belle continued to maintain close ties with her family and childhood home in Manitoba. Starting in 1935, she would take Murray, and later Murray and Paul, on an annual trip back to the family farm.[8] In the first half of the twentieth century, train travel was the only viable method of making the long trip from southern Ontario to Manitoba. Belle and the two boys would share a sleeper on the train that left Toronto for western Canada late at night. When observation cars were introduced the boys would enjoy looking at the passing scenery for hours. They would leave the train at Brandon, staying a few days in the city to visit with Murray's maternal grandparents, then going on to the farm near Souris. During these summer visits the boys threw themselves into the life of the farm, doing assigned chores or catching gophers to collect the two-cent bounty offered by the municipality for each gopher tail.[9] Even though Murray was raised and educated in the urban environs of Toronto, these fondly remembered annual trips to western Canada developed in the growing boy a love for rural life that would strongly influence both his life choices and his artistic output.

Figure 1.1. Murray and Paul Schafer. *R. Murray Schafer*

Murray received piano lessons from the age of six with a local teacher, Miss Lindsey. He later speculates that his parents, particularly his mother, thought that piano lessons would be good medicine for him.[10] The Schafer household was a musical one; his father had had no formal lessons but had taught himself to play some pieces on the piano, including the first movement of Beethoven's "Moonlight Sonata." His mother had had lessons and often played for the enjoyment of it.[11] His creativity and curious mind first evidenced itself primarily in non-musical ways. According to his parents, he had remarkable muscle control and coordination from an early age and was able to realize forms and shapes from age three, with the unusual habit of drawing figures from the bottom up, always ending with the head.[12] Both parents were supportive of their son's early artistic aspirations, and his passion for painting and drawing continued as he grew older, expressing itself at around age eight or nine through the medium of comic books. His creations, branded *Trigger Comics*, had stories about various heroes that Schafer created, including the Black Doom, Two-Gun Manitoba, and Hop Harrigan. The inspiration for the stories came from the serial stories that Schafer would hear in the evenings on the radio. Murray soon discovered that he could rent his creations overnight to other students to generate income, income which he was allowed to keep, and that he generally used to buy chocolate bars. Schafer's developing talent in the visual arts was all the more remarkable due to his handicap—he had been born cross-eyed and almost blind in one eye. Paired with his passion for the visual arts was an obsession with building things, whether a train and tracks or a church with celluloid stained glass windows, a full-size racing car or a human-drawn stagecoach.[13] Even though the Schafer household was not in need of extra money, it was still expected that both Murray and Paul would contribute to the family finances by taking various odd jobs. From the age of eight Murray variously held positions as a newspaper deliverer, and an odd-job person, first at the local drugstore, and later an apothecary.[14]

When he was eight years of age, Murray's bad eye started to constantly ache. The diagnosis was glaucoma and an operation was recommended. This first operation was unsuccessful, and in a second operation the surgeons removed the eye and put in an artificial one.[15] His return to school after a few weeks' recovery was expectedly tough. He would regularly be met by a gang of boys who would taunt him and beat him up because he looked different with his glass eye.[16] This situation was not helped by the fact that although Schafer wanted to play sports, his parents wished him to stay clear of rough physical activities. As a result he didn't play football or hockey growing up, which further separated him from his male peers.[17] Looking back on his often unpleasant grade school experiences at Humewood Public School in Toronto, Schafer is somewhat philosophical. He posits that this helped him develop mental and physical toughness, valuable assets for a creative person.[18] He remembers an isolated high point, winning a gold medal for public speaking in grade seven. He also remembers the at times severe discipline of the teachers and the strictly ordered regimen of the days.[19] His dislike of public school is confirmed by his parents, who mention that he was largely self-taught. After coming home from school he would read every book in sight, picking up the knowledge not taught at all or taught in a way that he could not grasp in school.[20]

Despite his physical limitations, Murray continued to develop his abilities as a visual artist. This pursuit was encouraged both by his father, who was also an amateur visual artist who sketched and painted, and his mother, although Murray doesn't recall his father ever asking him what he wanted to be when he grew up.[21] He and his brother also kept up their piano lessons, and by the middle of elementary school Murray was proficient enough to play pieces by Brahms and Beethoven along with such popular tunes as "Bumble Boogie."[22] He also enjoyed playing flashy, extended improvisations that explored the full extent and colors available to him from the keyboard.[23]

THE TEENAGE YEARS

If the young Murray's experiences in grade school were unpleasant, his high school experiences were much worse. He found high school "a revolting experience. I hated every moment of it. It was the most vile five years of my life."[24] Although he had scored highly on the IQ test given to the high school students, he remained at the bottom of almost all of his classes. He did not get on well with his teachers, who apparently had no appreciation for his artistic ambitions (the exception being his art teacher Miss Higgins) and thought him an academic failure. Some even went so far as to recommend (on several occasions) that he leave school altogether. A few comments from his report card from February 1950 bear this out.

> Miss Higgins: Art—possesses great talent in art; very much above average; has been slow in work but has improved also in art since Christmas.
>
> Mr. Harston: Physics—attitude—respectful, fairly attentive, sometimes mind wanders; work—just average; grasp of subject—indifferent; prognosis—uncertain.
>
> Miss Tighe: History—(grade 11)—this student consistently neglects his work and seemingly makes no effort. He is no problem in conduct since he simply sits in class. He takes my class period one, and has already been late three times. I believe he failed in his final examination in grade ten and suggest that he go back to Canadian History unless he shows definite and immediate improvement.[25]

At various points in high school he was failing all of his classes except art, and by grade eleven he had even begun to fail his art classes. He would later remark that the high school experience led him to feel that he was completely expendable as a human being.[26] It is likely that as a sensitive, artistically inclined teenager he was less adept at hiding his adolescent anxieties than some of his peers.[27] Coupled with this was his (most likely accurate) perception that the antagonism toward his artistic ability coming from his teachers and classmates was reflective of a general antagonism toward the arts in Canadian society as a whole during this time. He has in several interviews recalled an encounter with the guidance counselor at his high school, to whom Schafer expressed his desire to become a painter. When the counselor discovered that he meant an abstract painter, not a commercial, or even a house painter, his response was discouraging in the least. "Now look here, young man. You're going to have a wife and family and you're going to have to look after them. How are you going to support them with the kind of money you're going to make from those dizzy paintings?"[28] Outside of his achievements in the visual arts (he began to produce some very fine paintings in high school), the only other bright spot in his high school career was his interest in sports, in particular football, but primarily as a coach since his parents discouraged him from playing overly physical sports. For a few years Murray coached a team at the local High Park YMCA. Reflective of the young man's intense personality, he immersed himself in the study of strategy, reading several books written by American football coaches, and even going as far as to correspond with some of those coaches, including the legendary Frank Leahy, who was still at Notre Dame at the time.[29] He recounts with pride the phenomenal success of the team, which not only did not lose any games but did not give up a single touchdown.[30] He continued to coach football until about age twenty-one, when he left Toronto. Looking back he speculates that he applied the same level of craftsmanship to sports that he now applies to his art. As an adult, sports would bore him.[31]

Murray's first significant encounter with literature was reading Charles Dickens's *Great Expectations* in grade ten. From there he moved on to other classics, going so far as to commit the entire text of *Macbeth* to memory in grade eleven or twelve, proving his nascent ability to master a subject when it truly interested him. This interest did result in improved grades in English Literature, but not English Composition, where the assignments were too rigid and unimaginative to inspire effort.[32] A grade-twelve essay based on an imagined conversation between Schafer and the philosopher Nietzsche, whose writings he had been studying, was failed by his teacher, who simply wrote "Don't lie!" on the paper.[33] With all of these antagonistic figures in Murray's school life, it is truly fortunate that at home his family was supportive, if not entirely comprehending, of his focus on the arts.[34]

Perhaps the most remarkable thing about Schafer's high school transcript is the total absence of any music classes whatsoever, due at least in part to the limited offerings at the school (for example, the only ensemble was a brass band that was not as good as the one he had played in as a Boy Scout in elementary school). As with many of his other significant artistic experiences, his musical epiphanies occurred outside the school grounds. He continued lessons through adolescence on the instrument he called "an overdecorated hearse" and became proficient enough that it was expected that he would earn a piano degree. His mother had hopes for his advancement in this area and made certain that he studied with the best teachers in Toronto. His final teacher in high school, Douglas Bodle, preferred that he earn a piano Licentiate of the Royal Schools of Music (LRSM) from London, England, rather than the certificate offered by the Royal Conservatory of Music.[35] His examiner was Sir William McKay, who was at the time the organist at Westminster Abbey and who had traveled to Canada to administer the licentiate exams. After writing a theory exam and giving a full-length recital, the young Schafer passed with distinction and received what was to be his only formal music certificate. After the exam McKay apparently asked to come to

Figure 1.2. Early Illustration—"Lucifer." *R. Murray Schafer*

the Schafers' house so that he could listen to Murray play some more.[36] At some point during this process the young Murray made the mistake of confessing his love for French music, especially the music of Les Six, and lost out on his chance for a scholarship to study in England, to his mother's great disappointment.[37]

Murray's other significant musical activity was singing, from around age ten, in a men's and boys' choir at a local Anglican church, Grace Church on-the-Hill in Forest Hill, one of the more affluent areas of Toronto. Murray's brother Paul had been singing there for a few years as a soprano, and Murray joined as an alto. The choir was conducted by John Hodgins, who also for a brief time gave Schafer organ lessons. These years singing in the choir instilled in him a lifelong interest in composing and performing choral music. In addition to receiving excellent musical training,[38] he enjoyed the added benefit of getting paid two or three dollars a month to sing.[39] While there he was exposed to the standards of choral repertoire; the church choir did an annual massed performance of *Messiah*, and once gave a performance of Benjamin Britten's *St. Nicholas Cantata*, with the composer conducting.[40] He would remain active in the church choir through his time at the University of Toronto, somewhat remarkable considering his increasingly unorthodox views on religion and its place in his life. He had found companionship with several of the members of the group, who would go out after rehearsals to the village cafe and talk about music (mostly vocal music), literature, and philosophy until the cafe would close for the night. He made an even more significant connection to one particular member of the choir, Phyllis Mailing, the alto soloist. Although Phyllis was six years older than him and engaged to be married, that did not deter Murray, and the two became lovers when Schafer was nineteen and had joined her as a student at the Royal Conservatory of Music.[41]

Around the same time as Schafer's literary epiphany courtesy of *Great Expectations*, he also experienced a musical epiphany, courtesy of Beethoven's *Fifth Piano Concerto*, heard on the radio of his parents' new (and first ever) car. It is interesting that it was this, of all the musical experiences he had already had (he had gone to several Toronto Symphony Orchestra concerts as a child with his father, who for at least one year had season tickets), that first turned his interest seriously to explore music. After this revelation from Beethoven he turned his musical interests from jazz and pop music to classical music.[42] Another significant musical revelation was hearing a performance of Berg's *Wozzeck* by the New York Philharmonic. He was eighteen or nineteen years old at the time, and he hadn't realized that such music could exist. The chance to hear a piece like *Wozzeck* was unusual as there was very little contemporary music being performed in Toronto in the 1950s.[43] In his early teens Murray began theory lessons and after completing all of the offered theory courses was accepted to continue his studies with the noted Canadian composer and teacher John Weinzweig. It was through Weinzweig that he was first exposed to the music of the French composers who made up Les Six, which led to the unfortunate exchange with Sir William McKay that lost him his potential scholarship from the Royal Schools of Music. Weinzweig recalls of Schafer during this time that he had already developed an interest in the relationship of word and tone and was interested in the philosophy of language. By the age of nineteen, Murray was much more interested and involved in music, and he turned his hand for the first time to composition, beginning (but never completing) work on an operetta that he hoped would attract a lot of girls.[44] This operetta was called "Haddon Hall" and is firmly in the Gilbert and Sullivan vein, both in the existing libretto, which is almost complete, and in the three or four musical selections that are sketched out ("Tubal Cain" for men's chorus, "Maiden's Song" for women's chorus, and a duet between the two protagonists, the Colonel and Phyllis.) Other than this larger effort, Schafer wrote some other sketches and shorter pieces, including a setting of "If Ye Love Me" for chorus in 1950, a set of short piano pieces in 1951, and one or two songs for voice and piano in the same year.

Although Murray was growing as an artist and musician outside academia, he continued to struggle at Vaughan Road Collegiate Institute. By the end of the twelfth grade he had managed to pass enough classes to achieve what was then labeled a junior matriculation. This allowed him to leave high school early if he chose, but a junior matriculation would not qualify him to attend university in Ontario. Faced with the choice of leaving high school or spending at least another year in misery, he left.[45]

ACADEMIA (FOR A WHILE)

At age eighteen and finally liberated from the Ontario public school system, Schafer was now faced with what he should do next. He still considered the visual arts his primary passion,[46] and his high school art teacher suggested that he apply to the Ontario School of Art. He was granted an interview, to which he brought several of his sketches and paintings, but after looking at the young man's offerings, the interviewer asked about Murray's right eye. Murray replied that he had an artificial eye, and the interviewer responded by saying that he would not recommend a career in art with such a disability. (In later writings, Schafer has often wondered how many great artists have suffered from imperfect vision.)

With the Ontario School of Art now closed to him, the young artist was forced to reevaluate his career path. As luck would have it, that year the Faculty of Music at the University of Toronto had initiated a new course of study, the Artist Diploma Program. This course was designed for students with high musical talent who didn't have the academic credentials to enter a traditional university program. These students would study with many of the same faculty and take many of the same courses as those studying for the bachelor of music degree but would obtain a certificate at the end of the three-year course.[47] Schafer's certificate through the Royal Schools of Music made him a good candidate for this performance-focused diploma program. John Weinzweig, who had joined the faculty at the University of Toronto, was also instrumental in bringing Schafer into this program and obtaining a scholarship for him.[48] Schafer studied for a year at Toronto's Royal Conservatory of Music[49] then entered the Artist Diploma Program to begin what would be a very brief university career.[50]

Since Schafer entered the Artist Diploma Program in the fall of 1952 ostensibly as a pianist, his primary teacher was Alberto Guerrero, the Chilean concert pianist who was the teacher of many notable students, including Glenn Gould and John Beckwith. Born in 1886, Guerrero had come to Cana-

Figure 1.3. Early Painting—*Ecclesia Dei. R. Murray Schafer*

da at the age of thirty-two after a successful concertizing career in the United States.[51] Schafer remembers fondly the lessons he had with Guerrero for a year and one-half, which ended up mostly in discussions about music since it was clear to Guerrero that this particular student had no interest in being a concert pianist. By all accounts Guerrero was an inspiring teacher who focused not only on the technical but also on the musical development of his students.[52] He was well versed in a variety of subjects, including philosophy, art, religion, and literature, and he was a nearly perfect fit for the inquisitive Schafer. Guerrero would ask him each week if he had practiced. When Murray inevitably answered no, Guerrero would ask him what he had done. When Schafer answered, "I read a book" or "I visited an art gallery," Guerrero would say, "Oh, tell me about it." They would talk for the half-hour lesson, often without touching the piano.[53]

Schafer also studied with Greta Kraus, the German harpsichordist who served as the university's early-music specialist. In the early 1950s harpsichord was still an unusual focus, with the Early Music Revival still in its early stages. Schafer found her love of early music infectious, and his preference for harpsichord over piano lasted long after his studies were over.[54] Through Kraus, Murray was exposed to the music and writings of C. P. E. Bach and J. J. Quantz, whose influence can be seen in the embellishments and rhythm of his early works, in particular the *Concerto for Harpsichord and Eight Wind Instruments*.[55] This influence came in spite of the fact that his lessons with Professor Kraus took a very similar form to those with Guerrero, as he and she both recall that he actually learned only one piece while studying with her.[56]

Schafer continued his studies with John Weinzweig while in the Artist Diploma Program, now adding analysis, orchestration, and finally composition to their lessons. John Weinzweig was the first significant Canadian composer to embrace the music of Stravinsky and Schoenberg and allow it to influence his own compositions. In this he was a solitary figure since musical culture in Ontario during the first half of the twentieth century was dominated by the nineteenth-century Anglo-romantic tradition. Contemporary music was rarely heard and even when heard not appreciated. Weinzweig had left these stifling confines and traveled to the United States to study at the Eastman School of Music, where he was exposed to the major trends in contemporary composition coming from Europe and America. Upon his return to Toronto he began taking students and was eventually offered a position teaching theory and composition at the University of Toronto Faculty of Music.[57] He was responsible for training an entire generation of prominent Canadian composers in the contemporary techniques he had been introduced to in the United States. The list of his students included Harry Somers, Harry Freedman, Norma Beecroft, and Robert Aitken.[58] Through Weinzweig's tutelage Murray was introduced to a wide array of modern styles, and in the Faculty of Music library the young musician was able to listen to recordings of the dodecaphonic works of Schoenberg and Berg and some pieces of Ives and Bartok, who were just emerging as important twentieth-century figures.[59]

As Schafer's first tentative steps toward composition began during this time, to Weinzweig's credit he did not try to force his student to adopt his compositional style or philosophy.[60] Schafer realized that his technique was far behind his peers Somers, Freedman, and Beckwith, and this created personal uncertainty about the pieces that he was producing during this time. Since his teacher's dodecaphonic technique was still far beyond him, he began with timid forays into polytonality, reflective of his continued interest in Les Six.[61] He did make enough progress during his studies with Weinzweig that he began to produce the first works that he considered worthy to be performed and published. He also wrote other works, including a *Toccata* for organ from 1952 and a *Te Deum* for choir and organ, both intended for Grace

Church on-the-Hill and John Hodgins. During his last year at the university, he, along with other student musicians, put on a concert of new music, including the first performance of a piece that would later be published as *A Music Lesson*, with Murray at the piano and Phyllis singing.[62] Schafer has recounted on several occasions what happened following the performance. "After our performance, I mouthed Stravinsky's credo that music is a nonemotional medium. 'Is that the way you feel about it?' someone asked from the audience. 'That's how I feel,' I said. Everyone laughed. I have never forgotten the humiliation of that day."[63]

Murray's schedule allowed him to attend lectures by the noted media theorist Marshall McLuhan as part of a class called Poetry and Music, which he had enrolled in along with a friend who was a graduate English major.[64] This course was originally taught by Lister Sinclair, noted radio personality with the Canadian Broadcasting Corporation, but after McLuhan stepped in to take over the lectures, class attendance dropped to such a degree that McLuhan was able to invite the students over to his house. This was due, as Schafer recalls, to McLuhan's extremely poor lectures.[65] The events at the house took the form of question and answer—a student would ask a question, and McLuhan would answer with far-ranging expositions that often landed a great distance from the original topic. In class there would be discussions of aesthetics; McLuhan's (then) developing communications theories; and such authors as James Joyce, Ezra Pound, Roger Fry, and Clive Bell.[66] Of these authors, the works of Ezra Pound in particular caught Schafer's imagination. Murray also took a class with early electronic music innovator Hugh LeCaine, but this particular class didn't talk much about music so was less useful for the emerging composer. LeCaine would later visit Murray at Simon Fraser University, and he admired Schafer's mix of live and electronic sounds in several of his later compositions.[67]

As a break from his academic studies Murray spent the summers of 1953 and 1954 at Doon Art School, held in the converted former home of internationally known Canadian landscape painter Homer Watson. These summers were a welcome respite, although Schafer no longer had any illusions about making a living as a visual artist. Schafer's primary teachers there, John Martin and Carl Schaeffer, did not think of his glass eye as a handicap for a visual artist. Two significant benefits came from this study. First, he was exposed for the first time to such notable visual artists as Klee, Kandinsky, Matisse, and Picasso, among others.[68] His admiration for Paul Klee was long lasting and had an influence on several of his early compositions, including *Concerto* and *Three Contemporaries*, and also his early writings.[69] Many of the visual techniques he learned there would find their way into his later graphic scores.[70] It was also at the Doon Art School that Schafer met Bob Walshe, who would become a lifelong friend and significant influence. The two would correspond regularly for the next fifty years and meet several times in Europe, particularly in France, where Walshe ultimately settled.

Despite the many benefits of the Artist's Diploma Program on Schafer's development as an artist, not everything was going well for this particular academic. Diploma students also took academic courses with the bachelor of music students, and this is where Schafer ran into trouble. In these courses, attendance was compulsory, and a roll-call was taken before every lecture.[71] The young radical had the same difficulty fitting into these structured academic courses as he had had in high school. Looking back, Schafer is harsh on his colleagues and the "puerile attitudes of these people who were content to hug their professors and do whatever they had to do to get through their courses."[72] As in high school the young student was content to ignore these aspects of his academic life and continue to self-direct his learning. Fellow students recall that across his dorm room at the University of Toronto he strung a clothesline to which were attached philosophical notes and relevant ideas from whatever author he happened to be reading at the time.[73]

Things finally came to a head for the student radical during Christmas time of his second year in the program. Part of the degree requirements for the Artist's Diploma was to participate in the faculty choir or orchestra.[74] The young student had requested to be excused from choir since he already had extensive choral experience, but this request was denied by Arnold Walter, director of the Faculty of Music.[75] Schafer resented this requirement and felt that the level of the choir (and the instruction) was below that of his church choir, where he had been exposed to the canon of Anglican church music from Elizabethan times to the music of Healey Willan. The choir director at the University of Toronto at that time, Dr. Richard Johnston, was a man with a sharp temper and short patience who programmed what Schafer called "sappy pop songs" and a "repertoire of tasteless and toothless chorus music."[76] As a form of protest, Schafer would take large art-books into the rehearsal and thumb through them as the choir rehearsed. This led to an altercation that has often been repeated by Schafer, and appears in his memoirs.

> "Choir stand up!" commanded Dr. Johnston from the top of the chair he always stood on. The choir stood up. "Choir sit down!" came the abrupt contravening order. The choir sat down. "Choir and Mr. Schafer stand up!" bellowed the commander. Schafer calmly turned the pages of his book on Rouault or Cézanne. "Schafer!" screamed the doctor. "Stand up!" Several girls began to swoon, recognizing the symptoms of the well-known tantrum that would sour the mood for the rest of the evening. "Come up here!" Nonchalantly I wandered to the front carrying my precious book. "Sit there!" ordered El Duce, pointing to an empty chair directly in front of him. "Now, once again, CHOIR AND MR. SCHAFER, STAND UP!" The choir stood up. Schafer opened his book and began to read. "SCHAFER!" It was the loudest sound the

school had ever heard. The dust rose from the windowsills and the lights flickered. Dr. Johnston leapt in the air, landing with such force that his feet went clear through the seat of his chair. I looked up to see him furiously waving his baton only a few feet in front of my nose. I did the only natural thing. I got up and ran away. He lunged after me but the legs of the chair tripped him and he came clattering to the ground. As I darted to the door, I saw girls hurrying to pick him up off the floor.[77]

An alternate account of this incident appears in Stephen Adams's biography of Schafer, in which Johnston stamps on the chair and falls through. Schafer then laughs when Johnston lunges forward and falls on his face.[78] Whatever the actual story, this incident was one of the reasons that the young student was called into Dr. Walter's office to account for his behavior. A second reason was a rather insulting essay he wrote for an American faculty member who taught a music education course that Schafer was required to take. This took place during the final exam for the course, which was in the fall semester. Schafer considered this exam to be particularly full of stupid questions, and after answering the questions somewhat flippantly, he attempted to leave. He was told that he had to stay in the room for at least an hour, and he used the time to write his opinion on how music education might be "more inspiringly taught." He expected to fail the exam but didn't expect the faculty member to bring the bitingly sarcastic essay before Dr. Walter, who summoned him into his office.

Schafer was instructed to apologize in writing to the two offended faculty members or he would be expelled from the Faculty of Music. In their initial meeting, Walter contrasted Schafer's fate if he remained in the university, perhaps going on to graduate school, with what would happen if he left the university and was forced to do menial work the rest of his life. He was sent away for twenty-four hours to think about it. Schafer returned the next day without having thought it over much and fell into a nervous laughing fit when he saw the sun from the window behind Dr. Walter shining through his ears. Dr. Walter yelled at him to get out, and Murray's formal university training officially came to an end.[79] Schafer recalls in later interviews that he left the University of Toronto whistling, and for many years after would whistle whenever his thoughts turned back to his alma mater.[80] Schafer would later be reconciled with Dr. Walter, who even wrote him a letter of recommendation in 1956 in support of Schafer's studies in Europe, in which he lauded his ability as a composer. The expelled student would eventually receive an honorary degree from the University of Toronto. In his address to the graduating students at the University in 2006, he reflected on his academic experience.

> I spent years in school trying to get out. It seemed to me that so much education was devoted to answering questions that no one had asked while the real

questions slid by unanswered. Plato taught that there was an answer to every question. Socrates taught that there was a question to every answer, but that was something my teachers didn't want to deal with. For that reason I never completed my education but set out to travel the world and educate myself.

It was only after many years of travelling, first as a sailor, then a journalist, a broadcaster and composer that I began to question seriously why my life at school had been so futile. The failure of the music program concerned me in particular because I had musical talent . . . and had eventually adopted music as my vocation.[81]

Many of Schafer's future explorations in music education would flow from these questions, generated during his brief tenure in academia.

After attending Doon Art School for a second (and last) summer, Murray returned to Toronto in the fall of 1954 with a pressing need to make a living. His first short-lived job was in an ice-house, crushing ice for cocktail bars. Fortunately his father, still working for Imperial Oil, was able to get Murray a job on a Great Lakes oil tanker. He was to work on the S. S. *Imperial Windsor* for nine months, saving up money to begin the next stage of his life.[82]

Chapter Two

Uncertainty, the Temporal Muse, and Wanderlust

LOOSE ENDS AND THE LIFE AQUATIC

Murray came on board the SS *Imperial Windsor* as a deckhand in March 1955, the only novice seaman on board a ship with a wide range of veteran characters. The crew would work forty-eight hours a week in shifts of four hours on, eight hours off. When the weather demanded or the ship was discharging or taking on oil, the men would work upward of twenty to thirty hours without a break but were at least paid overtime for those long stretches. After a few months, Schafer began to be accepted by the crew, whose isolation from the rest of the world naturally drew them together. Many of the crewmen read books since there was no television and radio reception was spotty at best. Schafer's roommate, a veteran sailor from England named David Price, had an extensive library, including works by Kant, Dylan Thomas, and Schopenhauer.[1]

Schafer came away from his first nautical experience with a thorough knowledge of knots, the ability to work hard, and vivid memories of such events as the backbreaking task of guiding the tanker through the old St. Lawrence canal system and being violently sick after a night of drinking and a day of rough seas. He left the *Imperial Windsor* at the beginning of November 1955, having saved a few thousand dollars, and returned home to Toronto to plan his next step, visiting Europe (or perhaps more accurately, getting away from Canada). His first thought was to go to Vienna, and he picked up as much of the German language as he could from a neighbor in Toronto.[2] He set sail from Halifax on March 3, 1956, aboard the SS *Ascania*, which would dock at Portsmouth, England. The young, restless man was more than eager to leave his native country. Looking back, he recalls having headaches every day toward the end of his time in Canada, headaches that disappeared the day he left the country.[3] In a letter to Bob Walshe later in 1956, Murray outlined his desire to be free of his previous life, despite personal and emotional connections to home.

> Mine was probably so complete a break as one can make without going to ridiculous or suicidal lengths. I mean, to leave one's country, friends and family, and only with the greatest feelings of guilt, a girl, in order to stumble into a cage of the most severe loneliness—and all because of one's work desires.[4]

The girl referred to in the letter of course was Phyllis Mailing. She had been hinting at marriage, and he was not yet ready to make that commitment.

A CANADIAN IN EUROPE

His time aboard the *Imperial Windsor* had prepared him for rough seas, so he was able to enjoy the crossing while many of the passengers were forced to their bunks. After his arrival he went straight to London to stay with a cousin who was also a painter, Scott Medd. Scott was Murray's guide through the various galleries, theaters, and opera houses in London and helped him gain access to the Reading Room of the British Museum.[5] In Schafer's letters to his mother he complained about the quality and variety of music available to listen to in the great British metropolis,[6] and by the end of March he was tired of sightseeing and had decided to move on to Vienna in early April.[7]

There were multiple reasons for Schafer's desire to reside in Vienna. Greta Kraus had family there and had given him the contact information of her brother. Murray wrote to the brother, and found out that Greta's nephew was living in an apartment in Heitzing, on the outskirts of Vienna, and had a room to rent. Schafer went to look at it, found it small but acceptable, and began renting the space. The nephew, whose name was Uri, had no objections to Murray having a piano in the room, and the young composer found a grand piano he was able to rent for a dollar a day. Overall he found it quite cheap to live in Vienna and was able to keep his expenses down to about $40 a month.[8] He taught English to two of Greta's other nephews and became quite close to Uri. (His major composition of that year, *Minnelieder*, would be a wedding present to Uri.[9]) He enjoyed Vienna, and there were some musical highlights, including concerts of music by Hindemith and Stravinsky.[10] Unfortunately these highlights were rare and he generally found the musical scene to be not what he expected and extremely disappointing. Schafer had naively thought that Vienna would still be the center of new music in Europe, with the spirits of Schoenberg, Berg, and Webern still walking the streets,[11] and that he could find one of their students to teach him

Figure 2.1. Self-portrait. *R. Murray Schafer*

the techniques of atonal and twelve-tone music.[12] But since he thought all the teachers he could find in Vienna were "imbeciles," his hopes of studying contemporary music in Vienna were not to be fulfilled.[13]

Unable to receive the musical training he wished to have at the Vienna Academy, Schafer focused his studies in other areas. He decided to study medieval German and found a woman at the university who agreed to teach him. Schafer also attempted to immerse himself in modern German, tackling such Romantic German poets such as Heine, Goethe, Rilke, and Novalis, some of whom were on the reading list of a German course he was taking at the university. The course focused on the language as a literary, not a conversational, idiom, so there was no conversation in the classroom. Schafer ultimately dropped the course to focus on the practical aspects of improving his spoken German[14] but continued to develop his reading knowledge of the language by struggling his way through German poetry and aesthetics, including such authors as Baumgartner and Kant.[15]

Despite his initial love of Vienna, Murray began to feel an increased sense of isolation. His flatmate and friend Uri was a medical student and was gone all day. His limited German made it difficult to make friends, so he spent most of his time alone in the apartment trying to get his piano chops back up. His increased restlessness led to a decision to leave Vienna for an extended period of time, and he considered his travel options. Austria was bordered by the (then) Communist states of Hungary to the east, Yugoslavia to the south, and Czechoslovakia to the north, so he traveled west, hitchhiking rides to whatever place his current driver was going. Upon arrival at his new location he would spend the night in a youth hostel or sometimes procure a free meal and bed at a farmer's house.[16] Through this method of travel he managed to visit Salzburg, Munich, Nuremberg, Frankfurt, Wiesbaden,

Figure 2.2.   Schafer in Vienna. *R. Murray Schafer*

Cologne and Aachen (to visit the cathedrals), Bonn, and Esterhazy, where he saw the bones of Franz Joseph Haydn.[17]

The one planned trip Murray took was to Brussels to visit a young woman named Nicole (he does not give her a last name in his journal) whom he had met on the boat-train on his way to Vienna. They had started to correspond, and after his arrival in Brussels they both went to Oostende, where Nicole had relatives, and spent several days together there. When Nicole returned to school in Brussels, Schafer made his way back to Vienna. For a time he thought of her as his muse, and to think of her inspired melodies, some of which found their way into *Minnelieder*.[18] Schafer had essentially returned to Vienna by June but still took additional trips to Brussels and made a short visit to London to engage in further studies at the British Museum.[19]

Refreshed by his travels, Schafer turned his attention back to composition. By early September he had finished a six-movement *Partita* (ultimately withdrawn), which he stated in a letter to Bob Walshe would "pretty well sum up 'en masse' my musical outlook up to the present."[20] The various influences in his life, including Nicole's inspiration, Uri's upcoming wedding, and his work with the German medievalist, inspired him in December to set the poetry of the German *minnesingers*.[21] *Minnelieder* was initially titled *Jahrezeiten de Minne (Seasons of Love)* in the composer's autograph. As he turned his attention to this piece, Schafer wrote,

> My instrumental means are simple and I want these songs to be as delicate as Klee drawings. My style is undergoing a great change, for I feel that to express nobly or religiously one must first begin with the simplest means and work outwardly, adding complication only as his maturity and mobility of expression merit them.[22]

Schafer has often remarked that he considers *Minnelieder* the first piece he wrote that was a finished piece of art, although he would also characterize it as conservative.

In December Schafer also received a kind letter from Benjamin Britten, which the composer had written in November, about Schafer's biographical song about the composer, which the young man had, with some temerity, sent to him. It read as follows:

> Dear Mr. Schäfer,
> Thank you for the charming compliment you pay me by the writing of the little biographical song; I was very pleased with it. I am sorry I was so elusive when you were visiting this country, but I am afraid that I am only in London for business reasons, and always very occupied. However, I shall be in Vienna in April (14th–24th) and hope to meet you then.
> With best wishes,
> Yours Sincerely,
> Benjamin Britten, 8th November 1956

Encouraged by Britten's positive feedback, Schafer decided to add a song about Ezra Pound and one about Paul Klee to finish off the set, which he initially called *Three Contemporary Portraits* but which was later renamed and premiered as *Three Contemporaries*.[23]

Schafer's close friend Bob Walshe arrived in Vienna just before Christmas of 1956, and Uri was able to rent him a bedroom at an inexpensive rate. The winter of 1956 was the high point of the Hungarian Revolution, and Schafer and Walshe were witnesses to the streams of Hungarian refugees escaping over the Neusiedler See to Austria. Bob, an aspiring (and later published) author, initially spent much of his time sketching out a novel based on those events.[24] Bob was much more gregarious than Schafer and tried to lure Murray into a more active social life, including attempting to get the two of them involved with "various daughters of Latin American diplomats living in Vienna."[25] These attempts met with mixed success since Murray usually preferred to stay home and read (mostly Kafka at this time) or listen to concerts on the radio.[26] After Walshe left in April of 1957, Schafer found himself again isolated and without much social interaction. In June he again visited his Belgian acquaintance Nicole but found the relationship becoming increasingly uncomfortable and complex. He also seriously considered joining the German Marine Agency, the *Schiffartsvermittlung*, which would accept his Canadian credentials of seamanship, but the pay was not enough to convince him to again set sail since he still had sufficient money saved up.[27]

TRAVELS EAST AND NORTH

He determined to travel to Greece and then hopefully on to Egypt. The train ride from Vienna to Thessaloniki involved a forty-eight-hour journey through communist Yugoslavia, and because of the political situation, the coaches were locked from the Austrian border to the train's arrival in Thessaloniki. Since the passengers were not even allowed to go onto the station platforms, they had to take their own food for the journey, and Schafer packed a bag with beer, rolls, and sausage links in preparation for his journey. The train arrived in Thessaloniki late on the second day. After a night in that town, which made an immediate impression on Schafer with its picturesque scenery, warm weather, and delicious food, he boarded another train for Athens. There he was transfixed by the Parthenon, spending a whole day on its steps reading about it. He brought back a piece of stone he chipped off with his penknife along with other small artifacts one could cheaply purchase from the young boys who offered to sell them to tourists.

One day he was approached by a young Parisian woman who asked if she could sit with him since she was being bothered by some Greek soldiers. He kept her company for the day, and she offered him a place to stay if Schafer was ever in Paris since she and her husband had a large apartment there. At another time he met a young Greek woman named Vasiliki, who approached him, recognizing him as a tourist. After a few hours of chatting at a coffee shop, they exchanged addresses and a passionate kiss. After he left Greece she (now nicknamed Vicki in Schafer's mind) sent him a letter, beginning an extended correspondence. When the rain continued for several days, Murray decided to go to Crete to see the Palace of Minos. The myth of the labyrinth, with its associated characters of Ariadne, Theseus, and the Minotaur, fascinated Schafer during his daily visits to the palace, and many of these characters would find their way into Schafer's later compositions.[28] He also went to Turkey to visit the archeological site of Troy. While visiting Athens and Knossos, Schafer was taken by the folk music he heard there, writing down (and later arranging) several tunes.

Schafer was back in Vienna by May and by mid-June he was back in Oostende and Brussels to visit Nicole.[29] His relationship with Nicole still seemed complicated to the idealistic and naive young Schafer, and in his mind Vicki, who was writing him passionate letters, was beginning to supplant Nicole as his muse.[30] Shortly after his visit with Nicole and her parents he once again went to Cologne then for several days in July used his credentials of seamanship and worked as a sailor on the Rhine to get away from things and to earn a little more cash.[31]

After his few weeks of sailing he visited relatives he had succeeded in tracking down, cousins of his father by the name of Hilgendorf who lived in the village of Hildesheim.[32] After a week with these relatives, Schafer continued his travels, including a stop in Lüneberg and a visit to Copenhagen, where he had a little room a short distance from the center of the city.[33] At the end of the month, when Murray was back once again visiting his relatives, he received a letter from Nicole informing him that she had found someone else.[34] This news intensified his loneliness, and he decided to return to Vienna since his flatmate Uri had recently also gone through a breakup and they might be able to console each other. His restlessness soon returned, and he decided that he should visit Paris to experience the culture there and to get away from German-speaking lands. As he prepared for his trip, he found solace in literature and listening to music on the radio, although he discovered that his tastes had changed, finding that most classical music annoyed him and that he preferred the folk music of Greece, Arabia, and Eastern Europe. His dislike for Mozart in particular had intensified, and he wrote in his journal, "Above all others I find him the most loathsome. His nervous little twitchings, like a fly buzzing on the windowpane, do nothing but annoy me."[35] As his sense of isolation and lack of interest in socializing increased, he continued his preference of books over people, reading a wide variety of authors including Mann, Joyce, Kafka, Tolstoy, and the poets Rilke and Pound.36

TO PARIS AND SOUTHERN FRANCE

In mid-August Murray took the overnight train from Vienna to Paris. He found a hotel on the Rue du Panthéon but was unsatisfied with it and remembered the Madame Delvert he had met and helped in Athens. She had offered her apartment, so Schafer found the address and, upon arriving there, discovered that the concierge was expecting his arrival. Schafer was able to stay in the luxurious penthouse for a few weeks since Madame Delvert was holidaying in Les Vosges with her husband, and upon the couple's return he moved into a boardinghouse to continue the search for a reasonably priced apartment while exploring the city and attending classes at the *Alliance Française* to improve his French.37 His search for accommodation, including checking out university housing, proved futile, so he considered moving to a smaller town such as Lilles or Reims in hopes of having an easier time of finding something affordable.38 Growing frustrated, he took a break from his search and crossed the channel to England to spend a few days with Bob Walshe and to spend some time in the British Library. By the end of August, when the fall term began in Paris, Schafer had only managed to find a pension for the steep price of 1,300 francs a day, the only benefit being it was near the *Alliance Française*.39 As chance would have it, Schafer fell in with a group of French students one afternoon, ending up conducting them in an informal choir when they discovered that he was a musician. After the afternoon's activities they all dispersed, but one of the students, François Tivoli, kept in touch. Through this new friendship Schafer found his way to Angers in October, invited to spend a weekend at the Tivoli family residence outside the town.40 While there he met François' friend Bernard, whose father owned a large hotel in the town itself. It was decided that Schafer would move to Angers and stay at the hotel for a while, which he agreed to in early November, only intending to say about three weeks.41 Just before returning to Angers he made a quick trip to Germany with Charles Rush, a student he met at the *Alliance Française*, at least in part to escape his intolerable room in Paris. The only notable part of this trip was the resulting self-realization that he was not cut out to travel with anyone but preferred solitude.42

In Angers Murray was able to stay free of charge in a small room on the top floor of the hotel, and he would receive free dinner cooked by François' sister Madeleine. In exchange for this, he would give the children an hour of conversation in English each day.43 In the old building the heat did not reach up to the top floor, so by November he was forced to go to bed early and read under the covers, introducing himself to such authors as Carlyle, Breton,

Cocteau, and Frazer.[44] He took short trips to other parts of France, including Rodez and Narbonne, and in early December obtained a Spanish visa so he could travel by train to Barcelona.[45] He went to the city to see works by Antonio Gaudi and to try to escape the reality that in a few weeks he would be returning to Canada for Christmas where he, among other things, would have to see Phyllis, with whom he had corresponded on and off for the past year.[46] While in Barcelona he accidentally knocked his glass eye off the night stand onto the floor, where it smashed. He had no choice but to check out of the hotel early next morning and take the train back to Angers and then to Paris, where he had a spare eye in his trunk.[47]

THE WANDERER RETURNS HOME (UNHAPPILY)

Unable to delay his return to Canada any longer, on December 10 Murray traveled from Paris to London, staying again with Bob Walshe and making certain to visit the British Museum library once more. A few days later he boarded the boat-train for New York. Once again the crossing had rough weather, but Schafer had retained his sea legs. On his arrival he took a train from New York to Toronto. During the course of this homeward journey he felt a strong reluctance to be returning to Canada, with the only possible bright spots being his close family members and Phyllis.[48] Once back in Canada, he began immediately to work on getting away once more since the only two things keeping him there were a lack of money and Phyllis, with whom he felt "so close and yet so far" as they began to get to know each other after his absence.[49] Since he was, at least for the time being, stuck in Toronto, he began to work and create a name for himself in the Canadian musical community.

Soon after his return to Toronto he was approached by the director of BMI Canada (now Berandol Publishing) about publishing several of his works, and Terrance Gibbs from the Canadian Broadcasting Corporation (CBC) also expressed interest in recording and broadcasting both the *Concerto for Harpsichord and Eight Wind Instruments* and *Minnelieder*. The Toronto Wind Quintet and Phyllis Mailing began preparation of *Minnelieder* to premiere it later in the year, and Schafer and fellow composers Milton Barnes and Morris Eisenstadt decided to put on a concert or two of their compositions, with the first one scheduled for May.[50] After creating a piano version of *Minnelieder* for Phyllis to perform in February, he turned back to composition, and by the end of March he had completed his first new piece in two years, *Kinderlieder*, for voice and piano. Seven of the nine songs set texts by Bertolt Brecht, with the final two setting German traditional texts that are in the same vein as the Brecht texts. Some of the Brecht settings are taken from that poet's collection *Kinderlieder*, published in 1956. They reflect Brecht's socialist leanings and were chosen by Schafer because they matched his own socialist leanings, which were then reaching their highpoint.

Schafer's next three compositions remained unpublished and unperformed. *Five Greek Folk Dances* for violin and piano used five of the folk tunes he had gathered during his trip to Greece. His *Sonata da Camera for Two Celli Alone*, dedicated to Bob Walshe, and *Petit Divertissement Angevin*, a five-movement suite for flute, oboe, clarinet, and cello based mostly on piano compositions from 1952, were also withdrawn. As a side project, he began preparing the text for what he called an "Ishtar cantata," which ultimately did not come to fruition.[51] He also turned his hand back to writing, producing a recording review of Glenn Gould for the Canadian Music Journal.

John Weinzweig was impressed enough with his former student's progress to invite Schafer to join the newly formed Canadian League of Composers, an advocacy group for Canadian composers and their music.[52] On the tenth of May the planned Schafer/Barnes/Eisenstadt concert took place, the first time that a Schafer composition received public press. His contribution to the program was *Trio for Clarinet, Cello and Piano* from 1954, and *Three Contemporaries* from 1956. John Beckwith, who reviewed the concert in the Canadian Music Journal, was cool toward the trio but admired *Three Contemporaries*, considering it the success of the concert.[53]

Despite these encouraging creative and professional developments, Schafer was still dissatisfied with Toronto and determined to get back to Europe, and he began writing letters looking for work there.[54] In order to earn some money and not be such a financial burden to his family he took a job teaching new Canadians English. He also started to learn Italian and Arabic to prepare for planned trips to Italy and Egypt, and he worked to further improve his German and French. He was able to find an Italian to teach him Italian, a Lebanese priest at the local Syrian Orthodox Church to teach him Arabic, and a French pianist to help him with his French.[55]

By June things had reached a breaking point, with Schafer feeling that a significant decision lay before him to either settle down in Canada and marry Phyllis or to leave Canada and return to Europe. He was torn between his desire to be free of any ties and his sense of connection and obligation to Phyllis, whom he had known for so long and who had done so much for him. His decision was to try to leave Canada, and he applied for a grant from the Canada Council of the Arts as a way to escape before Christmas.[56] Despite his decision, during the summer months he was indecisive and unproductive, taking until September to complete his next composition, *Sonatina for Flute and Harpsichord (or Piano)*, dedicated to his friend, flautist, and composer Robert Aitken.[57] By October Schafer was still in Toronto but had not committed to Phyllis through "his own selfishness,"[58] and by November it was clear that marriage was not in their immediate future. They both decided to get away from Canada for a while. Phyllis made plans to travel to Germany in January in order to continue her performance career. In preparation for his travels, Murray got $2,000 from his father (with the understanding that this would be the last loan he would receive), and he finished his application for a Canada Council grant for another $2,000, proposing to study the literary and musical influences on troubadour and *Minnesinger* music to determine which were local and which were oriental.[59] This proposal was denied but Murray still booked a ticket to fly from Toronto to London on February 10. In December Schafer managed to finish one more composition, an unpublished piano set called *Three Ideograms for Walter Ball*, and in the second half of January he traveled to Montreal to oversee the recording of his *Concerto for Harpsichord* for the international service of the CBC, which would broadcast the piece on February 4.

BACK IN EUROPE

Upon arriving in London in February, Murray was able to stay with his friend Bob Walshe, sharing his basement apartment. After some time there he journeyed to Trieste, remaining there for a while, teaching conversational English at the Berlitz Language School. Upon his return to London Murray again stayed with Bob, produced some articles, and began to look around for other money-making projects that would allow him to stay in Europe. He conceived of a plan to travel to Eastern Europe, and by July was in Vienna, preparing for his trip into communist Eastern Europe as a guest of the International Folk Music Council (IFMC).[60] He had heard that the IFMC was planning a conference in Romania, and he proposed to attend the conference with a newly purchased tape recorder to make some radio programs to sell to the CBC or perhaps the BBC. He was also hoping to be able to interview people about life in communist Europe since he had socialist leanings and wanted to find out more. The president of the IFMC suggested that he approach the Romanian Embassy to see if they would fund his trip and arrange some interviews.[61] In his interview with a person at the embassy he claimed, with technical accuracy, that he had connections to the University of Toronto Press and the *Globe and Mail* newspaper. (He had written articles for the university student newspaper and had a letter to the editor printed in the *Globe and Mail*.) He convinced the embassy to give him money, and emboldened by his success, he approached the Bulgarian and Yugoslavian embassies. He was able to craft and fund a trip in which he would visit the Romanian town of Sinaia, where the conference was to be held, then Bucharest, Sofia, Belgrade, and Zagreb.[62] He left Vienna on August 10, his destination Sinaia by way of Bucharest.

Chapter 2

ADVENTURES IN THE EASTERN BLOC

On the train from Bucharest to Sinaia Murray met an attractive girl and as the night progressed Schafer found himself alone with her in the train car. They began to communicate through pictures, since she spoke only Hungarian, and he learned her name was Erzsébet, and that she was visiting a town named Tusnad Bai, where she had relatives. At her stop they embraced and said goodbye, and Schafer thought he would not see her again, even though she had given him her address. Schafer arrived in Sinaia, where he attended the conference. He liked its organization but thought many of the lectures were quite boring. He kept thinking about the girl he had met on the train, and on an impulse he packed a small bag, went to the train station, and to his surprise was able to get a ticket to Tusnad Bai simply by asking for it, no identification required. Once he arrived in the town he found someone who could show him the cottage where Erzsébet was staying with her family, and he remained there for several days, eating the wonderful homemade food, going for hikes with his hostess, and enjoying the celebrity of being from an exotic country such as Canada.[63] Schafer returned to Sinaia in time to attend the end of the conference and to prepare to travel to Bucharest, where the conference delegates would attend several concerts of folk music from the different regions of Romania.[64] On his return to the conference he was asked by one of the organizers of the event (who was likely also a communist official) where he had been for the last several days. Schafer dissembled, mentioning that he had friends in Romania, but pretending to forget where they lived and making up a name. A day later he was asked the same question by one of his translators, and it became clear to him that attempts were being made to find out the details of his unauthorized trip. The interpreter continued to occasionally ask him about his whereabouts but Murray was able to steer the conversation to other topics, including literature, listing several poets and authors she had never been exposed to in her studies. One night the interpreter, named Corina, pressed him again, saying that she would lose her job if he didn't tell her where he had been. His disappearance had caused significant trouble since the police, fearing that he had been in the Carpathian region stirring up revolution, had been rounding up people for questioning. Schafer then told her that he had been visiting a peasant family, relatives of a girl he had met on the train.[65] That seemed to satisfy her, and they continued their time together, growing closer and closer. One night he and she were followed, and she told him to go to the conference hotel, while she went home. Two men followed him to the hotel, stayed for a while, then disappeared. Schafer spoke of his experience to a fellow conference delegate, who strongly advised him to go to the Canadian Embassy and tell them the story, but since there was no Canadian Embassy in Romania, Murray had to go to the British Embassy instead. The man there said he would try to speed up Schafer's departure since he could not leave except on the day listed on his visa. When Schafer went back to the hotel, he was met by another woman who said she was his new interpreter. Murray insisted on seeing Corina. The new interpreter eventually reluctantly agreed, and she and Schafer went to a restaurant where Corina was at another table. She was able to slip him a note through a musician who was going from table to table, letting him know that she would meet him at the train station tomorrow, when he would be leaving. Since Murray himself had heard no news of when he would be leaving, he was greatly unsettled but relieved to be leaving what was increasingly becoming a dangerous situation.[66] The next day Corina was able to briefly meet him at the train station so they could say goodbye. He would not see her again, although for some time after they would keep up correspondence, having worked out a written code to send each other messages buried in the banal texts of their letters.[67]

Schafer's next stop was Sofia on September 7, where he was the guest of the Bulgarian Composers' Union. His time there was both less adventurous and less pleasant. He was asked to lecture on Canadian music, and he introduced them to pieces by his teacher John Weinzweig and his friend Harry

Figure 2.3. Romanian Shepherd. *R. Murray Schafer*

Somers, and his own *Concerto*, which paled in comparison to the other pieces and was not enthusiastically received.[68] He also found the city drab. He was still reeling from the events in Bucharest and worried that his creative desire was waning, leaving him nothing but articles and radio talks and interviews to occupy his time.[69] To top it off, his tape recorder broke while he was recording a service in the Alexander Nevsky theater. Since the technician in Bulgaria did not have access to parts to fix the British-made machine, Schafer could no longer fulfill his purpose for traveling in Eastern Europe. The officials in Bulgaria arranged for him to leave for Yugoslavia a few days early, and after a shortened stay there[70] he traveled back to Budapest for the Franz Joseph festival, where he met the then seventy-seven-year-old Zoltán Kodaly and the younger composer László Lajtha, whom he was scheduled to interview.[71] He and Lajtha kept in contact, and Schafer arranged performances of several of the Hungarian composer's pieces after he returned to Canada.[72] This journey to Eastern Europe helped Schafer determine that he was not comfortable fully embracing Marxism, at least as it was practiced in the countries he visited. He also was profoundly affected by the peasant music he heard in Romania, Bulgaria, and Hungary. He turned his experiences into a contribution on Balkan folk music to the CBC program *Assignment*, an article for *Romanian Cultural Magazine*, and an article for the publication *Queens Quarterly*.[73]

THE SAFETY OF LONDON AND JOURNALISTIC AMBITIONS

Once safely back in London, Schafer began serious work on an extended project he had conceived earlier in the year, a series of interviews with British composers, which was the second reason he had purchased the tape recorder he took with him on his journey east.[74] Having made some progress on the project, he was able by the end of the year to persuade the CBC program *Music Diary*, produced in Vancouver, to broadcast his series of interviews with prominent British composers.[75] This willingness on the part of the CBC to invest in this project was due in part to the continuing strong connections between this former British colony and England, and with this surprising agreement in hand he applied for Canada Council funding. These interviews would later be edited and result in Murray's first published book, *British Composers in Interview*, issued in 1963 by Faber Music. In the project Schafer interviews sixteen of the most prominent British composers working at that time, using his newly repaired portable tape recorder. One of his subjects, the famed composer Benjamin Britten, had not responded to the young interviewer's written request to meet. After Schafer had the temerity to take the train to Aldeburgh and knock on Britten's door, the esteemed composer agreed to an interview, but only through written correspondence.

The radio programs and book were well received, and through this project Schafer was able to make interesting connections and establish long-lasting friendships, in particular with Michael Tippett and Peter Racine Fricker. In Schafer's second year in London, he would choose to study with Fricker, leading to important developments in his compositional style.

BACK TO COMPOSITION?

Schafer's literary and research endeavors were masking a continued uncertainty on the young man's part as to whether he wished to even be a composer, despite the warm reception of his earlier pieces back in Canada. Although he felt that he had produced pieces of good quality, his interest in musical composition was at best intermittent during this time, and the radio documentaries, composer interviews, and articles all served to distract him from focusing intensely on his music and to help him avoid a growing depression over the fact that he had still done nothing he considered significant with his life.[76] It took an important personal event to force him to pick up the pen again to compose: the death of Alberto Guerrero, his influential piano teacher from his days at the University of Toronto. Schafer's response was to compose *In Memoriam Alberto Guerrero* for string orchestra, in only five days. In the tribute the composer says "This little memoriam . . . is a tribute to a great musician, whose influence I shall never forget."[77]

Schafer once again applied for a grant from the Canada Council in the spring of 1960, this time proposing to study composition with an established teacher. His interviews with British composers allowed him to procure letters of support from Malcolm Arnold, Peter Fricker, and Michael Tippett, and he was also able to cite performances of his *Concerto for Harpsichord* and *Sonatina for Flute and Harpsichord* and an upcoming performance of *Minnelieder* in London in the spring of 1960.[78] His application was accepted, with the stipulation that it be with a well-established teacher. Schafer first wished to study with Michael Tippett, but that composer was not accepting any students.[79] His next choice was the noted Hungarian composer and teacher Matyas Seiber. Seiber agreed to take Murray on as a pupil but later that year died in a car accident, so Schafer turned to Peter Racine Fricker, a former pupil of Seiber and himself a well-established composer.[80] Schafer would later say that Fricker's compositions did not influence him directly (other than perhaps in their strong emphasis on form), but through the Englishman Murray was exposed to the adventurous composers and techniques that were happening during that time.[81] Often their "lessons" would happen in a London pub where they would analyze Webern, Dallapiccola, Machaut, Berio, and Boulez.[82]

Chapter 2

TAKING THE PLUNGE

Schafer's studies with Fricker were interrupted mid-year by an important personal event. After many years of indecision, Murray had finally decided to commit to Phyllis, and they were married in June of 1960, in the town hall of Chelsea. It was a double wedding as his long-time friend Bob Walshe was married that same day to an English woman named Pamela.[83] After their wedding, Schafer and his new bride honeymooned first in Trieste, then in Verona, before making their way to Merano where Murray was planning to visit Ezra Pound.

Schafer had first been introduced to Pound in Marshall McLuhan's class back at the University of Toronto, and his interest in the poet had been deepened after reading Pound's translations of medieval lyric poetry. In London in 1959 Schafer had met the poet's wife Dorothy, and through that connection he had reached out to Ezra and begun corresponding with him. Pound had moved back to Italy in 1958 after being released from St. Elizabeth's Hospital (a psychiatric hospital in Washington, DC) and now resided in Merano, in a castle belonging to his son-in-law, Prince Boris de Rachewiltz. Schafer had discovered that Pound had written an opera, *Le Testament*, based on texts by the fifteenth-century poet François Villon. No one seemed to know anything about this piece, and it had become one of Schafer's goals to produce it.[84] Schafer had been discussing the project with Alexander Goehr, one of the composers Schafer had interviewed. Goehr was now a part-time producer at the BBC, and there was strong interest there in producing the opera. Schafer had written to Pound about his proposal, asking if he could visit. Pound replied that he shouldn't come, but the persistent scholar still decided to try. After arriving in Merano, Schafer left Phyllis at the hotel, traveled up to the castle, and knocked on the door. After repeated loud knocking, Pound appeared up in the one of the towers and told him to come up, saying to the intrepid visitor, "I have learned from my wife that you are one of the few people who ought to be let in here."[85] Murray and Phyllis would visit with the poet, his wife Dorothy, and daughter Mary for several days. They talked of his opera, of various kinds of music, and of politics. Pound sang several passages from his opera for Schafer and recited many unpublished poems. They were invited to stay longer but Murray had already arranged an interview with Sir William Walton in London so they could not stay. Before he left, Murray received permission from Pound to produce the opera, and the poet typed up a letter instructing the director of the Library of Congress to give Schafer the manuscript to the work.[86] Pound also gave Schafer an envelope, with the instructions to give it to T. S. Eliot upon his return to London. In the envelope was the final installment of the *Cantos*, Pound's great lifework. It was not to be published for another twelve years, so Schafer was one of the first to find out how the poem ended. Upon his return to London, Schafer obtained the copy of Pound's opera, and with the help of Sandy Goehr and D. G. Bridson (another BBC employee and a long-time Pound admirer), he began to prepare the opera for a radio production.[87]

HOME IS CALLING

In early 1961 Schafer and his new bride were settled in London. Schafer continued to work on his edition of Ezra Pound's opera and was finding it a frustrating process, given his questions about the amateurishness of the opera and his doubts as to whether Pound was serious about all that he put on paper. These issues, coupled with the piece's lack of stylistic unity, made editorial choices difficult.[88] He coupled his work on the opera with articles and essays, including several about Pound, the first of which, "Ezra Pound and Music,"[89] would later serve as the introduction to his book of the same title. He also wrote articles on other subjects, including one on Thomas Mann and Romain Rolland called "Two Musicians in Fiction."

In the midst of this activity he finally found a renewed interest in composition, and focused, through his studies with Fricker, on mastering serial techniques, motivic manipulation, and structure. He also threw himself into analyzing a wide variety of music from different periods and styles to learn various approaches to tonality, counterpoint, harmony, orchestration, and form. This process was made easier by the vibrant music scene in London, where he was able to hear performances of everything from Heinrich Schütz to Jean Sibelius to Arnold Schoenberg.

In March Murray traveled with Phyllis to Paris for a week, meeting up with fellow Canadian composers Srul Irving Glick, Walter Buczynski, Bruce Mather, and Harry Somers. Schafer had several profitable discussions with Somers, discussing their respective approaches toward serialism. Somers also suggested during this visit that since Schafer was still waiting for a libretto from Bob Walshe for an oratorio called *The Judgement of Jael*, Schafer should read a chronicle of the adventures of Jean de Brébeuf. Schafer began working on the libretto for the piece when he returned to London that month,[90] and the resulting piece was a cantata for solo baritone and orchestra called *Brébeuf*. This composition would serve as a homecoming present for the reinvigorated composer. Murray and Phyllis had decided to go back to Canada, and by the beginning of 1962 they were settled into an apartment in Toronto, ready to begin the next chapter in their lives.

Chapter Three

Homecoming and Education from the Other Side

TORONTO—FOR THE TIME BEING

The beginning of 1962 found the newlyweds back in Toronto, in an apartment on St. Clair Avenue, ready to get reacquainted with their home country.[1] Although it would take some time to adjust to Canada (Schafer had been in Europe for the better part of six years), the young couple immediately threw themselves back into the city's musical life. Phyllis did extensive concertizing and also sang in the newly formed *Festival Singers*, Canada's first professional choir directed by Elmer Iseler (the group would later be called the Elmer Iseler Singers).[2] Schafer would later recount hearing Phyllis practice for her recitals, remembering that

> simply listening to this creature practicing in the background was very useful to me in learning what the voice could do—what was suitable for the voice and what was unsuitable. I could try out techniques with her and of course all my major vocal works were all written for her voice . . . they suit her range, her tessatura; they suit her rich and dramatic quality.[3]

This is certainly true of Murray's two major vocal works from 1962 and 1963, *Five Studies on Texts of Prudentius* and *The Geography of Eros*, even though both were ultimately premiered by Mary Morrison.

Schafer initially worked as a librarian for the Canadian Music Center (CMC) and also did some contract work for the CBC. The CMC was an initiative of the Canadian League of Composers, founded in 1951 by John Weinzweig, who invited Murray to become a member in 1958. The CMC served as a score repository, a lending library, and a general resource of

Figure 3.1.   Murray and Phyllis on their wedding day. *R. Murray Schafer*

music by living Canadian composers. Schafer's work included filling orders for perusal scores, and he would make certain to include avant-garde pieces if the request was not specific. He would also contribute an introductory essay called *A Short History of Music in Canada* to the CMC's pamphlet *Catalogue of Canadian Orchestral Music.*

In January of 1962 Schafer received the final signed contract from Faber for *British Composers in Interview*, which was published the following year. With that book now in its final stages, Schafer was able to turn to other projects. "The Limits of Nationalism in Canadian Music" appeared in the *Tamarack Review* that year, written as a response to perceived pressures to write "Canadian" music after his homecoming.[4] He also wrote concert reviews, did interviews of Canadian musicians,[5] and excerpted portions of *British Composers in Interview* as articles for such publications as the *Canadian Music Journal* and *Music Across Canada*.[6] Two other achievements in the spring of 1962 were the BBC recording and broadcast of the Ezra Pound opera *Le Testament*, which Schafer had so painstakingly edited in 1961, and the premiere performance of *In Memoriam Alberto Guerrero* in Vancouver.[7]

Schafer's most significant contribution to the musical life of Toronto during this time was cofounding the Ten Centuries Concerts series. This innovative concert series was the brainchild of Schafer and his composer colleagues Norm Symonds, Harry Freedman, Harry Somers, and Gordon Delamont. To this forward-looking group, the musical scene and concert offerings in the city were much too conservative and monochromatic, so in the spring of 1962 they decided to create a series that would construct its programs using unusual or neglected repertoire ranging from medieval chanson to newly composed works.[8] It was decided early on that no non-musicians would be on the board, so everyone donated time and energy to keep the series going, and Schafer held the post of president for two years before passing it on to fellow composer Norma Beecroft. During those two years, Schafer devoted much of his time and energy to the practical workings of the organization, including procuring the new recital hall at the University of Toronto as the main venue of the series.[9] The initial series sold five hundred subscriptions on the basis of a vigorous phone campaign, and Ten Centuries Concerts was off and running. The series would continue for six years, entirely run by the musicians and composers, who chose the music and executed the day-to-day operations.

In the minds of the founders, the choice of music came first, and programming was painstakingly discussed, with hours spent discussing how different pieces from different genres and eras would fit into a cohesive whole, much like the theory of montage in a film. In the various programs of the concerts, audience members could hear a thirteenth-century chant-fable juxtaposed with Schoenberg's *Pierrot Lunaire* or listen to Schumann's *Kreisleriana* coupled with readings from E. T. A. Hoffmann's stories about Kriesler, all performed in costume by candlelight.[10] Schafer would have two pieces premiered as part of the series, *The Geography of Eros* in 1965 and *Five Studies on Texts of Prudentius* in 1966.[11] The concert series exposed large audiences to music that had never been performed in the city, and as the series grew other musical organizations joined them.

With all of these activities consuming much of his time, Schafer used his spare moments to complete several pieces he had begun in London, starting with *Canzoni for Prisoners*. His first purely orchestral piece, it was dedicated to prisoners of conscience, "non-violent objectors in any land who are imprisoned merely for their beliefs."[12] Schafer was a founding member of Amnesty International in 1961, and his continued involvement in social justice found expression in his music. Along with the earlier *Protest and Incarceration*, *Canzoni for Prisoners* is the first of several socially or politically motivated musical statements that Schafer would produce throughout his life, reflecting his conviction that one responsibility of a composer is to be a "secretary of his own time, recording what is happening around him."[13] At the premiere performance of *Canzoni*, given in 1963 by the Montreal Symphony Orchestra in collaboration with the Canadian League of Composers, Schafer met the composer and CBC producer Serge Garant for the first time. Garant was very enthusiastic about Schafer's music and would be instrumental in the production of Schafer's first large theatrical work, *Loving/Toi*. The other significant piece Schafer finished during this year, *Five Studies on Texts of Prudentius*, most clearly shows the influence of his study under

Fricker in its strict canonic writing and use of isorhythmic techniques. The set also calls for spatial separation of the performers, with the singer in the middle of the room and the flutes in the four corners of the room, creating not only temporal canons but also spatial canons. At the premiere soprano Mary Morrison sang to a recording of the four flute parts created by Robert Aitken. This use of prerecorded material intrigued Schafer, and he began to write compositions that used recorded sounds. Two of his first attempts at this, *Opus One for Mixed Chorus* from 1962 and *Divisions for Baroque Trio* from 1963, were ultimately withdrawn. *Four Songs on Texts of Tagore* for women's chorus, written in 1962, does not use electronics but is notable for being Schafer's first setting of the poetry of Rabindranath Tagore.

SCHAFER THE EDUCATOR?

Although busy and productive in Toronto, Murray felt that he needed a more financially stable position so he applied for, and to his surprise received, an artist-in-residence position at Memorial University in St. John's, Newfoundland, which was scheduled to begin in September of 1963. While preparing for the move to Canada's easternmost province, the couple continued their active participation in the musical life of Toronto, and Schafer became involved in a significant project that would shape his career, compositions, and creative focus. This was an educational initiative begun by John Adaskin, then secretary of the CMC. Initially called the Graded Educational Music Plan, it would be renamed the John Adaskin Project after Adaskin's untimely death in 1964. The project was created in 1961 as a response to the concern of several public and high school teachers that they were unable to find music by living Canadian composers appropriate for grade school students, and its purpose was to identify and create music appropriate for use in schools. It started with a $10,000 grant from the Canada Council for the Arts, and before commissioning new pieces, its initial focus was on collecting existing music and grading it for suitability.[14] Schafer was involved in this stage of the project, and he promoted the goals of the project in an address he gave to secondary school music teachers in Toronto in October of that year. In this talk, titled "A Perspective of Music Appreciation," he advocated for a teaching method that went beyond the narrowly defined canon of pieces appropriate for children to contemporary, avant-garde pieces and pieces from other time periods of music, paralleling the goals of the Ten Centuries Concerts.[15] By 1963 a committee of music educators had compiled a "recommended list" of current music compositions appropriate for educational use, and the project moved to its next step, identifying where gaps existed in the available music and filling those gaps with commissions. John Adaskin proposed that instead of simply commissioning composers, it would be valuable for the composers receiving the commissions to meet with music educators and work with the students to ensure that they would write effective pieces for young musicians.[16] In May 1963 the CMC asked Schafer to write an introductory article about the project for the publication *Music Across Canada*. In this article he outlined the project's history, plan, and potential application for Canadian teachers, composers, and students.[17]

The initial Seminar for Graded Educational Music took place in November of 1963 in the school districts of Toronto and two of its suburbs, Scarborough and North York. One of the fifteen participants in the inaugural project was Schafer, who flew back from St. John's for the event.[18] After a day of discussion with the composers and the leaders of the school districts, the composers spent three days working with the students. The composers then came back for additional discussion, and on the last day of the seminar the pieces created by the composers with the students were performed. Schafer's contribution was the first form of *Statement in Blue*, and was quite different from what the other composers produced during this time since the students had a hand in the creation of the piece, facilitated by the use of graphic notation.[19] The whole project was declared a success and generated enthusiasm for repeating it in future years. Schafer wrote a letter to Peter Dwyer at the Canada Council after the seminar, stating that

> enthusiasm grew from day to day as the composers worked with the children, wrote little pieces for them, and the educators had a chance to experience Canadian music of our time at first hand. Speaking personally, I can honestly say the week spent at the seminar was one of the most exciting of my musical career.[20]

Two discussions that Schafer led during this 1963 seminar would later be incorporated into his first music education pamphlet, *The Composer in the Classroom*,[21] and Schafer would later cite his time spent in the Toronto schools as the inspiration behind his involvement in music education, which became a constant throughout his career and garnered international acclaim.[22] More immediately it resulted in several instrumental and choral pieces for youth over the next few years, including the two early pieces *Invertible Material for Orchestra* and *Statement in Red* for wind and percussion instruments. Given his own negative experiences with educational institutions, it is somewhat surprising that Murray would so eagerly throw himself into this field, but in many interviews he would cite his own aborted musical education as the reason he wanted to change how this subject was taught both in secondary and post-secondary institutions.[23]

Chapter 3
LIFE ON THE ROCK

At the beginning of September 1963, Phyllis and Murray were settled in St. John's, Newfoundland. As Schafer began his first year as artist in residence at Memorial University, he was given an office (the desk would arrive several days later) and a wide-open job description. There was no music program or program in any of the arts at Memorial University at that time, and Schafer's meeting with the university president did not shed any light on what he was supposed to do. He had no specific teaching responsibilities so he and Phyllis began working with some of their fellow faculty members to improve the musical life of the city.[24] The initial going was a bit rough, and Murray recounts in particular a party they attended just after their arrival in the city where they were thrust among English faculty members who did nothing but complain about being at St. John's.[25] Through persistence they began to find like-minded colleagues and slowly build a musical community. Murray led a musical discussion group that would meet to explore such topics as folk music and the evolution of jazz. He also became chairman of the Music Committee, which promoted musical awareness and appreciation, and the Orchestra Committee, which consisted of a group of conductors eager to form an orchestra in St. John's since there was no orchestra in the entire province at the time.[26] Phyllis formed a small madrigal group that consisted mostly of faculty members and their wives and gave a few recitals of *lieder* that were well received. Phyllis had continued to develop her performing career, even winning a competition in New York for recitalists, which included an extensive tour. After a few weeks, she realized that she preferred the quieter life in St. John's to the frantic life that touring involved.[27] The school music programs in Newfoundland had strong brass band ensembles, so Schafer was able to form a good amateur brass ensemble with interested students, giving performances of baroque and renaissance pieces with them[28] and bringing them to the point where they could do a recording and broadcast for the CBC.[29] At some point there were even discussions of forming an Institute of Contemporary Arts.[30] Murray also procured money from the university to bring performers in from the mainland to do concerts. All these efforts were successful enough that when Murray's initial one-year appointment was due to expire, several people lobbied to have his residency extended, and he was asked to stay for a second year.[31]

Schafer continued to write, research, and lecture. In addition to writing several articles and lecturing, he began to work out over the next two years the basic concepts of his first educational pamphlet, *The Composer in the Classroom*.[32] The following year he would begin work on a booklet on musical life in Canada using some of his published articles,[33] but he would ultimately set this project aside for several years. The most important writing project he undertook during his first year at Memorial was a collection of

Figure 3.2.   Schafer at Memorial University. *R. Murray Schafer*

translations of writings by E. T. A. Hoffmann on music, paired with his own essays on Hoffmann. The rough draft of this project was completed by June of 1964, although the book *E.T.A. Hoffmann and Music* would not be completed and published until 1975. Schafer would later admit that this project was his version of a doctoral thesis, written to prove that he was worthy to teach and work at a university even though he never completed a formal degree.[34] He also began a graphic-art novel that he would later publish as *Smoke*.

At Memorial University Schafer was able, for the first time, to have what he called an "established pattern of creativity."[35] He began to think of large compositional projects that could extend over several years while he was simultaneously producing pieces in the short term. The first fruits of this newfound creativity were two pieces for orchestra, *Untitled Composition for Orchestra no. 1*, described as "one of a series of pieces where he tried to work with strict devices,"[36] and *Untitled Composition for Orchestra no. 2*, a study in contrasting sound masses. His continued focus on structure and the manipulation of space is reflected in several other compositions that were ultimately not completed. *Untitled Composition for Voices* had as its basic premise the "correspondence between the aural counterpoint and a form of spatial counterpoint, where the singers move."[37] *Composition for Four Players* was based on the realization of such Klee drawings as *The Flying Seed* through glissando strings.[38] The first rough sketch for what would become *Statement in Blue* was completed by mid-September in preparation for the November Adaskin Project session in Toronto,[39] and he began to consider a work for young musicians based on the nuclear bombing of Nagasaki during World War II, which he would later name *Threnody*.[40] In addition to these smaller explorations of technique and forms, Schafer began to work on larger projects. A major composition called *Antigone* took up much of his time in 1964. Although he finished the libretto and sketched out some chorus parts, he ultimately chose not to finish the piece, and the score is lost.[41]

The other large-scale work he began at this time, *Loving*, would ultimately be completed through a commission from the French television wing of the CBC. The first section he wrote was *The Geography of Eros* at the end of 1963, and it premiered as a stand-alone composition by Mary Morrison as part of the Ten Centuries Concerts. *The Geography of Eros* marked another strong compositional development for Schafer and set up several compositional processes that would characterize his approach to large-scale theatrical compositions such as the use of the term "editing units" to mark divisions of a work and finishing and premiering shorter segments of a work before folding them into a larger composition. Schafer would continue to work on *Loving*, next finishing *Vanity's Aria* in 1964, a setting for mezzo-soprano and four tapes, which included prerecorded material of the same voice.[42] Ironically, his request to access the University of Toronto's electronic music studio in order to work on the piece was rejected on the grounds that he was not a student. When he asked if he could take a seminar in electronic music, and re-enroll as a student to do so, he was turned down for lack of academic qualifications.[43] This initially prevented him from carrying out some ideas he had for the composition, but by September he had completed the libretto draft of the first part of *Loving*, with the intent to sketch out the rest of the music for that part then begin the libretto for the second part of the piece.[44]

In the summer of 1964 Schafer continued his work with young students. C. Laughton Bird, the director of music education in North York, had been involved in the initial seminar of the Adaskin Project and had invited Murray back to teach a two-week summer course for students thirteen to seventeen, which Schafer simply called "Musicianship." The course would be repeated the next summer, and Schafer's discussion and work with these students, along with the sessions he had done in 1963 as part of the Adaskin Project, would form *The Composer in the Classroom*, published in 1965.[45] During one of the trips from Newfoundland back to Toronto, where they stayed with Harry Freedman and his wife Mary Morrison, Phyllis experienced increasing pain during the long train ride. Once they arrived in Toronto, Mary took Phyllis to the hospital, and Murray and Harry stayed at the Freedman's home to talk about music and other things. Late at night, Mary returned to inform Murray that Phyllis had had a miscarriage. This was the closest that Schafer would ever come to being a father, and looking back, he regrets not having the courage to speak to Phyllis about what happened and so wasn't able to ask her how she felt about it.[46]

In November of 1964 Murray received a letter from Pierre Mercure mentioning the possibility of commissioning *Loving* for television, with an anticipated broadcast date the following May. This was a serendipitous occurrence since he had already earlier speculated that the first part of *Loving* could be performed on radio or television.[47] He turned his attention back to finishing the libretto to take to Montreal in December to show Pierre and the officials at the CBC. In response to the commission from the French radio network, he began to think of making the piece bilingual, mixing English and French, which would open up a new dimension in the work and make it feasible for performance anywhere in Canada. The name of the piece was changed to *Loving/Toi*,[48] and Schafer was put in contact with Gabriel Charpentier, Pierre's assistant at the CBC, who had taken *The Geography of Eros* to a conference of radio broadcasters in France, where it had been well received. Gabriel would work on the libretto with Schafer, helping him translate the French portion of the text.[49]

By January of 1965 Schafer had developed his ideas for his new music drama enough to give a lecture to the Humanities Association at Memorial University about the composition, which he called "Aspects of *Loving*: A Work in Progress." Although he kept working diligently on the piece, he was often of two minds about its value. He found himself experiencing a dearth of ideas and distracted himself by reading voraciously.[50] He began the final copying of the piece by April and started to have ideas for another epic theater work, this time for the stage, called *D.P.* (Displaced Person), which would eventually emerge as *Patria 1*.[51]

As a result of the preparations for the upcoming broadcast of *Loving/Toi*, Schafer traveled several times to Montreal in the beginning of 1965 to work with the producers, and while he was on the mainland he usually took the opportunity to teach and arrange performances of his other compositions. A typical trip occurred in February when he first journeyed to Montreal to meet with Mercure and the CBC producers to work on *Loving/Toi* and to teach at the University of Montreal. From there he went to Toronto to oversee a performance and recording of *Canzoni for Prisoners* by the Toronto Symphony Orchestra then attend a performance of *Statement in Blue* by the Dufferin Heights Junior High School. The student players enjoyed *Statement in Blue* but at least two teachers the next day "condemned it as totally useless and contrary to the purpose of education,"[52] which only further confirmed the composer's belief of the need for the new approaches that he was currently espousing in his compositions and would later promote through his writings.

These constant trips to the mainland reminded him of his continued discontent with life in St. John's where, despite having renewed his contract for a second year, they were not using him to his full potential. He considered the university to be stuck in the past century and not interested in new things, and he referred to himself as "the only 20th-century man in the Arts Faculty at Memorial."[53] At the beginning of 1965 he and Phyllis began preparations for the move from St. John's, not yet knowing where they would be. They made their final preparations for departure in April, including attending several goodbye parties, and Schafer copied as much of *Loving* as he could before packing up his books and manuscripts. He arrived in Montreal in early May to begin serious work on the production of *Loving/Toi* with Pierre Mercure and composer/conductor Serge Garant.[54] Rehearsals were in progress by July although Pierre, who was producing the project and in particular leading the taping of the scenes, began to act strangely, drinking heavily and missing deadlines in rehearsals, and failing to check with the technical people.[55] After one visit to his hotel with one of the producers, it was decided that Pierre's behavior was erratic enough to take him to a hospital. A few months later, Pierre died in an automobile accident in France. It was discovered after his death that several scenes had not been filmed, despite Pierre's assurance that everything was completed.[56]

Murray and Phyllis spent the summer of 1965 in Toronto. Murray had been approached by an acquaintance, Bruce Attridge, about coming on to the faculty at Simon Fraser University in Burnaby, British Columbia. He had gone for an interview there but had to wait to see if they would hire him, given that he had no university degree. The couple received word in the summer that his hiring had been approved, and they moved to British Columbia, the opposite end of the country from Newfoundland, so that Murray could begin a new career in the Center for Communications and the Arts at the province's newest university.

Chapter Four

Academia, Notoriety, and New Endeavors

LIFE ON THE WEST COAST

By early September of 1965, Murray and Phyllis were settled into their new home in the Vancouver area, as Murray prepared to begin his teaching responsibilities at Simon Fraser University (SFU), perched on a mountaintop just outside of the city. Murray viewed his new job with a mixture of excitement, trepidation, and annoyance. The trepidation was from the prospect of teaching full-time, and the annoyance was from having to move to and be based in Vancouver in the midst of the final serious preparation for *Loving/Toi*.[1] Despite these initial misgivings, the decade Schafer spent in Vancouver would prove to be an exceptionally productive time for him.

At SFU, Murray was a member of the Center for the Study of Communications and the Arts. At its inception, SFU was eager to test out new ideas about university education and willing to hire teachers who were specialists in their fields but did not have multiple academic degrees, so Schafer found the center to be an ideal place for both his temperament and his academic outlook. He was a member of an interdisciplinary department designed by Archie MacKinnon to bring together the arts, media, and the sciences. MacKinnon was a student of the noted media theorist Marshall McLuhan,[2] and in addition to Schafer, MacKinnon also hired a television producer, a biologist, a theater director, a mechanical engineer, and a social psychologist. Most of the faculty embraced the chance to unite their fields of study, and Murray personally relished the opportunity to develop his growing theories in these various disciplines.[3] There was great flexibility and freedom in the teaching load and what classes the faculty could offer, and with the wide-open advancement policy in the early history of the university, Schafer achieved full professor rank in a mere five years.[4] As an added bonus, the university offered Schafer and his composer colleague Jack Behrens the opportunity to build one of the best electronic sound studios in North America, and the later addition of sound analysis equipment assisted Schafer's developing work in acoustics and psychoacoustics.[5] Since the center was originally housed in the Faculty of Education, Murray would also be able to further develop his theories on music education.

In his first fall at SFU, he published his first music education pamphlet, *The Composer in the Classroom*. This pamphlet grew directly out of his experiences working with students in the greater Toronto region, both in the summer of 1963 as part of the Adaskin Project and in the summers of 1964 and 1965 as part of a course offered by the North York School District.[6] As part of his initial duties at the center, Schafer co-taught with other music education faculty a course on music for first-year students. Two results of his work on this course were an article espousing the advantages of using graphic notation as an educational tool, "The Graphics of Musical Thought" (it would not be published until 1975), and his second music education pamphlet, *Ear Cleaning*, in 1967. The first nine sections and the final section of *Ear Cleaning* are reproductions of lecture notes and exercises Schafer prepared for the first-year experimental music class at SFU.[7]

In addition to the education course, Schafer also created what he called a new "sensitivity course." This class would meet on Saturdays, beginning at ten in the morning and often lasting until the later afternoon or even early evening.[8] Activities included holding a session in darkness to study the effects on conversation or blindfolding the students so they could have an unimpaired sonic experience in the lecture.[9] He later described his approach to the course in this way: "When we wanted to study the eye, we gathered together a physiologist to tell us about the physiology of vision, and a painter and an architect to share with us their insights into the aesthetics of vision."[10]

Schafer also had the opportunity to bring in guest lecturers, and early on in his time at SFU he brought in John Cage, who gave his famous "Lecture on Nothing." When Cage was at Schafer's house for the reception after, he noticed some of Schafer's graphic scores and commented positively on them. The two kept in touch, although not meeting often, and Cage followed Schafer's work on music education.

Eventually the Center for the Study of Communications and the Arts was moved from the Faculty of Education to the Faculty of Arts, which severed Schafer's links to his fellow education faculty but opened up new opportunities.[11] He began to teach a course called Communications 100, which introduced students to the connections between technology, the arts, and society at large. Typical assignments included such things as during the course of the semester, go to one of the following two corners in Vancouver, and remain there for a minimum of one hour. At the top of your assignment, give the date and time that you were there. You may record your impressions, observations, reflections, in any form you wish: written, taped (oral), visual photographic, cinematographic, etc., etc., etc. Use your imagination.[12]

One of these blocks was in a seedier part of Vancouver, and he gave the students total freedom in their projects, provided they put some effort into it. When one student brought in a leaf pasted on a piece of cardboard, Murray told him that he failed. When the student threatened to go to the dean of the school, Murray said, "Then don't forget to show your project."[13] Another location was a block in Burnaby, which included an empty church at one end. The students were to study an aspect of this rather ordinary block and create something to be exhibited in that church hall at the end of the semester. Projects included study of the architecture and a book of recipes gathered from the Italian immigrant women who lived on the block. On another occasion, a small seminar class was given one assignment: "You may do anything you want in this course provided you all do it together."[14] He then sat back and watched the students work out over the course of the semester what they would do.

MOVING BEYOND LOVING (AND BITTERNESS)

In the midst of his oft-times radical explorations into the pedagogy of teaching, Schafer continued his travels east to finish *Loving/Toi*, and even after the piece's unsuccessful premiere he maintained his musical ties to Ontario and Quebec. At the end of October he took an extended trip to Montreal, where he visited friends, including fellow composer Istvan Anhalt, and guest taught for the first time at McGill University. He then stayed to plan and execute, with Serge Garant, Gabriel Charpentier, and officials from the Canada Council, a seminar on the arts. These activities kept him away from Vancouver until the end of the year.[15]

The completion of *Loving/Toi* also allowed him to turn his attention to new compositions.[16] In addition to developing his "Displaced Person" work, he turned his attention to a large commission from the CBC for Phyllis. Initially called *Requiems*, it was performed and published as *Requiems for the Party Girl* and would become one of the core elements of *Patria 2*.[17] For voice and chamber ensemble, *Requiems for the Party Girl* sets thirteen brief text fragments of contrasting character, including multiple languages and nonsense syllables (all written by Schafer), divided over ten short arias.[18] He had completed this major commission by the end of 1966, and the premiere took place in February 1967 at SFU. After a second performance in Vancou-

Figure 4.1. Schafer in the Electronic Music Studio, Simon Fraser University. *R. Murray Schafer*

ver in 1968, *Requiems* enjoyed great success, was recorded three times, won a Fromm Foundation Music Award, and was championed by such great conductors as Bruno Maderna and Pierre Boulez. Two other pieces written in 1966, *Festival Music for Small Orchestra* (a commission from the Charlottetown Festival) and *Sonorities for Brass Sextet* (written for the St. John's Brass Consort as part of a Centennial Commission from the CMC) were later withdrawn.

His next choral piece, *Gita*, was written for the 1967 Tanglewood Festival through a commission from the Fromm Foundation. Two electronic pieces were written for the 1967 World Exposition in Montreal, one for the Man and Life Pavilion and one for the Pavilion of Chemical Industries. *Threnody* was written for the Vancouver Junior Youth Symphony Orchestra. Schafer had for a few years been contemplating this piece based on the bombing of Nagasaki, and when he received a commission from the Vancouver Junior Youth Orchestra, it spurred him to complete what has become one of the most performed pieces that Schafer has written for young musicians. He continued to travel to Toronto and Montreal to guest teach and to attend performances of his works. He and Phyllis also found time to vacation in Mexico.

The year 1967 was Canada's centennial year, and Schafer felt some bitterness that he received only three small commissions related to the celebrations—*Sonorities for Brass Sextet* and the two pieces for Expo '67. In particular, the success of Harry Somers's opera *Louis Riel*, which was a centenary commission, opened old feelings of bitterness about the unsuccessful production of *Loving/Toi* two years prior. In his journal he noted that he still had

> anger at the publicity Harry Somers' opera Riel is getting, not because I begrudge Harry his celebrity but because Loving, despite of or perhaps because of its innovatory qualities (also its enormous production difficulties and shortcomings) gained practically no attention at all, particularly in the English language areas of the country. Loving was the biggest "letdown" of my life from which it took two years to recover. Almost no one felt it succeeded. I could not reconcile these reactions with my own feeling that the opera is an important work with really significant things to say. A glance at my own works since Loving shows the long time I look in overcoming and fighting back. I have totally recovered now but I still get damn mad.[19]

His mood would lighten somewhat when in 1968 he applied for and received a Canada Council grant. After discovering that the grant also included money for travel, he decided to visit, with Phyllis, a place he had wished to see as early as the 1950s—the Middle East, and in particular Iran. He obtained a leave of absence from SFU for the spring semester of 1969 and began to look forward to and prepare for the trip.

Murray became increasingly productive in 1968 as the sting of being overlooked the previous year slowly receded. In March he wrote over the course of a few days his most popular choral composition, *Epitaph for Moonlight*. Schafer then turned his attention to a piece for Phyllis called *Sappho* but was interrupted by an unexpected commission from the Montreal Symphony Orchestra to write a work for the fall of that same year. He was notified of the commission by a letter, which gave no details as to the length of the piece or what he was to be paid for his efforts. After working out the details through several phone calls and agreeing to accept the commission, he happened to listen to a recording of Richard Strauss's tone poem *Don Juan*, which inspired him to use one of that composer's tone poems as the basis for his own composition. He chose *Ein Heldenleben* and began working steadily on his own piece, which he called *Son of Heldenleben*.[20] In April he traveled to Regina, Saskatchewan, to attend a performance of an opera by his colleague Jack Behrens, then continued east to Toronto then to Chicago, where he lectured at Northwestern University and heard a performance of *Threnody*.

STRUGGLES AND DISSATISFACTION

Once Schafer was back in Vancouver he kept working on *Son of Heldenleben*, began to go through his notes on the writings of Ezra Pound with the idea of preparing them for publication, and sketched out a third music education pamphlet. *The New Soundscape* would be published the next year as a reflection of his growing interest in environmental sounds and acoustic ecology.[21] These activities kept him busy until July, when he traveled to Quebec to teach at a camp for amateur musicians and where he celebrated his thirty-fifth birthday. He considered it a significant milestone, and wrote in his journal,

> Tomorrow is my 35th birthday and I can reveal a silent pact I made with myself many years ago that if I had not accomplished something truly significant by the 35th year I would commit suicide. I shall not commit suicide. What I have accomplished is certainly no degree "truly" significant; neither, I feel is it insignificant.[22]

As part of trimming away those things which he didn't consider significant, he decided to withdraw almost half of his existing compositions, including more recent works that he considered to be of insufficient quality, stating that "to be known perhaps as the author of one or two unique and uncounterfeiting works would be preferable, in this age of supersaturation, to classical ambition of seeing all works in print and on record."[23] The pieces he ultimately withdrew were *Sonorities for Brass Sextet*; *The Judgement of Jael*; *Dithyramb for String Orchestra*; *Invertible Material for String Orchestra*; *Festival Music for Small Orchestra*; *Opus One for Mixed Chorus*; *Divisions for Baroque Trio*; and *Four Songs on Texts of Tagore*. Such notable pieces as *Three Contemporaries*; *Partita for String Orchestra*; *Protest and Incarceration*; and most remarkably *Epitaph for Moonlight* were saved from this fate, although he initially considered withdrawing them as well. Even with this extensive compositional housecleaning, he continued to be very dissatisfied with his work. These feelings were compounded when in early August Phyllis performed a program that included both his *Requiems for the Party Girl* and Schoenberg's *Pierrot Lunaire*. In *Pierrot* Schafer heard everything he had sought to do in *Requiems* and found his own piece wanting.[24] Still, facing the Montreal commission, he forced himself to continue intensive work on *Son of Heldenleben*, and in an effort to find a new path he approached the composition of the piece quite differently, composing and copying the full score simultaneously, without any idea of where the piece was going, and resisting the urge to go back and revise or re-order.

Once that piece was finished and sent off, Schafer first took a break from composition to prepare *The New Soundscape* for publication then wrote the choral piece *From the Tibetan Book of the Dead*, using texts from the *Bardo Thodol*, a set of instructions to a dying person preparing them for their stay in the after-death state. Schafer interrupted work on the piece in early November to travel to Montreal to meet with Franz Paul Decker, the conductor of the Montreal Symphony Orchestra. When he arrived he discovered that Decker hadn't looked at the piece or listened to the electronic sections. When rehearsals began the maestro was purportedly ill so Murray had to take the first day of rehearsals until Decker arrived the second day. The premiere on November 12 was canceled due to weather, and since Schafer had already booked a plane ticket to London on November 13, he was at the airport waiting for his flight when the premiere took place. His friend and fellow composer Istvan Anhalt attended the concert and called him after, ecstatic about the piece.

TRAVELS IN EUROPE AND THE MIDDLE EAST

Schafer had planned this latest trip to Europe to do additional research on Ezra Pound. He spent a few days at the British Library then traveled on to Italy to visit Pound's widow and to search out additional writings Pound had done on music, many of which had been published in obscure Italian journals.[25] After this visit he made his way back by way of Rome and London to Toronto in early December for a performance of *Son of Heldenleben* by the Toronto Symphony Orchestra (TSO) then finally traveled home to Vancouver to supervise rehearsals for the upcoming premiere of *From the Tibetan Book of the Dead*. Once home he was approached by John Roberts, who was then director of music for the CBC, to write a one-hour radio drama for the network's submission for the Italia Prize, an international prize for radio programming. The piece that Schafer proposed was called *Dream Passage*, which incorporated the earlier *Requiems for the Party Girl*. The setting would be an asylum, where the singer would be surrounded by doctors and psychiatrists who would only speak foreign languages so that there was no hope of her being cured.[26] He spent the rest of the year working on the tape passages for this new piece at the electronic studio at SFU.[27]

Murray and Phyllis spent the first few months of 1969 preparing for their departure to the Middle East, and Murray focused on finishing up various writing and composing projects and immersing himself in the Koran and other Islamic writings. At the end of March they departed, traveling first from Toronto to Istanbul via Frankfurt. They did some sightseeing in Istanbul before going on to Tehran, where Murray found the pre–Islamic Revolution city overrun with American imperialism and rampant commercialism and bemoaned what he saw as a loss of the traditional culture. Most disturbing was that the muezzin, who led the call to prayer, had been replaced by a loudspeaker in one of the mosques in the city. They visited the ruins of Persepolis then went on to Isfahan to visit the mosque there, which he would later describe as the most beautiful building in the world. After Isfahan they went on to Konya, Turkey, to visit the Rumi mausoleum and to see relics of the dervishes. He immersed himself in the discourses of Rumi, the founder of Sufism, and also studied the tenets of Zoroastrianism, the other religion native to Iran. From Konya they traveled to Mersin, then to Side to enjoy the beach. The friendliness of the people there and the natural beauty of the countryside confirmed Murray's growing disgust for urban life. After several days at Side, they boarded a coastal cruiser which took them to Bodrum, Pergamon, and Izmir. He took the opportunity to once again visit Troy, then continued to Bergama, then Ephesus, and finally Athens by the middle of May. They then made the long trip back to North America, where their first destination was Chicago to attend a performance of *Requiems for the Party Girl* by the University of Chicago Chamber Players, with Neva Pilgrim as the soloist and Ernst Kreneck as the conductor. He found out that they were recording the piece without consulting him, with help from the Fromm Foundation.[28] He was initially angry but was able to stay in Chicago for a few more days to observe the recording session, and he was pleased with the result. He was offered a teaching position at the University of Chicago but ultimately decided that the rough urban life of Chicago during the late sixties was not to his taste. The couple traveled to Toronto to see Murray's parents, his brother Paul, and sister-in-law Joan.

THE RELUCTANT PROFESSOR

Murray was reluctant to return to Vancouver and decided that he would stay away as long as he could, perhaps even until September, even though this would mean being separated from Phyllis, who had immediate singing engagements on the west coast. He took advantage of this quiet time to jot down more thoughts about the themes he would include in future compositions, including re-workings of the Theseus and Ariadne stories. At the end of May the performance of *Dream Passage* by Phyllis, the University of British Columbia Singers, and the Vancouver Symphony Chamber Players was broadcast on the program *CBC Tuesday Night*.[29] The success of the piece encouraged Schafer to return once more to this material with the goal of expanding it into a full-length production. He also began writing another extended composition based on Rumi texts, *Divan I Shams I Tabriz*, using a three-week retreat at a cottage on Georgian Bay, northwest of Toronto, to complete the initial sketch. He would return to the sketch at the end of the year, revising it to fulfill a commission from the Vancouver Symphony Orchestra.

Schafer returned to Vancouver in June, where he worked on the final proofs for *The New Soundscape*, which was to be published later in the year, and began to put together the first draft of *When Words Sing*, his fourth music education pamphlet.[30] In July he began to work with fellow composer Harry Somers on the *Music Media Box*, a creative, interactive, mixed-media resource for the public school music classroom commissioned by the Ontario Arts Council.[31] This was interrupted by his late summer residency at the Maryland Summer School for the Arts, where he created the composition *Minimusic* as an ear-training exercise for the group of five students he was coaching.[32] That same summer Schafer's work with a seventh-grade class on his ideas about music education was filmed by the National Film Board of Canada and turned into a documentary, *Bing Bang Boom*.[33] His first composition project in the fall was two anthems for choir, organ, and electronics titled *Yeow and Pax*, commissioned by the First Congregational Church in Old Greenwich, Connecticut.

A NEW ENDEAVOR

Schafer reluctantly returned to SFU for the fall semester, where he was now professor in the Department of Communications Studies.[34] In addition to his compositional activity and work in music education, he was preparing to launch another initiative—the World Soundscape Project—and he began revamping a former electronic music studio at SFU into a Sonic Research Studio.[35] Schafer had been developing his ideas on acoustic ecology as early as 1966, and given his growing concerns about noise pollution and its effects on human health and communication, it seemed time to focus on this new project.

The World Soundscape Project (WSP) was officially named and launched in 1969, and for its first year was a project run chiefly by Schafer, with occasional help from his students, as part of the SFU curriculum. Schafer had first taught a course on noise pollution at SFU in the 1968 spring semester, which had not been met with much enthusiasm. When he returned back to work in September of 1969, Schafer incorporated his next series of classes on noise pollution into his Communications 100 class, and one of the class projects created the WSP's first document: "Results of a Social Survey on Noise—Vancouver 1969." Schafer describes the project as follows:

> About 650 people were interviewed on a door to door basis selected at random over a grid including Vancouver, Burnaby and New Westminster. . . . The answers for the first questions have been broken down into general age and occupation categories to facilitate cross-sectional analysis. This did not seem so necessary with the final questions.[36] Eight questions were asked of the people surveyed, and the following conclusions were reported—
>
> Well over 50% of the people polled regarded noise in modern life as an important or even major problem. Of those familiar with noise abatement procedures and legislation in their community, 66% were dissatisfied. 76% of those polled are in favour of more research to combat noise . . . and perhaps most interestingly of all, 60% were not convinced that noise was a necessary consequence of progress—an ancient and, thankfully, dying myth.[37]

This was an important first step for the project in that it not only gathered information about people's opinions but it also raised the issue in people's minds. The second document to come out of the project was *The Book of Noise*, drawn together in 1969 from lectures Schafer had given at meetings of the Scientific Pollution and Environmental Control Society (SPEC). Schafer had the sense that the idea of noise pollution was not being considered seriously, even by a group such as the SPEC, and he realized that he would have to be the main advocate for increasing awareness of this issue. He initially self-published (and paid for) the first printing of five thousand copies, giving copies to people interested in the issue of noise pollution.[38] It is the first publication where the Schafer formally defines the concept "soundscape," although he had already put this term and concept out into the public through *The New Soundscape*. In *The Book of Noise*, noise is placed in the context of the soundscape and as part of a discussion about the relationships between society and environmental sounds.

In 1970 Schafer sent a successful funding application to UNESCO, which included the specific aims of the WSP.

1. To undertake an intensive interdisciplinary study of contrasting acoustic environments and their effects on man.
2. To suggest ways of changing and improving acoustic environments.
3. To educate students and field workers in acoustic ecology.
4. To educate the general public in acoustic ecology.
5. To prepare reports as guides to future studies.

With funding in place, the WSP was ready to include national and international projects as part of its studies.

In the midst of this new activity Schafer continued to work on *Divan I Shams I Tabriz*, now a commission from the Vancouver Symphony Orchestra. He returned to his initial sketch in November and worked diligently to complete it for a scheduled performance in the spring of 1970. In March he learned that due to fire marshal regulations and double booking of the space, the piece would not be performed at all by the orchestra, despite being commissioned by them. He had already gotten resistance from both the symphony's manager and conductor due to the size of the piece (large orchestra, seven singers, tape), and its complexity (an orchestra divided into fourteen mixed quintets, a stage string group, and four percussion batteries), but logistics were the "evil mischief [that] succeeded in eliminating a year of my hopes and expectations, not to mention effort."[39]

CONTINUED SUCCESS

After this profound disappointment Schafer was able to get away from Vancouver, going on a previously planned visit to Europe to meet with a representative of Universal Editions and gauge their interest in publishing his compositions and translating his music education pamphlets into German.[40] He first went to Lausanne to see if the Recontres Culturelles would be a good place for him and Phyllis to stay and work for the summer, then on to Bern, Zurich, Saarbrücken, and finally Vienna to meet the Universal Editions representatives.[41] He waited several days to have a brief meeting with the director Herr Schlee then waited several more days to meet with the head of the project, Dr. Harpner. Harpner was not particularly encouraging, and Schafer assumed that nothing would happen, so he continued his journey, visiting friends in Paris and spending a few days in London before returning to Vancouver in late April. Just after his arrival back home he received a phone call from a Universal Editions employee, Friedrich Saaten, who indicated that he had been charged with translating Schafer's books into German and wanted to begin the process.[42] Included in this project would be Schafer's recently completed music education pamphlet, *When Words Sing*.

Schafer had two months back at home before leaving again for Europe to attend a UNESCO conference on music and so he turned his attention to a commission that he had received from the TSO, due in large part to the critical success of *Son of Heldenleben*. At the end of May he traveled to Ottawa for a CMC conference in the newly opened National Arts Center. The theme of the conference was "The Performer in 2001," and Schafer's contribution was to take the delegates on a sound walk through Ottawa to introduce the concept of the performer's need to expand his listening to include all environmental sounds.⁴³ He then went to Toronto, where he turned his full attention to another commission, a string quartet to be performed by the Purcell String Quartet in July. He stayed for a while in Ontario, working on the commissions and shuttling back and forth between Toronto and Ottawa for a performance of *Son of Heldenleben* and a performance and recording of *Threnody*.⁴⁴

Once the Purcell Quartet commission was finished (his *String Quartet no. 1*) Schafer turned his attention to the several other commissions he had received, including *Enchantress*, commissioned by the CBC for Mary Morrison; *Music for the Morning of the World*, commissioned by the Société Contemporaine for Phyllis; *East* for the National Arts Center Orchestra; and of course the TSO, which he was now calling *No Longer Than Ten (10) Minutes*.⁴⁵ He worked frantically to make progress on all of these pieces, traveling to Stockholm for the UNESCO conference where he was to speak on acoustic ecology. From there he traveled to Switzerland to have additional meetings with Universal Editions, which would keep him away from Canada until July.

He made it back to Vancouver in time to attend the successful premiere of his *String Quartet no.1* by the Purcell String Quartet at the Vancouver Art Gallery. As he returned to composing, he first turned back to an earlier piece he intended for Phyllis, *Sappho*, and also began work on an extended electronic piece with Bruce Davis and Brian Fawcett at SFU's Sonic Research Studio. Called *Okeanos*, the composition would be a study of the sounds and symbolism of the sea, commissioned by CBC Vancouver for broadcast the next year.⁴⁶ These projects were an excuse to not work on the TSO, which he was finding difficult, but when Phyllis was away for much of the month of October, traveling and performing, he focused on finishing the Ezra Pound book, working on the TSO commission, and sketching out ideas for the third movement of the *Lustro* triptych, which he would call *Beyond the Great Gate of Light*.⁴⁷

At the beginning of 1971 Murray took the train to Toronto to visit his parents, since his father was ailing, and on the trip back to Vancouver he stopped for a while in Brandon, Manitoba, to teach and also to visit his mother's relatives. The snow-covered prairie landscape, marred visually and aurally by recreational snowmobilers, gave him the idea to write a piece where the snow was completely obliterated by the roar of snowmobiles, which he would call *North/White*.⁴⁸ Back in Vancouver in February he began the second part of the *Lustro* triptych, which he called *Music for the Morning of the World*,⁴⁹ working diligently until his next trip, only a few weeks away. This next trip started with yet another train ride to Toronto, where he attended the premiere of *No Longer Than Ten (10) Minutes*, a rather scandalous event for both the audience and the critics. After the premiere Schafer worked his way east, teaching in Quebec, New Brunswick, and Newfoundland, then he took a flight from St. John's to London in early March.[50] Once in England he gave a series of lectures at the University of York on several topics, including music, sociology, religion, science, and the environment. He then went on to Salzburg and Paris then back to Canada, returning home after being over a month away.

He returned home to several projects, including *Enchantress*, *Beyond the Great Gate of Light*, and a new commission for Dartmouth College, which he had decided to base on Zoroastrian thought and call *In Search of Zoroaster*. He also, on a whim, decided to write another graphic notation piece for youth choir inspired by his soundscape work, in which he was still deeply immersed. He called the piece *Miniwanka, or The Moments of Water*, and used words for water in various Native American languages.[51] These activities kept him busy until October, when he traveled to Moscow to lecture at the meeting of the International Music Council of UNESCO,[52] stopping in London along the way to finalize publication arrangements with Universal Editions. Once back in Vancouver he worked on finishing an article for the UNESCO *Journal of World History*, "The Music of the Environment." He also finally completed *Enchantress*, deciding to reuse the text from his earlier piece *Sappho*, which he had decided to withdraw. As he turned his attention back to *Beyond the Great Gate of Light*, the third part of *Lustro*, he had serious misgivings about the triptych. Although he was worried that it was too "pretentious" and demanding and therefore would likely never be performed, he decided to finish the piece since he had come this far. He then completed *In Search of Zoroaster* and finally finished *Okeanos*.[53]

PERSONAL TURMOIL AMID PUBLIC SUCCESS

Schafer was experiencing a level of productivity and public success unmatched in his life so far, but he was also experiencing serious personal turmoil. As early as 1968 there are mentions in Murray's journals of "meeting someone." This "someone" was Jean Reed, a recent divorcée who had just moved to Canada from England with her two teenage sons, and had begun to work as a secretary at SFU.[54] Schafer fell almost immediately in love with Jean but hesitated for a long time as to whether he should leave Phyllis to move in with her.[55] His relationship with Jean continued to grow in intensity over the next several months, but he was still uncertain as to what to do by the beginning of 1971, and as late as June of that year he thought he would stay with Phyllis.[56] This resolution was short lived as by July he was with Jean for good. "I shall never forget the day I moved out, leaving Phyllis sobbing on the floor of our apartment and, as the years pass, I accuse myself more and more."[57] On his way to the UNESCO conference in October he had to stop by Toronto to let his parents know about his breakup with Phyllis and new relationship with Jean. The next day he wrote,

> I have for so long suppressed thoughts of Phyllis because I did not want to become sentimental; but there is no doubt that, whether merely because of my upbringing, or because of some deeper sense of duty, my behavior over the past few months has cracked my life to pieces—and I can say this in spite of the fact that my life with Jean has been uncommonly happy. Perhaps I never had integrity, I think probably I didn't; but in the midst of those family scenes which I thought stupid or boring I realize now there was something more sacred, for which all the recent successes of my career can never compensate.[58]

By January of 1972, Murray was settled in with Jean and her two boys, and more than ready to put the past tumultuous years behind him. That month *Requiems for the Party Girl* was performed by the New York Philharmonic under the baton of Pierre Boulez, and he had multiple commissions waiting to be filled, including *North/White* for the National Youth Orchestra of Canada, the earlier National Arts Center Orchestra commission (*East*, still not completed), a vocal piece called *Arcana* for the Montreal International Competition, and a piece for youth orchestra called *Train*. Between working on these pieces, he was revising and combining various earlier pieces (including *Requiems for the Party Girl*; *From the Tibetan Book of the Dead*; and *Dream Passage*) to create *Patria 2: Requiems for the Party Girl* for an August production at Ontario's Stratford Festival.[59]

Schafer was able to complete *Patria 2* by the end of April, then he took a much needed break from composition to turn his attention to writing. He wanted to finish his first full-length soundscape publication (*The Tuning of the World*), gather his current thoughts about *Patria* into an article called "The Theatre of Confluence," and make progress on his fifth music education pamphlet, *The Rhinoceros in the Classroom*. He turned back to composition in July, first writing a shorter choral setting of Psalm 148 (originally titled *Tehillim* but renamed *Psalm* when he revised the piece in 1976) then finishing *Arcana* and finally sketching out *East*. In June was the broadcast performance of *Music for the Morning of the World* and in August was the highly successful production of *Patria 2* on the third stage of the Stratford Festival. It was directed by his SFU colleague Michael Bawtree, with the orchestra conducted by Serge Garant, and Phyllis playing the role of Ariadne.

The year 1972 was also (in the opinion of Keiko Torigoe, among others) the official founding of the WSP as a stand-alone organization since Schafer and his assistant Bruce Davis, with funding from UNESCO and the Donner Foundation, were able to hire a group of paid researchers.[60] With the hiring of research assistants, the WSP began regular meetings to further develop their missions and goals and begin field research by the end of year.[61]

After a year of frantic personal and professional activity, Murray and Jean began 1973 with a boat trip to New Zealand and Australia, stopping in Honolulu on their outward journey. There Schafer was met at the dock and taken out to lunch by people from the Music Department at the University of Hawaii, then he gave a two-hour lecture at the university on music education. Once in New Zealand he worked for two weeks, lecturing and teaching. From there they sailed to Sydney, and while on the boat Schafer took the opportunity to write a few paragraphs for the celebration of John Weinzweig's sixtieth birthday for the journal *Cahiers de Musique*. Once in Australia he taught in Sydney, Adelaide, Perth, and finally Melbourne, where he was also one of four speakers at an International Society for Contemporary Music meeting. From Australia they traveled back to Vancouver, stopping at Fiji along the way.

Murray was only in Vancouver for a few weeks in April before he traveled east to attend several premieres, the first being *In Search of Zoroaster* in New Hampshire. Upon his arrival in Dartmouth he was thrust into the role of musical director for the performance and was also asked to oversee the staging and lighting of the piece, which he was not expecting to do but found to be fairly easy, and the positive experience renewed his belief in the power of his compositions.[62] From Dartmouth he went directly to Ottawa to attend a rehearsal of *East* by the National Arts Center Orchestra then to Toronto to see the Canadian premiere of *In Search of Zoroaster* and even more significantly the premiere performance of *Lustro* by the TSO. These various works represented three years of intense compositional toil, and it was a crowning achievement for his career thus far to see all of them come before the public. He was also able to listen to the performances of *Arcana* from the Montreal International Competition. The effect of hearing so many new pieces in such short succession encouraged Murray, and he felt that he was finally producing pieces of significance that would remain in the canon of contemporary classical music. While still in Ontario Schafer completed his next major commission, *North/White*, for the National Youth Orchestra of Canada, using the initial sketches he had prepared on the long boat ride back from Australia to Vancouver. He initially struggled with the idea of including a snowmobile in *North/White* and placing it prominently on the stage but decided to leave it in to reinforce the environmental message he wished to convey:

> The North is not described by the adjective "pretty" and neither is this piece. *North/White* is inspired by the rape of the Canadian North. This rape is being carried out by the nation's governments in conspiracy with business and industry. The instruments of destruction are pipelines and airstrips, highways and snowmobiles.[63]

Chapter 4

GROWING RESENTMENT AND A FRESH START

Schafer was finally free of commissions for a time, which allowed him to work on pieces he was interested in, including a piece based on the New Testament Book of Revelation (*Apocalypsis*), and *Patria 1: The Characteristics Man*, which he was determined to bring to the public even if he had to produce it himself. He began to experience a growing resentment about the time that he had to devote to his teaching and soundscape research, which robbed him of valuable composing time. He reluctantly turned back to finishing both *The Tuning of the World* and *The Rhinoceros in the Classroom*, and at the beginning of August began to prepare his fall semester courses for SFU. With several members of the WSP, both associates and research assistants,[64] he worked to complete the WSP's next large project, *The Vancouver Soundscape*, a set of recordings with an accompanying booklet.[65] Two WSP members, Bruce Davis and Peter Huse, spent almost all of October and November traveling across Canada from Vancouver to St. John's and back again, collecting sound data to begin research on a national level.[66] In addition to these major initiatives, the WSP had collected data on other sonic concepts, using it to produce several articles in local newspapers to get the word out about what they were doing.

Murray's frustration with his lack of time for composing continued into 1974, when all of his non-teaching energy was devoted to finishing up various writing projects. He brought *The Tuning of the World* into final draft form, readied *The Rhinoceros in the Classroom* for publication, oversaw of completion of the *Acoustic Ecology Dictionary*, edited by Barry Truax, for the WSP, and produced ten one-hour broadcasts for the CBC, titled *Soundscapes of Canada*, which would be broadcast from October 21 to November 1 of that year and included compositions by Bruce Davis, Peter Huse, Barry Truax, and Howard Broomfield.[67] Finally at the end of June, with the semester over, he turned his attention back with some apprehension to *Patria 1* since he had set it aside for so long. The libretto was now complete, and he knew that he was going to incorporate the choral piece *Gita*, but the rest of the music still needed to be composed. He was able to finish the first draft by the middle of September, when classes began again, and during an October trip to Ontario to teach at McMaster and Brock universities he took the opportunity to meet with representatives of the National Arts Center to talk about possibly producing the piece.

Murray had been working hard to finish up these non-composition projects for a reason—he and Jean had decided to leave Vancouver and move to a farmhouse in rural Ontario. This would allow Murray to focus on composing while supplementing his income as needed through guest lecturing and teaching. They had vacated their house in the Vancouver area at the end of September in preparation for the move, and on November 18, 1974, Murray officially submitted his letter of resignation to SFU, listing his reasons for leaving the teaching position he had held for ten years.

> As the University has developed many changes have taken place. I do not know whether they are for the general good or not, but their cumulative effect has been to alienate me. Money and space are both in shorter supply than formerly and the continual scramble one must indulge in to obtain minimal facilities is tedious and wasteful of energy for everyone.
>
> Much of my early work at the University was in music education and I developed here what is now considered by many to be a valuable new approach to that subject. My books on music education are having a considerable influence in many countries of the world. It is a deep personal regret that my work in this field has been completely ignored by our own Faculty of Education.[68]

He closed the letter with the following words:

> I have often wondered how long it would be possible for me to combine an active career as a composer with teaching responsibilities and research work. I have always known that, of the many kinds of work in which I am engaged, musical composition is the most important. When it becomes threatened, I suffer. Therefore I recently bought a farm in Ontario and it is my plan to make that the centre of my future life.[69]

As 1974 ended Murray was ready, with Jean, to turn the page on the most fruitful decade of his life and begin a new career as a full-time composer and homesteader.

Chapter Five

Country Life, Renewed Creativity, and Change

THE BIG MOVE AND UNEXPECTED COMPLICATIONS

As 1975 dawned Murray and Jean were in the midst of preparations to abandon Vancouver for the rural community of Bancroft, Ontario. Having already wrapped up his responsibilities at SFU, Schafer divided his time between helping Jean with the practical aspects of the move and wrapping up several professional and creative projects, including editing *Patria 1* and preparing several works for publication. He would soon be off to Europe to give multiple lectures on music education and soundscape and also engage in a research project with several members of the WSP. During the trip he found the often repeated, nearly identical lectures he had to give physically and emotionally draining in combination with the extensive soundscape research conducted by him and the other WSP members. The materials they gathered would need months of organizing for publication and would not be publicly issued until 1977 as *Five Village Soundscapes*.

Murray returned from this grueling trip to an equally grueling task: the reconstruction of the rundown farmhouse that he and Jean had purchased, which was in much worse shape than either of them had realized. It would take almost the rest of the year to make it truly livable, and it was a most unpleasant process, as he noted in his journal.

> But the worst experience was to rebuild the farmhouse without the skills required so that only now within the last two weeks or so has it become inhabitable. It was not so much the sheer physical work of reconstruction that drove us to exasperation, for that was probably good for us. It was the delays, the mistakes, the mounting cost. Twice I had to revise my estimate of the

> amount of time it would take. It would deprive me of all intellectual pursuits (reading, writing, letters) not to mention all creative work. (I have not composed a note since the completion of Patria I last January.) It has only been during recent weeks that we have finally been able to unpack our effects and sort them out, for now at last we have heat and plumbing. The painting is finished and the wood is cut for winter. We still spend about four hours a day working at the house (today it was tiling the bathroom floor) but the heavy work is all behind us. I never experienced anything so frustrating in my life. For many of the jobs we could not get workmen and so we (Jean did as much and more than I) stumbled through them ourselves, learning from mistakes, cursing the mistakes and taking no pride in what we had learned.[1]

The couple did manage to find time in the midst of the renovations and general chaos to be officially married in September, when their respective divorces were finalized, and at Christmas they were able to go to Toronto to visit his family. By New Year's Eve the farmhouse was in good enough shape for his dear friend Robert Aitken to visit with his family.[2] Murray considered 1975 a lost year as he was only able to bring to publication two significant projects that he had completed the previous year. The first was his fifth music education pamphlet, *The Rhinoceros in the Classroom*. The second was *E. T. A. Hoffmann and Music*, the first draft of which had been largely completed while Schafer was in Vienna in the late 1950s. It was only now, after many delays and several years of editing and rewriting, that he felt it was ready to be presented to the public.[3]

Schafer began 1976 by intensely working on several projects, the largest of which was *Apocalypsis*, his earlier conceived piece based on the biblical Book of Revelations. A second project was a piece for voice and orchestra commissioned for the noted Canadian contralto Maureen Forrester, which he had already titled *Adieu, Robert Schumann*. The third project was his *String Quartet no. 2: Waves*. He worked quickly on all three pieces, finishing first drafts by the middle of February. The rest of his energy was devoted to revising the novella *Smoke* and fleshing out *The Tuning of the World*.

In the middle of February Murray and Jean began to take tentative steps to integrate into their new community, first by visiting the church services offered by the local congregations. Although neither Murray nor Jean were particularly religious, they viewed church attendance as a way to connect to the community around them so that they would not become more and more isolated and grow stir crazy over the long winter months.[4] They would eventually decide to regularly attend the Maynooth Lutheran Church. As winter turned into spring, he found time to relax into country life, connect further with people (although he noted in his journal, "It is hard to stand around until the country people decide what they think of you"),[5] and let his creative life be influenced by the physical countryside, mentally modeling himself after Canada's Group of Seven painters. Although this idyllic life was too often interrupted by trips to the city that he called "pisspot Toronto," he continued to be productive, finishing both *Adieu, Robert Schumann* and *Waves* and starting two new compositions, *La Testa d'Adriane* and *Hymn to Night*, with ideas of folding them into another *Patria* work. He worked more seriously on *Smoke* and started to gather together a collection of essays about music in Canada.

LOOKING BACKWARD, LOOKING FORWARD

In August Murray reluctantly journeyed back to Vancouver to finish two soundscape projects, the *European Sound Diary* and the *Five Village Soundscapes*, and to raise money to get them published. He felt he was coming back to SFU as a defector, and even though he was concerned by what he saw as an increasingly academic and less socially conscious focus to the WSP, he didn't feel he had the right to take back leadership from the new director, fellow composer and teacher Barry Truax. It took the entire month of August to bring the two projects into shape, and when Schafer returned home he found it difficult to get back to composition. He spent much of his time reading, and in order not to be completely unproductive he corrected earlier scores and parts for publication. He would not fully turn his attention back to composition until November, completing *Hymn to Night* later that month and then turning his attention to *La Testa d'Adriane* and *Apocalypsis*. Since his only professional engagements toward the end of the year were a lecture in Toronto called *Music in the Cold* and the premiere of the educational piece *Train* by the Victoria Park School in Toronto, he was able to make significant progress on the two pieces.

The Schafers were now well settled into their life at the farm, and the past year had been more productive for Murray, who was able to complete five significant compositions and the novella *Smoke*. Despite this, the composer faced 1977 with anxiety about his continued progress as a composer, as reflected in a "prayer" he wrote in his journal in January.

> Let me be young again, not in energy or strength, but in daring. . . . Give me the courage to abandon the comfortable style of maturity and to hammer out new shock-thoughts, gristly dialogue with the environment, instead of fat monologues with myself.[6]

Despite these internal struggles, Schafer continued composing, focusing almost exclusively on the first part of *Apocalypsis*, called *John's Vision*, after having finished the second part, *Credo*, the previous year. He was now under a deadline to complete the piece since there was a planned fall production at Toronto's Metropolitan Church involving multiple churches as part of the annual Dayspring Festival, which Murray had been involved with for a few years. He focused exclusively on writing, rewriting, and copying this enormous work until the beginning of May, only pausing to do the lectures and interviews necessary to support himself and Jean.[7] Only a week after finishing the work and copying out the parts for the choirs, he discovered that the full production would not be performed as scheduled due to lack of money since the Faith and Arts Commission had decided to not support it. There had been resistance to the project for some time since the minister at Metropolitan who had initially agreed to the project had left for another position, and the Dayspring Festival had begun to falter, despite Murray's personal efforts to keep the project going. He also began receiving letters and complaints from the governing bodies of the various churches, including a letter from the wardens at St. Paul Anglican Church withdrawing their participation in and support of the project.

Schafer's immediate response to this bitter disappointment was to go outside and put in some fence posts because work on the property needed to continue, but the cancellation of the full production of *Apocalypsis* affected him almost to the same level as the public rejection of *Loving/Toi* several years back. He fell into a deep depression, the symptoms of which were frequent and extended headaches and a general lethargy that made it difficult to do anything other than some scribblings on the beginnings of another book, which would eventually become *Dicamus et Labyrinthos*.[8] This lasted for nearly a full month, and Murray was only able to break out of it by doggedly working on *Dicamus* and returning to an earlier planned series of essays on the musical scene in Canada, beginning with expanding last year's lecture *Music in the Cold*.[9] Even after the depression lifted he was not able to return to composition for several more weeks, despite the pressure of a looming commission for the National Arts Center Orchestra. Although he outwardly blamed his lack of productivity on the summer heat, he inwardly realized that he was experiencing a mental crisis that had been steadily building over the last several weeks, ever since the completion and subsequent rejection of *Apocalypsis*. His confidence was shaken, and he would awaken each day with a type of mental paralysis, fearing that he was going nowhere and lamenting that "I am seeking new forms of expression, but I lack precise direction and am not yet fortified with enough confidence to really tackle them."[10]

To outside observers, life and success seemed to continue apace for Murray. Both *The Tuning of the World*, Schafer's first extended book on acoustic ecology, and the long-awaited *Ezra Pound and Music*, in process for over a decade, appeared in print. Schafer also distracted himself by succumbing to the pleas of the leadership at the Maynooth Lutheran Church, who had been asking him for some time to start a choir at their parish. The stated purpose of the group was to help improve the singing at the church, and Murray found the training he had received as a boy and young man in his church choir in

Toronto useful as he began this new endeavor with six singers, hardly any of whom read music. The choir quickly grew to fifteen members, and he soon had the choir singing in harmony, taping the lower parts to well-known hymns and lending the cassette player out to a member each week. He also took to visiting the choir members to make sure they stayed involved and even would drive to pick up those choir members who did not have a way to get to the church for rehearsal.[11] By the fall he had gotten the choir up to forty enthusiastic and dedicated singers who were ready to take on larger projects.

By September Schafer's compositional energy had finally returned, and he was able to make progress on the commission for the National Arts Center Orchestra in Ottawa, which he titled *Cortège*. Due to his extended period of depression and inactivity he was now pressed for time and was only able to leave a week between the first draft and the rewrite. This was much less time than he usually allowed himself, but he had to complete the piece by the beginning of November before he left for an extended lecture and teaching tour in Europe. His travels took him first to London to visit old friends then on to continental Europe, with Poland as his first stop. After teaching there he went to Portugal, where his first engagement was in the capital city of Lisbon, working with students under the auspices of the Gulbenkian Foundation. From there he went to the city of Coimbra where he taught a large group class on creativity, folding into the planned lectures and activities some of the pressing issues he was exploring in the fields of music education and acoustic ecology.[12] He would not return to Canada until later December, in time to mail copies of *Music in the Cold* as Christmas presents to friends. He was refreshed by the trip, feeling for the first time that people in that continent were interested in what he had to offer.[13]

COMPOSITIONAL MALAISE AND SOUND SCULPTURE

Schafer began 1978 still profoundly disappointed at the failure of *Apocalypsis*. He had managed to produce a performance of a greatly reduced and truncated version because he had personally agreed to manage and direct it himself, a task that he never wanted to take on again. He also was discouraged by the overall tone of the reviews that had come out about *The Tuning of the World*. He had hoped for the book to be a Eureka! moment for modern humanity around such issues of sound, acoustic ecology, and noise pollution, but it had not happened, even though some of the reviews did give him some hope that the book would gradually have some influence in this area.[14] He was able to move on from both disappointments and, after attending the successful premiere of *Hymn to Night*, turned his attention to revising *La*

Testa d'Adriane, hoping to finish this final commission so that he could devote his full creative energies to the *Patria* cycle.

Schafer could not begin serious work on the cycle for a few months as the whole of February and part of March would be broken up by various travels to see performances and premieres of his pieces. In Toronto were the premieres of *Hymn to Night* and the first stage production of *Loving/Toi* (which would tour Ottawa, Montréal, and Halifax). A ballet was being choreographed in Montreal to his *String Quartet no. 1*, and the premiere of *Adieu, Robert Schumann* was happening in Ottawa. His parents were able to come to Ottawa for the rehearsals and performances of that piece, driven there by his brother Paul.

After this flurry of activity he was able to return home and turn his attention back to composition, although he initially had no ideas for new pieces and no commissions to force him to his desk.[15] Inspiration would be a long time coming, as Schafer fell into another period of creative stagnation and depression, although this time it was not accompanied by the severe headaches as in the past. He kept busy through his involvement in the recording and editing of *Loving/Toi* after the tour was finished and then correcting the scores and parts for publication. The early summer was taken up by a project for Yehudi Menuhin and the CBC. Menuhin had written a letter to Schafer outlining a series of shows he was producing with CBC television titled *The Music of Man*. Since Menuhin was a great supporter of Schafer's soundscape work, he wanted to devote one of the eight shows to an exploration of soundscape. They decided on a date in June, and Schafer suggested that as part of the show he would create a sound sculpture. The previous owner of their farm had left several pieces of junk metal in a barn and drive shed, and in the previous year Schafer and a student who was driving up from Toronto every two weeks to study with him had decided to make a sound sculpture out of those pieces of junk. The sculpture they constructed in the old barn did not survive the winter, but the process had given Schafer several ideas for a new creation. He solicited the help of Rosemary Smith and Harry Mountain, friends of his who were respectively a composer and a sculptor, and the three of them built the sound sculpture over the course of three days. The sound sculpture was activated by Schafer and Menuhin riding up and down on a seesaw.[16]

By the middle of the summer Schafer was finally able to turn his attention to future projects, including a commission for a trombone ensemble that he had decided would be set around a lake at dawn and dusk as a new type of environmental composition. He still found it hard to focus on composition and made slow progress throughout the summer and into the fall, when he took an extended teaching trip to the United States in October, lecturing in North Dakota and Wisconsin. At the end of the month he was back in Ontario, and he began to look for sites for the piece for the trombone ensemble, which he was calling *Music for Wilderness Lake*. He also focused on expanding two *Patria* segments, one of which would be based on the idea of a circus sideshow, the other on the Greek myth of Theseus, Ariadne, and the Minotaur. He also helped bring to publication *The Handbook for Acoustic Ecology*, a compilation of terms and concepts related to the field of soundscape studies. It would be the last WSP publication that Schafer would be involved in.

As the year ended, Murray was frustrated at what appeared to be another lost year. He had devoted much of his time to *Patria*, and although he now had the outline of the next three segments of the cycle, he had only sketched out a few preliminary drafts of the text or music, including some of the harp music for *Patria 5*. *Apocalypsis* was his only completed piece, which had not even received its planned performance. The only other things he had to show were some work on *Dicamus et Labyrinthos*, the first ten pages of an essay called "Ursound," and the beginnings of a graphic novel called *The Chaldean Inscription*.[17]

COMMUNITY ENGAGEMENT AND A NEW KIND OF MUSIC

As 1979 began he didn't have much time to brood as he had to finish the final corrections and copying of *Loving/Toi* and edit and complete several items for a special double issue of the literary journal *Open Letter* that was devoted to his work. He rushed to complete usable drafts of *Dicamus et Labyrinthos* and *Ursound* while also selecting various previously written pieces to round out the issue. He also edited the harp music he had written last year, which was written for the harpist Judy Loman and intended for inclusion in *Patria 5*. He called the stand-alone piece *The Crown of Ariadne*. After its successful premiere in March, Murray was inspired to go back to *Patria 5* and work further on the music.

At the beginning of May Schafer traveled to New York to lecture at the New School of Social Research at New York University, giving various lectures and classes and speaking at a conference on soundscape.[18] Upon returning he fell once again into depression, this time with the accompanying symptomatic headaches and eye pain, which he tried to ignore through such physical activities as digging in the garden.[19] These episodes had happened enough by now for Murray to clearly see a pattern.

> I've been through this before. Momentary resolutions to do something; inability to sustain interest in any topic for more than 10 minutes, guilt at not composing or doing interesting creative work, headaches and eyeaches so that I can't even read. It has lasted many days.

This malaise was compounded by Jean's accompanying depression. She found the black flies of rural Ontario relentless and was confined to the indoors.

As spring turned into summer and his depression continued, Schafer distracted himself by focusing on the inaugural concert of the Maynooth Community Choir, which took place in early July, and for which he had written two pieces, *Hear Me Out* and *Gamelan*. The choir now had close to forty members and had grown into a true community group, and for the performance there was an audience of almost two hundred, an exceptional turnout for such a small community.[20] Encouraged by this success he began to work on a larger project for the choir, a collaboratively created piece based on the Old Testament story of Jonah. *Jonah* was created largely through improvisation by the choir members, with guidance from Schafer. The instrumentation was modest, using the people available in the area, including organ, flute, and clarinet. The performance in August was once again a true community event, involving about forty performers from an area whose total population was a little over two hundred. The church was full for both performances.[21]

As well as working on *Jonah* in July, Schafer also turned back to *Music for Wilderness Lake* and settled on an unfrequented lake close to his farmhouse for the site. Some film students (who were to later form Rhombus Media) were engaged to record the performance in order to make a documentary about the piece and the process,[22] to be broadcast later as part of the CBC Spectrum Series. Despite the mist at the lake on the day of the performance in late September, they were able to get two good takes of the morning portion and enough of the evening portion to make it worthwhile.[23] Inspired by the success of the piece and the possibilities of this new compositional direction, Murray began to sketch out initial ideas for a larger piece based on and around a lake, which would eventually become *Patria Prologue*. After a quiet October Schafer traveled to Ottawa in November to attend a performance of *Hymn to Night* with the National Arts Center Orchestra, and while in Ottawa he went to view Canadian landscapes at the National Gallery by painters from the Group of Seven, seeking inspiration for future compositions. The rest of the year was spent sketching out a piece for Maureen Forrester to sing with string quartet called *Beauty and the Beast*, working at a humorous/satirical choral piece called *Felix's Girls*, and serving on an awards jury for the Canada Council of the Arts.[24]

A NEW VENTURE AND PERSONAL LOSS

The beginning of 1980 was again a busy time for Murray. He first went to teach for a few weeks in Southern California, returning to Ontario in early February. He had additional shorter engagements through February and

March, which took him away a total of five weeks. When he was home in April, he and Jean began a new venture. Murray had grown increasingly frustrated over the past few years with his two publishers Berandol and Universal Editions, who did not seem interested in either promoting his current published works or accepting new works. He decided to create his own company to promote and distribute his music, and he and Jean spent several hours creating promotional materials announcing the launch of Arcana Editions before they left for Europe at the beginning of May. Schafer's lecturing took them to Italy, Switzerland, Vienna, and Paris (having to lecture in English, French, and German) before they returned to Canada at the beginning of June. Once back Schafer was able to briefly turn back to composition, devoting his energies to a piece for Maureen Forrester to sing with orchestra called *The Garden of the Heart*.

In July he launched into intensive preparations for the first full performance of *Apocalypsis*, which the University of Western Ontario had agreed to produce. The performance was scheduled for November, and since Murray ended up again directing the work himself the project took his full attention until early December. Although the full production was originally supported by the CBC and was broadcast by them, Schafer felt that the production team that the CBC sent out to London was of no help and seemed to be wishing for the project to fail.[25] He later learned that they destroyed all of the tapes of *Apocalypsis* after the broadcast before he had a chance to make copies to even listen to them. He found the whole process exhausting, and in the midst of this intense period his father entered into the final stages of his battle with cancer. This meant that when Schafer was not in London for *Apocalypsis*, he was in Toronto in his father's hospital room. The death of his father at the end of the year was painful for Murray, especially the final visits in the hospital. A few weeks later he heard about the passing of Marshall McLuhan, whom he considered to be a spiritual father.

With all the distractions of the past year, Schafer had only managed to complete *The Garden of the Heart*, a choral piece called *Snowforms*, many of the texts for *Patria 3* and one composition intended for it, and a duo for speaker and clarinet called *Wizard Oil and Indian Sagwa*. Despite this, Schafer was surprisingly positive, feeling that he was at the peak of his powers and having fewer doubts about the value of his compositions.[26]

A NEW DECADE AND NEW DIRECTIONS

The new decade saw Schafer again traveling west, first to Vancouver for the premiere of *Snowforms* (he considered the piece a failure), then to Alberta to discuss ideas for a new environmental piece, his *Patria Prologue: The Princess of the Stars*, with the directors of the Banff Centre for the Arts. He also visited the University of Calgary library, which had obtained some of his manuscripts from Phyllis, and saw some things that he had completely forgotten about. From Calgary he flew to Kansas City to lecture, then traveled by train to Chicago for another teaching engagement before finally arriving back home in February.

Although he had three commissions to finish, he put off working on them since he had no upcoming professional engagements until May (a soundscape course at Montreal's Concordia University) and wished to focus on *Patria* material and other projects. As a bridge back to composing he began to correct and prepare several scores for printing with Arcana Editions, including the major task of putting *Apocalypsis* into its final form.[27] After a few days of this work he also began sketching out new pieces, including a choral composition called *Sun* and his *String Quartet no. 3*, and began working on texts for *Patria 6: Ra* which he began to conceive as a dramatic tableau lasting all night. Later in March he began to lay the groundwork for a production of *The Princess of the Stars*, which would happen outside of Toronto in September, hoping that having a deadline would force him to complete the piece since hardly any of the music and only some of the text was in its final form. He devoted his energy to planning the production and working on the score for the rest of March and into April, only interrupting the work to travel to Montreal to attend the rehearsals and premiere of *Beauty and the Beast* by Maureen Forrester, which the audience enjoyed but the critics did not.[28] At the beginning of May Schafer attended the premiere performance of *The Garden of the Heart* at the National Arts Center in Ottawa, then went on to Concordia University, first leading a series of workshops and presenting the lead paper in a seminar on acoustic space then teaching a two-week course with the students.[29]

Schafer's mood upon his return to Monteagle Valley at the end of May was far less optimistic than at the beginning of the year. Although he had finished a draft of *String Quartet no. 3* by early June, he had misgivings about its value and was feeling a general uncertainty about his work as he passed into middle age, concerned that his present efforts lacked the vitality of his earlier pieces and wondering if the critical reviews of his last few compositions were valid. He also had been turned down for a Canada Council grant and had not been paid for several commissions worth about $17,000, which also made him worry about his financial future. He wryly notes in his diary,

> In introducing the French Radio program on Lesconil, the official from Radio France referred to me as "the eminent Canadian sociologist." Jon Whyte in an article just received from the Banff newspaper has called me "one of our best poets." Richard Johnston in an article in the Alberta composers' magazine referred to me as "one of the world's greatest calligraphers." Now I have just

returned from Stratford where the Art Gallery is planning an exhibition of sound sculptures next summer. I am beginning to feel twinges of identity crisis.[30]

Despite his doubts, Schafer continued work on *String Quartet no. 3*, finishing it along with a commission for the Canadian Brass, *Situational Music for Brass Quintet*, by the end of June.[31] With these projects finished, he turned his attention to the rewrite of *The Princess of the Stars*, but the pressure of finishing it and his growing self-doubt began to affect his health, with the symptomatic headaches and eye pain returning. He was able to push through the rewrite, finishing it by September and looked forward to a period of no commissions or teaching obligations. He decided to take a break from composition for the month of September, devoting his energies to other writing projects. He first gathered together all his notes on music education and soundscape exercises for the book *A Sound Education* then saw through the final proofs and printing of his next graphic novel, *The Sixteen Scribes*. At the end of the month were the final rehearsals of *String Quartet no. 3* and *The Princess of the Stars*. He was pleased with the quartet, and *Princess* was also a success, produced by Robert Aitken and New Music Concerts at Hart Lake near Brampton, Ontario. Even though it rained during the premiere there was still a crowd of three hundred. Inspired by these successes, he finished the year working intensely on the music for *Patria 6*, first completing the aria *Amente Nufe* for a separate performance by Maureen Forrester.

Murray started 1982 teaching and traveling, first at Queen's University in Kingston then at the University of Western Ontario before going to Stratford, Ontario, to prepare for an upcoming exhibit of his sound sculptures. After talking with his producers in Toronto about a possible production of *Ra*, he decided to delay it until May of 1983, largely to allow for more time to raise the needed funds to make it happen. He was not too upset by this decision since it would take the pressure off him to finish the piece by the spring. He decided to turn down several possible commitments (other than a lecture called *Radical Radio* for a conference in New York) so he could compose uninterrupted for a few months before his next European tour, which would take him to Rome, Vienna, Graz, Paris, Goteborg (a lecture on soundscape), and Stockholm (a repeat of his *Radical Radio* lecture). He completed a commission for the Toronto Mendelssohn Choir, deciding to rework the "Sun" section of *The Princess of the Stars*.[32] He also took out the old draft of *Patria 5* to see how he could make it into a workable piece since it had sat dormant in draft form since 1977. He worked diligently on the revision, working primarily on simplifying the libretto, but once again hit a creative impasse after rewriting about half the text and about thirty minutes of music and had to put it aside.[33] When he returned home from Europe he turned his attention back to *Ra* with the goal of putting it into some kind of shape by the beginning of the next year. Another bout of depression began, but he was able to work through it to finish the dramatic outline and the draft of the music by the end of the year.[34]

After a short break over the holidays, Schafer started 1983 with the *Ra* rewrite, finishing it by the middle of January. After this concentrated effort he immediately succumbed to the expected period of emotional and creative exhaustion, distracting himself with reading and menial tasks. As the depression began to stretch over several weeks, he realized that he would not be able to start anything significant until after the production of *Ra*, scheduled for the beginning of May, was over. The end of February was taken up with the rehearsals, performance, and subsequent recording of *Amente Nufe* with Maureen Forrester and the percussionist John Wyre.[35] After that he passed the time by revising and copying out *String Quartet no. 3* in preparation for its publication.

PROFESSIONAL SUCCESS AND PERSONAL UPHEAVAL

The production of *Ra*, held at the newly opened Ontario Science Centre, experienced one of the greatest successes of any of the *Patria* segments, bringing in a wide variety of audience members. It also brought upheaval into Murray's personal life. The Canadian mezzo-soprano Eleanor James had auditioned for and won the part of Hasroet, Goddess of the Necropolis, in the production. By his own admission, Murray had had flirtations with other women who were involved in his other major productions, seemingly needing the energy of that attraction to help him push a particular project to its limit. His attraction to Eleanor was different, and much deeper than usual. They would not physically consummate their love until after the production, but there was no doubt that this was a significant and potentially long-lasting relationship. Eleanor reciprocated Murray's feelings, and he was so drawn to her that in the last days of rehearsal for *Ra* he felt that he had to tell Jean. Her simple response was "What did I do wrong?"[36] After *Ra* was over, Murray and Jean returned to the farmhouse with their future in doubt and no clear idea how to deal with this development. Murray wanted to be with Eleanor, or at least be on his own so that he could see her when he wanted. He had a reason to get away from the farm in June, a residency at Stratford, Ontario, as part of his sound sculpture exhibit. Jean stayed on the farm, and Eleanor was able to regularly visit Murray in Stratford before he left for Newfoundland in July in order to prepare and perform his *Harbour Symphony* in St. John's harbor.

When Murray arrived in Ontario later that month, he and Eleanor decided to rent a house in Toronto in September. This decision proved to be a bad one, and the arrangement would last for only three months. Eleanor was a

Figure 5.1. Eleanor James. *R. Murray Schafer*

founding member of the Canadian Opera Company Ensemble in 1979 and a member of the ensemble through 1981. This had been followed by two additional contracts to play various small roles, but as was typical for the ensemble her contract was not going to be renewed for the fall. Murray was at loose ends given the situation with Jean, and he felt uncomfortable going out much in Toronto with Eleanor since his circle of friends and acquaintances knew him and Jean as a couple. He began to drink a little too much and gloomily pondered his future. In early November Murray told Eleanor that he was moving back to the farm, essentially abandoning her and their life together, although he would continue to pay the rent for their house in Toronto. Jean in the meantime had decided to begin studies at the University of Ottawa, so Schafer was alone (and extremely lonely) on the farm. He was torn between Jean and Eleanor, feeling strong emotions for both and visiting both frequently. These strong emotions and the turmoil of his situation were reflected in his *Flute Concerto*, written for and premiered by Robert Aitken and the Montreal Symphony Orchestra. He escaped the almost unbearable situation for a while by traveling, first to Amsterdam to talk about the possibility of doing some productions there as part of their new music festival,[37] then on to an extended teaching engagement in California, where he also laid the groundwork for a workshop production of a new *Patria* segment he had been sketching out, *Patria 4: The Black Theatre of Hermes Trismegistos*.

The situation had not improved by the beginning of 1984. Murray was still living on the farm himself and traveling to visit both Jean in Ottawa and Eleanor in Toronto. He and Eleanor had slowly restarted their relationship as they realized that they couldn't bear to be apart, but Murray kept his visits to Eleanor a secret from Jean. Eleanor stayed in the house until June and continued to develop her career, winning the Toronto Met auditions and finishing second in the Detroit auditions. She also traveled back and forth to New York to audition for roles, and in May she arranged a European audition tour to England, Holland, Austria, and Germany.[38]

In late January Murray himself began another extensive travel sequence, lecturing in Winnipeg and Banff and attending the rehearsals of *A Garden of Bells*, which he had composed the previous year for the Vancouver Chamber Choir. From there he went south to California to begin rehearsals for *Patria 4*, which he had completed quickly in the last few months, the one benefit of being alone on the farm for such an extended period of time. The production at Cal Arts in Valencia would keep him in California from the middle of February through the end of production in the middle of March. From there he traveled east to teach at the University of Colorado at Boulder before returning to the farm.

In April he and Jean had reconciled enough that when he asked her to go to Japan with him for an extended trip, she agreed. In Japan they were the guest of noted composer Toru Takemitsu, who introduced the Canadian couple to Japanese culture, including the many beautiful Buddhist temples and the tea and incense ceremonies. Murray taught several seminars on soundscape theory and practice and also did various interviews for Japanese media outlets. He and Toru became good friends over the course of the visit, and Murray was commissioned to write a piece for the Kyoto Symphony the following year. After he and Jean returned to Canada, Murray felt compelled to confess to her that he had been not only visiting her but also seeing Eleanor since he had returned to the farm last fall. A few days after hearing this news Jean officially separated from him, and Murray realized that his life in Monteagle Valley was over. He arranged to sell the farmhouse, put his things in storage, and move out.

HAPPINESS AT LAST?

Eleanor had received a contract with the opera house in St. Gallen, Switzerland, through her audition tour and would leave in August for Europe. After Schafer had moved off the farm, he and Eleanor were able to be together in a rental in Kirby, a town northeast of Toronto, until her departure. While there he managed to compose a piece for the Toronto Children's Chorus called *The Star Princess and the Waterlilies*. In August Murray sadly saw Eleanor off, then moved himself into a bachelor apartment in Toronto, calling her every week, writing her often, and finding that his mental state allowed him to accomplish nothing creative. After a few weeks he decided that he couldn't bear it any longer and decided to go to be with Eleanor, who had found an apartment in St. Gallen that had a studio for Murray to work in. By the middle of October he was with her, and they both were happy to simply be together, as Murray noted in his diary:

> What I love in you is the voice, not the stage voice that flashes through the theatre, but the sotto voce voice, reserved especially for me. I have heard it so much more frequently since we have been together here. Strange that only after two years of knowing you, you are allowing it to come out.[39]

In order for them to be together as much as possible, Murray would keep a place in Toronto and spend regular time with Eleanor in St. Gallen, traveling other places as needed to teach, lecture, and generate enough income to support him and Jean, to whom he had financial obligations while she was attending the University of Ottawa. When Eleanor was off from the opera house in the summer they would be together in Canada for those months. Murray was able to make this arrangement work for almost two years, and was able to begin composing again. He first wrote a piece for Eleanor called *Sun Father, Sky Mother* that he had first conceived while in Banff, then he turned to setting several letters he had received from her, which he titled *Letters from Mignon*.

As 1985 began Schafer's focus was the looming commission from the Kyoto Symphony Orchestra which he had received during his visit to Japan the previous year. He decided to base the piece on an incense ceremony he had participated in while there, giving the composition the title of that ceremony, *Ko wo kiku*. He was able to travel to Japan for the premiere, which was conducted by Seiji Ozawa, whom he found pleasant to work with and a congenial colleague. His only other piece that year was another commission, a piece for Robert Aitken that he decided to call *Buskers* and to include in

Patria 3. The summer of 1985 was taken up with the production and performance of *The Princess of the Stars* in Banff National Park, where Eleanor sang the part of the princess.[40] For the rest of the year Murray continued completing the structure for *Patria 3*, which he was now calling *The Greatest Show*. His pattern of composing, guest teaching, and visiting Eleanor continued into 1986. His creative efforts were still focused on *The Greatest Show*, with Schafer taking occasional breaks to complete other compositions. *Fire* was written for the Vancouver Chamber Choir for their performances at Expo '86, and *Tantrika* for voice and percussion and an orchestral version of his early *Minnelieder* were written for Eleanor. An orchestral piece, *Dream Rainbow, Dream Thunder*, was based on a late-night piano improvisation after a visit with Eleanor to Neuschwanstein Castle in Bavaria.

After spending the last two years traveling and seeing Eleanor in Switzerland as much as he was able, it was becoming clear to Murray that he would not be able to maintain this nomadic life much longer. As the summer approached, he began preparations to settle more permanently in Canada, called back not only by financial constraint and homesickness[41] but also by the demands of the upcoming production of *The Greatest Show*. His life was about to change again.

Chapter Six

Two Loves, Financial Concerns, and the *Patria* Cycle

BACK TO CANADA AND *THE GREATEST SHOW*

Despite his best efforts, Murray was unable to make things work financially with being so frequently in Europe, and Arcana Editions, which he had left in the hands of an associate, was nearing bankruptcy. He needed to go back to manage it himself, and so he reluctantly returned to Toronto in the spring of 1986 and procured a coach house apartment so he could get access to his papers, which had been stored near Bancroft since selling the farmhouse. The coach house was large enough for him to comfortably set up operations for Arcana, and he focused on bringing it back to profitability and procuring lecturing and teaching engagements in order to offset both the high cost of living in Toronto and his financial obligations to Jean. He still felt the loss of being estranged from Jean, who was continuing her schooling at the University of Ottawa and was speaking of getting a job but had not yet found one. As in previous summers, Eleanor was able to come spend the summer in Canada after her obligations to the opera house were over. Her contract in St. Gallen had been renewed for another year, and Murray was saddened at the thought of being separated from her when she left in August. In addition to devoting energy toward getting himself on a better financial footing, he focused his attention on completing *Patria 3*, which kept him busy through the end of the year.

Schafer approached 1987 with some trepidation. Despite the productive last two years, he was worried that his creative powers might be diminishing, comparing his recent works unfavorably to the pieces he had produced a decade ago.[1] His concerns would be justified since the next year would be difficult and nonproductive, and in addition to bringing *Patria 3* to completion he would only complete two other compositions, both commissions. Murray's first professional engagement in 1987 was a semester-long teaching residency in San Diego. Eleanor was able to spend significant time with him there, and his light teaching load allowed him to begin *Harp Concerto* for Judy Loman, for whom he had written *The Crown of Ariadne*. The genre of the concerto was antithetical to Schafer's philosophy of what music should be, and he struggled both with the general concept and with writing more music for the harp, fearing he had grown tired of the instrument and of writing concert orchestral music in general.[2] He came back to Canada in April to hear Eleanor perform *Letters from Mignon*, in Calgary, a performance made even more meaningful by the fact that only he and Eleanor knew who the author of the texts was. He then returned to San Diego until May, where to mark the end of his residency the students and faculty put on a concert of several of his pieces.[3]

After his residency was over Murray continued to travel to teach and lecture both in North America and Europe since he needed the income. This did not leave much time for creative activities, and most of his free time was devoted to producing *The Greatest Show*. Since the show was being produced in Peterborough, Ontario (northeast of Toronto), the couple rented a house in the countryside close to that city. Eleanor helped him coach the singers up until the time she had to leave for Europe.[4] Murray stayed until the show was over then went back to Toronto and the coach house for the fall. The success of the production encouraged Murray to refine the show over the winter and spring in preparation for another production in 1988. Growing tired of city life, and looking to reduce his expenses, Murray decided to permanently move out of Toronto, and in November he purchased a farm in Indian River, a short distance away from Peterborough, where the second production of *The Greatest Show* would be held. After the production was over Schafer drove from Toronto to Memphis to lecture at Memphis State University until the beginning of October. At the beginning of the month he attended a production meeting for *Patria 1*, which the Canadian Opera Company had decided to produce in order to tap into a government grant.[5] The assigned director was not interested in receiving any input from Schafer, not even returning his calls, so the composer ultimately decided to stay away from all of the staging rehearsals and not to attend any of the performances.

Despite the money he earned from his teaching engagements and the success of *The Greatest Show*, Murray still had significant financial concerns. The profit margin for Arcana Editions was very slight, even with him doing most of the work, and he realized that he was in worse shape financially now than he was twenty years ago even though he had many more compositions to his credit and a national reputation. His concerns were somewhat alleviated by a piece of unexpected good news. He was being awarded the

Figure 6.1. Schafer in Southern California. *R. Murray Schafer*

inaugural Glenn Gould Prize for Music and Communication, which came with a $50,000 prize. He would later find that this award was through the intercession of his friend and colleague Yehudi Menuhin. At the end of November he attended the awards dinner for the prize with his mother, brother, sister-in-law, and Eleanor, who was back in Canada for the holidays and would stay through the end of the year.[6] The $50,000 that came with the award turned out to be timely as toward the end of the year Schafer received a letter from PROCAN (Canada's royalty-gathering organization, now called SOCAN) stating that he would no longer be receiving royalty checks due to changes in how royalties for classical music would be determined and collected, losing him almost $18,000 annually.

A YEAR OF TURMOIL

During this time Jean and Murray had kept in contact and had visited regularly since she had finished her studies at Ottawa and had found a position at a law firm in Toronto. She had been having problems with her eyesight, and when her employer refused to give her time to go see a doctor, she resigned from her job in order to attend to the problem, which was diagnosed as cataracts. She had surgery in the summer, and since she had no job and was now recovering from cataract surgery, Schafer suggested that Jean stay on the farm with him until she could get back on her feet, and she agreed at the beginning of 1988 to move back in with him. When Eleanor called Murray in January he broke the news to her. She was devastated. For the foreseeable future she would remain in Europe, and they would continue to create lives apart from each other. One of Eleanor's colleagues in Europe, the tenor and stage director Robert Hoyem, had been courting her for some time. Thinking that her relationship with Murray was over, Eleanor began a relationship with Robert that would continue for several years.

Murray continued to accept teaching and lecturing engagements in Canada and Europe through 1988, which forced him to fit his compositional work into spare moments. Outside of bringing *Patria 4: The Black Theatre* to its final form, the only other two pieces he would be able to finish this year were two choral commissions, *The Death of the Buddha* for the BBC Singers and *Magic Songs* for Orphei Dränger. His first significant engagement in the new year was a semester-long position at McGill University in Montreal. After the term was over he traveled to Europe, stopping first in Brussels, his first visit to that city since 1956. He went on to Amsterdam to have meetings with members of Jim Henson Productions about his possible involvement in a television series on the theme of music (he ultimately would have little to do with the production).[7] From there he went to Liège to find both financial backing and a suitable place for a production of *The Black Theatre*, then on to Bologna to lecture for two days,[8] then to Paris to visit his old friend Bob Walshe. From Paris he traveled to Brussels for more preparations for *The Black Theatre*, then finally returned home to prepare for the next production of *Patria 3*.

The production would be seriously marred by poor weather. Rain cancelled the dress rehearsal and the preview night and saturated the ground so badly that running electrical cables for the lighting was impossible, forcing them to essentially do half a show. The weather reports also reduced the crowds for the first several days, causing panic among the board, which Schafer allayed by putting in a substantial amount of his own money to make the production work. The greatest disappointment was that the community of Peterborough did not come out to support the work even though he had deliberately produced it there in order to make the city a thriving arts community. The show finished its run on September 4, and Murray was so exhausted and discouraged that he didn't even go to the closing-night party. He stayed at the farm with Jean through September and October, leaving in mid-November for Bonn, Germany, for rehearsals and a performance of *Adieu, Robert Schumann*, where the English portions were sung in German translation. The performance gave him a chance to adjust some of Clara's texts in order to reconcile the original German and his own English version. From Bonn he went back to Liège to move preparations along for *The Black Theatre* and then on to England for the British premiere of his *Flute Concerto*, with Robert Aitken as the soloist. He then returned home to the farm for the rest of the year.

Murray spent the beginning of 1989 finishing his *String Quartet no. 4*, commissioned by the Orford String Quartet, before leaving for Belgium in February to prepare for the first complete production of *Patria 4*. Murray was excited to have the full production finally realized and equally excited to see Eleanor for the first time in over a year. Eleanor had been cast in the role of Melusina, and he had some trepidation as to how they would be with each other. The production was successful, and when he and Eleanor first saw each other they fell into each other's arms and spent as much time together as possible during the several weeks of rehearsal and performance. When it was over they had to say goodbye. Murray was traveling to Sicily, where Jean already was, and Eleanor was traveling to Munich, where she was a guest artist for the Staatstheater am Gartnerplatz (she would be hired permanently there in September). Even though they were to once again be physically separated, they were committed to continue their relationship, seeing each other during the summers when she was back in Canada and having weekends together when he was traveling in Europe. Murray would set up a post office box under the name Richard Wagner where Eleanor could send him letters, and he would write back to her at the Staatstheater.

When Murray and Jean returned to Canada in April, they participated in a presentation of English country dances, madrigals, and readings at Art Space in Peterborough, which reminded him of an earlier idea of basing a piece on a planting and harvesting ritual. He eventually would turn this idea into *Patria 10: The Spirit Garden*.[9] At the beginning of May he heard the recording of the premiere of the *String Quartet no. 4* and was inspired to begin a fifth quartet for the Orford String Quartet to play. He heard the premiere performance of *The Death of the Buddha* by the BBC Singers as part of the Toronto International Choral Festival in June. He continued work on the quartet and a guitar concerto for Norbert Kraft, and he began to have initial meetings exploring two new *Patria* segments. He gathered together a group of artists to explore work on initial ideas for *Patria 8* and had the first meeting of people interested in creating *Patria Epilogue: And Wolf Shall Inherit the Moon*, which he had begun sketching out in St. Gallen. Schafer had inserted an ad in the program newspaper for the second *The Greatest Show* production asking for interested people to join him in the creation of this new work. Eleanor was the first to sign up even though her European engagements prevented her from being involved in the initial planning stages, but five others also responded, and they and Schafer met to discuss how the work might develop.[10] Murray also took some time in the summer to be involved in the annual Peterborough Festival of the Arts, where he did a production of *Jonah*. Once these summer activities were over he focused on the string quartet and the concerto and spent as much time as possible with Eleanor, who was in Canada for the summer.

Murray had a brief teaching engagement at Duke University in North Carolina at the beginning of the fall then spent the rest of the year at the farm. He worked on *Patria 5* to see if he could finish the music and drum up interest in a production with the Peterborough Arts Association. He also applied for a Canada Council Grant with the hopes of gaining enough funding to work exclusively for a while on the *Patria* cycle,[11] but since he still had significant financial concerns about the next few years and couldn't count on the grant to come through, he reluctantly took on several orchestral commissions. As the year drew to a close, Murray reflected on how he had enjoyed having Jean back on the farm, which had taken away much of his loneliness as they had settled into a life very reminiscent of what they had in Monteagle Valley a few short years ago.[12]

STABILITY AND PRODUCTIVITY

The first two months of 1990 were consumed with travel. Murray started the year with a brief teaching engagement at Queen's University in Kingston, then he traveled to France at the beginning of February to see the Vancouver

Children's Choir perform a concert of his music at the Nantes Music Festival, finally spending a few days visiting Paris. He was home for only a few days before embarking on his first teaching trip to South America, centered in Brazil. He first flew to Rio de Janeiro, where he had lunch with music educators from Argentina and Brazil and did a workshop with about sixty teachers, many of whom had already read his books in Portuguese translation, which eased the process. From there he went to São Paulo where he did a week-long workshop with 140 music teachers from all over Brazil, teaching six hours each day, and having almost daily interviews with reporters.

He returned to Indian River at the beginning of March physically and mentally exhausted, with no creative thoughts, and so took a few days of rest before turning back to composition. He had three orchestral commissions due by the end of the year: *Scorpius* for the Esprit Orchestra, *The Darkly Splendid Earth: The Lonely Traveller* for Jacques Israelievitch, and *Gitanjali* for Donna Brown and the National Arts Center Orchestra. He also wanted to finish a series of articles on the *Patria* works and knew that his work on these projects would soon be interrupted by more travel. He worked steadily until the end of April when he traveled to Seattle for four concerts of his music, then to San Bernardino, California, as part of the Music of the Americas conference. No one came to his scheduled lecture on *The Princess of the Stars*, but the festival rescheduled the talk, and there was a decent audience for the second attempt. As the summer began he continued to work diligently on his compositions, focusing most on finishing a complete draft of *Patria 5* before leaving with fifteen other interested people (including Jean) in August for the first camping expedition for the *Patria Epilogue*.

Happy to have finally finished *Patria 5*, Schafer decided to produce in Toronto a November showcase performance of about three quarters of the music to try to find a sponsor to support a full production of the segment. He was bitterly disappointed but not completely surprised when no sponsors or producers showed up, including no one from such major arts and funding organizations as the Canadian Opera Company, the National Ballet, and the Canada Council for the Arts. He was happy with the music, however, and invigorated enough to continue to work on his commissions, finishing *Scorpius* by the end of November and generating rough sketches for *The Darkly Splendid Earth* and *Gitanjali*. As he worked he couldn't help but contrast his dislike of writing orchestral works with the passion he felt for the *Patria* cycle, and he brooded on his position in his home country, which (in his mind) didn't support him or his music, forcing him to look for work regularly in other countries, which seemed absurd.[13]

After finishing the three commissions at the end of January, Murray immediately fell into a month-long period of depression, vowing never to do three commissions so closely together again and not convinced that any of the three were any good. He was still unable to compose in March and passed the time proofreading the collection of essays he had written on the *Patria* cycle until he left for his next tour. His travels over the next few months took him to Grenoble and Vézelay in March, Vancouver in April, Kalamazoo in May to teach at Western Michigan University, and Montreal and Vancouver again in June. Once his travels were over he worked on the final copy of *Patria 5*, taking a break at the end of July to search out camping sites for the second iteration of *Patria Epilogue* and also attend the farewell concerts of the Orford Quartet, where all five of his string quartets would be performed. Eleanor was again in Canada for the summer, and they spent as much time together as they could manage.

He continued the work on *Patria 5* in the fall, interrupting it only for a week's residency at Arizona State University in October and a week in Munich in November for a conference on acoustic design, where he gave a lecture and workshop and was able to spend time with Eleanor. After the conference was over he went to Paris for a few days to see Bob Walshe. After almost a year of intensive work, *Patria 5* was finished by the middle of November, and he turned his attention to a commission for the city of Montreal called *Musique pour la parc Lafontaine* before taking a well-deserved Christmas vacation with Jean at Wells Beach, Maine.

After the gargantuan task of finishing *Patria 5* over the course of 1991, Schafer doubted that he could finish another part of the cycle in 1992, but he doggedly set to work revising the text of *The Enchanted Forest* (*Patria 9*) while struggling to finish and polish *Musique pour le parc Lafontaine*. After completing the piece at the end of January he was again struck with a bout of depression, noting,

> The thought has occurred to me that my vocation as a composer has survived merely as a habit, like smoking my pipe or picking my nose, that as time goes on the pleasure it evokes decreases, though the suggestion that it be given up would involve a willpower in contradiction with laziness and the prospect of a battle at the late stage in life is never something willingly contemplated.[14]

He distracted himself by sorting through old soundscape files with the idea of producing a book of essays in time for next year's Banff Acoustic Conference. His next round of journeys took him to Calgary to lecture to music educators, to Montreal to meet with the musicians who would perform *Musique pour la parc Lafontaine*, and to Toronto to begin rehearsals for the indoor version of *Patria 5*. The performance at the beginning of March drew a crowd of 300–400, and he was generally pleased with the performance, although he felt they could have used more rehearsal time.

A SIGNIFICANT SOUTHERN TRIP

Immediately after the performance Murray and Jean left for a second trip to South America—a two-month engagement to teach in Brazil, Argentina, and Uruguay organized by his Brazilian colleague Marisa Fonterrada.[15] He began with a four-day course in Rio de Janeiro and São Paulo, followed by events in Londrina, Gramado, and Porto Alegre, where he met the Brazilian minister of education. At the beginning of April he left Brazil for Buenos Aires, Argentina, where he continued his intense schedule, working with large groups of students six hours a day. While in Buenos Aires he had the opportunity to meet senior Argentinian composers and performers and play them some of his music. From Buenos Aires he went on to Mendoza to teach even larger classes of students, some whom had traveled more than six hundred miles to attend, including a group that had come from Chile. While he was at Mendoza the University of Cuyo gave him an honorary doctorate. After the exhausting week was over he and Jean had a few days off in the countryside with no responsibilities[16] before returning to Buenos Aires, where he spoke to the students of the National Conservatory about acoustic ecology, lectured, and participated in a panel discussion. The next leg of their journey took them to Tucuman, in the remote northern part of Argentina, to lecture and give a three-day course. While there he was treated like a foreign dignitary, meeting the governor's wife, the province's minister of education, and the rector of the university in Tucuman.[17] Murray and Jean's return to Buenos Aires was delayed due to the airport losing power so his schedule became even more crowded once he made it back to the capital. He did a lecture, attended a concert of his music, and did one more day-long course, with people mostly from the south of the country. From there they went finally to Montevideo, Uruguay, to do a workshop with 170 music educators as part of an annual meeting of Uruguayan music educators before returning home by way of Rio.

Once the Schafers were back home in May, Murray went to Ottawa to oversee the rehearsals and performance of *Gitanjali* at the National Arts Center then took several trips to Toronto to prepare for the first Canadian production of *The Black Theatre*, to be performed at Union Station at the beginning of June. From there Murray went to Montreal for the production of *Musique pour la parc Fontaine.*

After the last few exhausting months, Murray was glad for an extended period of time at home.[18] He worked on a commission for an accordion concerto and made rapid progress on his second soundscape book, *Voices of Tyranny: Temples of Silence*. Once he had sketched out the concerto by the beginning of August he began to work on his next commission, a choral piece for the King's Singers called *Tristan und Iseult*. He unofficially dedicated the piece to Jean, telling her "it was reflective of their romance, now much more secure after a period of enmity, reminiscent of the change that occurred between Tristan and Iseult after they drank the Love potion."[19] Even though things on the surface were better with Jean, Murray and Eleanor were still regularly writing and had seen each other over the summer when she was back in Canada.

DISAPPOINTMENT AND DEPRESSION

At the beginning of August, Murray was informed that a *The Princess of the Stars* production planned for the Banff Center in 1993 would not happen. His response was anger and depression, once again questioning the value of his works since his home country wasn't interested in supporting him. He even went so far as to consider destroying the work and even destroying his whole *Arcana* catalog. He brooded on the farm until it was time to leave for the *Patria Epilogue* week and was only able to compose again when he returned home, finishing final versions of *Concerto for Accordion and Orchestra* and *Tristan and Iseult*. He then was able to relax for a few weeks before traveling with Jean in December to Finland where he did a seminar in Seinäjoki, presented at a Nordic soundscape conference at Virrat, and attended a choral conference at Espoo where the Vancouver Chamber Choir was performing. After the conference he and Jean were invited to vacation for a few days at a cottage above the Arctic circle. Not having any new ideas for compositions, he began to rewrite an earlier novel, *The Journey*, renaming it *Wolf Tracks*.

Schafer's lack of productivity continued in 1993 up until he and Jean left at the end of January for Costa Rica, where he was to teach a group of fifty music educators for a week. The work was less demanding than the South American courses he had taught last year, with the sessions lasting only four hours a day, and after the course they were able to spend a few days at an ocean-side resort. While watching Jean do Tai Chi in the amphitheater at the resort by moonlight, he had an idea for his *String Quartet no. 6* and had sketched it out by early March.

On March 11 Murray went to Toronto to attend an eightieth birthday concert for John Weinzweig[20] and also spent time with the accordion player Joseph Macerollo, working on and refining the solo part for the concerto for the premiere in April. Later in April Schafer went to Cobourg, Ontario, to hear the youth choir La Jeunesse sing his composition *The Star Princess and the Waterlilies*. He wanted to hear them live since he was considering using them in the production of *Patria 9: The Enchanted Forest*. There was already a workshop of some of the music scheduled for the next month with his good friend Barry Karp and singers from Barry's high school. He next went to Toronto to hear the King's Singers' performance of *Tristan and Iseult*.

Figure 6.2.   Schafer with Score Illustrations. *R. Murray Schafer*

A BRIEF REVIVAL AND MAKING A LIVING

After a brief time at home Murray had to travel to Halifax, Nova Scotia, to serve as artist in residence at the Scotia Festival. He was able to take Eleanor with him since she was back in Canada. As part of the festival he gave several lectures and organized concerts of some of his environmental pieces, which were well performed although sparsely attended. Once back home he worked hard to finish the first complete draft of *The Enchanted Forest* by the beginning of July since he knew he would have a busy summer and an extended teaching engagement in the fall. The summer would include celebrations for his sixtieth birthday including the Tuning of the World Conference in Banff, which would result in the formation of the World Forum for Acoustic Ecology. Since membership in the annual *Patria Epilogue* event had grown to over forty it would need much more organization than in previous years. Before the *Patria* week he had the inaugural Music and Environment Workshop at the Haliburton Forest and Wildlife Reserve. There were fourteen attendees from Canada, the United States, Brazil, and Argentina who came to experience various events and short seminars offered through the week. Although the week went well, it was personally marred by a bad argument between him and Jean, which began over something fairly small but led into deeper issues and ended with Jean screaming obscenities at him and leaving without telling him where she was going. Once the week was over, they were able to reconcile. In September Schafer started a semester-long teaching engagement at the University of Ottawa, using the time when he wasn't teaching to rewrite and copy *The Enchanted Forest*, otherwise remaining unproductive for the rest of the year, taking a few brief trips in December before spending Christmas on the farm with Jean.

Murray began 1994 by traveling to serve for a semester as Brandon University's Stanley Knowles Visiting Professor in Public Policy. Jean went with him to help him settle in then left to go back to Peterborough when classes began. Once she had gone, Eleanor was able to come to Brandon and be with Murray for a while. His arrival in Brandon was met with indifference, with no meetings with other faculty scheduled, few public lectures, no press, and hardly any students other than the twenty-two in his music education class. With so much unexpected free time, he was quite productive, beginning work on a commission for the Tokyo Symphony and starting another graphic novel, *Shadowgraphs and Legends*. He also took the opportunity to delve more deeply into his family history, journeying to the nearby towns of Hamiota and McConnell to find out information about his father and his father's family.

Toward the end of January he was able to take six students from Brandon University along when he went back to Costa Rica. On arriving in Costa Rica they attended a luncheon hosted by the Canadian ambassador, which gave the Brandon students and the Costa Rican educators a chance to meet each other before the beginning of the course. At the end of the month and the completion of the course he and the students enjoyed some time at the beach before going back to wintery Manitoba, where he wrote a choral piece based on some of the work he did with the students in Costa Rica called *Beautiful Spanish Song*. He continued his residency at Brandon University through

February and early March, only taking a short break to drive to Winnipeg to attend the Winnipeg New Music festival. In March he went to Toronto where he was to receive the Molson Award at a concert of his music performed by the Esprit Orchestra. He also wanted to see his mother since his brother had called to warn him about her quickly deteriorating health. Upon arriving he was shocked to see her emaciated condition. She was obviously in much pain even though her speech was so slurred that he could not understand what she was saying. Murray was deeply disturbed by the long, slow process of her passing. He tried to comfort her by saying that she would soon see his father, and at the same time he wished "it would end quickly so that the torment might pass from her frail carcass and I could feel the flight of her soul away towards the paradise I know she still believes in."[21] He then went to the gala concert with Eleanor, and the next day his brother called to say that their mother had passed away early that morning. There would be a family service at the funeral home, which he would miss because he could not change his plane ticket back to Brandon without great expense.[22] His mother's death strongly affected him and had brought back memories of his father. Murray obsessed that he would become like his father, who at retirement age had let his brain decay and his life shrink to mowing the lawn and waiting for meals.

After his residency was over in April, Murray was able to return home for a few weeks before leaving with Jean at the beginning of May for a week in France, where he taught at Marseille and went to Aix en Provence to hear a performance of some of his pieces. At the end of May, Paul, his wife Nancy, and their girls came to visit Murray and Jean and to place their mother's ashes in the Warsaw cemetery next to their father. At the beginning of June he focused intently on the piece for the Tokyo Symphony, which he had given the title *Manitou*, only interrupting his work to supervise meetings and rehearsals for the upcoming full production of *The Enchanted Forest*, which was experiencing numerous problems, including financial, even though Murray had personally already committed $16,000 to it. The first *sitzprobe* was at the end of June and went fairly well, with an informal audience of about five hundred people. Maureen Forrester, who had premiered several of Murray's pieces and had been contracted to sing the role of Earth Mother, arrived without having learned her part, which made him furious.

Schafer's summer was interrupted by many trips and obligations, including a journey to Banff to see a ballet choreographed to his *String Quartet no. 5*, the teaching of a second environmental course at the Haliburton Forest and Wildlife Preserve, and the annual production of *Patria Epilogue*.

A DIFFICULT CHOICE, A DIFFICULT RELATIONSHIP

Upon his return he turned his full energies to *The Enchanted Forest* production, still experiencing troubles with Maureen Forrester who hadn't yet learned her part properly. (He would find out after the production was over that Maureen was experiencing the early stages of dementia.) Despite this the production was a great success with substantial crowds every evening. After the production was over he briefly went to Kansas to lecture and teach. Once he returned to Canada, he was faced with a dilemma. The TSO had programmed his *Flute Concerto*, but he was considering refusing to allow them to perform it since it was the only piece by a Canadian composer in their whole season. He was conflicted only because his good friend Robert Aitken was scheduled to perform the work, and he hated for him to lose his performer fee since he had worked hard to convince the symphony to include the piece in their season. Ultimately he decided not to allow them to perform the piece. The whole episode threw him into a deep depression as he meditated on the fact that he was supposed to be famous and rich, but the reality was that his work was so rarely performed that at the age of sixty-one he still had to travel, mostly out of the country, to find work to support himself. This depression lasted until the end of October, when he left for Argentina to present a major lecture on soundscape theory.[23] When he returned from Argentina he finished the final ink version of *The Enchanted Forest* even though there were no immediate prospects for another production and finally returned to composition at the end of the year, sketching out ideas for his next commission, a trumpet concerto that he was calling *The Falcon's Trumpet*.

Murray started 1995 with an underlying sense of discontent and anger as he brooded on the events of the last year. He had a short teaching engagement in Quebec City early in January, and once he returned home he began preparations for a more extended trip to Europe at the end of February. Realizing that he was no longer able to take on the full burden of the *Patria* cycle, he began to gather support to set up an advisory board to help with future projects. His creative focus before he left was sketching out more music to use for that year's *Patria Epilogue* and making a better start on *The Falcon's Trumpet*. He and Jean arrived in Paris by the end of February, where they visited Murray's longtime friend Bob Walshe and his wife. While they were in Paris Jean fell ill, which was an inauspicious start to a trip that they had both hoped would help further heal their still damaged relationship. While he nursed her back to health, he sketched a choir piece based on the wind, *Once on a Windy Night*. Once Jean was well enough they traveled to Strasbourg, where Murray had an extended residency. In the middle of the month they traveled to Vienna to hear Robert Aitken play *Flute Concerto* with the Vienna Philharmonic. It was well received, with three curtain calls.

This success and his seeming ease in finding teaching work in Europe made him speculate how his life would have been different had he chosen to remain in Europe instead of returning to Canada. He and Jean also took the opportunity while in Strasbourg to travel to the south of France and into Spain. Much of May was taken up with rehearsals with various students for *Le Paysage Sonore*, a sonic street festival in Sélestat that was one of the main events associated with Murray's residency in Strasbourg. After the festival was over, Murray went to Hannover, Germany, to do a soundscape workshop, then the couple traveled to Poland at the beginning of June for his final teaching engagement before returning home.

After this extensive absence from home, the Schafers came back to Canada at the beginning of June but only had a few weeks at home before leaving for Japan at the end of the month, where *Manitou* would be performed by the Tokyo Symphony. The hope that they both had that traveling together would help their relationship was proving unfounded. Murray felt that things were still not right between him and Jean, who complained (he thought justifiably) that he did not pay enough attention to her. It was becoming clear that they had different goals and outlooks on life and were having trouble finding common ground. Deciding to give it one more try, Jean accompanied Murray to Japan. They arrived in Tokyo at the beginning of July and had a few days to adjust to the time change before the first rehearsal of *Manitou*. The premiere of the piece was not until July 9, and in the meantime Murray was scheduled to do lectures on music education and soundscape, and he also had the opportunity to meet with the conductors of some of the leading Japanese choirs to talk about possible commissions. After the premiere he had a few days to visit with Toru Takemitsu in the hospital, where he was undergoing therapy for lymph node cancer. After they arrived back home, the rest of the summer was spent preparing and executing the latest *Patria Epilogue*, which was up to fifty-four participants.

At the end of August, all of the traveling over, Murray turned back to composition, working on *The Falcon's Trumpet*; *Once on a Windy Night* for the Vancouver Chamber Choir; and texts for two new *Patria* segments, *The Spirit Garden* and *The Palace of the Cinnabar Phoenix*. At the beginning of October, three courses he had planned to teach in Toronto over the winter, Music and Your Child, Acoustic Ecology, and Music and the Arts (a discussion of *Patria*) had insufficient registrations to go forward, and were canceled. This news, and the news that a plan to remount *The Enchanted Forest* had fallen through brought back the old feelings of bitterness as he realized once again that he would have to go outside the country to find work to support himself. He continued to work on his commissions *Once on a Windy Night* and *Deluxe Suite for Piano*, which he had accepted not out of desire but out of necessity. These activities took him to the end of November, when he started to prepare for the second part of his residency in Strasbourg in early December. Shortly before he left for France, he was notified of a planned recording session involving his voice and orchestra pieces by the National Arts Center Orchestra. Schafer communicated back and forth with them, wanting to know whom they had chosen as the singer and pushing to have the recording delayed until he was back from Strasbourg early in the next year. The orchestra management offered to fly him back for the sessions, and he decided to let the project go forward.

Murray's residency in Strasbourg took him into February of 1996, and he had time while there to work on several pieces, including music for the upcoming workshop version of *The Spirit Garden*. His quiet time in Strasbourg was followed by a two-month whirlwind teaching and lecturing tour. In Switzerland he presided over the formation of the Swiss Soundscape Association. In Paris he lectured to music therapists and architects. In Hamburg he lectured and did a week-long session with film students. He lectured also in Copenhagen, Stockholm, Tampere, and Gothenburg, and he visited Cologne for a discussion about a possible radio program.

Once back in Canada he continued his travels, lecturing at the University of Victoria and the University of British Columbia before attending the premiere of *Once on a Windy Night* by the Vancouver Chamber Choir. From there he went east to Toronto to attend rehearsals for *The Falcon's Trumpet* with Stuart Laughton and the Esprit Orchestra and give a lecture to the English department at York University. Upon finally returning to the farmhouse at Indian River to stay for a while, he heard the University of Strasbourg had decided to award him an honorary doctorate. He used his down time to make final copies of several pieces, finish some commissions, prepare a children's version of *A Sound Education* for translation into Japanese, and write additional music for *The Spirit Garden*. He managed to finish all of this by the middle of April, despite having growing difficulties with both his good eye and his bad eye socket.

At the beginning of May he found that several of the people involved in the *Patria Epilogue* had decided not to return. The project was not developing as he had hoped, which meant he would have to continue to be involved to make certain things moved forward as they should. He also had worries about the workshop production of the "Spring" portion of *The Spirit Garden*, which was also faltering, requiring him to travel to Ottawa to observe rehearsals and make certain everything was stable. Eleanor was back in Canada, and she traveled with him to Ottawa.[24] Once he was able to come back to Indian River, he continued to work on additional music for *The Spirit Garden* and put together the first draft of *Patria 7: Asterion*. He pondered whether he should take Jean's suggestion to abandon the *Patria* projects and accept the multiple commissions that he was being offered but concluded the boredom of writing only concert music would kill him within a year, although the money would be useful. The first part of August was broken up by a trip to

Toronto to prepare for a recording of some music from *And Wolf Shall Inherit the Moon*, a trip to Montreal to try to find support to produce *The Princess of the Stars*, and a trip to Ottawa to raise money for *The Spirit Garden*. After that was *Patria Epilogue* week.

He had received a commission from the Tokyo Philharmonic Chorus to write a piece on a nature theme, with Latin as the preferred text, but was unable to start work on it because of a severe bout of depression, which was accompanied both by urges to burn everything he had written and a sense of complete futility in starting anything new. This lasted into November, when he was finally able to begin on the commission and sketch out ideas for the second part of *The Spirit Garden* before traveling to France to speak at the University of Strasbourg's convocation and receive his honorary doctorate. His first task when he returned home was to revise *Manitou* since the Winnipeg Symphony Orchestra had decided to program several of his orchestral pieces as part of their New Music Festival in February. After that was complete he worked on *Vox Naturae*, his *Viola Concerto*, a commission for the Japanese choir Utaoni, and his radio program *Winter Diary*.

Murray's first engagement in 1997 was the Winnipeg New Music Festival in February so he was able to rest at the farm until then. After the festival was over, he went on a trip through the province with his friend Claude Schreyer to record audio for *A Winter Diary* and gather supporting materials. After his return to Ontario his time was taken up by meetings for upcoming productions of *The Princess of the Stars* and *The Spirit Garden*, copying and correcting completed pieces, and beginning a piece for Jacques Israelievitch called *Wild Bird*.

At the end of March he traveled to Europe. His first stop was Frankfurt, where he met with the organizers of the Hessischen Rundfunk Conference, who wanted him to do a four-day workshop and give a lecture. From Frankfurt he went to Portugal to teach two days in Faro and three days in Lisbon. From there he went to Cádiz, Spain, to teach a music therapy course, then finally to Madrid before returning home. April was divided between composing the "Harvest" section of *The Spirit Garden* and traveling to Ottawa to help with the production of the "Spring" section of the piece. The premiere at the end of May had a small audience and he returned home discouraged since there might be no money left in the production budget to produce the second section later in the year. He was at a loss as to what to do because both the music and the subject matter of *The Enchanted Forest* and *The Spirit Garden* had been created to appeal to a broader public, but the support didn't seem to be there. His mood brightened somewhat when he received a phone call informing him that he was to be awarded a Governor General's Award for Excellence in the Arts, which included a $10,000 prize.

At the beginning of June he went to SFU to receive an honorary doctorate, a strange experience he felt, since he had only returned once or twice since leaving in 1975. While he was there SFU reissued the *Vancouver Soundscape Project*, including in it compositions based on the old material, which Schafer thought did not align with the original purpose of the project. At the reception after the ceremony he saw his first wife, Phyllis, which was bittersweet. After returning home he finished the "Harvest" section of *The Spirit Garden* and began serious work on *Viola Concerto*, now an official commission. He finally finished the first draft by the middle of July then took a break to go to the beach with Jean, his brother Paul, and Paul's family. Copies of *Wolf Tracks* arrived at his house in time for his birthday, and he gave a few away as gifts to those he invited to his party. The rest of summer was spent preparing and executing that year's session of *Patria Epilogue*.

September was taken up with the latest production of *The Princess of the Stars*, presented this time at the Haliburton Forest and Wildlife Preserve. He was anxious about the success of the production since he had promised Jean that this would be his last production of a *Patria* work without having sufficient financial backing in place beforehand. The production was an artistic triumph, but the audience was poor, creating a deficit that put everything in serious financial jeopardy. He came home exhausted but had to continue work on his *Viola Concerto*, finishing the rewrite by the middle of October so he could begin reworking the text of *The Palace of the Cinnabar Phoenix*. At the end of November he and Jean traveled to Japan to hear the premiere of *Seventeen Haiku* by the Utaoni choir, staying for a few days after to help them prepare their full-length concert of his music, and he gave a lecture at the university of Gifu City. After the trip they returned home for a few days then went south to Brazil for the rest of the year, laying the groundwork for a production of *The Enchanted Forest* planned for the following October.

A BIRTHDAY YEAR AND A TURNING POINT

Murray started 1998 by reworking *The Enchanted Forest* into a children's book, which would also be translated into Portuguese and printed in Brazil to accompany the upcoming October production of the piece. After this was finished he was unable to compose, falling into another period of creative inactivity that lasted until the beginning of March. Once he was able to write again he started working on two commissions: *Four-Forty* for the St. Lawrence String Quartet and orchestra, and *String Quartet no. 7*. He also started sketching out the music for *The Palace of the Cinnabar Phoenix*, finding it hard going since he wasn't feeling any inspiration and had to continue by sheer force of will. He ended almost every day with a headache and often had a day where he simply couldn't write anything. At the end of March was the premiere of *Viola Concerto*, and after he returned from the performance his struggles continued so he focused on working on the string quartet in small assignments. He filled in the rest of the time with revisions to *Viola Concerto* and created new pamphlets for Arcana Editions since sales had dropped precipitously over the past few months. In April he could not continue to force himself to compose so he switched his focus to writing essays and lectures for two upcoming conferences and updating his early soundscape publication *The Book of Noise*.[25] These activities kept him distracted until he left for a June soundscape conference in Stockholm, which would include a tribute to his work in the field of acoustic ecology. After his return from the conference he was finally able to compose. He took a break around his birthday, driving with Jean out to see their old house in Monteagle Valley and spending the night of his sixty-fifth birthday at a nice inn. The rest of the year was spent composing and revising, and preparing for yet another European lecture tour in early 1999.

Murray and Jean left for Europe at the end of January, first stopping in Paris, where he taught and they visited friends, then traveling to Hannover, Cologne, Stockholm, Turku, and Malmo. The couple returned to Canada in April, where preparations were underway for the premiere of *String Quartet no. 7*, which would happen at the beginning of May. Due to various logistical concerns, it ended up being a simplified version, and Murray, disappointed, went to the rehearsal to fulfill the requirements of the commission but did not attend the actual concert. In the middle of April Murray and Jean were back in Europe, but on separate trips. Jean had decided that she did not want to accompany Murray to Germany again and instead went on a walking tour of France. She and Murray had begun to live increasingly separate lives. A few years prior he had gotten her a condo in Peterborough since she didn't like living on the farm. She would spend the week in the city and come out to the farm on weekends.

Murray spent a week in Germany, doing a lecture, workshop, and concert cycle in Wiesbaden, and a lecture in Marburg, and taking the opportunity to spend precious time with Eleanor. On arriving home Murray received notification he would be the first recipient of the Lou Applebaum award. Although pleased with the award, he realized that there were no scheduled performances of his music for the rest of the year at which the award could be presented. He continued to struggle with *Four-Forty* until the August *Patria Epilogue* and was also able to write two short choral pieces, *Alleluia* and *You Are Illuminated*.

To further complicate things, Eleanor returned to Canada at the end of July to be with her dying mother, who was living in Burlington, Ontario. She stayed with her mother until her death and remained for a while after to settle her mother's affairs. Although Murray initially tried to keep Eleanor's presence and their meetings a secret from Jean, she immediately suspected that something was happening. Eleanor insisted that Murray be honest with Jean, and when he admitted what was going on, Jean filed a formal separation agreement. Murray was left alone on the farm but felt that he could not invite Eleanor there so they arranged to meet elsewhere as often as possible, often at an inn, before she returned to Munich in December.[26] Eleanor had established herself in Munich, having an established voice studio with her partner Robert, who was aware of and accepted her relationship with Murray. After her contract was over at the Staatstheater she began to teach at the Bavarian Theater Academy and sang as a guest at several other opera houses in Germany. After Eleanor and Jean had both left, Murray felt a sense of loneliness but also felt a sense of relief that he no longer had to lie to anyone about his continuing relationship with Eleanor.[27] They would continue to write, and he would often travel to Europe to see her perform. As 1999 drew to a close he settled once again into life on his own.

Chapter Seven

Loneliness, Reconciliation, Happiness, and New Challenges

ALONE AGAIN

As 2000 dawned Murray was still alone at the farm, experiencing such great loneliness that at times it paralyzed any desire to work or compose. As the winter dragged on he slowly adjusted to his situation and was able to compose, turning his attention to a commission for the Nexus percussion ensemble and University of Toronto orchestra he called *Shadowman*. It was difficult work as he was still recovering from the stress of completing *Four-Forty*. He pushed through on a first draft in order to complete it before his next European trip, which took him in March first to Munich then to Sélestat, where he was helping prepare the festival *Deux milles sons pour deux milles ans*. He was in Europe until April, and since he was able to spend significant time with Eleanor in both Munich and Sélestat, he returned home feeling refreshed and enjoying the emergence of life on the farm as spring progressed. The rest of the year was spent composing, taking breaks to enjoy his garden, and of course participating in the *Patria Epilogue* week in August. Eleanor came to visit him when she was in Canada for the summer but had no immediate plans to leave her life in Munich and her partner Robert.

The winter months at the end of 2000 and the beginning of 2001 were again lonely and difficult. Murray was in another creative depression, which he was not able to shake off through the rest of the winter and well into the spring. In May he went to Winnipeg (albeit without much enthusiasm) because the St. Norbert Arts Center was mounting a new production of *The Spirit Garden*, and the "Spring" portion of the production was scheduled for that month. He would be in Winnipeg for the full month, and (somewhat ironically) he resented leaving his garden for that long during the spring planting season. When he was able to return to Ontario, he immediately had to go to Toronto for a Patria Music Theatre Productions board meeting, making certain that plans for the upcoming fall production of *The Palace of the Cinnabar Phoenix* were moving forward. He then gave the keynote address for the 2001 Chorus America conference, which was being held in Toronto in June.

Schafer went back to the farm still feeling creatively barren and wondering if he should simply stop writing music altogether. It wasn't until the beginning of July that he was able to begin to focus on an upcoming commission for the Tokyo Philharmonic Choir called *Imagining Incense*. He alternated that work with a rewrite of *Shadowgraphs and Legends*, and he continued preparations for the September production of *Patria 8*, with Eleanor, who was again back for the summer and involved in the production, singing the role of Shen Nü. After production was over, Schafer had some time to himself, using the time to write a lecture on silence for a presentation at Wilfrid Laurier University, revising his *String Quartet no. 8*, and finishing up two other choral commissions, *Rain Chant* for the Taipei Philharmonic Choir and *Winter Solstice* for the Vancouver choir Chor Leoni. He was worried about his financial future since the alimony he had to pay to Jean was rising, and he had sunk almost $30,000 of his own money into *Palace of the Cinnabar Phoenix* without any sense of what he would recoup once all of the bills were paid. One evening he took a break from composition to entertain his friend and fellow composer Harry Freedman, who came to visit with his wife Mary Morrison. It would be the last time Murray saw his friend before Harry died. Toward the end of October Murray had to return to Winnipeg for the "Harvest" portion of *The Spirit Garden*, rehearsing with the performers for two weeks leading up to the November 1 performance. After that production he returned home, still without many creative ideas and still feeling a profound loneliness since Eleanor was back in Europe.

This loneliness continued into 2002. Even though the weather was mild and Eleanor was with him every time she came to Canada, he found a third winter by himself very difficult and felt a strong need to have a companion. He desperately wanted it to be Eleanor, but he felt he couldn't ask her to surrender her life with Robert and be with him permanently. These feelings continued to affect his creative life. Since completing *Cinnabar Phoenix* the previous year, he had had no strong desire to compose even though he had managed to complete the two short choral commissions and the rewrite of *String Quartet no. 8*. He had begun a ninth quartet simply to break up the tedium of his life on the farm and had also projected some ideas for a tenth quartet,[1] but most of his time was spent preparing a new edition of *Patria 1* using photocopies of the score he had sent to the National Library of Canada as his template. His thoughts were often on Eleanor, and he began to sketch out initial ideas for a piece intended for her to sing, *Thunder: Perfect Mind*.[2]

He looked forward to the summer when Eleanor would be back and would sing the role of Earth Mother in that fall's production of *The Enchanted Forest*.

HOPE, HAPPINESS, AND *THE FALL INTO LIGHT*

The summer was busy with travel. In July he went to Toronto to hear the Tokyo Philharmonic Choir perform some of his music, including the commissioned piece *Imagining Incense*, as part of the Toronto International Choral Festival. After attending that performance he next went to Mexico for the Foro Latinoamericano de Educación Musical (FLADEM) conference, staying there for a few weeks and giving a series of workshops.[3] After a few days at home he traveled to Minneapolis for the 2002 World Symposium on Choral Music to attend the premiere performance of *Rainchant* by the Taipei Philharmonic Choir and serve on a composers' panel.[4] From his return home until September he was in rehearsals for *The Enchanted Forest*, which opened September 13. By the end of the production Eleanor was openly talking about returning permanently to Canada to be with Murray after her engagements were finished the next spring.[5]

After *The Enchanted Forest* was finished, he and Eleanor traveled together to Portugal where he was overseeing preparations for the 2003 soundscape week in Coimbra, called Coimbra Vibra.[6] When they returned to Canada they traveled to Sackville, New Brunswick, to create a piece in partnership with the Sackville United Church called *Remember Susanna*, to be performed the next year. When the couple returned to Indian River for the remainder of the year, Murray began serious work on an extended commission for Soundstreams Canada. He had been asked by Lawrence Cherney, the director of Soundstreams, to write an extended choral piece for six choirs, children's chorus, and percussion for performance in the atrium of the CBC's Broadcasting Center in Toronto in February of 2004. He had agreed after some internal debate since he thought that organization's performance of *Zoroaster* the previous year had been a disaster. He only agreed after Cherney agreed to a price high enough that Murray could focus on that commission and turn down a semester-long teaching position at the University of Michigan. He worked on the piece through the end of 2002 and into 2003, finishing the first draft of *The Fall Into Light* (the title thought of by Eleanor) by the end of January before going to Montreal to lecture at McGill University. At the beginning of March, Murray dropped Eleanor off at the airport in Toronto for her flight back to Munich then went to John Weinzweig's ninetieth birthday celebration at the CMC offices. He then flew to Australia to do a session with children, Ear Cleaning, as part of the World Forum for Acoustic Ecology conference in Melbourne, returning at the end of March.[7]

Once back on the farm, he was cut off from the rest of the world for several days by a snowstorm at the beginning of April, which allowed him reread some of his old diaries and to focus on the rewrite of *The Fall Into Light*, hoping the revision would be finished in May before Eleanor returned even though he still hadn't received a written contract from Soundstreams.[8] When Eleanor was back in Canada they went to Sackville at the beginning of June for a concert of Murray's music, including *Remember Susanna*, the collaborative piece they had worked on with the local musicians the year before.[9] Eleanor then returned to Munich while Murray traveled to Portugal for a few days, preparing for the soundscape event in Coimbra. It was scheduled for October, but after this latest visit Murray came home concerned that the project wouldn't happen at all due to various delays and some difficulty in getting enough groups involved. Back home by the middle of June, Murray worked in his garden and on *Thunder: Perfect Mind*, finishing it by the end of June and presenting it to Eleanor as a welcome-home gift when she returned to the farm at the beginning of July. She would now be living in Canada with Murray, although for several years she would still be traveling to Europe for professional singing engagements.

After Murray and Eleanor had spent the months of July and August on the farm, they traveled together to Portugal to oversee the final preparations for Coimbra Vibra. Even in the midst of the preparation the relaxed schedule allowed them to take side vacation trips to Salamanca, Avila, Segovia, and Rouen and for him to give lectures in Madrid. After Coimbra Vibra was over in October he attended a radio conference in Nuremberg, then he and Eleanor finally returned to the farm at the beginning of November. At the end of the month he was back in Montreal doing master classes, including a workshop on his most recent string quartets and a course called Soundscape and Mythology.[10] After a very busy year, the couple were able to take the month of December off, enjoying life together on the farm. Murray took that month to write *Tanzlied* for voice and harp for her.

At the beginning of 2004 Murray's time was taken up doing outreach events for the upcoming production of *The Fall Into Light*. It was an intense schedule as he taught in a dozen places in four days. There was a wide range in both the ages of the students and sizes of the classes so he had to constantly change his approach, which was exhausting. After these workshops were over he returned home and turned his attention to other projects, with the main focus being starting his *String Quartet no. 10*, which he had given the title *Winter Birds*. He and Eleanor drove back to Toronto for the premiere of *The Fall Into Light* at the end of February, which was wonderfully received.

Eleanor traveled to Montana for the first part of March to visit her former partner Robert, and Murray was himself travelling back and forth to Montreal to observe rehearsals of *Beauty and the Beast* by the Molinari Quartet, who had dedicated themselves to performing and recording all of his music

Figure 7.1. Eleanor James and Murray Schafer. *R. Murray Schafer*

for string quartet, and to show them sketches of the two quartets he was working on. At the beginning of May Eleanor sang Mahler's *Lieder eines fahrenden Gesellen* with the Peterborough Symphony Orchestra, and while watching her, Murray was reminded how she looked on the stage at St. Gallen when they were first together so many years ago. May was spent largely working on the tenth quartet.[11] In the middle of the month he made the long drive from Indian River to Winnipeg for the release of the recording of the St. Norbert Arts Center's production of *The Spirit Garden*. In the later part of July Eleanor premiered *Tanzlied* with Judy Loman at the Ottawa Chamber Music Festival. On the day of the performance Eleanor became quite ill, and when she went to a doctor after the performance, he diagnosed her symptoms as the result of a gall bladder attack. The doctor advised her to go home, but she had a performance the next day of *Adieu, Robert Schumann* with the Orchestre de la Francophonie at Domain Forget and felt obligated to do the concert. After returning to the farm she became so ill that they had to rush her to the hospital for emergency surgery. Murray went late to the *Patria Epilogue* so he could remain with Eleanor until her sister could come to be with her.

ARCANA EDITIONS AND FURTHER TRAVEL

In September Jean told Murray that she was no longer willing to do the accounting and banking for Arcana Editions even though he had been paying her extra for the work. He was upset since he would now have to take on all the financial aspects of the publishing company and decided that the best option was to purchase the necessary equipment to run everything out of the basement of the farm house. Later in the month he traveled to São Paulo where he again presented at the FLADEM conference and discussed with some of his colleagues the possibility of a soundscape study in Amazonia the following year. The end of the year he devoted to composition, finishing *String Quartet no. 9* and a short piece called *Flew Toots for Two Flutes*, written for Robert Aitken to commemorate Bob's retirement from his university position.

In January of 2005 Murray traveled to Winnipeg with the hopes of persuading the New Music Festival to mount a performance of *Apocalypsis* in 2006 and to show the score of his *String Quartet no. 9* to Gwen Hoebig, the concertmaster of the Winnipeg Symphony Orchestra, since she wished to program it for next year's festival. On arriving back at home he spent the rest of January and February finishing the tenth quartet, starting an eleventh quartet, and completing a choral commission for Soundstreams Canada called *The Death of Shalana*.

Eleanor left again in March to visit with Robert and Murray himself left that month for Mexico to give a weeklong course on designing soundscape radio programs for Radio Educación. He returned home to an empty house and felt the isolation keenly. He took a trip to Concordia University in Montreal to look for a suitable venue for the course he would teach in September.[12] He found it difficult to compose after returning but worked on and off on his two commissions, a string trio and his next string quartet, until July when he left for Portugal in the middle of the month to give the keynote speech at a conference on acoustics and vibration in Lisbon. Upon his return Eleanor was away so he celebrated his birthday alone, brooding over what he perceived to be his growing physical and creative deterioration.[13] At the end of July Murray traveled first to St. John's, Newfoundland, then to Hiroshima with the Newfoundland Children's Chorus, who had initiated the Threnody Peace Education Project with partner organizations in Japan. He was in Japan through the beginning of August,[14] attending the chorus' performance of *Threnody* and other choral works in Hiroshima on Hiroshima Day. While in Japan he also gave a lecture on *Threnody* and a workshop on music education and met with the organizers of the World Forum for Acoustic Ecology conference planned for 2006 in Japan.

A RARE SUCCESS, AND RECOGNITION

After he returned home his energies were devoted to another production of *The Enchanted Forest*, in which Eleanor sang Earth Mother. The production gave eight performances in September to sold-out audiences and great reviews. Initially buoyed by this rare success, Murray traveled to Montreal for his semester residency at Concordia University, traveling back on some weekends to the farm and Eleanor. Eleanor would also come regularly to see him in Montreal and was involved in a Theatre of the Senses class he was teaching. Between his teaching responsibilities and regular trips back to the farm to see Eleanor and take care of Arcana business, he found all desire to compose gone and wondered if it would ever return. His time at Concordia wrapped up at the beginning of December with a performance of the pieces he had helped students in his class create. Having recovered from the stress of the fall, he was able after Christmas to start on another commission for Soundstreams Canada, a piece for fifteen brass instruments that he called *Isfahan*.

In January of 2006 Murray traveled to France to give a lecture called "Acoustic et la vie urbaine" at IRCAM, a French institute for electro-acoustic and music research, and he repeated the same lecture at Chalons sur Saone as part of a weeklong conference called "La Semaine du son."[15] Once back on the farm he resumed work on *Isfahan* and had several meetings to prepare for *Patria Epilogue*, which kept him busy until the beginning of May,[16] when he traveled to Mexico for a week to give a talk at the Bianale of Radio Educación and teach a six-day course.

After he returned home from Mexico he had no desire to write, even though the deadline for completing *String Quartet no. 11* was quickly approaching. At the beginning of June he traveled with Eleanor first to Montreal for the premiere of the *String Quartet no. 9* by the Molinari Quartet then to Toronto for the premiere of *Isfahan* at St. Anne's church. He was happy with *Isfahan* even though he had a few ideas to tighten up the piece but was discouraged by the poor reviews of the string quartet. That same month he received an honorary doctorate from the University of Toronto, where he gave several classroom lectures and a speech to the graduating class recounting how he had been expelled from the university so many years ago. Once all of these activities were finished, he had a break until August and took the opportunity to visit John and Helen Weinzweig, who were now in a nursing home in Toronto.[17]

In June and July he watched the development of the labyrinth for *Patria 7: Asterion* out in the field beside his house and struggled with *String Quartet no. 11*, knowing what he wanted to express but not finding the right way to put it down on paper. In the beginning of August Eleanor's former partner Robert was hospitalized in Denver with a brain tumor, and she decided she should go to attend to him. It was unclear how long she would be gone, and to be safe they arranged for someone else to be ready for the performance of *Patria 8* planned for the beginning of September. As she left, Murray couldn't help contrasting Robert and Eleanor's congenial relationship with the relationship he and Jean had, which was so rancorous that Jean refused to even talk to him. In the middle of August he went to Haliburton to help with the move-in of *Patria Epilogue*, but for the first time he chose not to stay for the whole week, only returning for the final day ceremonies and to help move everything out.

Although the preparation and performances of *The Palace of the Cinnabar Phoenix* went well in September and Eleanor was back to reprise her role of Shen Nü, the production was marred by rain for most of the weekend, which reduced audience numbers and canceled some nights altogether, plunging the project into $40,000 of debt, which was all the more concerning for Murray since he had personally put $30,000 into the project.[18] He had to set these concerns aside, however, since he and Eleanor immediately embarked on a recording project with Esprit Orchestra of the voice and orchestra pieces Murray had written for Eleanor: *Minnelieder*; *Letters from Mignon*; and *Thunder: Perfect Mind*. Once this was complete, Murray went to Berlin where he had several speaking and teaching engagements.[19] He returned home for a few weeks then left alone for a three-week engagement in Tokyo since Eleanor's engagements did not allow her to join him. While in Japan he heard a performance of the revised version of *Manitou* and gave the keynote address for the World Forum for Acoustic Ecology Conference. He was also able to spend some time at the Aomori Contemporary Art Center in Nagasaki before finishing up his time in Japan at Kyushu University in Fukuoka, where he lectured on soundscape. He was able to return home to Canada and Eleanor at the beginning of December, where he worked to finish a commission for the Canadian soprano Stacie Dunlop, *Six Songs from Rilke's "Book of Hours,"* taking a break to write a little choral piece called *Lilies, Water, Carp* that he imagined would become part of a larger choral collection.[20] The end of the year was overshadowed by concerns about the collapse of the Patria Music Theatre Productions board due to several resignations, which he feared would put next year's August production of *The Princess of the Stars* in jeopardy.[21]

DISCERNMENT AND UNCERTAINTY

These concerns extended into 2007 until the board was reconstructed and the decision made to go ahead with *The Princess of the Stars* at the Haliburton Forest and Wildlife Reserve. As the New Year began, Eleanor, who had been taking a year of discernment in 2006, decided that she would begin degree studies in divinity with the view of becoming an ordained minister.[22] Murray focused on finishing three commissions (*Rilke Songs*; *Trio for Violin, Viola, and Cello*; and *String Quartet no. 11*) and sorting some of his manuscripts and recordings for deposit at the National Library of Canada until he left for Freiburg at the beginning of February to teach and lecture. Once he returned he focused his compositional energies on two large pieces, the first a commission from Soundstreams Canada for the Canadian Opera Company's Children's Chorus called *The Children's Crusade*, the second a commission from longtime patron Michael Koerner for the rededication of the concert hall at the Royal Conservatory of Music, which Murray would call *Spirits of the House*. These projects kept him busy until August, when he went in for the final day of the *Patria Epilogue*. After *The Princess of the Stars* production in September was over he was able to complete the first draft of *The Children's Crusade* before succumbing to mental and emotional exhaustion, which continued through the rest of the month. At the beginning of October he managed to work a bit more on *Spirits of the House* before leaving for Tucson to attend the premiere of *Trio* and teach at the University of Arizona.[23] At the end of the month he began a term as composer-in-residence at the University of Toronto, a position funded by the Koerners. He had no interaction with any of the composition faculty there,[24] and with his ample free time he sketched out ideas for several smaller pieces.

That fall Eleanor began her master of divinity classes at Emmanuel College at the University of Toronto, which meant she needed to live in the city even though she was part time. She was also directing the workshop production of *The Children's Crusade*, planned for the fall. Murray would come to visit her and also be involved as needed in the production.[25] At the beginning of November he was informed of the cancellation of three possible *Patria* productions over the course of a few days. The Canadian Opera Company decided not to program *Patria 5*, the Banff Center canceled their *The Princess of the Stars* production, and the *Patria* board decided to suspend, at least for the time being, any further productions. He wondered if he would see another professional production of a *Patria* work during his lifetime and was despondent until the end of the November (when he traveled to Greece to teach and lecture) and even after.[26]

Chapter 7
A MILESTONE AND ANOTHER DISAPPOINTMENT

The beginning of 2008 was broken up into various events, the first of which was performance of his *Quartet no. 6* as part of a concert in the foyer of the Canadian Opera Company Theater, with the Koerners, who had commissioned the piece, in attendance. At the end of the month he was made an honorary fellow of the Royal Conservatory of Music. He struggled to finish the violin and piano duo, now a commission from the CBC for the violin and piano duo he had started the previous year then set it aside and focused on finishing his most recent novella, *The Garden of the Heart*.[27]

At the beginning of February Murray traveled to Winnipeg for the New Music Festival, which was celebrating his seventy-fifth birthday with several performances. After the festival he was able to travel further west to Brandon to visit relatives, then he returned home for a short time before traveling west again, this time to Victoria to attend performances of the ninth, tenth, and eleventh string quartets by the Molinari and the Lafayette String Quartets. Once back in Ontario he attended a celebration of his music in Ottawa by the National Arts Center Orchestra, where his only responsibilities were to attend the concerts and give a few lectures and sessions with students. As part of the celebrations in honor of his seventy-fifth birthday, Eleanor performed *Letters from Mignon*, the Molinari Quartet played several of his string quartets, and five high school choirs performed some of his choral pieces. The rest of March was taken up with a visit to Stratford to prepare for a performance of *Music for Wilderness Lake*, a short teaching engagement at the University of Toronto, rehearsals and performance of *Threnody* at St. Elizabeth High School in Toronto, and a talk for the Toronto Music Festival.

Schafer rested and recovered for much of April, not able to write much before leaving at the end of the month for Mexico to present at the FLADEM conference. Once he returned he spent May finishing edits for *The Garden of the Heart* and revising *The Children's Crusade*, both of which he was able to complete by the beginning of June.[28] From the end of June until September the farmhouse was invaded by contractors, who were adding a studio space, a longstanding dream of Murray's. Despite the disruptions, Schafer was able to continue working, focusing on several projects over the next few months, including a commission for the Tokyo Philharmonic Choir based on passages of Ovid's *Narcissus and Echo*,[29] a choral commission for the University of Cincinnati called *Make Room For God*, and a short choral piece called *The Searching Sings*. The rest of his time was spent preparing for the *sitzprobe* for *The Children's Crusade* scheduled for mid-September, which was quite successful. Murray was looking forward to the production, with Eleanor directing and long time *Patria* collaborators Jerrard and Diane Smith doing the costuming and set designs. After the *sitz* was over, Murray was able to work on *Trio for Violin, Viola, and Cello* and a commission for the Vancouver Chamber Choir's fortieth anniversary, *The Love That Moves the Universe*.[30]

In November Eleanor was told that she would no longer be directing the production of *The Children's Crusade* since the producers, the Luminato Festival and Holland Festival, wanted a better-known director. Jerrard and Diane Smith were also let go. Murray was furious and considered cutting any ties to the project,[31] confirming this decision after Lawrence Cherney brought the new director Tim Albery up to Peterborough to meet him. There was to be no place for Eleanor or the Smiths on the production team, and therefore he would not participate further in the project.[32] After this disappointment, Murray was unable to focus on composition until the beginning of 2009, which meant that he was short of time to complete a commission for the National Arts Center Orchestra. The performance was in May and he was traveling in March, so he took the approach of writing it as if he were in a dream state, writing one minute of the work each day and not trying to relate the previous day's work to that of the next day. Sticking with this approach, he was able to finish *Dream(e)scape* in twenty-six days, leaving a full month to tidy it up before leaving to give a lecture at a World Forum for Acoustic Ecology conference in Mexico City. In April he fell again into depression and noticed to his increasing anxiety that he was starting to suffer from significant short-term memory loss, which he managed to keep hidden from people when talking to them although it made him increasingly reluctant to accept new lecture engagements.[33]

In May he was awarded the Governor General's Performing Arts Lifetime Achievement Award as part of a three-day event that proved to be more enjoyable than he thought it would.[34] Late May was the premiere of *Dream(e)scape* and early June the premiere of *The Children's Crusade*. He was not going to go to any of the performances of *The Children's Crusade*, but at Eleanor's insistence he went to one performance without letting anyone know beforehand. In July Jean called him to relate that she had had a terrible fall and was in a recovery home. Murray loaned her $6,000 to help defray her expenses and visited. This reconciliation was short-lived, as soon thereafter she asked him to not call her again, still resentful and blaming him for their separation.[35] In August he again went to the final day of *Patria Epilogue*, and in September he attended the premiere of *Spirits of the House* at Koerner Hall. Not having written anything since spring, he forced himself in October to sketch out ideas for a commission for the TSO, a piece for which he did not even have a title as of yet. At the end of October he traveled to Mexico, where he met with several contacts who were thinking of planning a festival similar to the Coimbra Vibra event he had organized a few years before.[36] After that trip he and Eleanor flew to Linz, Austria, as part of that city's celebration as the cultural capital of Europe.[37] When they returned home he spent the rest of the year working on the TSO commission and a second piece for Music on Main in Vancouver.

MEMORIES AND MEMOIRS

As 2010 began Schafer focused first on finishing the choral set *Landscapes and Soundscapes*. In March he traveled to Vancouver by train, where he worked with Heidi Krutzen on the harp part for *Trio* and then attended the rehearsals and performance of *The Love That Moves the Universe*, which was enthusiastically received by both the audience and the critics.[38] When he returned to Ontario, Eleanor was away visiting Robert so he decided to drive north to Bancroft to visit old acquaintances, and he found out that the farmhouse that he and Jean had purchased for $25,000 was now for sale for $200,000. In May a representative from the TSO called, asking for the title of piece he was writing for them. Murray gave the tongue-in-cheek reply "Symphony no. 1 in C Minor."[39] In June he traveled with Eleanor to Finland for the annual World Forum on Acoustic Ecology conference and was told that the World Forum on Acoustic Ecology World Listening Day would now be held annually on July 18, his birthday.

Upon his return to Canada he was awarded his tenth honorary doctorate, this latest one given to him by Concordia University in Montreal. The remainder of the year was spent gathering together materials to publish a memoir; finishing another choral piece, *The Soul of God*, as a commission for Soundstreams[40]; and working on *Quintet for Piano and Strings* for the ARC Ensemble, who were also teachers at the Royal Conservatory of Music, and a set of songs for the marriage of his niece as a wedding gift, which would become the core of the later *Four Songs for Harp and Mezzo-Soprano*.[41]

At the beginning of 2011 Schafer began to teach a class at the Royal Conservatory of Music in Toronto, which took him into the city every Wednesday for most of the spring. This also allowed him to see Eleanor more often during the week since she was continuing her studies in Toronto. He and Eleanor traveled on Saturdays to Kingston, where they were involved in creating another community theater piece, *Job: A Tapestry*. His main creative focus was finishing his memoir, which he originally wished to call *My Life* but changed to *My Life on Earth and Elsewhere* when his editor suggested the first title wasn't catchy enough. In March was the premiere of his *Symphony no. 1 in C Minor* by the TSO as part of their New Creations Festival. A few days after that he traveled to Vancouver, where he did a workshop at the University of British Columbia and attended the premiere of *String Quartet no. 11* by the Lafayette Quartet.[42] After the May production of *Job: A Tapestry* and the completion of his class at the Royal Conservatory,

Murray sketched out an orchestral piece called *Figures in the Night, Passing*, even though he had no commission for it or any prospects of having it performed.[43] This was all he could manage until the end of July, when he left for Vancouver and the World Harp Congress, where July Loman gave performances of *The Crown of Ariadne* and *Wild Bird*, and he and she gave a masterclass. As part of the conference, the Verlaine Trio gave a performance of *Trio for Flute, Viola and Harp*.[44]

Murray had extensive travels planned for the fall and into the next year, and Eleanor decided to take a year's break from her divinity studies at Emmanuel College so that she could travel with him. Their first trip was in September to São Paulo to attend the FLAMA conference. He lectured, Eleanor gave workshops, and she also performed *Tantrika* with two Brazilian percussionists.[45] They both participated in the final event, a rainforest soundscape walk. After a few days at home they then flew on to Greece, arriving in Athens and then traveling to Corfu to attend that year's World Forum for Acoustic Ecology conference. From there they went to Aix-en-Provence to visit Bob Walshe, returning home on October 9 for the rest of the year. Murray continued teaching every Wednesday at the conservatory, completed another piece for Eleanor, *Four Songs for Harp and Mezzo Soprano*, and attended several performances of his pieces, including *The Falcon's Trumpet* with the Kelowna Symphony in British Columbia and *Isfahan* at Koerner Hall at the Royal Conservatory of Music.[46] On Christmas Eve Murray and Eleanor continued their annual tradition of attending the candlelight service at Westwood United Church,[47] and after many years together, they were quietly married on December 30.[48]

The year 2012 passed quickly, and relatively productively. In July the newlyweds traveled to Dieburg, Germany, for the annual World Forum of Acoustic Ecology conference.[49] They then took a ten-day driving trip along the Rhine as their honeymoon. Throughout the year Schafer worked on various commissions, including *Wolf Returns* for the Esprit Orchestra and another choral piece for Soundstreams, *Here the Sounds Go Round*, for three choirs. In October was the premiere of *Wolf Returns*, and that concert also served as the official launch of his memoir *My Life on Earth and Elsewhere*.

DIAGNOSIS AND REPERCUSSIONS

The following year would be full of celebrations for Murray's eightieth birthday, but the year did not start in the way that Murray and Eleanor had intended. As early as their trip to Corfu in the fall of 2011, Eleanor had started to notice changes in Murray's behavior, with an increasing forgetfulness and other symptoms that started to cause her concern. These continued and increased over the next year, and Murray was given an official diagnosis of Alzheimer's disease. It was decided at that point to not make it public knowledge and to let Murray continue to drive until his driver's license expired on his birthday in July. Murray decided to continue to work and compose as long as his symptoms allowed, and he continued to teach weekly classes at the Royal Conservatory of Music, easing his responsibilities by regularly bringing in guest performers. The birthday celebrations went on as normal, with several performances. In March he went to Toronto for John Weinzweig's 100th birthday celebration at the CMC national office. In May, as part of another Soundstreams project, he began working with the Gryphon Trio, preparing for a series of concerts and composing for them his *Trio for Violin, Cello and Piano*. He took a break from this work in the middle of May to travel to Montreal to hear the Molinari Quartet give the premiere performance of his *String Quartet no. 12*, which had been commissioned for them by Phyllis Lambert and which he had completed the previous summer. In June was a performance of *Music for Wilderness Lake* in New York's Central Park by the Tilt brass ensemble and a TSO performance of *Scorpius*, during which performance he was honored as part of the celebration of Wagner's and Verdi's 200th birthday, and Murray's 80th birthday.[50] After this he traveled to Stratford for a summer festival based on his music and soundscape writings. July and August were particularly busy, with the premiere of *Tanzlied* by Eleanor and Judy Loman at the Ottawa Chamber Music Festival at the end of July and the weekend-long performance that celebrated the completion of *Patria 7: Asterion* out on the farm at the beginning of August. The completion of *Asterion* was a great satisfaction for Murray as it meant that all the parts of *Patria* had now been produced at least in partial form. As the summer ended, Eleanor and Judy Loman recorded *Tanzlied* as part of Judy's project to gather together into one recording all the music Murray had written for harp.[51] The most rewarding part of 2013 was when Schafer was properly recognized for his contributions to his home country and given the highest civilian honor that can be bestowed on a Canadian citizen when he was made a Companion of the Order of Canada.[52]

The year 2014 started with Murray staying on the farm with Eleanor, recovering from the previous year and further winding down his activities as his symptoms continued to progress. In March he traveled to Mexico for one last time, agreeing to go only if he could bring an assistant, Doug Friesen, a friend and fellow musician and educator who was also a proponent of Schafer's approach to music education. They were in Mexico for a week, and things went well enough that Murray felt comfortable letting Doug take over the traveling and teaching in Latin America from this point forward. After he returned home, he gave only one more significant lecture for the rest of the year, for a conference at Conrad Grebel College at the University of Waterloo titled "Hearing Our Earth as Song."

April saw the premiere of *Trio for Violin, Cello and Piano* by the Gryphon Trio. The Winnipeg Symphony Orchestra performed his *Symphony no. 1 in C Minor* at the beginning of May then repeated the piece as part of their Carnegie Hall performance the next week, with Murray and Eleanor in attendance. At the end of the month he was given a Sing! Legacy Award, presented to him for his significant contribution to the vocal arts in Canada. August was quiet, apart from his visit to the last day of *Patria Epilogue*.

Over 2015 and 2016, Murray's symptoms continued to progress, and he managed to complete only one more piece after *Trio*, to which he gave the official title *Alzheimer's Masterpiece* and the unofficial title *String Quartet no. 13*. He no longer accepted teaching or speaking engagements but continued to travel to attend performances of his pieces, including the June 2015 production of the complete version of *Apocalypsis* by the Luminato festival in Toronto. The highlights in 2016 included a January performance of *The Falcon's Trumpet* by the Esprit Orchestra, the launch of a remastered and remixed recording of *Loving* from the 1970s, and a reprise of *The Love That Moves the Universe* by the Vancouver Chamber Choir. June saw the premiere of *Alzheimer's Masterpiece* at the Montreal office of the CMC, which also served as the official public announcement of Murray's condition. In August Murray still managed to go out for the final day of *Patria Epilogue*, accompanied by Eleanor, who now accompanied him everywhere as his condition worsened. On November 11 Murray had a bad fall down the stairs from the second floor to the first floor and had to be hospitalized for two weeks, which was an extremely disorienting and upsetting experience for him. After he returned home, it was decided that it would be safest to set up a bed for him on the main floor.

In 2017 Murray's Alzheimer's continued to progress, although he and Eleanor were able to still take short trips to Toronto to attend performances of his pieces. The highlight of the year was the announcement in November that Murray had been inducted as an honorary member of the International Society for Contemporary Music, the first Canadian composer to be so honored.

As 2018 begins, Murray and Eleanor continue to live quietly on the farm, often taking a drive in the middle of the afternoon. They regularly visit with his brother Paul and his family and continue to visit and receive visits from other family and friends. Although it is difficult, Eleanor is at peace as Murray enters this last stage of his life, noting, "Murray's life on earth is nearing its end, but the 'elsewhere' is just beginning."[53]

Part II

The Writings

Chapter Eight

The Educational Writings

As Stephen Adams notes in his biography of Schafer, "Schafer's commitment to music in society shows most clearly in his contributions to music education. Here, in simplified form, all his ideas come together."[1] The titles of his early music education pamphlets and the titles of the two books in which he has collected and expanded those pamphlets reflect his approach to teaching music. His approach has taken a strong hold in many parts of the world (including Europe, Asia, and Central and South America) and his publications have been translated into multiple languages. His educational philosophies have had a direct influence on both his compositions for amateur youth or adult performers and also several aspects of his work on acoustic ecology.

EARLY FORAYS INTO EDUCATIONAL THEORY

It was largely because of his work at the CMC that Schafer was asked to join the John Adaskin project in 1962 and given the task to identify, grade, and promote existing contemporary Canadian compositions suitable for performance by children. He also gave a talk to secondary school music teachers in Toronto titled "A Perspective of Music Appreciation," where for the first time he publicly advocated for music education instruction that went beyond the narrowly defined canon of pieces deemed appropriate for children to include contemporary compositions (including avant-garde pieces) and lesser-known works from other eras.[2]

As Schafer continued his involvement in the Adaskin Project, he began to sketch out an article that he would later publish under the title "The Graphics of Musical Thought." In this article he argues for the effectiveness of graphic notation as a tool for the early facilitation of music creation in children (a central tenet in his philosophy), particularly those who have not yet mastered traditional notation. The article begins with a brief history of the development of the graphic and symbolic elements of music notation. Schafer then posits that conventional music notation is largely symbolic, static, and "tells us a great deal about specific musical thoughts, but little about how these thoughts are linked together." In contrast, graphic notation "tells us less about specific thoughts but more about their general relationships and formal shapes."[3] In Schafer's view,

> the value of conventional musical notation is its objectivity. A musical sign can be transformed into a musical act only when it is understood or can be easily explained. Conventional notation is a complex system sanctioned internationally for the communication of musical thought and it is therefore unambiguous and objective. If it has one severe disadvantage this is its complexity, for it takes many years of practice to obtain fluency in reading music.[4]

Schafer then expounds on his view of the value of graphic notation in the classroom, arguing that in the school curriculum, where time is always precious, it is inefficient in the early stages to focus on the development of music reading skills, on silent exercises.

> What we need here is a notational system, the rudiments of which could be taught in fifteen minutes, so that after that the class could immediately embark on the making of live music. Several of my own graphic scores are engagements with this problem. Such scores may be less specific than those notated in a conventional manner, but this is in keeping with an important trend in modern education where the objective is no longer to give children exact recipes for execution but to set them free on discovery-paths of their own.[5]

In the article Schafer cites as examples several of his own compositions, including *Statement in Blue*; *Minimusic*; and *Epitaph for Moonlight*.

In November of 1963 Schafer was involved in the Adaskin Project's initial Seminar for Graded Educational Music in the school districts of Toronto and two of its suburbs, Scarborough and North York. After an initial day of discussion with leaders of the school districts, the composers spent three days working with the students,[6] and on the last day of the seminar the pieces created by the composers during their residency were performed. Schafer's contribution was the initial form of *Statement in Blue*, the first compositional outworking of the theories expressed in "The Graphics of Musical Thought": using graphic notation as an entrance into music creation and bypassing the inherent difficulties of reading traditional notation for players just learning that language. In addition, Schafer gave the eighth-grade students that he worked with an active role in the creation of the piece, a very different approach than that taken by the other composers involved in the project.[7] The seminar was declared a success, and Schafer wrote the following about the experience:

> The enthusiasm grew from day to day as the composers worked with the children, wrote little pieces for them, and the educators had a chance to experience Canadian music of our time at first hand. Speaking personally, I can honestly say the week spent at the seminar was one of the most exciting of my musical career.[8]

In the summer of 1964, C. Laughton Bird, director of music education in the Toronto borough of North York, invited Schafer to teach a two-week course for students age thirteen to seventeen, which the composer simply called "Musicianship." The course would be repeated the next summer, and Schafer's discussions and activities with these students along with the earlier seminar sessions would form the sections of his first music education pamphlet, published in 1965 with the title *The Composer in the Classroom*.[9] The texts in this pamphlet are condensed transcriptions of these earlier sessions, arranged to reflect a progression of ideas and accomplishment even though they were gathered from different situations and even different years.

Schafer's first task in "Getting Acquainted" is getting the students to relax so that they will be more likely to engage in dialogue with him and each other. We see Schafer drawing answers out of the students about what kind of music they like and dislike, which leads to a discussion about the value of certain types of music and of music in general.

In "What is Music?" Schafer notes,

> A very large area of misconception is exposed in this discussion by asking a basic question. The interesting conclusion reached is realistic with regard to the musical scene today; and although it does not seem to be compatible with ... pamphlets on music appreciation, it does seem that students studying the subject deserve the benefit of a useful and "living" definition of music.[10]

The attempt to create an accurate description of what music is is carried out over several class periods and covers such topics as the difference between music and noise, how to write music for a horror movie, Arnold Schoenberg's *A Survivor from Warsaw*, and the nature of melody and rhythm.

In "Descriptive Music" Schafer observes that

> the real purpose of this discussion was to discover a way of releasing whatever improvisatory gifts the students had. It relied in the first instance on the trick of "imitating nature" to accomplish this. This seemed an expedient method to relax the students and prepare them for some of the more subtle improvisatory experiments to follow.[11]

Schafer immediately begins engaging the students in using their instruments to experiment with sound, guiding them in their improvisations and assuring them that they are creating actual compositions through these experiments.

In "Textures of Sound," Schafer continues to work with the students to refine their improvisations, moving from the fairly simple depictions of nature to expressing emotion and using Debussy's *Afternoon of a Faun* and Mussorgsky's *Night on Bald Mountain* as examples of creating contrasting moods or emotions. Schafer then leads guided improvisation with the class by using various gestures, which he first explains.

"Music and Conversation" is the final extension of these progressively more complex improvisation exercises. Schafer notes,

> It is difficult to decide whether the real value of an experiment such as that to follow is in drawing out latent talent for improvisation or merely as an exercise in ear training. Probably it serves both uses. Certainly it was discovered that most students never listen at *all* to one another when they play in bands and orchestras where there are twenty clarinets or sixteen flutes all tootling away at the unison line of their Beethoven-Browns or Handel-Jacksons. Thus, to force students to listen, as was necessary here, would seem to constitute an important "break-through" in their musical education.[12]

The exercises in this discussion use a standard wind quintet, and the smaller number of musicians facilitates more sophisticated experiments where the only means of communication between the players is their instruments. Schafer works intensely with the players to help them listen to each other and craft effective improvisations.

"Mask of the Evil Demon" was the only one of the sessions included in the pamphlet that was undertaken with sixth-grade students, which allowed Schafer to move more quickly toward creation and improvisation than with the older students. In his observations he explains a possible reason why.

> It is the duty of every composer to be concerned with the creative ability of young people. But he has to be quick to catch it. For our system of music education is one in which creative music is progressively vilified and choked out of existence. . . . Any public school class will improvise uninhibitedly, but by the time they have reached grade 12 or 13 this ability has completely soured into nervous laughter at the prospect of playing four notes that weren't given to them.[13]

Schafer works with the students to create a piece using a mask that the class has earlier made, which is hanging on the wall of the classroom. Once the exercise is in motion, Schafer is able to gradually draw back and let the class take over, with continual suggestions for changes and improvements.

THE SIMON FRASER YEARS

Once Schafer began teaching at SFU, he transferred the concepts he had developed with young students to his university classes, in particular to an experimental music education class designed for first-year students. As Schafer notes in the preface to his second music education pamphlet published in 1967, *Ear Cleaning*,

> I felt my primary task in this course was to open ears: I have tried always to induce students to notice sounds they have never really listened to before, listen like mad to the sounds of their own environment and the sounds they themselves inject into their environment. This is why I have called this a course in ear cleaning. Before ear training it should be recognized that we require ear cleaning.[14]

The sections of *Ear Cleaning* largely consist of Schafer's lecture notes for this experimental music education course. These notes functioned as work points for Schafer, upon which he would expand and improvise with the students before moving to various exercises intended to test the theories and answer any questions that were raised. The actual interactions between Schafer and the students in the class are not recorded, but *Ear Cleaning* shows a deliberate and progressive study of the elements of sound and how they can be combined and studied. Schafer notes in the preface

> As a practicing musician I have come to realize that one learns about sound only by making sound, about music only by making music. All our investigations into sound should be verified empirically by making sounds ourselves and by examining the results. . . . An actual contact with musical sound is made and this is more vital than the most gluttonous listening program imaginable. Improvisatory and creative abilities—atrophied through years of disuse—are also rediscovered, and the student learns something very practical about the size and shape of things musical.[15]

The first two sections are closely related. "Noise" creates a discussion of the definition of noise as "undesirable sound" or a sound that interferes or destroys. Various exercises place the same sounds in different contexts to determine how much the concept of noise is based on context. "Silence" attempts to find a definition of silence, then asks if silence is even possible and how silence functions to protect musical events from noise. The exercises that follow focus on deep listening and attempts to find silence.

The next three sections move us into the realm of sound. "Tone" focuses on sound's fundamental nature as it grows out of silence in a horizontal line at a constant altitude (frequency). To this basic tone is added "Timbre," the tone's color and overtone structure, and "Amplitude," the loudness-softness that adds "the third dimension to this tone by the illusion of perspective."[16]

The next three sections move us further into musical concepts. Schafer describes "Melody" as "taking a tone for a walk,"[17] achieved by moving the tone to different frequencies, and "Texture" is created by dialogues of lines with each other. Schafer's definition of rhythm is direction, which in its broadest sense divides the whole into parts.

"The Musical Soundscape" concludes the first part of the pamphlet with several suggested activities for the class, including combining several of the exercises from the previous sections into various choral compositions, using graphic notation as a notational model. In this section Schafer describes a musical composition as a musical journey back and forth through a cone of tension where all the preceding elements are interacting in that cone. The appearance of the word "soundscape" in this section looks ahead to Schafer's work in acoustic ecology.

The next two parts of the pamphlet serve almost as appendices and differ from the first section in that they are transcriptions, similar to the chapters in *The Composer in the Classroom*. The first transcript, "Charles Ives and Perspective," draws again from Schafer's experience at North York Summer School and is the culmination of two or three sessions discussing Charles Ives's composition *Three Places in New England* with a group of string players. It is included because Schafer saw similarities between this session and the issues raised in the sessions at SFU. The second transcript is "Music for Paper and Wood." The exercises in this part are based on using paper as a musical instrument, followed by exploring the sounds of Japanese wooden wind chimes.

Once students have cleaned out their ears enough to hear the sounds around them, they can go a stage further and begin to analyze what they hear. It should be possible to reconstruct synthetically, or at least effectively imitate, a sound one has heard, provided the analysis has been accurate. This is the point where ear cleaning gives way to ear training.[18]

The last section of *Ear Cleaning* is called "Four Postscripts," and it is a collection of shorter notes describing additional activities the class undertook over the course of the semester, including listening for silence, bringing an interesting sound to class, recording environmental sounds, and writing poetry about sound and silence.

In 1969 the National Film Board of Canada filmed a documentary called *Bing Bang Boom*, which recorded a series of eight sessions that Schafer did with twelve-year-old children. The final film shows the progression, through edited segments, of the class that experiences Schafer's method of exploring their creativity in the classroom, not simply parroting back what the teacher tells them or learning études. In the documentary, two important things happen. First, through the various exercises, the class is brought to the point where they create and perform their own piece of music without the use of any traditional notation. The second, and just as important in Schafer's mind, is his own transition from being the central figure in the classroom at the beginning of the classes to being almost invisible as the class members themselves began to take the lead, criticizing their own work and planning new compositions.

That same year, *The New Soundscape* was published as "a handbook for the modern music teacher," and in this collection of short essays and transcripts we see the growing synergy between Schafer's theories on music education and his developing thoughts about acoustic ecology.

The short essay "Yes, But Is It Music?" serves as a preface to and apologia for the entire pamphlet, referencing the section of *The Composer in the Classroom* where Schafer and some high school students wrestle with a definition for music. After that experience, Schafer wrote John Cage for his definition and received the following reply: "Music is sounds, sounds around us whether we're in or out of concert halls."[19] With a new definition of music emerging, Schafer gives several notes to the music educator as to what the new student of music will have to know, and he says the following about his pamphlet:

> One of the purposes of this booklet is to direct the ear of the listener towards the new soundscape of contemporary life, to acquaint him with a vocabulary of sounds he may expect to hear both inside and outside concert halls. It may be that he will not like all the tunes of this new music, and that too will be good. For together with other forms of pollution, the sound sewage of our contemporary environment is unprecedented in human history.[20]

He then goes on to list a second purpose, paralleling his work with the World Soundscape Project.

> I am about to suggest that the time has come in the development of music when we will have to be concerned as much with the prevention of sounds as with their production. Observing the world sonograph the new music educator will encourage those sounds salubrious to human life and will rage against those inimical to it.[21]

What follows in the booklet takes a variety of forms, mostly transcriptions of class discussions or class plans from his sensitivity class ("The Sonic Environment"; "Schizophonia"); classroom activities ("A New Definition of Noise"; "Three Thresholds of the Audible and One of the Bearable"; "Beyond the Audible"); essays ("Concerning Silence"; "The Sound Object"; "The New Soundscape"; "Epilogue"); and in one case ("Sound Sewage: A Collage"), a selection of quotes about noise.

"The Sonic Environment" is based on an extended exercise where Schafer had the students take ten minutes to sit quietly and listen to the environmental sounds around them then choose a historical document and list all the sounds or potential sounds in it, whether the document be a painting, novel, or biblical scene. "Concerning Silence" flows out of the previous exercises and leads students to the realization that in modern society, silence is elusive. This flows into a discussion of silence in traditional music, which now must mean the absence of traditional musical sounds, not absolute silence.

"A New Definition of Noise" flows directly out of the previous discussion when the students were in an apartment discussing how "noisy" it was, basing their dialogue on a redefinition of noise by the nineteenth-century physicist Hermann von Helmholtz: "The sensation of a musical tone is due to the rapid periodic motion of the sonorous body; the sensation of a noise to non-periodic motions."[22] Schafer posits a new definition: "Noise is any undesired sound signal,"[23] so any sound that interferes with the accurate transmission and reception of a message is noise. The next chapter, "Sound Sewage: A Collage," is a collection of quotes about noise ranging over several centuries and situations.

"Three Thresholds of the Audible and One of the Bearable" as defined by Schafer is sounds so soft they cannot be heard, sounds so high they cannot be heard, and sounds so low they cannot be heard. "Beyond the Audible" explores frequencies that are higher and lower than audible sound, leading to an exploration of the hearing abilities of other animals, the microcosmic world of molecules, and the macrocosmic world of "The Music of the Spheres" in a discussion of the theory traced through the writings of Boethius, Kepler, and Shakespeare that the planets and stars make perfect musical sounds as they move.

"Schizophonia" is a word invented by Schafer that describes the modern phenomenon of how a sound can originate in one place and be heard (even simultaneously) in a completely different place that is perhaps miles away. This new term is the basis of a discussion of how it now seems more natural for someone to listen to electronically reproduced music than to listen to live music, and how sound can be electronically manipulated. "The Sound Object" is defined as "one completely self-contained acoustic event."[24] Schafer and his class explore the various aspects of a sound object, including tone, preparation, attack, decay, reverberation, death and memory, and morphology. These sound objects are then included in a musical composition.

The penultimate section of the pamphlet, "The New Soundscape," summarizes and pulls together the various preceding sections. Schafer returns to his new definition of music and the need for the music educator to help his or her students navigate recent developments in the approach to musical composition and society's approach to music and sound. "Epilogue" is a tongue-in-cheek eulogy for the piano based on Schafer's view that the piano has passed out of vogue and is dying as an instrument in modern society.

Schafer's fourth pamphlet, *When Words Sing*, was published in 1970. Schafer sets this pamphlet in the context of the previous three publications and in particular *The New Soundscape*, where he expressed the concern that the sound of the human voice might be in jeopardy of being overwhelmed by the mechanical and technological sounds of modern society. In this publication Schafer returns to the most intimate and basic producer of sound, the human voice. He notes,

> I have not begun with traditional singing. If anything we leave off at about the point this begins. My purpose was to work with raw vocable sound.[25]

He encourages the reader to perform the book with their voice, and he structures it as a series of short notes with suggested exercises for the reader to do.

"Voiceprint" and "Melisma" encourage the reader to first explore a single tone based on the practices of Mantra Yoga then to explore the expressive range and potential of their individual voice, using a graphic score to encourage this free exploration.

"Nature Concert" is based on a group exercise that Schafer first used at a summer camp when several groups were sent off to create different realizations of nature sounds. At the end the reader is encouraged to create their own sound chronicle. One of the sounds discussed in that section is further explored in the next chapter, "Thunder-Word," using James Joyce's attempt to write a visual/sonic expression of thunder in *Finnegan's Wake*.

From textless sounds Schafer turns to an exploration of the basics of language in the next four sections. "The Biography of the Alphabet" leads the listener through the various phonemes of the English language based on the alphabet but unrelated to any words, simply exploring the sonic character of each sound. "Onomatopoeia" encourages the listener to find words with different sound characteristics. "Vowels" is an exploration of the frequency of certain vowel sounds and how they can be paired with various tones. "The Psychographic Curve of the World's Soul" moves to setting a word to music, working from the premise that you must work up from the word's natural sound and meaning.

"Pianissimo Secrets" and "Sound Poem" explore the more extreme sounds of the human voice, first the softest sounds possible, then the variety of expressions possible when declaiming text. This leads to exercises in creating sound poems using various word combinations to truly express their meaning.

"Words and Music" is placed at this point to let the reader reflect on the similarities and differences between words and music. Schafer defines language as "communication through symbolic arrangements of phonemes called words" and music as "communication through arrangements of tones and sound objects."[26] He explores the scale of tension when words and music are combined, giving eight stages of vocalism leading from maximum sense (stage speech) to maximum sound (electronically manipulated vocal sounds).

The next four sections move on to communal (choral) vocal expressions. "Choros" uses the chorus texts from Sophocles' *Antigone* as the basis of a classroom exercise in expressing the meaning and sonic impression of text using untrained voices. "Choric Textures" introduces the use of graphic notation to express certain events and moods ranging from chaos to clouds. "Haiku" suggests the usefulness of this short poetic form as a source of choral improvisation. The culmination of this part of the book is "Manitoba," a collaborative composition with an eighth-grade class that realizes through graphic notation the geography of the Canadian province of Manitoba.

The final section of *When Words Sing* is a reproduction of Schafer's most famous work for young singers, *Epitaph for Moonlight*. The text for this composition, which Schafer calls a "study piece for youth choir,"[27] is based on words created by a seventh-grade class for moonlight in newly created languages. Musically, the piece summarizes the composer and educator's philosophy of the use of a simplified graphic notation to encourage music making. At the end of the pamphlet, Schafer includes an appendix titled "Texts without Comment." Some of these groups of words ("War-Words," "Raindrops") were created by different groups of students, ranging from grade seven through university. He also includes various quotes about words and speech, ranging from Homer and Virgil to Schoenberg and Berg, and texts from various other sources.

The Rhinoceros in the Classroom, published in 1975, was the last pamphlet to grow out of Schafer's time at SFU. Its collection of essays serves as a summary of Schafer's efforts over the past ten years and an embellishment of a list of maxims for educators that he had placed above his desk at SFU:

1. The first practical step in any educational reform is to take it.
2. In education, failures are more important than successes. There is nothing so dismal as a success story.
3. Teach on the verge of peril.
4. There are no more teachers. There is just a community of learners.
5. Do not design a philosophy of education for others. Design one for yourself. A few others may wish to share it with you.
6. For the 5-year-old, art is life and life is art. For the 6-year-old, life is life and art is art. This first school-year is a watershed in the child's history: a trauma.
7. The old approach: Teacher has information, student has empty head. Teacher's objective: to push information into student's empty head. Observations: at outset teacher is a fathead, at conclusion student is a fathead.
8. On the contrary, a class should be an hour of a thousand discoveries. For this to happen, the teacher and the student should first discover one another.

BLOCKS: SLABS

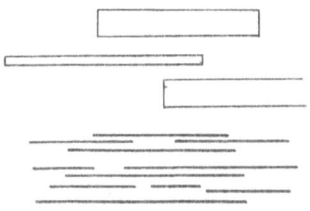

Blocks or slabs of sound are sustained chords or clusters. Sonorities can be built up in this way either by adding or eliminating different groups of voices on different chords or by adding or eliminating individual voices on individual notes. Extra plasticity is given to the rather dull sound of sustained chords or clusters by the careful use of dynamic shadings.

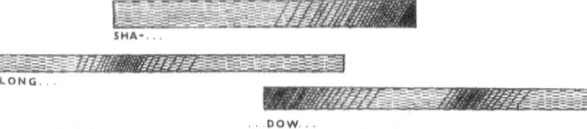

WEDGES

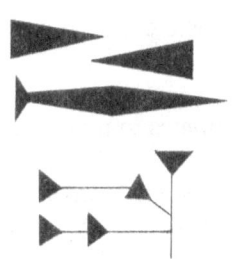

A chord or texture may appear to "grow" in size as a result of its dynamics. It may also grow by the gradual addition of more tones. Choric textures of this sort might be called *wedges* after cuneiform writing which is angular and shaded in this way. A text for vocal experimentation might therefore come from the Babylonian cuneiform.

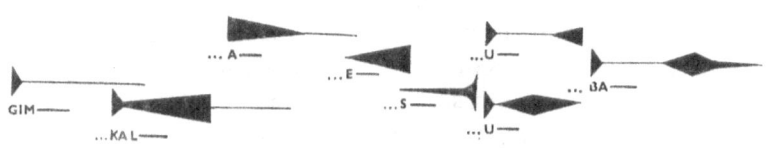

(See **Texts Without Comment** at the close of this booklet for more Babylonian words.)

Figure 8.1. Choric Textures from *When Words Sing*. R. Murray Schafer

9. Why is it that the only people who never matriculate from their own courses are teachers?
10. Always teach provisionally: only God knows for sure.[28]

After this preface, Schafer moves into the "Introduction," reflecting on what he has learned from the past decade of teaching, traveling, and lecturing, and he argues that creative music making should have a place in mainstream music education, whose focus up to this point has been improving the facility of young musicians.

"A Statement on Music Education" is a transcript of a lecture that Schafer gave at the Seventh International Music Congress of the International Music Council of UNESCO in 1971. This essay expands upon the three fields he has concentrated on in his work in music education.

1. To try to discover whatever creative potential children may have for making music of their own.
2. To introduce students of all ages to the sounds of the environment; to treat the world soundscape as a musical composition of which man is the principal composer; and to make critical judgments which would lead to its improvement.
3. To discover a nexus or gathering-place where all the arts may meet and develop together harmoniously.[29]

To this field he adds the use of Oriental philosophies to train Western musicians.

"Another Statement on Music Education" attempts to give Schafer's answer to four basic questions about music and education: Why teach music? What should be taught? How should it be taught? Who should teach it? After discussing the various traditional answers to the first question, he simply states, "Music exists because it uplifts us."[30] Schafer's answer to the second question is that the teacher should teach to preserve past musical experiences and to expand the repertoire, including involving the students themselves in creating (not simply reproducing) music. His response to the third question is to advocate for the reduction of the role of the teacher as authority figure in favor of cooperative problem solving and creation, allowing models from other subjects to influence the learning process. The final question is answered with a strong statement that traditional music should only be taught by professionals, no compromises.

"A Note on Notation" returns to the topic Schafer first broached in his earlier article "The Graphics of Music Thought." He reiterates his resistance to teaching music notation in the early stages of education, which encourages a departure from sound to paper, and states his desire to let the subject of notation come up naturally, usually when the class is already composing pieces. At that point the students should devise their own notation, refining it as they discover what information needs to be added to their system.

"The Music Box" is the author's take on educational kits that had become fashionable in North America as a partial replacement for the textbook. He goes on to describe what he believes should be included in a kit used for music education, referencing the kit that he and fellow composers and artists created at the request of the Ontario Arts Council in 1969. The completed box had nearly three hundred items, and the remainder of the essay describes some of the elements of this kit.

"Threnody" is a reproduction of an essay he wrote in 1970 that discusses his most ambitious piece for young performers and how he tailored his contemporary idiom to the age group for which it was intended. "Departing in New Directions" is a collection of exercises that Schafer and his composer and visual arts colleagues did as part of a communications course at SFU between 1965 and 1971, and it also references the sensitivity course he taught at the university, both classes being an attempt to break down the natural barriers between the various arts forms.

The closing essay, "Curriculum Vitae," first critiques academic institutions and their unwillingness to change. Schafer references his own difficulties at the University of Toronto that resulted in his expulsion from the school and reflects on his own teaching career at SFU and as a guest lecturer at multiple institutions. He ends with listing what he would consider the ideal curriculum for music.

MAYNOOTH AND AFTER

In 1976 Schafer gathered the preceding five music education pamphlets into one book, *Creative Music Education*. The only new material was an extended preface, "A Note to the Teacher," where he briefly describes the focus of each pamphlet and gives a short apologetic for this new publication.

> In the past few years, as I have tried out similar teaching ideas in a dozen other countries on three continents, I have noticed a growing number of music educators moving out in similar directions. An encouraging sign, though the area is still rather bleak. And that, I would say, is the only justification for the reappearance of my "diary of personal experiences" in a format that looks suspiciously like a textbook.[31]

In 1986, Schafer sat down once again to gather together a definitive edition of his writings on music education, taking as the basis of this new book the five original pamphlets and adding additional essays. *The Thinking Ear: On Music Education* supplants *Creative Music Education* as the definitive edition of his music education writings.

The preface to the book is closely based on the preface of *Creative Music Education*, only altered to allow for a sixth section, a collection of new essays and writings, gathered under the heading "Beyond the Music Room," that were written after that book was published. All five sections are given short, updated introductions, and all but one of the original pamphlets are presented unaltered. *The New Soundscape* is given an additional segment, which appears after the epilogue. It is titled "Middle-East Sound Diary" and consists of notes from Schafer's journal entries during his trip to Turkey and Iran in 1969 while on leave from SFU.

Beyond the Music Room contains a variety of materials, mostly in essay form, outlining Schafer's continued exploration in music education and soundscape studies after his departure from SFU. In the preface to this section he describes the reasons for his departure from Vancouver and concludes by saying that although he was not reclusive, "the time I spent in the country changes a lot of my attitudes, and these changes are reflected in the music I wrote there as well as in the essays which follow."[32]

"Bricolage" is an extended essay on the possibilities of sound sculpture. It describes the first sound sculpture that Schafer created with a composition student in a barn on Schafer's rural property and the second created for Yehudi Menuhin's CBC series *The Music of Man*. At the end of the essay (which includes detailed drawings of both sound sculptures), Schafer speculates as to the usefulness of creating sound sculptures with students in an educational setting.

"Jonah and the Maynooth Community Choir" speaks to Schafer's work with adult amateur musicians. The opening of the essay laments the focus of music education on training children, usually in a well-equipped classroom with many accessories. Schafer counters that what is more needed are teachers who might be called "community music animators" able to work in less-affluent situations and with abandoned groups of people, many of them adults. The remainder of the essay describes Schafer's experience in the rural Ontario community of Maynooth, creating and developing the Maynooth Community Choir made up of singers of all ages and abilities. The culmination of three years of work was the creation, with the choir, of a piece called *Jonah*. The piece is described in detail, and Schafer reflects on the value of such an undertaking for a situation that is often considered infertile ground for the arts. He advocates again for every community to have a career person to guide the arts and engage the population in creating and performing music that is grounded in the community.

In "Letter to the Portuguese," Schafer reflects on his time teaching in Lisbon, where he worked with both students and teachers, describing the various events and exercises that he undertook with them.

"Edward's Magic Orchestra" was written in response to an enthusiastic card from an eight-year-old boy named Edward. This essay imagines a class-

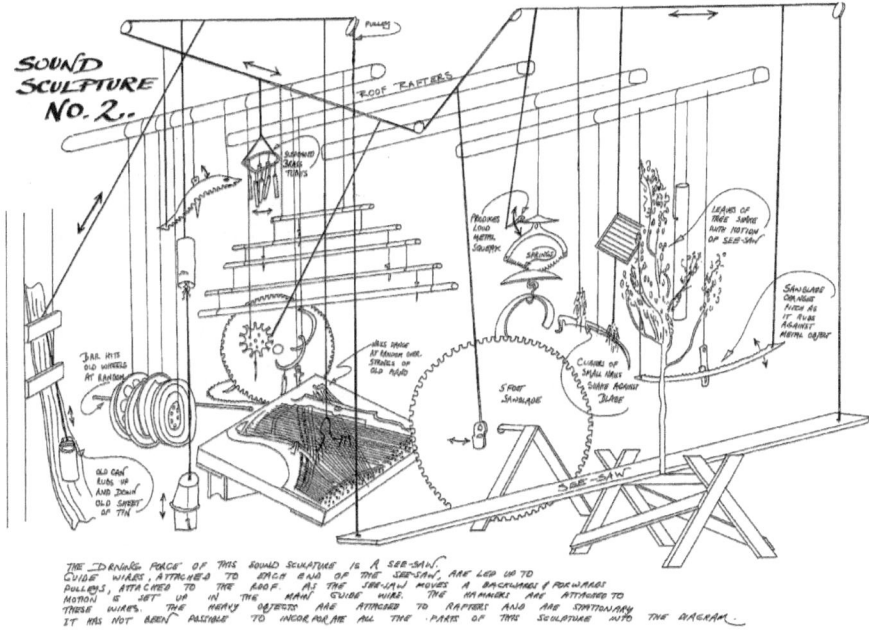

Figure 8.2. Diagram of *Sound Sculpture no. 2* from the essay "Bricolage," *The Thinking Ear*. R. Murray Schafer

room setting with Edward as a main character. The music teacher, Miss Chirp, takes the class through a typical listening exercise, playing various instruments and asking the class what they think they sound like. Edward begins to daydream, which changes his interaction with the teacher and the class, setting in motion exercises more similar to what Schafer would advocate for music education classrooms.

"Here the Sounds Go Round" is an extended poem written and recorded on one half of a vinyl disc as part of an exhibition of some of Schafer's graphic scores and small sound sculptures that traveled across Canada.

Schafer would not publish his next book, *A Sound Education*, until 1992. Subtitled *100 Exercises in Listening and Sound-Making*, it was intended to be

> useful to every teacher concerned with improving the listening skills of children and young people. The exercises could serve as a foundation for music but they are intended to have a broader application than this. In today's noisy world, it is more important than ever for whole populations to begin to listen more carefully and critically. Here are exercises dealing with soundmaking

and listening, gradually leading on toward the designing of soundscapes, both personal and public.[33]

He expands upon this concept in the extended preface to the book. After discussing briefly the history of the founding of his soundscape concepts and the realization that a negative approach to the issues of noise pollution (focusing on the reduction of problem noises) would be ineffective, Schafer explains his years-long focus on helping society in general to listen better so to effectively engage in positive soundscape design. Toward the end of the preface he asks,

> How could I put all this in the most cogent manner for teachers and individuals who might be interested in such a program? I decided the simplest form would be best: a collection of exercises—I would call them Ear Cleaning Exercises. I have used them all in my own teaching with both children and adults. The vast majority require no special training to undertake. Many could be performed alone, but a group would be best for most of them.[34]

Although the book is laid out in a logical progression, the exercises within are not meant to be performed front to back but to be adapted to the needs of the group and serve as an inspiration for new exercises. The progression of the exercises is similar to that found in *Ear Cleaning*, starting with simple (and not so simple) exercises concerned with aural perception and imagination then progressing to the creation of sounds and leading to the exploration of the place of sound in our society. The exercises take place in a variety of settings (such as the classroom or on a busy street corner) and ask the reader to create new sounds, discover sounds long gone, or make no sound at all. At the end of the final exercise is a simple instruction: "We have reached the end of our exercises for the present. Now it is up to you to extend the work begun with these experiences in any ways your imagination might take you."[35]

For his final educational booklet, *HearSing*, published in 2005, Schafer gathered together seventy-five additional exercises in a similar format to those of *A Sound Education*. The two books are related, but in this book the exercises are less focused on sonic awareness and aural acuity and more focused on music making and creation. Accurate listening (ear cleaning) is one of the themes of the book, and Schafer carries over a few exercises from *A Sound Education* into this publication. The primary theme of the book is creativity, reflective of Schafer's long-term teaching philosophy, which he suggests is fundamentally different from what most professors of music do.

> The professors always explain first and do afterwards. Sometimes they don't even get that far. I always want the experience to happen first and the decision

as to its usefulness to come later. I keep telling my students, "Don't discuss it, just do it. Then we'll talk about it."[36]

Schafer goes on to further explain his nonlinear method of music education and lists his indictments against music education as it is still currently taught. He ends the preface on a philosophical note.

> The music room is neither the beginning nor the end of music. Music is the whole sounding universe. We are all simultaneously listeners and performers and composers of the universal symphony.
> And occasionally, we may find that we are lifted out of this world to enter the mists of the Divine Being Who inspires us all.[37]

The exercises contained within the book are divided into various sections. "Games" and "Outdoor Games" both contain activities to be played by groups of people. "Drawing Sounds" includes such exercises as taking a note for a walk and creating a media canon. "Language" is one of the larger sections, exploring everything from creating new languages to onomatopoeic words to new sound for water. "Listening" brings us closest to the activities found in *A Sound Education*, with various focused listening exercises to increase sonic awareness.

"Time and Rhythm" outlines various activities to increase awareness in the ears and in the body of the passage of time, change in tempo, and coordination between different musicians. "Counterpoint" links sound and gesture, both individual and coordinated, and leads to more complex exercises in which students must simultaneously create and be aware of sounds.

The next sections lead the student from "Improvisation" to "Composition." The first few exercises explore the sonic possibilities of various objects, such as a piece of paper or shoes, then leads to freely improvising with sounds. This leads to realizing simple graphic scores and exploring the possibilities of one tone. "Song" is in many ways the culmination of the book, containing only one command, to create your own song, and simple suggestions are given for inspiration.

The final section of the booklet, "Stillness and Silence," brings us slowly away from sound. It serves as a coda to the book and also to Schafer's career as a music educator with its focus on listening not only closely to sound but finding and appreciating rare silence in our modern society. The final exercise within this closing section encourages the student to sit quietly and imagine sounds, as listed in the book.

Chapter Nine

Soundscape Publications

Schafer's work in the field of acoustic ecology and as a founder of the WSP has earned him an international reputation among architects, scientists, musicians, and environmental activists. He has produced pamphlets, articles, books, and audiovisual materials on this subject over the course of his career and has lectured around the world on the subjects of noise pollution, acoustic design, and sonic awareness. The materials in this chapter are presented chronologically, reflecting his several decades of effort in this field. Many of his first publications were created with the involvement of members of the WSP or, if written by Schafer himself, were inspired by his work on the project.

DOCUMENTS OF THE WORLD SOUNDSCAPE PROJECT

The first document to come out of the WSP was the article "Results of a Social Survey on Noise—Vancouver 1969." About twenty-five students in Schafer's Communications 100 class interviewed Vancouver residents about their views on community noise.[1] Schafer describes the project as follows:

> About 650 people were interviewed on a door to door basis selected at random over a grid including Vancouver, Burnaby and New Westminster. . . . The answers for the first questions have been broken down into general age and occupation categories to facilitate cross-sectional analysis. This did not seem so necessary with the final questions. Eight questions were asked of the people surveyed, and the following conclusions were reported:
>
> Well over 50% of the people polled regarded noise in modern life as an important or even major problem. Of those familiar with noise abatement procedures and legislation in their community, 66% were dissatisfied. 76% of those polled are in favour of more research to combat noise . . . and perhaps

most interestingly of all, 60% were not convinced that noise was a necessary consequence of progress—an ancient and, thankfully, dying myth.[2]

The privately published *The Book of Noise* was also written in 1969, although not released until 1970. Torigoe considers *The Book of Noise* to have two main themes—to provide adequate knowledge and understanding of the problems of modern acoustic environments, and to propose solutions to noise pollution.[3] These two themes also imply a concern for the social aspect of the issue, not simply a scientific or an acoustic one. In the book Schafer introduces some interesting concepts, including the idea of the "acoustic space" of an object, which in modern society can be much larger than the physical space of the object. This allows objects or people to invade others' privacy without stepping into their physical space.

In 1998 Schafer, almost thirty years after its publication, returned to the book, redrafting and slightly revising it. He notes in the new edition that

> thanks to the sustained efforts of countless people, solutions to some of the worst problems are being found or now seem attainable, though a larger effort is still necessary, particularly in the area of public education, if we are to succeed in restoring a balanced and ecological soundscape to the world.[4]

The book begins with "Howl!" and ends with "Yeow!" (the same word in Hebrew), linking the concept of noise pollution faced by modern society (discussed in terms of decibels in "Howl!") and the noisy, apocalyptic ending of society itself (in "Yeow!") as described in the Hebrew scriptures, in the writings of the Sufi mystic Rumi, and in the Koran. This structure connects the scientific and spiritual dimensions of the problem of noise.

The book's second section, "The Soundscape," introduces in language accessible to the lay reader the concept of acoustic ecology, encouraging the cultivation of the habit of listening. From this general concept the focus narrows to a discussion in the third section titled "What Is Noise?" giving several possible definitions followed by a discussion of modern sources of noise. How this problem has developed is explored in "How Sounds Are Spreading," and the newly added "Same Story" discusses how this problem has been constantly addressed in articles for almost forty years.

The next several sections look at the hazards of noise pollution from several different angles and in several different contexts, including "Noise: A Killer," "The Deaf Teenager," "The University," "Do Africans Hear Better?" "Other Effects of Noise on Health," "Psychological Disturbance: Social Complaints," and "Sonic Weaponry." From a discussion of some effects of noise pollution, the booklet looks to some of the root causes of the problem in Western society in "Sound Imperialism," "The Modern City as a Blitzkreig," and "Sound Symbolism."

The focus once again narrows for the next several sections, first to motor vehicles in "The Car: A Noise Machine or . . . ?" then moving on to aircraft. A discussion of the history of noise regulation in the airline industry occupies the next several sections ("The Big Sound Sewer of the Sky," "The Deaf Ear of the Aviator," "And Now the Bottom Line," and "Big Birds and Little Birds").

After these extensive discussions of the modern problem of noise pollution, the booklet moves on to possible solutions, beginning with looking to other cultures and historical epochs in "Progress and Restraint," consumer advocacy in "Ears for Sale," and the possibility of communal observances of silence in "Observing Silence."

At this point the pamphlet turns its attention from society as a whole to the individual, human aspect of noise. This discussion covers several sections, beginning with "The Basic Module" (which in the human environment is the human being). "Quiet Groves and Times" equates the human need for quiet with the need for sleep. The intersection of the individual and the soundscape is explored in "Jitters and Brouhaha," "Acoustic Space," and "Sound Walls" and culminates with "A UNESCO Resolution," using the 1969 statement of the General Assembly of the International Music Council,

> We denounce unanimously the intolerable infringement of individual freedom and of the right of everyone to silence, because of the abusive use, in private and public places, of recorded or broadcast music. We ask the Executive Committee of the International Music Council to initiate a study from all angles—medical, scientific, and juridicial—without overlooking its artistic and educational aspects, and with a view to proposing to UNESCO, and to the proper authorities everywhere, measures calculated to put an end to this abuse.[5]

The final portions of the book list what the individual can do to improve the situation. "A Tourist in the Soundscape" suggests personal awareness when one is traveling through the world. "Noise Abatement" urges the individual to be aware of local noise ordinances, and "A Time for Voices" encourages advocacy by joining (or founding) a Noise Abatement Society and lobbying elected officials. But it is not only advocacy that is important—" . . . And a Time for Quiet" encourages the reader to be aware and respectful of their effect on the soundscape and of how to minimize their personal impact, and "sama" (the Sufi word for "listening") encourages an individual exploration of deep silence and listening as the most profound way to engage with this issue. After "Yeow!" the reader is given a list of other publications as a resource and a list of organizations to contact.

The Music of the Environment was written for the UNESCO *Journal of World History*, but while Schafer was waiting for it to be published he issued it privately under the auspices of the WSP. The article was later published both by UNESCO and also by Universal Editions in late 1973.[6] In this substantial article, Schafer discusses sound not from the perspective of noise pollution (as in *The Book of Noise*) but from an educational perspective, similar to the approach in *The New Soundscape*. This substantial article is made up of three sections, dealing respectively with natural sounds, recent changes in the acoustic environment, and future potential changes to that environment.[7] Schafer begins by discussing the concept of God as a voice in many world religions and the idea of water as the first sound heard by humankind. The second and third sections of the article deal with modern sounds, particularly man-made, but in a broader sense than *The Book of Noise*. The concepts of "hi-fi" and "lo-fi" systems of noise (hi-fi being the old rural environment, lo-fi the broadband noise of the modern urban environment) are introduced, as is the concept of "schizophonia," where modern technology can separate a sound from its initial context, in particular through the ability to record sound. In the final section Schafer introduces concepts of acoustic design such as "signals" (a sound that is a significant feature of a soundscape, important because of its individuality or domination), and "acoustic community" (the medieval concept of a parish being the area within which the church bell could be heard). In this publication are found the first drafts of the theoretical underpinnings of the new field of study launched by the WSP, the field of acoustic ecology.[8]

A Survey of Community Noise By-laws in Canada was completed and compiled in 1972. All communities in Canada that at that time had a population over 25,000 were contacted and asked for copies of their noise bylaws as well as comments from public officials involved in the enforcement of the bylaws. The introduction to the published results talks about the issues and effects of noise pollution and the responsibilities of the three levels of government (municipal, provincial, and federal) in facilitating noise abatement. It discusses what measures have (or have not) been taken by various levels of government and criticizes, where needed, the lack of effort. It then describes the forms of legislation taken by various municipalities across Canada to combat noise pollution, highlights inconsistencies and perceived faults in the various bylaws of the different municipalities, and proposes possible solutions to these issues. It cites authorities from other countries as possible examples of effective noise abatement legislation, and advocates for the federal government to set national standards for municipalities; for provincial governments to provide money to municipalities to purchase effective measuring equipment; and for municipal governments to raise the level of fines.[9]

One of the crowning collaborative achievements of the WSP, *The Vancouver Soundscape*, was issued in 1973. Unlike previous efforts, it was a mixed media effort, two LP discs with an accompanying booklet, that were intended to augment each other. The booklet is divided into six parts ("Some

Earwitness Accounts," "A Thumbnail Historical Sketch," "Features of the Vancouver Soundscape," "Hi-fi to Lo-fi Soundscape," "Vancouver's Noise Pollution Problems," and "Towards Acoustic Design") and includes three types of material: text written by members of the WSP, quotations from literature, and maps and graphics. The two discs are divided into four distinct parts. Side 1 of LP 1 is given the title *Shoreline and Harbour* and has four tracks: "Ocean Sounds," "Squamish Narrative," "Entrance to Harbour," and "Harbour Ambience." The second side is given the title *Signals and Soundmarks* and has three tracks: "Homo Ludens: Vancouverites at Play," "The Music of Horns and Whistles," and "Vancouver Soundmarks and the Music of Various City Quarters." LP 2 side 1 is given the title *A Conversation Piece* and is an informal discussion among Schafer and his research assistants about their experiences while doing the sound recordings. Side 2 is called *On Acoustic Design* and is an introduction by Schafer to this new field of study, including several audio examples.[10]

The 1974 series of radio programs titled *The Soundscapes of Canada* is the first occurrence of an acoustic ecological study on a national scale, based on materials gathered in 1973 during a cross-country research trip (with the exception of two of the segments). The use of radio allowed the WSP to broadcast an acoustic environment into homes across Canada and eventually internationally when it was broadcast in other countries such as Sweden and Australia. Unlike earlier projects that if not exclusively print media at least included a printed element, this project was strictly aural and educational in nature, raising people's awareness of their acoustic environment. The materials for this series of broadcasts was drawn mostly from the materials gathered the previous year during a cross-country trip.[11] The programs of *The Soundscapes of Canada* can be broken into three categories: narration illustrated with examples, sound collages, and tape compositions.

Programme I: Six Themes of the Soundscape serves as Schafer's introduction (along with his SFU colleague Barry Truax) to the program for the radio audience. The six themes he outlines are rhythm and tempo, ambience and acoustic space, language, gestures and textures, the changing soundscape, and silence. *Programme II: Part One: Listening* serves to further prepare the audience to listen to the soundscape. It is explained as "a half hour of ear cleaning activities and relaxation exercises, in preparation for the kind of concentrated listening required for this series of programmes."[12] The next several segments, from the second part of *Programme II* through the first part of *Programme VIII* are collages of sounds. There is a wide variety of sonic topics in this section, ranging from sounds of work and sounds of play to developing on a national scale several of the WSP's central concepts. They include contributions by Bruce Davis, Peter Huse, and Barry Truax. Of particular note is Program V (Summer Solstice), a groundbreaking recording of a bioacoustic habitat. *Programme III: Signals, Keynotes, and Soundmarks* deals with "the characteristic sounds of a community or region [that] often go unrecognized and unvalued, until they disappear or are changed."[13] *Programme IV* focuses specifically on soundmarks where it combines "the important and unique sounds of Canadian communities in an hour-long sound profile of the country."[14] The last three segments (*Programme IX* and the two parts of *Programme X*) are soundscape compositions by Howard Bloomfield, Barry Truax, and Bruce Davis.

Five Village Soundscapes was completed and published in 1977 although it was based primarily on research undertaken in 1975 by Schafer and several members of the WSP, including coauthors Davis and Truax. After visiting several European villages, they chose five to be the focus of their research, staying in each village for seven to ten days total. Their goals were to

1. Investigate local and regional history.
2. Study local archives for references to sound (town crier, post horns, noise bylaws, etc.).
3. Create morphology charts of all significant changes in the soundscape.
4. Record and measure the intensity of all village signals.
5. Draw profile maps for prominent community signals.
6. Record all antique sounds in the village (blacksmith, old tools or artifacts, etc.).
7. Make extended recordings of characteristic ambiences in each village.
8. Take regular sound level recordings day and night both in and outside the village.
9. Enumerate and measure the frequency of specific types of transportation sounds.
10. Make lists of sounds heard throughout the village at different times of day.
11. Run a Sound Preference Test in the village school(s) in which we ask children to list their favorite and most disliked sounds in the community.
12. Conduct interviews with elderly people concerning the past soundscape of the village.
13. Focus special attention on any unusual features of the soundscape.[15]

The results were published in seven chapters. "The Five Villages" introduces the five villages (Skruv in southern Sweden, Bissingen in southern Germany, Cembra in northern Italy, Lesconil in western France, and Dollar in southern Scotland) from a visual perspective, giving a history of each location and how each met the criteria for inclusion in the study. Chapters 2 through 5 ("Soundscape Character," "Acoustic Rhythms and Densities," "Acoustic Materials," and "Acoustic Definition") discuss the acoustic attributes of each village. "Community Attitudes to the Soundscape" lists the result of a sound preference survey conducted in village schools and with elderly villagers to determine their perceptions of local sounds.[16] "Conclusion" gives several suggestions for improving the soundscape through design and education.

The *European Sound Diary* was published in 1977 as a companion to *Five Village Soundscapes*. At Schafer's suggestion, each member of the research team for *Five Village Soundscapes* kept a sound diary during their trip. At the end of each week Schafer would gather them together, selecting and combining certain passages to create an experiential account of their soundscape expedition. The publication is divided into several sections according to the geographical areas the team visited, sometimes focusing on a specific city, sometimes a country, and sometimes the journey from one region or country to another. Schafer provides an introduction and conclusion to this document, providing context to the personal commentaries which have been combined to create the *Sound Diary*. The publication concludes with two appendices. The first is a collection of sound walks from Vienna, Paris, London, and Stuttgart that the reader could easily reproduce. The second is a table of measurements of European sirens, comparing police and other emergency vehicle signals from Stockholm, Stuttgart, Vienna, and London.

The *Handbook for Acoustic Ecology*, issued in 1978, is the last WSP project that Schafer oversaw. The *Handbook* was edited by Barry Truax and was designed to be a reference book. In addition to gathering together existing concepts and terms in the field of acoustic ecology (and often explaining and interpreting them from the WSP perspective), the *Handbook* also contains concepts and terms that the WSP had created as a result of their work. The purpose of this publication is to help educate the layperson who has an interest in the field of acoustic ecology and who might want to contribute to this (at the time) emerging field of study.

POST–SFU AND POST–WSP

Schafer's first publication after leaving SFU and giving up his leadership of the WSP was also his most substantial. *The Tuning of the World*, published in 1977, is the first book-length discussion of the topic of acoustic ecology. As he acknowledges in the preface to the book, the book borrows from Schafer's individual publications and WSP publications, including *The New Soundscape*, *The Book of Noise*, *The Music of the Environment*, and the *Vancouver Soundscape*. In this publication Schafer attempts to draw together this earlier material with more recent materials and thoughts to create the first cohesive and comprehensive discussion of this still-emerging field. Schafer would later reprint this work in 1994 as *The Soundscape: Our Sonic Environment and the Tuning of the World*. The book is in four parts, with an introduction and an epilogue, and it includes two appendices, which list sample sound notation systems and an international survey of sound preferences, and a glossary of soundscape terms.

The extended introduction to the book serves as an introduction for the lay reader to the concept of environmental acoustics, listing the various branches of the study that Schafer believes will come together to create the new interdisciplinary field of acoustic design. The main part of the introduction is the listing and explanation of ten principles and practices that will underpin the following materials. "From Industrial to Acoustic Design" discusses how this new interdisciplinary subject will draw together musicians, acousticians, psychologists, and sociologists, and it lists several activities that researchers in this field might do. "Orchestration Is a Musician's Business" describes the world as a type of musical composition where "all sounds belong to a continuous field of possibilities lying *within the comprehensive dominion of music.*"[17] "Dionysian versus Apollonian Concepts of Music" argues why the contemporary musician should be concerned with this field. "Music, the Soundscape and Social Welfare" notes that the music, and beyond that the general acoustic environment, of a society is an indication of social conditions. "The Notations of Soundscapes (Sonography)" discusses inherent difficulties in notating acoustic events, whether contemporary or historical, and how these might be overcome. "Earwitness" expands the previous concept to discuss how to recreate historical soundscapes. "Features of the Soundscape" details how to analyze a soundscape by distinguishing between "keynote sounds," "signals," and "soundmarks," and it also defines those three terms. "Ears and Clairaudience" discusses how the ear was supplanted by the eye in Western society but is regaining prominence over concerns about noise pollution. "A Special Sense" discusses the unique features of hearing and the ear itself.

After this extended introduction, the next two parts of the book ("The First Soundscapes" and "The Post-industrial Soundscape") "take the reader on a long excursion of soundscapes throughout history, with a heavy concentration on those of the Western world."[18]

The "First Soundscapes" is divided into four chapters, each of which is itself divided into several sections. "The Natural Soundscape" discusses the sound of water, both as the first sound in nature and the womb and in its influence in various forms on ancient civilizations and poets. It then discusses the sounds of wind and other natural phenomena before discussing soundmarks, what sounds might have accompanied the beginning of the world, and what might accompany its end. "The Sounds of Life" turns to animal sounds, first discussing the vocalizations of birds then the sounds of insects, water creatures, and other animals. It concludes with a study of the simultaneous development of both speech and music in humankind and such linguistic concepts as onomatopoeia, through which man can unite himself with the soundscape. "The Rural Soundscape" first introduces and defines two terms: "hi-fi soundscape" ("possessing a favorable signal-to-noise ratio")[19] and its opposite, "lo-fi soundscape." The countryside is hi-fi, allowing the listener to hear farther into the distance. From this definition the chapter moves on to discuss various rural soundscapes, including pastures, farms, and hunting. The invasive noise of war and the place of sound associated with sacred or religious activities is then explored. "From Town to City" discusses the change from rural to urban life that has occurred in the more recent centuries and how the soundscape has changed as a result. Several important sounds, such as that of a medieval church bell, a fourteenth-century mechanical clock, and a water mill and blacksmith shop are considered as well as how different construction materials can make sounds unique to that city (keynote sounds) that are rarely listened to consciously by the populace. The focus shifts further to urban noise, including night watchmen, street criers, horses and wagons, and most importantly to how the Industrial Revolution began to divorce work from song.

"Part Two: The Post-industrial Soundscape" begins with "The Industrial Revolution," which discusses the sonic changes that happened with industrialization and continued with the electric revolution that followed it, including a list of inventions that created more sound. How these new industrial noises were slowly accepted and eventually even promoted as evidence of progress and power is considered. From this point in part 2, Schafer focuses in on specific sounds that characterize modern society (trains, the internal combustion engine, and airplanes) and explores society's relationship to them. "The Electric Revolution" discusses how the themes of the Industrial Revolution were extended by the telephone, the phonograph, and the radio and their expansion of the reach of sound and creation of "schizophonia," "the split between an original sound and its electroacoustical transmission or reproduction."[20] The impact of radio on a community's sonic space and how radio programing should be studied in the same way one would a poem or composition is next explored, and the use of sound as a device to isolate people or to serve as background noise and how the resonant harmonics of various electrical devices have found their way into our sonic unconsciousness closes part 2.

"Music, the Soundscape and Changing Perceptions" serves as an interlude between part 2 and part 3, connecting the book's early focus on soundscape description to soundscape analysis, which is the concern of the latter part of the book. In delving into the relationship between music and the soundscape, Schafer first focuses on the history of European music to gather evidence of the shifting aural habits and perceptions of society since, as he argues "music forms the best permanent record of past sounds."[21] Nature descriptions in music, the incorporation of the hunting horn motif, and the parallels between the development of the orchestra and city industrial life leads us to the twentieth century with a discussion of the work of Honegger, Russolo, and the theories of "musique concrète." Twentieth-century composers who returned to the natural soundscape for inspiration (Debussy, Ives, Messiaen) lead to a discussion of the influence of the soundscape on music from the seventeenth century to the present time. Schafer plots the move of sound from the church to the factory to the rock concert hall, the growth of intensity and frequency range in Western music over this time, and the low pitch, continuous sound of modern society reflected in the bass focus of much contemporary popular music. How listeners now experience music (the modern stereo system and headphones) and its implications end the interlude.

The six chapters of "Part Three: Analysis" describe the various ways in which the sonic environment can be catalogued. "Notation" discusses the various advantages and shortcomings of any written notation system used to analyze a soundscape and introduces three graphic notational systems: (1) acoustics, describing the mechanical properties of sounds; (2) phonetics, to project and analyze human speech; and (3) musical notation. In addition to warning against placing too heavy a visual focus on the sonic field since "no silent projection of a soundscape can ever be adequate,"[22] Schafer describes in some detail the terms "sound objects," "sound events," and "soundscapes." "Classification" first asks and answers why we need to classify sounds and the ways in which we can do so, citing the work of Pierre Schaeffer and Schafer's own efforts in this field. The ways to classify sounds as discussed in the chapter include their physical characteristics, aesthetic qualities, cultural meanings, and effects.

"Perception" begins by showing the potential value of using terms from visual perception, such as "figure" and "ground," to describe aural perception. The focus then shifts to the usefulness of musical terminology, including ear training, perspective and dynamics, and gestures and textures. "Morphology" is concerned with the study of forms and structures. Schafer adapts this word to mean the "study of the changing forms of sound across time and space."[23] This allows various types of studies, such as the study of the evolution of train whistles, a comparison of different sounds used in different cultures for the same purpose, and changing construction materials, modes of transportation, and communication. The chapter then lists the benefits of such studies.

"Symbolism" discusses how a researcher must consider the referential or symbolic meanings of sound, which take it beyond isolated acoustical events. It circles back to part 1 of the book, reflecting on the symbolism given to the sea and wind by ancient cultures as well as bells, horns, and sirens before closing by demonstrating how all acoustic symbolism is constantly undergoing modification.

"Noise" draws heavily on WSP research and quotes extensively from *The Book of Noise* as it discusses the issues of noise pollution and ambient noise.

It summarizes various noise abatement laws around the world and discusses an additional concept, the regulation of certain words and sounds in the public arena around the world.

"Part Four: Toward Acoustic Design" takes the reader through the final seven chapters in the book, giving practical suggestions and solutions to several of the issues raised in part 3.

"Listening" defines the term "acoustic ecology," which is "the study of sounds in relationship to life and society,"[24] and explains the term "acoustic design" by comparing the soundscape of the world to a musical composition. The human ear and human voice are put forward as the basic modules for measuring the acoustic environment, and the reader is encouraged to learn how to listen, use a tape recorder, and keep a soundscape diary. "The Acoustic Community" begins by discussing the legal and environmental implications of private acoustic space and promotes the idea that communities can be designed along acoustic lines. This leads into a discussion of the retreat of humanity indoors as part of the noise phenomenon and highlights the inherent differences and meanings of indoor and outdoor sounds. How ancient architects took sound into account is contrasted with how modern architects often do not.

"Rhythm and Tempo in the Soundscape" moves from the rhythms of the human body (heart, breath, footsteps) to the daily and annual cycles of noises in nature and what they can tell us. Reference is made to the WSP's *Five Village Soundscapes* and what it told us about circadian and seasonal rhythms, and the chapter closes with a discussion of the lack of a governing rhythm in large cities and the frantic tempo of radio broadcasting.

"The Acoustic Designer" starts by stating the need for acoustic design in society, respect for the ear and voice, an awareness of sound symbolism, a knowledge of the rhythms and tempi of the natural soundscape, and an understanding of the balancing mechanisms by which an eccentric soundscape may be turned back on itself. Suggestions for acoustic design include the preservation of soundmarks (sounds that are important to or reflective of their communities), fixing the mistakes of earlier poor design, and imagining how future societies might be acoustically improved. "The Soniferous Garden" discusses one possible improvement, an acoustically designed park adapting the historical use of water, the Aeolian harp, and an opportunity for visitors to play instruments.

"Silence" appropriately closes the main part of the book, advocating for the return of silent sanctuaries where those weary of sound can retreat, and reintroduction of quiet times, the deliberate celebration of stillness by a society. Western society's fear of silence (which to this society symbolizes nothingness) is contrasted with the need for silence for true concentration and health.

The Tuning of the World closes with "Epilogue: The Music Beyond," a discussion of the parallel Eastern and Western concepts of music vibrations as the basis of the world's existence and the idea of the music of the spheres representing the perfection of the universe as posited by Pythagoras, Boethius, and Kepler. Schafer closes the book by reiterating that the need for all research into sound should conclude with silence.

It would be several years before Schafer would attempt another major publication in this field. *Voices of Tyranny, Temples of Silence* was written in 1992 and published in 1993, and it is Schafer's last full-length book on the soundscape. In the preface to this second book Schafer remarks,

> When *The Tuning of the World* was first published in 1977, book-sellers said it opened up such a new subject that they could find no appropriate place for it on the shelves. Had I been consulted, I might have suggested they leave it in the display window.[25]

This second volume grew out of Schafer's realization that there were still many issues surrounding the concept of the soundscape and noise pollution, and he published *Voices of Tyranny* simultaneously with *A Sound Education*, closely linking the concepts of awareness of and education on this subject. Unlike *The Tuning of the World*, *Voices of Tyranny* is a disparate collection of essays without any unity of style and tone, which Schafer acknowledges:

> So these essays explore soundscapes I've tried to inhabit, either personally or by examining documents from other places or times. The main concern is to try to discover clues that might be useful, so that, as future soundscapes evolve, they might, in a limited way at least, be rendered more satisfying and conducive to the better life we all hope lies ahead.[26]

"Ursound" (first published in *Open Letter*) begins by exploring in detail the appearance of sound in many creation stories, focusing first on the acoustic announcement of intention that occurs before each creation act in the Hebrew scriptures ("And God said . . . ") and the concept of the voice of God as the sonic collision of wind and water. He then cites other mythologies that also include the concept of creation through spoken word, including Ptah in the Egyptian stories, the Greek/Christian concept of Logos, and Mayan, Maori, and Brahman traditions. Schafer reinforces the idea that in all these cases creation arises out of the recitation of magic words, and the concept of God as an acoustic phenomenon can be traced through the monotheistic religions.

He notes that the deity would often speak to followers in dreams and then he segues into a discussion of the value of dreams as windows into the subconscious, as found in the work of Freud and Jung. He then speculates on the development of consciousness in *homo sapiens*, how that may have led to the loss of the voice of God, and how humankind attempts to recreate a sense of sacred sound through other means, such as music and ritual chanting. Schafer closes the essay by saying,

> Somehow we retain a faint acoustic memory trace of God's ordering and creating presence, even though we cannot grasp it completely. The elements are there—wind, water, fire, thunder, music and the voice—but that is all we know.[27]
>
> Sound is the original creative force, and we instinctively long to go back to it. In order to do that we "must return to the waters of instinct and the unshatterable unity of the unconscious."[28]

"Acoustic space" is a term that was first used by Marshall McLuhan and Edmund Carpenter in the middle of the twentieth century, but it was eventually supplanted by Schafer's own term "soundscape." In this essay Schafer attempts to define what acoustic space is, how sound operates in a space, and what the physical properties of sound actually are. An initial tracing of the concept of sacred and secular sound (or noise, as the case may be) leads to a discussion of the concept that those who experience the outdoors can hear the sounds of nature with an enlarged meaning, and if they could imitate a sound they could influence the natural world. Seeing and sounding are contrasted, with the first being analytical and reflective, the second active and generative. Schafer returns at the end of the essay to the original concept of acoustic space as known in natural (non-urban) and urban societies.

> In the one, everything sounds and has its sound presence, but like a spirit, incorporeal, without precise extension or shape. In the other, this resonating life is beaten down, first in the inner spaces of the church, the concert hall and the factory; then, by extension, through the external soundscape. In the past, it was the parish; today it is broadcasting that conquers space with sound. The first form will be more difficult for indoor man to comprehend, as he hides today behind glass windows listening to the radio and peering out at the silent cacophony of the streets.[29]

"Three Documentary Studies" discusses the possibility of studying soundscapes that existed before the invention of sound-recording devices, as evidenced by three examples. The first ("The Dialectical Soundscape") references the 1559 Pieter Brueghel painting *The Battle between Carnival and Lent*. This painting depicts two Shrovetide processions—one for Carnival, one for Lent. Schafer describes the painting in great detail and lists what sounds could be suggested by it, starting with the shape and size of the square, the faces and instruments, the multiple acoustic centers. The second study ("The Closed Soundscape") is taken from Victor Hugo's novel *Les Misérables*, book 6 of the Cosette section. The scene is an enclosed community of Benedictine Nuns sheltered behind eighteen-foot walls in the middle of Paris. As in the previous section, Schafer goes into great detail about what can be surmised from the written description of the area, in particular noting multiple references to bells even when the inhabitants are enjoined to silence. The final study ("The Open Soundscape") relies on a description from Anton Chekhov's novel *The Steppe* whose two keynotes are the sounds of nature and of a rumbling wagon carrying the travelers. Schafer compares the description to the orchestration of a composition where certain sounds are highlighted at certain points.

The first section in "Three Reflections" ("The Deceptive Soundscape") describes the time the author lived in a coach house in Toronto in one of the nicer parts of the city where the soundscape did not match the visual beauty. The unexpected noises included constant construction on both houses and utilities, pools, air conditioners, snowplows, and the unexpected absence of the sound of children playing. The section study ("The Glazed Soundscape") refers to a discussion in the *Tuning of the World* about the changing use of materials in the city, leading in this essay to a discussion of how glazed windows were an important invention for the soundscape, separating the interior from the exterior in a way that had not been possible before. This created the concept of noise as something that could (and should) be kept outside. The final study ("Crowded Soundscape") discusses the sonic impact of protests, crowds, and the army, all of which use sound as a unifying or terrifying tool. Schafer contrasts this approach to the need he sees for people to have rituals in large assemblies where their emotions can be expressed without destructive or disfiguring actions.

After an opening story recounting his effort to have the call of the loon as a spacer between radio programs of the CBC, "The Canadian Soundscape" becomes a discussion of some of the sounds that Schafer has strong associations with, including the particular sounds of the Canadian prairies (including the droning of combines at harvest time and the noises associated with horseback riding). He refers to descriptions of prairie soundscapes by such authors as F. P. Grove and W. O. Mitchell and notes how the Canadian soundscape has been little studied and celebrated, giving several excerpts from his diary where he recorded the sounds around him. He talks about the possible influence of the Canadian landscape and soundscape on his compositions and those of fellow composers Istvan Anhalt (an immigrant) and John Beckwith, and he concludes by discussing parts of the mythology of Canada's indigenous peoples that involve sound and how this can still have meaning in a modern society.

"The Soundscape Designer" begins with a historical event from the eighteenth century, a letter to an English newspaper that suggested a regulation of the sounds of the London soundscape. The author's approach was to improve the sounds of London through education and regulation. This story serves as background to the founding of the WSP, which Schafer maintains was a first attempt to put the earlier author's ideas into practice. From the founding of the WSP, Schafer goes on to discuss the classes he taught at SFU, the exercises he would give to his students, the project's study of the Vancouver soundscape, and the founding of the concepts of acoustic ecology, and he looks ahead to future developments.

At the beginning of "Music and the Soundscape," Schafer notes that he had suggested in *The Tuning of the World* that by the end of the twentieth century, music and the soundscape would draw together. He revisits this theme, still maintaining that it could happen, and he outlines how it might be possible. To set the stage for his discussion, he outlines how Western music is different from music in many other parts of the world because it is an abstract entertainment for the pleasure of the ears alone with no association with any function or purpose beyond enjoyment. This focus required music be disassociated from the soundscape by putting it in the concert hall and the music room, and it resulted in new musical forms and increased complexity. In contrast to this indoor music, Schafer lists various types of historical outdoor music, such as street processions, or elaborate Italian and French gardens where entertainments would have been held, and temples in Japan. He closes by discussing his approach to writing and performing his outdoor composition *Musique pour le parc Lafontaine*.

"Radical Radio" began as a lecture that Schafer gave several times in different parts of the world. In the lecture (and essay) Schafer defines "radical" as pertaining to roots or origins and he reconsiders the medium of radio by first going back to before the technology existed, "whenever there were invisible voices: in the wind, in thunder, in the dream."[30] He then explores how the old event of an "audience" with a king implied hearing (not seeing) and also obeying. Two early models of broadcasting are contrasted: the political model as employed by Hitler and the "enlightenment model" set up in opposition to this. Turning to the present, Schafer argues that contemporary models of radio have profaned its original concept. Radio is tuned to Western society's governance by the clock, "the pulse of a society organized for maximum production and consumption,"[31] but Schafer imagines that it could play a different role, following the rhythms of nature to help society reconnect with it. How we listen to radio has also changed since with the rise of societal background noise, we overhear it rather than listen to it. At the end of the essay he calls for a method of analyzing radio programing in a similar way to the way in which art and poetry are analyzed, and he speculates on what would happen if radio became an art form, replacing its humanistic approach to broadcasting with a phenomenological approach.

"Musecology" is a meditation on the musician's need to relate to society. Schafer takes the 1990 statement "133 Ways to Save the Earth" written by the founders of Earth Day and applies some of their findings to music and the music industry. An excerpt from the section on reduction and recycling of waste supports Schafer's criticism of a consumption mentality in music, where music is now created for mass consumption and sounds are taken out of context and divorced from their original meaning for their exoticism and charm. Music is further commercialized through technology and copyright to gain as much profit as possible. A passage on energy talks about various appliances but (Schafer notes) makes no mention of radios or televisions or the constant broadcasting of music in shopping malls and other public places. These walls of background music serve the same function as drugs and can even result in hearing loss. Schafer compares the statement's section on food, which encourages gardening and buying food in season, to the center-to-margin music industry where music is created in larger centers (often far away and "exotic") and shipped to the margins. In response to the section on transportation, Schafer discusses how in earlier centuries, small cities such as Weimar, Leipzig, and Bonn would have thriving cultures and produce great poets and musicians, reducing the need for travel to larger centers. The section on the preservation of the environment, including the harvesting of endangered exotic woods, inspires a comparison between how native instruments are made using resources around them, and how classical instruments are made using imported materials. Schafer concludes the essay by noting that "an ecologically responsive music would reduce our dependence on foreign materials as much as foreign inspiration, and seek both closer to home."[32]

The book closes with "I Have Never Seen a Sound," a collection of short statements about the nature of sound itself, beginning with short statements about creation myths that reference sound, moving to comparisons between sight and sound, and finishing with thoughts on silence, an appropriate ending to Schafer's second (and final) extended exploration of acoustic ecology.

Commissioned for the Studio Akustischer Kunst of West German Radio, the hour-long *A Winter Diary* was the third soundscape composition Schafer created for radio (the first two being *Okeanos* and *The Soundscapes of Canada*). Schafer joined with his friend and sound engineer Claude Schreyer to travel through the prairie province of Manitoba during the winter months of late 1997. The focus of the program is the often sharp contrast between indoor and outdoor sounds as they

> travelled along the road, visiting small towns, farms, Indian reservations, and national parks. The contrast between warm and friendly interiors of dwellings, restaurants and churches with rough and quiet landscapes outside, acoustically drawn only by the wind, passing by distant trains or the howling of prairie dogs, is one of the main themes.[33]

In addition to the focus on the contrasts between these two groups of sounds, the program is given structure by certain recurring sounds, highlighted as hallmarks of the prairie landscape. The recurring outdoor sounds include the sound of someone walking on snow, calling across the landscape, the sound of trains, both from close up and far away, and the ever-present sound of the prairie wind, the sound of which opens and closes the program. The recurring indoor sounds include a hockey game, hymn singing accompanied by an organ, and Native American singing and dancing. Around these recurring pillars of sound are additional outdoor noises (a dog sled race, a swinging gate, ice breaking, children playing at recess, a snowmobile, the sound of prairie dogs, and birds) and indoor noises (the crackling of a fire, people talking). This sonic composition ties together aurally many of Schafer's personal and professional interests, including his connection to Canada, and in particular Manitoba—the source of many fond childhood memories.

Chapter Ten

Scholarly Writing and Nonfiction

Outside of his compositions, Murray Schafer is best known for his work in the fields of music education and soundscape theory but less known for his relatively few but significant writings on other scholarly topics. His book on Ezra Pound's writings on music remains the primary resource on this subject, and his exploration of E. T. A. Hoffmann's writings on music is also a significant achievement. The remaining nonfiction writings are collections of articles, in-depth discussions of his own compositions, or explanations of his theories of theater.

MAJOR SCHOLARLY WORKS

Schafer's first book-length publication, *British Composers in Interview*, began with a series of audio interviews he was able to sell to the CBC program *Music Diary*, which was produced out of Vancouver.[1] As indicated in the preface to the 1963 book, the majority of the work was completed in late 1959 and early 1960. As part of this project Schafer interviewed sixteen British composers (John Ireland, Egon Wellesz, Arthur Benjamin, Alan Bush, Edmund Rubbra, William Walton, Lennox Berkeley, Michael Tippett, Elisabeth Lutyens, Benjamin Britten, Humphrey Seale, Peter Racine Fricker, Malcolm Arnold, Iain Hamilton, Alexander Goehr, and Sir Peter Maxwell Davies).

Each composer on the list was chosen as a prominent representative of a particular school of composition in England during that time, whether the late-Romantic music of Ireland, the strict serialism of Lutyens, or the avant-garde approach of Davies. Schafer placed the interviews chronologically according to the composer's birth to allow the reader to gain a perspective of British music over the first half of the twentieth century. The book was well received, in part because the focus was not the career accomplishments of the individuals interviewed but on their compositional approach.[2] Schafer's ability as an interviewer is apparent, and it also is evident that he carefully studied his subjects before preparing the interview questions and so was able to talk to them from a place of musical and intellectual equality. In particular his choice of questions leads to fascinating conversations in the face-to-face interactions with the composers,[3] which were often done at the composer's home or studio, giving them a sense of intimacy. After the interviews were completed, Schafer would transcribe the texts and hand them back to the composers in order for them to alter or add to their statements.[4] Schafer was careful to vary his questions from composer to composer, approaching the same subject from different angles. Schafer explains his approach in the extended introduction that precedes the interviews:

> If most interviews share a common concern, it is the exploration of the creative process itself. Composers are often asked about the mysteries of their work. I have encouraged them to speak as freely as possible about this by plying them with questions like: Does music come as in a dream, or is it worked out systematically? What is inspiration, and how large a role does it play? How long can inspiration be sustained? Is it confined to a motif, or does it extend to a melody or a complete movement? If a composer conceives a melodic idea, does it inspire its own harmony and instrumentation: When a composer says he "hears" music in his mind, does he mean he literally hears it or only "thinks" it? What is meant by "form," and why is it of such great concern to the composer of serious music?[5]

The introduction closes with several tables that show the various composers' answers to some basic questions such as Do you compose at the piano? Do you revise extensively? Do you have a favorite composer? How many hours do you compose every day? At the beginning of every interview, Schafer provides a thumbnail biographical sketch of the composer, including whom they studied with. He also paints a picture of where the interview took place, usually the composer's home or studio. Throughout the book are interspersed photographs of the composers interviewed.

Schafer's next large project was an extensive collection of translations and accompanying essays that he called *E. T. A. Hoffmann and Music*. He finished the first draft as early as 1964 but wrestled with the subject through many years of revision until the publication of the book in 1975. Schafer would later admit that this project was his version of a doctoral thesis, written to prove that he was worthy to teach and work at a university even though he never completed a formal degree.[6] It remains the only book-length study in English of Hoffmann's musical writings. In the preface to the book Schafer outlines his goal, which is to alternate his own translations of writings by

Hoffmann with essays on aspects of Hoffmann's life and works. Schafer notes,

> The selection of passages for translation has necessarily been arbitrary. The selected extracts have served as points around which circles are made to vibrate. If the reader may not always feel that his sympathies are concentric with these points and circles, it may be, as I shall be suggesting in a moment, that it is because we are losing touch with the romantic era to a greater extent than is generally realized. If there are difficulties with the texts, they will be on the affective and philosophical level.[7]

The first essay is called "Introduction," and in it Schafer creates the context in which he places his study of Hoffmann.

> This book is about romanticism as it affects music. It is not a book about romantic music strictly speaking, but rather about the artistic and social climate that surrounded the birth of the music to which we now give that name.[8]

Schafer discusses the use of the term "romanticism," the debate about when that movement appeared both in literature and music at the turn of the nineteenth century, and how music from that time period has remained the core of the classical music tradition in the twentieth century. He then briefly lists what he considers some of the tenets of romantic philosophy that are pertinent to his study, including a turning away from reality toward a world of illusion, the pantheism of nature, and the desire to transform one art form into another.

"E. T. A. Hoffmann: Life and Credentials" is a brief biographical sketch of Hoffmann, tracing his career as a civil servant and lawyer and his secondary life as a musician and writer, quoting passages from Hoffmann's journals as supporting material.

"Ritter Glück" and "Five Romantic Concepts" are respectively a translation of a Hoffmann story and Schafer's commentary on it. In the first Hoffmann recounts a meeting with Glück, which he insists was based on a real event, even though the esteemed composer had been dead for twenty-two years. In his essay Schafer notes five concepts that provide the basis for Hoffmann's essay: night, mystery, dreams, madness, and music, which individually are perhaps not unique to romanticism but in their interaction are uniquely romantic. He gives context to these concepts with a discussion of the fall out of favor of the principles of the Age of Reason, and the rise of the *Sturm und Drang* movement at the end of the eighteenth century; then he explores each concept in greater detail, putting them into the context of German society at the beginning of the nineteenth century.

"Baroness Seraphina" and "Inspiritrice" is the second pairing of a Hoffmann story and a Schafer explanatory essay. The Hoffmann story paints a picture of a young musician first tuning and playing a harpsichord for a baroness, then making music with her. At the end, she allows him to kiss her hand. Schafer begins his commentary by noting Hoffmann's story shows the fusion of music and love in his mind, citing other examples from the author's work to support his assertion. At the end of the essay Schafer adds a sixth concept to the five mentioned earlier: Music is the beloved.

Hoffmann's "Ombra Adorata" is a short essay about a recitative and an aria and its effect upon the dissatisfied soul of the listener, a musician discontented with life. Schafer's response is "A Romanticist's *Don Giovanni*," in which he first explains Hoffmann's effort both in this essay and in the tale "Rat Krespel" to imply the total unification of music with the beautiful woman who sings it. Schafer's essay also looks ahead to the next Hoffmann piece, "*Don Juan*: A Fabulous Incident Which Befell a Traveling Enthusiast," by linking the heroine's sacrifice of life for art in "Rat Krespel" to the singer's sacrifice for her art in *Don Juan*. In Hoffmann's piece the singer playing the role of Donna Anna in Mozart's *Don Giovanni* has identified so strongly with her role that she becomes the melodies she sings. She appears at night to the author, whom she identifies as the composer, and states, "I have sung you, for I am your melodies."[9] Schafer explores Hoffmann's enthusiasm for Mozart's operas and how the author's *Don Juan* essay changed nineteenth-century perceptions of what the operas were about and how the *Don Giovanni* characters were received. Schafer further comments on this concept at the beginning of his essay "Composers" before moving on to a discussion of Hoffmann's view of the composer as a seeker of ideals in both the divine and the fiendish regions of the imagination.

The next Hoffmann essay, "Beethoven's Instrumental Music," is a compilation of various reviews that Hoffmann wrote for the journal *Allgemeine musikalische Zeitung*, with his discussion of Beethoven's *Symphony no. 5* providing the core of the essay. In the commentary essay that follows, "The Critic," Schafer further explores the relationship between Beethoven and his contemporary Hoffmann, but the main focus is on Hoffmann's skill as a critic apart from his stories about music. This is particularly evident in Hoffmann's essays on Beethoven, where, as Schafer states,

> the author, seized by the pure excitement of present-tense music, has focused his imagination on the music itself and abandoned all desire to frame his comments, as in the preceding translations (in the book), within the context of the story.[10]

Schafer notes Hoffmann's grasp of not only the harmonic details but also the form of Beethoven's famous symphony. At the end of the essay, Schafer prepares the reader for the next item by Hoffmann, "Ancient and Modern Church Music." Hoffmann structures this essay as a dialogue between various characters who debate whether sacred music of their time could achieve the same high distinction as the sacred music of such past masters as Bach, Handel, and Palestrina. Hoffmann gives us no resolution to the argument, and in the next essay Schafer will move past the debate to explore another topic.

"The Absolute Musician: Johannes Kriesler" serves as an introduction to Hoffmann's essay "Of Kapellmeister Johannes Kreisler's Musical Sorrows." Schafer begins by first completing the argument found in "Beethoven's Instrumental Music" that music must be dominant and that in any collaboration all else must be subservient, referencing Hoffmann's essay "The Poet and the Composer" (the text of which is not included in this collection), where the librettist is given instruction on how to create a text that will not inhibit the composer. From this argument Schafer moves on to a discussion of Hoffmann's fictional character Johannes Kreisler, whom Schafer believes Hoffmann created to epitomize the composer in the modern sense. The essay discusses the various parts of Hoffmann's writings that flesh out this famous fictional character, whether in *Kreisleriana* or in the novel that the author would eventually write about the Kapellmeister. Schafer characterizes Kreisler as

> the personification of the romantic soul in its struggle to bring to the surface the deepest of its personal feelings, often at the risk of madness or death. Plunging into the unconscious the true romanticist fights with equivocal and unpredictable forces and returns to give them form in the abrupt and contradictory moods and tempos of his art.[11]

This view of a character at war with both the court and the bourgeois and saved only by music, including his own, is reinforced by Hoffmann's own words in "Musical Sorrows," describing the Kapellmeister's miserable existence teaching and working with those who have enthusiasm but no talent.

Schafer's next essay, "Philistines," creates context for the Hoffmann essay that follows it, "Reflections on the High Value of Music." Schafer begins by speaking of the German treatment of the concept of philistinism before focusing on Hoffmann's distinctions between what he considered true artists and philistines. Hoffmann's character Kreisler expresses this concept as two groups of people in society, "'good people' who live righteously but are poor musicians, and 'true musicians,' for whom a secret knowledge of the mysteries of music compensates for all other deficiencies in living."[12] In "Reflections," Hoffmann satirically takes the perspective of the philistine, giving us such statements as

> How important it is that children should be kept at their music, even if they have only the slightest talent for art—for that, indeed, is not the issue here. Thus when they move out into society, even though they may be otherwise

ineffectual socially, at least they will be able to contribute something pleasurable and diverting.[13]

Schafer follows Hoffmann's satirical send-up of philistinism with "Ecstasy," delving deeper into Hoffmann's thoughts on perfect music and its place in society. In Schafer's opinion, Hoffmann was not guilty of ignoring the social implications of art, but for him ecstasy is the opposite of that music practiced by the earlier referenced "good people." Kriesler, as the spirit of music itself, has achieved this ecstasy but is unable to communicate it to others. This isolation and inability to communicate, this extreme vision, can lead to either expulsion from society or madness. The following Hoffmann story, "Kreisler's Musical-Poetical Club," gives us a last glimpse of the Kapellmeister. In this essay Schafer notes the composer

> will run the full gamut of musical experiences from reverence to eroticism, from tranquility to fear, from heroism to madness, seeking to embrace the absolute, while his friends and disciples with their limited range of emotional responses can understand little of these flamboyant displays and nothing of the total ecstasy.[14]

Schafer follows Kreisler's disappearance with "Synaesthesia." In this essay he explores Hoffmann's special ability to draw the senses together, relating the sense in one art to another. He cites passages from Hoffmann's writings to reinforce this point and expands the scope to show that this was a romantic preoccupation in other composers and even in scientists of that period. From there he turns back to Hoffmann's approach to this subject, where one sensation—music—is the root of all other experiences. "For Hoffmann, music was so wild and uncontrollable that it needed interpretation to be comprehended. Music is the absolute power in the universe."[15]

Schafer contributes one final essay to the book, "The Cosmology Configured." In this essay he explores for one last time Hoffmann's view of music, which he frequently states "is not of this world."[16] Schafer maintains that Hoffmann early on anthropomorphized the spirit of music as the voice of the beloved in song, expanding the concept with the creation of Kreisler after his discovery of Beethoven. Since music descends from a higher realm, those who wish to experience it must rise up to the spirit realm of music. Schafer closes by revisiting once more Hoffmann's view of the opposition of the artist and society, which was still underpinned by the author's inherent optimism.

The book's three appendices discuss Schafer's approach to translation and the sources that he consulted; discuss E. T. A. Hoffmann as a composer, citing examples of his music; and discuss Hoffmann's legacy, traced first through the German authors that followed, then authors in other regions of Europe, and finally through composers to the end of the nineteenth century.

Like his E. T. A. Hoffmann study, Schafer's final significant research publication, *Ezra Pound and Music*, was a project that developed over several decades. Schafer had first been introduced to the writings of Ezra Pound by Marshall McLuhan during the young composer's brief time at the University of Toronto, and his interest in the poet had been strengthened during his time in Vienna by studying Pound's translations of medieval lyric poetry. In London in 1959 Schafer met the poet's wife Dorothy, and through that connection he reached out to Ezra, began corresponding with him, and visited the poet in Merano, Italy. While in Italy Schafer also gathered examples of Pound's writings, which would become the basis of *Ezra Pound and Music*, published in 1977.

In the preface to the book, Schafer states that his goal was to collect Pound's criticism and theorizing about music into one place, and he expresses the hope that this will give Pound's writings on music the attention that they deserve. He also indicates that a second volume of commentary on Pound's compositions is planned, but this projected volume never materialized.

After the preface is an extended introduction, which the author admits is a reworking of a 1961 article titled "Ezra Pound and Music" for the *Canadian Music Journal*. In this introduction Schafer explores in some depth Pound's involvement with and approach to music, in how it relates both to poetry and to society in general. Schafer lists Pound's activities in relation to music, including the criticism Pound wrote, his development of an aesthetic known as "Great Bass," his compositions, including his two operas, and the influence of music on his poetry.[17] Schafer first explores the three kinds of poetry that Pound listed:

> *logopoeia*, roughly poetry of ideas and precise expression; *phanopoeia*, poetry of images, and *melopoeia*, "wherein the words are charged, over and above their plain meaning, with some musical property, which directs the bearing of trend of that meaning."[18]

Pound's appreciation of music went beyond its relationship to poetry, and in his middle years the poet had a particular appreciation of Vivaldi's concerti, which he helped bring to the public, and Mozart's keyboard sonatas. In the relationship between poetry and music Pound's early thought drew him to the troubadours' attempt to create a natural symbiosis of the arts where the technical brilliance of the poetry also stimulated musical invention. He argued that the divorce of the two fields caused both to suffer. In Pound's mind,

> the perfect song occurs when the poetic rhythm is in itself interesting, and when the musician augments, illuminates it, without breaking away from, or at least without going too far from, the dominant cadences and accents of the

words, when the ligatures illustrate the verbal qualities, and when the little descants and prolongations fall in with the main movements of the poems.[19]

Pound maintained that poets could learn from music, and he himself was an example of this, in particular with his intense study of Provençal poetry and the original melodies paired with the poems, and in his practice of working on his poetry with music directly in front of him. Schafer talks about Pound's efforts to free English poetry from its restrictions and how music played a part in convincing the poet of the necessities of that reform, including a study of Dolmetsch's book *The Interpretation of the Music of the 17th and 18th Centuries*. Schafer closes the introduction with a discussion of Pound's two main musical concepts—his theory of absolute rhythm, and the concept of Great Bass. Both of these are temporal concepts that govern form, and the Great Bass also defines the pace and forms of Pound's *Cantos*. Schafer quotes extensively from Pound's poetry to support this assertion, beginning with the first two of the *Cantos*, and he closes by arguing that the *Cantos* as a whole might be best appreciated by measuring them against such musical forms as the fugue.

Chapter 1 discusses Pound's early reviews while living in England during the years 1908–1917. Schafer places these reviews in the context of Pound's life there, where he was making a living by writing columns and reviews for various periodicals on a variety of subjects. Schafer also discusses the music that Pound would have heard and how his tastes were already moving to the edges of the timeline, toward both medieval and Renaissance music and forward-looking composers at the turn of the century. He also explores Pound's relationship with fellow poet W. B. Yeats and early-music scholar Arnold Dolmetsch. As with all the chapters, the last part of this chapter is the articles that Pound wrote during this time.

Chapter 2 looks at the years 1917–1921 when Pound was still in England, still working as a music critic—writing under the pseudonym William Atheling—and augmenting his meager income by providing translations of texts for song recitals and music publications.[20] Schafer discusses Pound's approach in his reviews as Atheling, with a focus on song, a dismissal of many of the leading British composers of the day, and an idiosyncratic support of certain performers. This is then followed by the most extensive collection of articles in the book.

Chapter 3 discusses the years 1921–1927, first giving a brief sketch of Pound's travels during this time. In 1920 Pound left London for Paris to join a community of writers who were already there, including James Joyce and the American writers Ernest Hemingway and Gertrude Stein. There he would hear the music of Ravel and Stravinsky, the works of Les Six and Satie, and upon their arrival, the compositions of Virgil Thompson and Aaron Copland. Pound also began serious work on his *Le Testament*, later helped by composer and pianist George Antheil, whom he met in 1923. In 1924 Pound published *Antheil and the Treatise on Harmony*, eventually reissued in 1962 simply as *The Treatise on Harmony*. Schafer reinforces the importance of Pound's work, maintaining that it is on the level of Schoenberg's *Harmonielehre* and Schenker's *Harmonielehre* in the history of twentieth-century theory. Pound's focus is on the element of time as it relates to harmony, bringing back the horizontal aspect of what has often been considered a vertical construction, maintaining that

> a sound of any pitch, or any combination of such sounds, may be followed by a sound of any other pitch, or any combination of such sounds, providing the time interval between them is properly gauged; and this is true for any series of sounds, chords or arpeggios.[21]

Schafer includes the full text of the treatise in this chapter as well as Pound's other short writings during this time. Before the shorter writings, Schafer again gives a further biographical sketch, noting the completion of the *Le Testament*, the shaping of the first thirty *Cantos*, and Pound's decision to settle in Rapallo, a town on the Ligurian coast of Italy.

Chapter 4 covers the years 1928–1941, first exploring why Pound and his wife may have left Paris for Italy. Schafer speculates it was twofold: to remove any distractions from his work on the *Cantos*, which he now knew was going to be his life work, and to find a community where he could put his ideas into practice. Pound became the central figure in Rapallo, imprinting his personality on the cultural life of the town, including organizing a series of concerts from 1933 to 1939 that focused on using local musicians and not trying to imitate what was happening in larger centers. Pound began to again write reviews while in Italy, first in English, having them translated, then writing them directly in Italian. These included first reviews of the concert series that he had started and other concerts that he had attended, all of which are included in the chapter.

Chapter 5 is the shortest chapter, although it covers the longest time period: 1942–1972. Due to his circumstances after the war, Pound produced no more music reviews but did keep up correspondence with several people, including Schafer himself.

The book closes with three appendices. The first attempts to trace the development of Pound's theories of absolute rhythm and Great Bass, gathering together all references to these concepts, whether from the treatise or from other writings, and placing them in chronological order to try to further define them and eliminate as much confusion as possible. The second appendix is a glossary of important musical personalities (each given a brief description or biographical sketch) divided into three groups: (1) those mentioned frequently by Pound in his reviews, (2) those who were personal friends of the poet, and (3) historical musical figures who were important to Pound in some way. The last appendix is a 1924 article about Pound written by George Anthiel for the Paris edition of the Sunday *Chicago Tribune*.

COLLECTED WRITINGS AND WRITINGS ON THEATER

R. Murray Schafer: A Collection was created for the fall 1979 double issue of *Open Letter*, a quarterly Canadian review of writing and sources. The variety of texts in the issue ranges from essays to articles to fiction. The issue includes a bibliography by Stephen Adams.

The collection opens with an introduction by two of the contributing editors, bpNichol and Steve McCaffery, who explain their reasoning for presenting this issue.

> Though well known as a composer, educator, music historian and soundscape researcher, a representative sampling of his truly wide-ranging achievements had never been collectively presented. This seemed to us a stunning example of cultural neglect. Schafer is part of an unrecognized Canadian tradition, of the multi-directed poly-conceptual artist who refuses to be confined by the strictures of habitual aesthetic categories. [22]

This *Open Letter* collection emphasizes the diversity of Schafer's approach: "The Listening Book" (music education), "Citycycles" (performance art and sensory awareness), and "Ursound" (soundscape theory). The other pieces suggest the range of his creativity. [23]

Schafer's opening contribution to this collection is "The Listening Book," created for and dedicated to the editors. Schafer gives the following preface: "Dear bp and Steve: This booklet is for you. It is a musical score. In performing it you will be required to make sounds . . . Neither the book nor the reader is silent. Listen to the sounds you can make together."[24] What follows are a series of instructions to the reader, over several pages, to make music with the book, whether flipping pages, drumming, or simply listening.

"Citycycles," although listed as a performance art and sensory awareness segment, is strongly based on Schafer's soundscape concerns, expanding sonic awareness to include several of the other senses as well. There are four citycycles given, graded from easy to hard, each including twelve tasks, which are to be performed at leisure, each taking about an hour. The reader is instructed to choose one city block, in the center of the city. Before beginning the tasks, which range from "Find a place where people seem to be talking louder than usual" to "Find someone and tell him (or her) what you are doing. Bring him (or her) back with you," the reader is told to walk around their chosen city block once, getting a general impression. After the tasks are completed the reader is to return and discuss what they found with another person.

"The Theatre of Confluence (Note in Advance of Action)" is placed next in the collection. This essay was renamed "The Theatre of Confluence I" and included in the collection *Patria: The Complete Cycle*. "*Loving*" is a brief discussion of the approach and procedures of Schafer's first theatrical work, followed by a transcript of the complete libretto. In the discussion Schafer describes the genesis and performance history of the piece and talks about how the piece is not an opera since there is no plot but is rather an audiovisual poem more closely related to medieval chant-fable.

The next segment of this collection is a complete reproduction of the score for *La Testa D'Adriane*, a theater piece for soprano and accordion that Schafer later incorporated into *Patria III: The Greatest Show*. The extended essay "Ursound" comes next, later reprinted as the opening essay of *Voices of Tyranny, Temples of Silence*. Schafer's final contribution to this collection was the first version of the novel *Dicamus et Labyrinthos: A Philologist's Notebook*.

Schafer next substantial collection of writings, *On Canadian Music*, was published in 1984 and consists of thirteen articles, essays, and works of fiction. Schafer writes an extended and wide-ranging preface to this collection. He notes,

> The essays to follow were written over a period of twenty years, from 1963 to 1983, and while they have been collected together here because they deal with aspects of the same subject, they display many deflections of thinking which I have made no attempt to reconcile. From the faintly prophetic containments of the first pieces to the bold demands and pronouncements of the last, the difference is largely that between a young man with hope as his only ally and an older man whose work has taken certain concrete shapes so that his words, whatever they may be, must be understood as real attempts to explain why and how the work has taken those particular shapes.[25]

Schafer talks further about the reception and health of Canadian classical music in the twentieth century, tying it into a larger discussion of Canadian culture and whether a true Canadian culture even exists. Schafer argues that it largely does not, or at least is only now beginning to emerge, and suggests the causes of this are due to his country's enslavement to cultural models that came from outside Canada, a natural result for a country of immigrants who will look back to their country of origin for their models. Schafer closes the essay by stressing the importance of Canadian climate and geography as a potential cultural unifier.

"A Short History of Music in Canada" opens the collection. One of Schafer's first articles upon his return home to Canada in 1961, it grew out of his work at the CMC, written as an introduction to the CMC's first catalog of orchestral music. The article, Schafer notes, was typical for "not only what we thought of ourselves in those days, but, through the mirror of foreign reference books, of what others were invited to think of us."[26] The article does what the title implies, giving a brief overview of Canada's musical history, beginning with early European settlement up to the mid-twentieth century. At this point Schafer turns to a discussion of whether there is a national style of composition in Canada, concluding that it is not as present as in other countries and listing several reasons as to why this might be. He does maintain that Canadian composers are now coming into national and international prominence and cites the various organizations that had been founded to support the arts and composition in particular, including the CBC, the Canada Council for the Arts, the Canadian League of Composers, and the CMC.

Another article written soon after Schafer's return to Canada was "The Limits of Nationalism in Canadian Music." This article, a partial outgrowth of his exposure to the folk music of Eastern European and Balkan nations during his sojourn in communist Europe, explores the possibility of Canada developing a national school of composition by drawing upon its own folk traditions. Schafer rejects this possibility, citing Canadian society in general and the nature of folk music itself as the two main reasons. He argues that Canada does not have a good reservoir of folk music available to it that is distinguishable from that of other countries. The only truly Canadian folk music is indigenous music, which for many reasons he believes is not usable by classical composers. He then goes on to argue that folk music by its very nature is "perfect," and the composer cannot hope to improve it but only increase its circulation through his or her arrangement. The form of folk music also makes it difficult to arrange without destroying the character of the original, and he maintains that the character of folk music in Canada is not of a character and quality generally to make it fruitful material for Canadian composers.

"What Is This Article About?" was written in 1964 as a response to an announcement that the TSO had received a substantial grant to fund a composition contest to celebrate the upcoming Canadian centennial in 1967. Schafer wrote the article to criticize this competition and competitions in general. The article is based on the repetition of two questions, which are given various answers: Is this an article about the wrong way to buy culture? and What is this article about? The final answer to the question is "This is an article about the wrong way to buy culture. Because you can't buy it. It grows."[27]

The next article, "Ten Centuries Concerts: A Recollection," documents the inception of this endeavor, the first composers and musicians involved in the project, and how the first season of seven concerts was planned. Schafer makes certain to note that the first thing they did was plan the music, then find a way to make it work logistically and financially, which was the opposite of what almost all other organizations were doing at that time. The article goes on to list the seven programs of that first season, with an in-depth discussion of how each program was conceived and executed, including graphs of the flow of each concert. The next article also flows from the Ten Centuries Concerts endeavor and is the program notes for a performance of *Anerca* by fellow Canadian composer Serge Garant. "Serge Garant and His Music" is an insightful discussion and apologia for the music of a then still underperformed and little known composer.

"The Future for Music in Canada" is a transcript of a lecture Schafer gave at the 1967 meeting of the Royal Society of Canada. In this lecture the young composer saw four major issues facing Canadian music:

1. How to bring the whole country solidly into the twentieth century before we reach the twenty-first.
2. How to facilitate the transition from provincialism to internationalism.
3. How to limit the power of patrons and art legislators.
4. How to plan for the extinction of the professional musician.[28]

He goes on to discuss possible solutions to these problems and concludes that the way forward might be abandoning specialization in favor of the relationship between the arts, which will characterize most of the creative thinking in the near future.

"Harry Somers' Riel on Stage and Television" was extracted from a report Schafer prepared for a Vienna-based research group who were interested in Canadians' reactions to the broadcast of Somers's opera during the centennial year of 1967. Schafer begins the article with a brief biography of Somers and a short description of his compositional style, then goes into a longer description of the life of the subject of the opera, Louis Riel, and how Somers's librettist Mavor Moore treats him as a sympathetic figure before discussing the structure and musical content of the opera, highlighting how Somers paints the different characters and locations with different approaches. He discusses the enthusiastic reception the opera received in its stage production before comparing in some detail the different receptions of the opera on stage and on the screen.

"A Birthday Tribute to John Weinzweig" is one of the shortest of the essays in this collection, written on a ship in the South Pacific in February of 1973 in response to a request for a tribute for John Weinzweig's sixtieth birthday to be included in the journal *Les cahiers Canadiens de musique*. In this article Schafer pays tribute to Weinzweig as a teacher and colleague and the one person who helped bring Canadian music into the twentieth century. While on that same ship Schafer began to write a piece for the National Youth Orchestra of Canada. The piece, and the article describing it, are both titled "North/White." The article is the program note for the piece, and in it Schafer describes his concept of the North and his concern about the destruction of Canada's northern territories through development and industry. He concludes,

> The idea of North is a Canadian myth.
> Without a myth a nation dies.
> This piece is dedicated to the splendid and indestructible idea of North.[29]

"Music in the Cold" is a short work of fiction or allegory. In the separate publication of that work, Schafer does not include a preface but he does include one here, where he indicates that the work grew out of his move with Jean to the abandoned farmhouse in rural Ontario. He notes, "The rhythms of this life were beginning to affect my musical thinking even though the influence was not yet precisely evident in the works I was writing. 'Music in the Cold' was written as a kind of manifesto in advance of the work I knew would follow."[30]

"Canadian Culture: Colonial Culture" was a lecture given at Conrad Grebel College in Waterloo, Ontario, in 1983. In this lecture Schafer decries what he calls the colonial regime, which "strengthens itself by pushing out from centre to margin. It takes raw materials from the extremities and ejects finished products from the centre."[31] He parallels this to the Canadian adoption and absorption of American culture, which was preventing a maturation of Canadian culture. He references the earlier "Music in the Cold" as his manifesto for what is possible when culture is shaped by climate and geography, which had been acknowledged by writers and painters but not by musicians. He holds up his own compositions *Music for Wilderness Lake* and *The Princess of the Stars* as examples of music that acknowledges this influence. He argues that it is not evident if there is Canadian music because this music is not heard enough in its own country. He accuses the main musical institutions in Canada of deliberately neglecting works by Canadian composers in favor of historical European compositions, showing data to prove this neglect. He lays out what could be done to overturn this current problem, returning again to the need to overturn what he calls the "centre-margin culture-philosophy."[32]

"Music for Wilderness Lake," is taken from the introductory notes to the piece of that name. It begins with a discussion of the historical contexts of music making, whether in the church, the concert hall, or on the radio. Schafer discusses his long-standing discontent with current music-making practices, citing some of his earlier pieces, including *No Longer Than Ten Minutes* and *In Search of Zoroaster*, and indicating that the piece *Music for Wilderness Lake* continues his experiments with music performance, this time referencing an era when music was performed outdoors and took its bearings from the natural environment. He then goes on to describe how he had to write this piece differently to allow for the distance and the way sound travels over water. The process of recording the piece is also described in the article.

The final essay in the book, "The Princess of the Stars," begins with a synopsis of the action before the piece begins at dawn. Schafer goes on to describe what happens during the piece itself and also how the piece should be performed. In the essay Schafer notes that he considers this piece to be the most radical of his efforts to date since it is "wedded to its time and place by indissoluble links which guarantee that no counterfeit experience could be a replacement for it."[33]

Patria: The Complete Cycle is another collection of essays written at various times and places, this time gathered together and published in 2002. It includes a description of each of the twelve segments of *Patria* along with a preface, two appendices and additional essays—one on *Loving/Toi* and three with the title "The Theatre of Confluence."

Schafer titles the preface to this book "The Labyrinth and the Thread." In this preface he talks about the cycle as a whole, including his first conception of a series of works (originally only three) that would be thematically linked under the generic title *Patria*. He indicates they are not intended to be performed sequentially but there is a natural order to the cycle, and although each part is complete in itself, all the works reference each other, with common characters and themes traced throughout.

The first essay is titled "My First Stage Work: *Loving*." Schafer includes this essay here to set the stage for the *Patria* cycle since many of the concepts and techniques he developed for this groundbreaking piece were adapted to use in that cycle. He introduces the essay with a brief description of the piece and its production by the CBC. The essay itself was written while the piece was still being composed, so Schafer focuses on the overall conception of the piece, which would not have a plot or characters in the traditional sense. He also writes of his wish to create a synaesthetic work that "employs a number of arts in extremely close, frequently interpenetrating relationship."[34]

"The Theatre of Confluence I" was first written in 1966 after the completion of *Loving* when Schafer was considering new works for the stage, and it was revised in 1972. The original essay begins with a brief discussion of the poor reception of *Loving* and some possible reasons for it. Schafer then explains that the purpose of this essay is to crystalize his own thoughts on a new work that he would call *Patria*. His goal in this work was as follows:

> Ideally what I want is a kind of theatre in which all the arts may meet, court and make love. Love implies a sharing of experience; it should never mean the negation of personalities. This is the first task, to fashion a theatre in which all

the arts are fixed together, but without negating the strong and healthy character of each.[35]

He then gives this effort its official title, "The Theatre of Confluence," differentiating it from other contemporary theater concepts such as "total theater" and "absolute theater." He explains in more detail how this type of theater could work by being conceived on all levels simultaneously unlike what he calls "rank-order" creations such as opera where one element is conceived (usually the libretto) then the other elements, such as music, are added. He imagines counterpoint, not parallelism, as the ideal technique, similar to the concept of film montage, where two pieces of film are combined to produce a third experience that is different. He also cites the Roman Catholic mass as an example of a ritual where all the senses are summed up without sensory overload, and the Merz stage of the Dadaist movement as a contemporary example. He rejects chance as the guiding force behind his theater of confluence, and notes that it should be open to the possibility that at certain points the audience for this type of theater could be required to participate in unusual ways or even play an influential role in the shaping of the production. Different settings would be chosen to be appropriate for each work—one room or many, indoors or outdoors, even mobile or processional. The essay concludes with a discussion of the senses and how they relate to the "Theatre of Confluence," explaining that the initial *Patria* segments would use the sense of hearing as the main information-bearing channel.

After descriptions of *Patria 1* and *Patria 2*, Schafer includes the essay "The Theatre of Confluence II," noting that the topics discussed in that essay are relevant to the next several *Patria* works (*The Princess of the Stars*, *The Greatest Show*, *The Black Theatre of Hermes Trismegistos*, and *The Crown of Ariadne*). "The Theatre of Confluence II" begins by discussing the purpose and nature of art itself. Schafer maintains that the first purpose of art is "to effect a change in our existential condition"[36]—in other words, to change us. He takes us back to the first visual and musical expressions of mankind to support this theory, to tone magic and miracles. He then traces the rise of civilizations and how reflective consciousness led to a disinvolvement in and desacralization of the world, ultimately leading to use of the word "art" to refer to entertainment. Schafer believes that what has been lost in this transition is the divine, the sensation of it and the ability to touch it. What he means by "divine" is everything that is mysterious, everything that is beyond our ability to construe or dominate. From this point Schafer moves on to the idea of context and environment, first beginning with a satirical description of how theater has been practiced for centuries and how consumers experience it. He then asserts,

> To accomplish an art that engages all forms of perception, we need not only to strip down the walls of our theatres and recording studios, but also the walls of our senses. We need to breathe clean air again, we need to touch the mysteries of the world in the little places and the great wide places in sunrises, forests, mountains and caves and if need be in snowfalls or tropical jungles.[37]

The idea of regaining ritual is closely tied to this return to the natural world in Schafer's mind. He compares the richness of the Japanese tea ceremony to the rituals of modern life, which seem crude and shallow by comparison; contrasts the concepts of celebration and art; and suggests that performers will need to learn new techniques to participate in these new environmental rituals that know no distinction between audience, performer, and creator—the new Theater of Confluence.

After discussions of *Patria Prologue*, and *Patria 3–5*, Schafer includes "The Theatre of Confluence III," written in 1997. This essay has the most strident tone of the three and begins by listing what is wrong with the various art forms (theater, opera, music, dance, literature, film, art) and with their relation to the environment and to audiences. He then goes on to list what he thinks is required of these arts in contemporary society, including the radical concept of eliminating opera and film altogether. He revisits his earlier assertion that in our society, art really means entertainment, and he suggests that a new word may need to be created to describe what once was the classic definition of art. He goes on to say that art now must be a hammer, a cry of protest against anything that is being threatened. One of the threats is the way that modern society can be used to extend the outreach of a work to the occlusion of other art forms. The biggest threat is everything that the media calls art.[38]

The next several chapters are discussions of *Patria 6, 7, 8, 9, 10*, and *Patria Epilogue*. The book concludes with two appendices. The first outlines some of the character relationships in the *Patria* cycle, and the second gives a brief synopsis of each of the *Patria* segments.

Chapter Eleven

Works of Fiction

Schafer's works of fiction, although relatively few in number, display a remarkable variety of content and genre, ranging from more traditionally arranged novellas and children's books to idiosyncratic graphic novels and calligraphic creations. Some of the books present themselves more as works of art than works of literature, and many of the novels explore in literary form the characters and themes of the *Patria* cycle (and although they do not necessarily need to be read with knowledge of that cycle, they help to further flesh out the details of those works).

NOVELS, CHILDREN'S STORIES, AND SHORT STORIES

Music in the Cold from 1977 is a fable, a literary companion to his orchestral piece *North/White* written four years earlier, and also a response to the exploitation of the North for its resources. It is a cautionary tale of the dangers of his home country adopting the ways of its southern neighbor and not embracing its nature as an arctic country. The following passage toward the beginning of the book clearly shows Schafer's view.

>   Northern geography is all form.
>   Southern geography is colour and texture.
>   A northern glacier is brute form.
>   A southern jungle is juicy.
>   Between them, rolling land masses become formal in winter and technicolour in summer as the claw of the arctic stretches south then leaps back to escape the flatulence of the tropics.
>   The art of the North is the art of restraint.
>   The art of the South is the art of excess.
>   It is the soft art of dancing girls and of the slobber.
>   Of necessity conservation of energy begins in the North.

> It begins with lean stomach and strong bow.
> Prodigality is centred in the South,
> And the waste of energy begins at the mouth.
> Some of this waste energy is called art.
> It is thought that warm climates are the best incubators of it.[1]

In Schafer's morality tale, Canada begins as a virtually unpopulated, poor yet tough society but learns to exploit its resources and become a dominant force in the world, rich and powerful, with its society the international norm—in short becoming the United States. Outsiders come in and bring their culture with them, setting up the usual cultural institutions, and growing in wealth and popularity until "we no longer went South. We *were* South."[2] But the winter returns and the dreams collapse under the weight of the new ice age. All that is not necessary is cut away, people flee, and only the rough remain, half-wolves themselves. It is time to build a new mythology.

Wolf Tracks, completed in 1997, is, along with *The Garden of the Heart*, Schafer's fictional tour de force, simultaneously two stories and one story told from two perspectives, a man's and a wolf's. The story can be read from front to back using the right-hand pages (the "Tracks" part of the title, from the man's perspective) then back to front using the left-hand pages (the "Wolf" part of the title, from the wolf's perspective), or the reader can choose to read the "Wolf" part first, then the "Tracks" part. Both stories describe a journey. In "Tracks," a man enters a second-hand bookstore, grieving the loss of his dog, and finds a book, which he begins to read. This book urges him to take a train journey from his joyless, dull city life out to the wilderness. As he travels farther away a snowstorm comes, and the people he is with slowly leave or vanish into the storm. He is forced to abandon the train and begins a transformation into wolf form, and at the end of his journey he meets Ariadne and is united to her physically and spiritually. It is only at the end of the "Tracks" portion of the novel that we see the explicit connection to the multiple myths that Schafer explores in the *Patria* cycle as the man is revealed as Wolf, the chief male protagonist.

The "Wolf" portion of the story is even more explicitly tied to the *Patria* mythos. Wolf discusses his (and Ariadne's) journey through multiple reincarnations in the *Patria* cycle as it had been completed by Schafer in 1996 (*Patria 10: The Spirit Garden* and *Patria 8: The Palace of the Cinnabar Phoenix* were not yet finished). Wolf references his various incarnations as the Displaced Person in *Patria 1*, as the accordion player and "wolfie" in *Patria 3*, as one of the chimerical elements in *Patria 4*, as Theseus in *Patria 5*, as Anubis in *Patria 6*, and as Wolf in both *Patria 9* and *Patria Epilogue*. He also recounts his time as a scholar of Ecto-Cretan (referencing the earlier novel *Dicamus et Labyrinthos*); discusses his various meetings with Ariadne in *Patria 1, 3, 4,* and *5*; and talks of her sorrow and madness in *Patria 2*. All of these references are entwined with Wolf's journey, which is opposite to that of the man. Wolf travels from the wilderness to the city, crossing paths with the man along the way. Wolf's goal is to write the story that the man will read, find a suitable place for it—in this case a second-hand bookstore—and place it for the man to find. Wolf watches the man start to read the book and then leaves again for the wilderness.

In keeping with the theme of the book, Schafer, with help from several friends, originally placed copies of *Wolf Tracks* unnoticed in second-hand bookstores with the hope that people would find and read them. He has since made it available through his publishing house, Arcana Editions.

The Garden of the Heart was written in 2008, and upon completing the work Schafer described it as "a strange tale, part fact, part fiction in which I find myself involved with, even confused with, Richard Strauss and E. T. A. Hoffmann."[3] Schafer had earlier written his study of Hoffmann (*E. T. A. Hoffmann and Music*), and references to and quotes from the German author abound in the novella.

The story begins with the protagonist attending a performance of Strauss's *Ariadne auf Naxos*, which links the novella to the characters of Ariadne and Theseus, who are also iterations of the male and female protagonists in the *Patria* cycle. With the introduction of Ariadne, Schafer takes the opportunity to incorporate material from his earlier graphic novel, *Ariadne*. In addition to the *Patria* references, Schafer weaves into the story elements of one of his own compositions, also called *The Garden of the Heart*, which he admits shows the strong influence of Strauss. He also weaves into the novella some of his own biography, in particular his extended stay in Vienna as a young man. The lines between what is actual biography and what is fictional are constantly blurred so that the reader who is not familiar with Schafer's life would not realize to what extent the novella is based upon the author's own experiences.

The story itself is three tales interwoven. The first is centered around the creation of an illustrated text ("The Garden of the Heart" from *A Thousand and One Nights*) by Darab Sasan, a young Persian immigrant to Vienna in the 1920s. Darab creates it for a girl, Milena, and their relationship is also explored. The second story is a blend of fact and fiction about Schafer's time in Vienna in the 1950s. The third story brings us to the present day and a graduate musicology student Anselm Weber, who had originally wished to study Schafer's Vienna period but has been sidetracked into a controversy surrounding the Viennese premiere of *The Garden of the Heart* in 1985, when at least one critic maintained that Schafer's composition was actually by Strauss. His research leads him to discover the origin of the illustrated text with Darab Sasan, and he also has a mystical encounter with Darab's granddaughter. These three stories interweave in an almost bewildering fashion, leaving even a reader knowledgeable of Schafer's life and creative output wondering what is fact and what is fiction in the account. It is a complex narrative, rich with imagery.

The Stones is a short story, based on one (or more) experiences Schafer had on his travels around the world while giving lectures, classes, and workshops on education. The story begins with the teacher's arrival at an airport in a country far away from his home country. He goes directly to the classroom where twenty students are waiting for him. He gives them a series of exercises (drawn from Schafer's educational writings), the majority of which use stones since he has asked each participant to bring with them a stone that they had found. At the end the students each take their stone outside to a garden and find a place there for it. From the class the teacher goes directly back to the airport to journey home. The story is highlighted with illustrations of the stones in the various patterns that the class creates with them.

The Enchanted Forest is a children's book version of *Patria 9*. The story is recrafted as a narrative by the composer, and illustrations are provided by Diana M. Smith. Also included is a CD on which the story is read by Schafer, and some of the children's songs from the production are also included.

Triangle, Circle, Square is a short story that exists in a few copies in the composer's home and has not yet been published. It is a children's story, which first appeared in sketches in his journal, about the adventures of three shapes (a circle, a triangle, and a square although they not named as such). The characteristics of each are described in simple and humorous ways. Another character appears (a star), who is accepted by them but is not happy. The other three shapes work to get the star back to the sky where it belongs and are successful.

GRAPHIC NOVELS AND CALLIGRAPHIC COMPOSITIONS

Ariadne (first published as *Smoke* in 1976 but republished as *Ariadne* in 1977) is Schafer's first effort in the genre of fiction, and it is a work that blurs the line between short story and graphic novel. There is a linear plot to the story, which is closely linked to the *Patria* cycle as it then stood (*Patria 2* was completed in 1972, *Patria 1* in 1974, and *Patria 5: The Crown of Ariadne* existed in sketches). The piece is structured as a dedication with multiple scenes of varying lengths, paralleling the editing units of the *Patria* cycle. The novella describes the journey of the protagonist to a place where he meets a woman, their time together, her abrupt departure, and his return to the place where he began. This imagery of travel and return will be further explored in the later *Wolf Tracks* and is also a theme of *Patria 6: Ra*.

The graphic novel is structured as follows.

Dédicace—This dedication begins in an unknown language that through multiple repetitions on the page is transformed into English.

Scene 1—The text "I was in a city I do not remember" is accompanied by visual wordplay on the text "It rained for exactly forty-two hours, and then it drizzled for forty-two hours."

Scene 2—The text "I walked under the enigmas of tall buildings" is accompanied by an illustration of a building with windows made up of multiple letters that contain another message. This is followed by a visual description of the wanderings of the protagonist with the words written to outline the many turns he takes.

Scene 3—The protagonist meets a character, whom he will also meet later, and who will identify himself as Dante. The exchange between them, with Dante looking out a window, is visually represented by the placement of the words on the page. The protagonist continues on, his journey alternating between darkness and the light from street lamps and illustrated by the use of dark shades on the page.

Scene 4 ("Canon Cancrizans")—This scene describes the first brief meeting between the protagonist and a woman, Ariadne. The canon is exhibited through the word combinations that describe the encounter. This is followed by a description of the protagonist's response to this meeting.

Scene 5 ("Boustrophedon")—An ancient visual device in which the words are written from left to right then right to left on alternating lines is used to show the protagonist's indecision as to whether to journey on or turn back in hope of meeting the woman again.

Scene 6 ("Mem")—here the protagonist meets Dante again, who ferries him in his book, with the promise that he will meet the woman again. "Mem" is a Hebrew word for "water."

Scene 7—The protagonist and Dante arrive on the other shore, where the protagonist gets off, seeing white stones that were not carved by man but that still seem to have patterns with meaning. The illustrations on this page pay homage to Mayan hieroglyphs.

Scene 8 ("Katun")—Katun is a Mayan measurement of time, and in this scene the character enters through a gap in one of the glyphs.

Scene 9—The character enters a discotheque with dancing people. The illustrations here include a map showing the positions of all the people, tables, and chairs in the room and a graph that once decoded gives another message.

Scene 10 ("Metathesis")—The text in this scene has correct consonants but incorrect vowels for each word. The text expresses the agitation of the protagonist at seeing the woman.

Scene 11 ("Marienbad")—This is a visual diagram of the various questions and choices the protagonist has as he is confronted with the prospect of walking over to talk to the woman. He chooses to go, and their brief dialogue is diagrammed so as to "narrative as objectively as possible what happened next."

Scene 12—This is by far the longest scene, covering several pages and illustrations. The first pages are visual representations of the protagonist trying to guess the woman's name. Once the stars reveal her name—"Ariadne"—the scene goes on to describe her and their time together over the summer. As part of this Schafer quotes Giuseppe Ungaretti, adding two additional lines of his own. He includes a reproduction of part of the score of his vocal piece *Hymn To Night*, written the same year as the novel, and includes over several pages florid illustrations of the text he would use for his later composition *The Garden of the Heart*. The scene ends with the abrupt departure of Ariadne, with no reason given.

Penultimate Scene—Autumn has come, and the protagonist returns to the shore to wait for Dante, who takes him back over the water and tries to console him.

Last Scene—The protagonist returns to the city where he started. The dark illustration accompanies the words "When Dante put me ashore I could see the dark outline of the city in the distance. As I drew near I could hear the shriek of its black teeth clattering. Gradually it blotted out the sky."[4]

The Chaldean Inscription (1978) was sketched out in a year when Schafer composed very little but focused almost exclusively on texts. This included sketching out the form and libretto of the *Patria* cycle, focusing particularly on *Patria 5: The Crown of Ariadne*. He also did significant work on *Dicamus et Labyrinthos*, although that would not be published until the following year.

The Chaldean Inscription is most closely paired with the later *The Sixteen Scribes* in that it is essentially a visual exercise with no plot or characters. In the case of the *Inscription*, it is simply laid out, with no preface, introduction, or description of what the book is meant to be other than the copyright designation on the inside cover. When the reader opens the book, he is confronted with the following text, written in capital letters on the right-hand page:

> I AM ALL THAT IS
> ALL THAT HAS BEEN
> ALL THAT SHALL BE
> AND NONE SHALL LIFT
> MY VEIL[5]

Over the course of next nineteen pages, the script is slowly transformed from English into an unrecognizable and florid script. The script is always on the right-hand side so that the reader must turn the page to see the next version. This technique helps the transformation reveal itself slowly, and no explanation is given as to the meaning of the transformation or why it occurs. The reader is left to draw his own conclusions.

SOMETIMES WE SPENT WHOLE DAYS
REPEATING ONE WORD, GRADUALLY
REVEALING NEW ASPECTS OF ITS
MEANING...

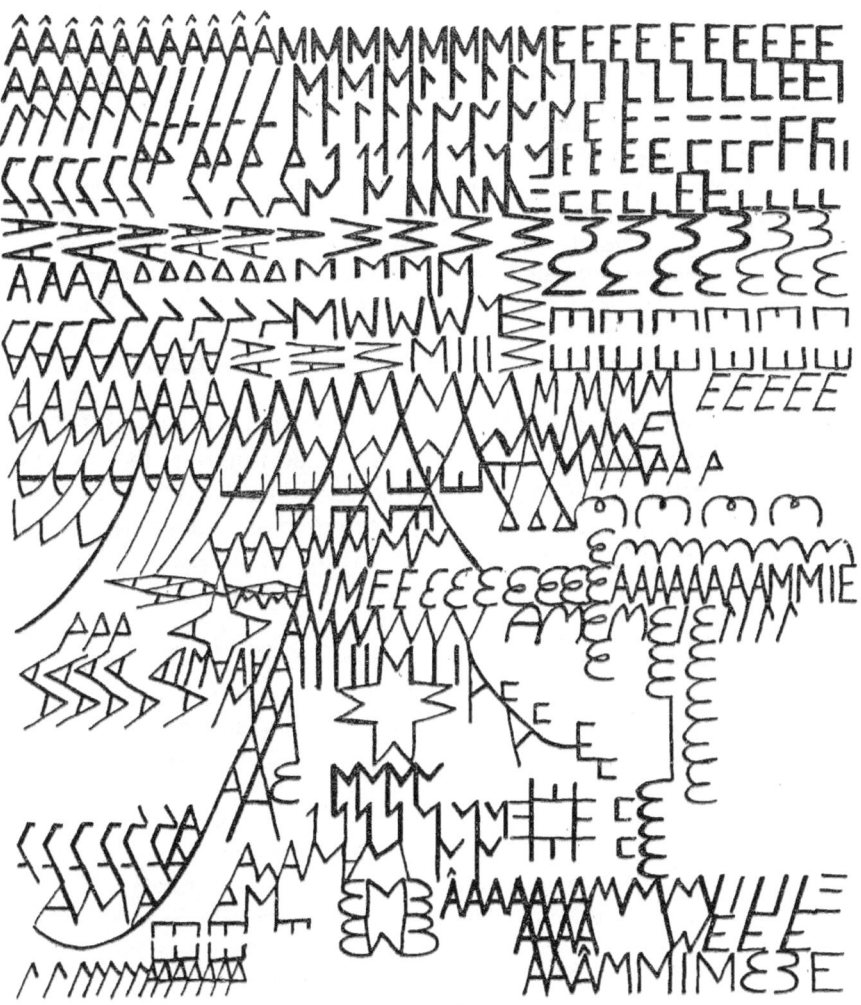

Figure 11.1.   Illustration from *Ariadne. R. Murray Schafer*

The Sixteen Scribes, written in 1981, is a collaborative effort, reflective of its text, which is based on a story that Schafer had encountered some time in the past.

> The king had sixteen scribes and everything he spoke was copied out carefully by each of the scribes to be sent to the most distant provinces where local governors were waiting to act on the orders contained in the sixteen letters. Each day the letters left the palace in the care of special messengers who sped out simultaneously in sixteen directions. It was absolutely essential for good government and the prosperity of the realm that all the governors should receive identical messages. For this reason the scribes were most carefully chosen for the accuracy and neatness of their writing style. For years this arrangement produced the most satisfactory results until one day a scribe made a fatal mistake which plunged the entire realm into tumult. It was not known at first which of the letters contained the fatal flaw. Allegations were piled on allegations, everyone pointing to one or another detail in the scripts and accusing one or another of the scribes of having precipitated the catastrophe; for by now every government in the realm was at war with every other government. There were unlimited theories but no one knew for sure and it was generally admitted that the matter would have to wait until the wars were over and historians could assemble and compare the sixteen transcriptions of the king's message. Only then would the matter be cleared up beyond all doubt.[6]

After the dedication and title page, the book consists of sixteen different calligraphic representations of this text, each appearing over the course of two pages. Schafer contributed one of the renditions himself and worked with his friend Victoria Artwell to solicit contributions from other calligraphers. What the reader is not told, but what is implied in the story of the text, is that there are also inconsistencies between the sixteen reproductions of the text.

Shadowgraphs and Legends (2004) is the longest of the graphic and calligraphic books that Schafer has written. It was published to give as a New Year's gift to friends, and it is a collection, not a unified story like *Ariadne*. Schafer opens the book with a text, accompanied by illustrations, discussing the genesis of the collection in the following way:

> And so I begin this little work which I will later call Shadowgraphs and Legends. I do not know what it will contain. All I know is that there is a piece of paper at my side and I intend to use it. I am not compelled to write. It is merely that my fingers have begun to twitch. Call it habit . . . agitation . . . nerves. All I know is that the paper invites the pen and that when ink flows from the nostril of the pen, patterns and words result.[7]

What follows for the rest of the book is a variety of illustrations and texts. The first two texts talk about the paper itself. The first is a love song to the page, the second ponders the sullying of the page by human hands. The next three pages are illustrations without comment, then a textual and illustrative meditation on "curve." As the book progresses we see a mix of such tongue-in-cheek short stories as finding an exact replication of a map of Poland in a wall stain at a restaurant, or a tale about a holy man to whose hands birds would come and eat (but the "saint" has cut off the birds' lower beaks so that they are dependent on him for their food), or a facetious tale of early experiments with books. At times different aspects of a drawing are explored. At the end of the book Schafer makes fun of his own book as well through various stories. One posits that the book is an archaeological find at the excavation of his house far in the future, and another speculates on what might happen to the last surviving copy of the book (it is destroyed in a hotel fire in Trieste).

The collection is visually stunning and is in many ways the most graphic of Schafer's literary efforts, freed from the constrictions of plot. It shows both his visual artist background and his affinity for wordplay and visual tricks.

Dicamus et Labyrinthos in its first form appeared in the 1979 edition of *Open Letter*. Schafer later revised it and published it separately. The book's full title is *Dicamus et Labyrinthos: A Philologist's Notebook*, and it is structured as the notebook (and diary) of a philologist who is working on deciphering a text.

The introduction to the book is purportedly written by Max Dorb, president of the Canadian Hellenic Association, who outlines the discovery of a third Ecto-Cretan text and discusses the various attempts to decipher it as well as the solution presented by the current notebook, which he indicates he is presenting unedited as the writings of a friend and fellow scholar who had been working on the project before his disappearance. After this introduction, the original Ecto-Cretan text, distributed over nineteen clay tablets, is presented.

What follows is the scholar's notebook itself in which he wrestles with the text, slowly revealing it to be perhaps by Daedalus, the famous architect who designed the labyrinth. Through various methods the text is revealed to be a cipher, and once it is solved the tablets tell the tale of Minos, Pasiphae, Ariadne, Theseus, and the Minotaur up to the point of Theseus entering the labyrinth. As the scholar deciphers the text, he also makes several speculative and philosophical entries discussing the nature of the labyrinth, exploring the meaning of the various characters in the story, and recounting various dreams he has had because of this work on the project. References in these speculations include Schafer's book *Ariadne*, written a few years earlier, and *Patria 5*, the first complete draft of which Schafer was working on at this time.

At the end, when the scholar has translated the text and found out to his dismay that it ends before it reveals what happens in the labyrinth between

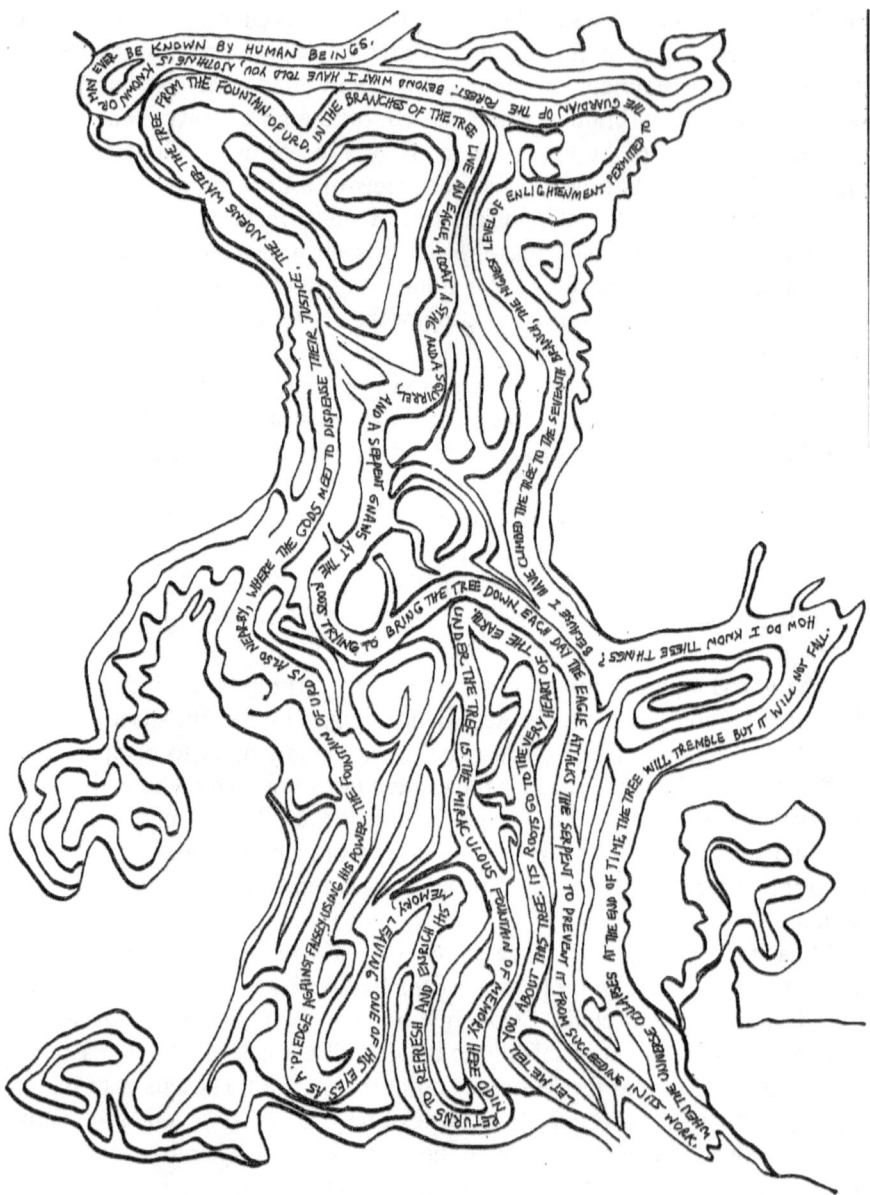

Figure 11.2.   Illustration from *Shadowgraphs and Legends*. R. Murray Schafer

Theseus and the Minotaur, he has a final dream, from which he does not return.

Part III

The Theatrical Works

Chapter Twelve

Loving and the Non-*Patria* Theatrical Works

In addition to his massive cycle *Patria*, Schafer has created many other theater pieces, whether community works created in collaboration with amateur musicians or larger works written for a combination of professional and amateur musicians.

THE COMMUNITY WORKS

Jonah was written in collaboration with the Maynooth Community Choir in 1979. With this group Schafer had the opportunity to practice in a community setting the educational theories he had developed at SFU. Schafer notes about the production,

> It was a community undertaking, involving about forty people. Considering that the total population of the Maynooth area is probably about two hundred, the per capita participation in this cultural endeavour probably exceeded the national average.[1]

Much of the spoken dialogue was created through improvisation by the characters themselves, including the sailors' dialogue and the storm scene. The king's speeches and the text of his song were written by the twelve-year-old who played the character. The man who played Job took basic material supplied by Schafer and fleshed it out into full text. The music was largely by Schafer, created or revised during the rehearsal process, with borrowings from two hymn tunes. He wrote for the instrumentation available—flute, clarinet, percussion, and organ.

Synopsis

Scene 1: "God Calls Jonah"; Scene 2: "Jonah and the Sailors"—In the short opening scene the unaccompanied chorus, representing the voice of God, calls Jonah to go to Nineveh. He flees in terror while the chorus narrates Jonah's travel to the shore to find a ship. He finds sailors who agree to take him on their boat.

Scene 3: "The Storm"; Scene 4: "Jonah in the Whale"—These two scenes are the most creative of the production. The chorus uses speech and other vocal effects (including sustained random pitches) to imitate the growing storm, with the chorus holding a rope around the prop of the boat. The organ joins in at the end to show the capsizing of the boat, which is turned sideways to represent the whale, and the instrumentalists improvise the effect of being underwater and in the belly of the whale, including props of phosphorescent fish, held by children. The choir sings a lament based on the text of Psalm 130, while Jonah speaks a different text, also lamenting.

Scene 5: "God Commands Jonah Again"—The choir again serves as narrator, this time singing the text accompanied by clarinet, indicating Jonah's positive response.

Scene 6: "The King of Nineveh"; Scene 7: "The Shady Tree"—A processional hymn (one of the borrowed hymns) accompanies the entry of the king, who dialogues with Jonah. The recessional hymn also uses a borrowed tune. Jonah waits for the judgment of Nineveh and argues with God. The flute player rises up in imitation of the shade tree, playing an improvised melody, then falls down as the tree dies.

Scene 8: "The Angel of God"—Accompanied by flute, organ, and percussion, the children's chorus sings simple unison melodies as the Angel of God to Jonah, who speaks his response. They are joined by the whole chorus, again playing the Voice of God, leading Jonah to understand God's will. The scene and the drama then end with an energetic, newly composed "Praise the Lord."

Remember Susanna was "improvised into existence by members of the Sackville Community Collaboration under the direction of Eleanor James and R. Murray Schafer."[2] The first performances of the piece were in 2002, in Sackville. It was repeated on June 4, 2003, as part of the Scotia Festival in Halifax. The story is based on chapter 13 of the Book of Daniel, and the story was created by first reading the text, with an added prologue and epilogue based on the story of Jesus and the woman accused of adultery in the Gospel of John, chapter 8. There are multiple characters in each scene and several minor characters and crowd members, reflecting the true community involvement of the piece.

Synopsis

Prologue: In response to a mob demanding that the woman caught in adultery be stoned, Jesus writes, "Remember Susanna" in the sand as a rebuke. There are two music cues in this scene, both written by Schafer with help from the actors: one for the crowd and one for the offstage choir, called the Holy Spirit Choir.

Scene 1: The scene opens with "The Ballad of Susanna," sung by the balladeer and mimed as it is sung. The two judges appear and are welcomed by Joakim, who introduces them to Daniel. There are two music cues, one a dance song to celebrate the festival of Sukkot, the other a setting of Psalm 118.

Scene 2: The scene begins with music playing softly in the background. Susanna reads a passage of scripture and speaks with her attendants and her mother about great women in the Old Testament.

Scene 3; Scene 4: As the music continues, the judges enter. They hear the various plaintiffs and show their corruption by taking bribes. They then accost Susanna in her garden as she prepares to bathe. When she rejects them, they accuse her of adultery, saying that they found her with a man, and the music continues to scene 5.

Scene 5: The Holy Spirit Choir sings to Susanna as she despairs, declaring itself to be the voice of Sophia, wisdom. Daniel overhears the conversation between Susanna and the choir.

Scene 6: The judges call forth the elders to sit in judgment on Susanna. As the elders condemn her to death, Daniel comes forward to accuse the judges of lying. He catches the judges in their lie, and Joakim, who has been watching, praises Daniel.

Epilogue: As Daniel leaves, Jesus returns and the scene shifts back to the gospel story. The accusers from the prologue leave, and Jesus tells the woman to go in peace.

Job (subtitled *A Cosmic Tapestry*) was premiered in 2011 in collaboration with Many Gifts One Spirit, a youth arts group supported by Sydenham Street United Church in Kingston, Ontario. The group had the previous year done a production of *Jonah*, with Schafer serving as a consultant, and wished to create a new piece. Schafer again took on the role of consultant but was less involved in the process since Kingston was two hours away from Indian River. The youth group improvised the piece into existence largely on their own after Schafer had provided the framework in collaboration with musical director Marie Anderson, who had worked with him before. In addition to coming to rehearsals with Eleanor, who was also an advisor, Schafer provided some of the music in order to tie the elements of the piece together.

Scene 1: "Evocation of the Cosmos, Dawn"—The Cosmic Chorus creates a soundscape using singing bowls, whirring tubes, and vocalizations from various groups in the chorus. Joined by Job, they chant a poem in praise of God and Creation.

Scene 2: "Job's Bounty"—The Cosmic Chorus becomes Job's family at a celebration, accompanied by klezmer music. A man from the audience, the Audience Man, reads the opening of the story from the King James Bible. God and Satan then address each other as the party scene freezes. As Satan draws Job aside, the soundscape turns more menacing, suggesting the disasters that are to follow.

Scene 3: "Job's Fall from Grace"—Four messengers rapidly appear, telling of the disasters that have befallen Job. The Audience Man comments on the action, questioning what type of God would allow this to happen, then he introduces the character of Sophia, who sings an aria. Satan and God discuss Job further, and God allows Satan to curse Job's flesh. Satan then taunts Job.

Scene 4: "Cold Comfort"—Job's friends come in, accompanied by the Cosmic Chorus. They try to convince Job that he has done something wrong to earn this punishment. God grows angry with the friends. Sophia and her son Rackam enter with a small group of children. Job does not see them but Sophia gives Rackam a necklace that the boy hangs around Job's neck.

Scene 5: "Litany of Woes"—The Audience Man speaks of Job's physical suffering, and Sophia responds that we are not only our physical bodies.

Scene 6: "God in the Whirlwind"—God comes to Job, asking him where he was when God made Creation. Sophia responds, and God and Satan also dialogue

Scene 7: "Job's True Comforters"—Rackam, along with Sophia and the children, approach Job. Rackam touches Job on the shoulder, who finally sees him. The children surround Job and give him new robes, while Sophia ascends to take her place beside God.

Scene 8: "Job's Restoration"; Scene 9: "Evocation of the Cosmos"—Rackam leads Job to each member of the Cosmic Chorus, who reveal themselves to be Job's children, alive once again. Job's wife is also restored to him. The entire cast and musicians create another soundscape, while Job speaks another poem.

LOVING

Schafer says the following about his first theatrical composition in his program notes:

> *Loving* was composed in 1963–65 while I was Artist in Residence at Memorial University in Newfoundland. *The Geography of Eros* and some other sections of the work had been completed when Pierre Mercure phoned with a proposal that *Loving* be commissioned for production on television. The only complica-

tion was that it would have to be produced in French since the producer would be the French network of the CBC.

I went to Montreal and met with Pierre and Gabriel Charpentier. The result was that we decided to make *Loving* a bilingual production so that it could be broadcast on both the French and English networks. And so its official title became *Loving/Toi*. But the production was never completed and it was shown in an abbreviated version.[3]

Although Schafer had written portions of *Loving* as stand-alone pieces, the form of the piece did not take final shape until he received the commission from Mercure. Adams describes *Loving* as a specifically Canadian allegory in which the protagonists each speak one of that country's two official languages, reflective of the tension between the two predominant cultures of Canada, and of the communication issues Lui (He) and Elle (She) face. He also states, "*Loving* is even more centrally concerned with sexual psychology"[4] since Schafer's original intent was to show multiple facets of both masculine and feminine psyches. In the end, *Loving* "dramatizes the female psyche from a decidedly male viewpoint,"[5] with Elle represented by four female singers but Lui only by himself and La Poète, both of which are speaking roles. The libretto of *Loving* is based on texts by the composer, who turned to his own adolescent love poems as inspiration, freely combining, altering, and augmenting them. Schafer published the full libretto as part of the *Open Letter* issue in the fall of 1979.

The Geography of Eros, the first section written, was a reaction to the formalist approaches Schafer had been taking in the works immediately preceding it, such as *Five Studies on Texts of Prudentius*. Schafer is quoted as saying about *Geography*,

> Quite frankly, I don't really think there is any musical organization to it. . . . I think really what I was interested in doing there was accompanying a text which I had created, and trying to find those points at which the nervous system of music and language touch.[6]

This approach is carried throughout *Loving*, which includes no formulaic or serial techniques. The musical material is intentionally fluid and responsive to the text. Only a few of the measures are metered, with the majority being free or given a stop-watch tempo in order to line up with the tape. Vertical lines are often given as reference points at which instrumentalists and singers should line up, allowing a great amount of freedom for the singer in between those points. The melodic and harmonic material is also quite free, with several passages of improvisation. Other passages give graphic sketches as an outline for pitches.

The orchestration includes no wind or brass instruments. The included string quintet plays a secondary role along with free-bass accordion, added for the 1978 revival of the piece. The dominant colors come from a large percussion section and the plucked instruments. Schafer uses different parts of the ensemble to reflect the personality of the four parts of Elle: strings and accordion without tape for Modesty, percussion and tape for Ishtar, plucked instruments and tape for Vanity, and resonant percussion for Eros. This instrumentation varies widely from section to section, ranging from just tape accompaniment to the full ensemble, the only addition being the recorded voice of La Poète.[7] Tape is used extensively in *Loving*, appearing generally as a mix of electronic and prerecorded sounds, spoken or sung texts electronically manipulated, and synthesized sounds. The character of the Poet is prerecorded by the character of Lui, and the spoken dialogue between Lui and Elle is generally not accompanied by the orchestra.

In a lecture on *Loving*, Schafer listed eight degrees of expressing text, most of which he used in *Loving*: stage speech; domestic speech (including slang or deliberately sloppy speech); *parlando* (slightly intoned speech); *sprechgesang*; syllabic song; melismatic song; vocables (pure sounds including humming, whistling, screaming); and electronically manipulated vocal sound.[8] In addition to these approaches to setting text, vocal writing in *Loving* incorporates many avant-garde techniques, including wide intervals and leaps, microtonality, and elements of non-Western music, including the folk music of the Balkans and pop and jazz music.

The structure of *Loving* follows more closely the outline of a traditional opera than one might expect given Schafer's statements on opera around this time. It is divided into scenes, as listed below, and within each scene that contains music one can see structures similar to ensemble pieces, arias, or recitative.

Synopsis

Scene 1: The scene begins with whispered voices in both English and French that overlap slightly the vocal quartet's entry on the text "Lover(s) suspended in mysteries confused vibrations" sung both in English and in French.

Scene 2: "A man wanders alone among the shapes of blue and green"— The vocal quartet continues, supported by the tape and the recording of the poet, who speaks of Elle, referencing their meeting and relationship.

Scene 3: "A man and woman are seen conversing. Perhaps they have been in silent conversation beneath the last words of the poet. They face slightly away from one another"—The spoken dialogue between the man and woman is interrupted by one short tape insertion. The woman reveals that she is "many people."

Scene 4: "The woman dissolves and the man is left standing alone. In slow motion he moves through a labyrinth of mannequins, accompanied by the voice of the poet"—In his travels he approaches first Modesty, accompanied by a brief statement of the music of her aria, then Vanity, then Ishtar.

Scene 5: "Quartet"—The stage is in darkness, and the quartet begins to sing an extended ensemble piece based on excerpts from their upcoming arias, accompanied first by the orchestra then by the tape. While this is happening a series of still photographs is projected on the screen, all depicting the various aspects of the woman as represented by Elle: Vanity, Ishtar, Eros, and Modesty.

Scene 6: "The man and woman are seen again conversing"—The man's voice is taken over by the poet while the man's lips keep moving. The woman's last line, "But I am afraid," turns into a scream.

Scene 7: "Modesty's Aria"—Modesty takes over Elle's scream to lead into her aria, which shows that Schafer's Modesty is hysterical rather than demure.[9] She is accompanied by the string quintet and, in the revised version, free-bass accordion. The text and accompanying writing express Modesty's interior turmoil over her attraction to Lui and her reluctance to physically consummate the relationship. Her aria ends as it began with the words "I am afraid," leading to repetitions of "No."

Scene 8: "The couple are seen again, the woman turning away from the man"—The woman rejects Modesty's portrayal of her. When the man leans toward her and whispers in her ear, she responds "Ishtar?" and laughs.

Scene 9: "Ishtar's Aria"—Ishtar takes over Elle's laugh at the beginning of her aria, which is sung in French and accompanied first by the tape and then by percussion before the aria is abruptly interrupted by scene 10.

Scene 10: "The couple are seen again, this time at a banquet table. Before them food, wine, etc."—The couple speak the texts simultaneously and are given dynamic indications as to how they should speak it.

Scene 9 (continued)—We return to Ishtar's aria, this time with the piano and double bass joining the percussion in imitation of a jazz trio.

Scene 11: "Phantasmagoria"—This is taken by the full instrumental ensemble, with the tape, but without the quartet of singers. Occasionally recorded segments by Elle, Lui, and La Poète appear overtop the texture.

Scene 12: "The couple is seen again. She might be seated at a vanity table and he on the edge of a bed"—The couple have a brief, spoken dialogue.

Scene 13—The voice of the poet speaks, accompanied by still shots from scene 5.

Scene 14: "Vanity's Aria"—The woman's place has been taken by Vanity at the vanity table. She faces a mirror. But this has been fragmented into a thousand pieces. Vanity's aria can be sung to either a French or English text and is focused on her physical, self-centered beauty as she applies makeup and looks at herself in the mirror. Her aria is accompanied by plucked instruments and prerecorded voices.

Scene 15—The poet's voice again enters, commenting on the text of Vanity's aria.

Scene 16: "The woman reclines on a bed or a sofa. The man is seated on the edge, bent towards her"—The couple's dialogue is interrupted by the voice of the poet, accompanied by Spanish guitar. At the end of the scene Eros begins to sing, leading into the next scene.

Scene 17: "The Geography of Eros"—Eros represents the reconciliation of the three previous characters and their conflict, referencing all three.[10] She is accompanied by resonant percussion, piano, and harp.

Scene 18: "The man and the woman are seen in exactly the same positions they were in during Scene Three"—They dialogue, accompanied by the poet. At the end of the scene they each say, "Are you coming?" in their own language and move off in opposite directions.

Scene 19—The scene begins with the voice of the poet accompanied first by the same ensemble that accompanied Eros, and this slowly expands to include the other instruments. The voice of the poet is eventually accompanied by the vocal quartet, which sings text in both languages.

APOCALYPSIS PART I: JOHN'S VISION

John's Vision was conceived initially as a community work involving volunteers, but the scale and complexity of the piece necessitated significant professional involvement in the two complete productions that have taken place.

> The first part of *Apocalypsis* describes John of Patmos' vision of the end of the world, as described in *Revelation*. To depict this epochal event I knew I would need enormous forces. For two or three years I had been involved in the *Dayspring* Festival at Metropolitan United Church in Toronto, and it was to this church that I made my proposal. My idea was that the new work would be undertaken by a consortium of churches, each providing choirs, soloists, actors and volunteer help of all kinds as they were able We were off to a good start; women were sewing banners, and choirs and dancers were rehearsing in various church basements when the minister at Metropolitan left for a new appointment. His successor had no interest in the arts; the *Dayspring* Festival withered, and my hair was turning grey trying to keep the momentum going. When I began to receive angry letters from church wardens about untidy rehearsals, and one of the ministers complained that the Apocalypse was not "Christocentric"(!), I knew that my original production plan would have to be given up.

The full production of both parts of *Apocalypsis* was given in London, Ontario, in 1980.

The text for *John's Vision* is taken from the last book of the Christian scriptures, the *Revelation of John*, with an insertion of Schafer's earlier piece

Psalm, a setting of Psalm 148. Schafer in his adaptations remains quite faithful to the original text and in the score indicates the location of the texts in the Book of Revelation. The three sound poets—bpNichol, Paul Dutton, and Steve McCaffery—embellished the texts of the characters they played (John of Patmos, Archangel Michael, and Antichrist), and Leo del Pasqua assisted in preparing the final text for this section.

Given the text, it is not surprising that *Part I* is a dramatic and theatrical work. Schafer turns not only to Christian texts but also to Christian theatrical tradition, drawing in particular from the pageantry of the Catholic Mass and from the medieval mystery plays that were performed in towns and cities in Europe during the Middle Ages.

The forces required for *John's Vision* are staggering, explaining why the piece has only been produced in its entirely twice. In addition to sound poets, solo singers, mime artists, and dancers, the piece also requires six different sung or speech choruses, percussion, wind and brass instruments, an extensive percussion battery that includes several newly created percussion instruments, and a Middle Eastern instrumental ensemble. To this is added organ, which is used mainly for sustained pedals, and electronic tape, used only at the beginning and the end of the piece. Schafer suggests that a minimum of seven conductors is required, each assigned to a different ensemble. The size of the piece and the extensive stage directions demand that it should be performed in a large church or cathedral in a cruciform design, although a large concert hall could also suffice. A wooden stage at the front is suggested along with platforms to elevate John, Michael, and the living icons. Seven large banners need to be constructed and hung at points throughout the church.

The music of *John's Vision* pays homage to the numerology found in the Book of Revelation, where two numbers have great significance: 7 (the seven seals, the seven trumpets) and 12 (the twelve gates of the New Jerusalem). These numbers conveniently line up with the diatonic and chromatic scales, creating extensive possibilities that Schafer takes full advantage of. Much of the piece is based on two pitch sets. The first is a seven-note exotic scale based on F, the second a "row" based on the remaining five pitches. These two pitch sets alternate, sharing any material other than the keynote F, which is often sustained as a pedal underneath. In addition to being a source of melodic and harmonic material, the numbers 7 and 12 also strongly influence the timing of the piece, both on a large scale and a small scale. The numerology additionally affects the number of performers. There are seven leading parts: the three sound poets and the four living creatures. Seven mimes represent the angels, and many of the choral and instrumental groups require a minimum of twelve or seven musicians.[11]

196   Chapter 12

Synopsis

A. Introduction—"As the audience gathers, the lights are low throughout the hall. Monks cross the floor with incense burners. One by one the performing groups enter and quietly recite texts in which the imminence of the Apocalypse is described."[12] The performing groups in this instance are the mixed chorus divided into four groups, the women's chorus, and the speech chorus (Chorus of the Lost). The texts are from the Old Testament books of Isaiah and Joel.

B. "The Cosmic Christ"—At the beginning of this section, seven torches are lit to reveal John. A crash of waves is heard on the tape, accompanied by the organ, which outlines the exotic scale. The instrumentalists do controlled improvisations on the scale, with each group having a different metronome marking, based on multiples of seven. John begins to chant, "In the midst of life I have had a vision of the one who was and is and is coming" as the adult choirs enter, also improvising on the scale, first using vocables, then gradually joining John's text or having their own texts based on verses from the first chapter of Revelation. Their meters are either seven or five, and the rhythmic patterns, arrangement of vowels, and arrangement of syllables also fall into

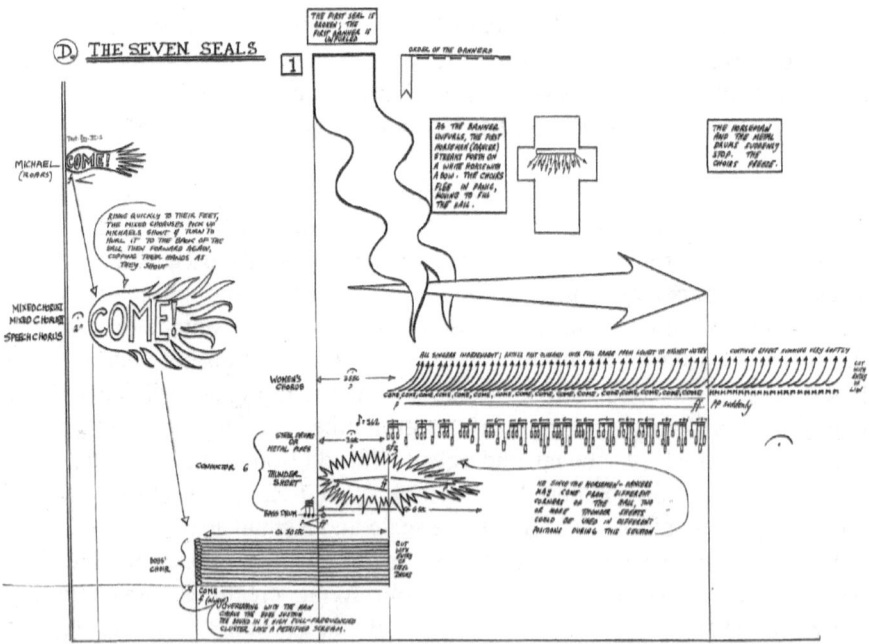

Figure 12.1. "The Seven Seals," *Apocalypsis Part 1: John's Vision.* R. Murray Schafer

patterns of seven. The underlying wave sound crescendos for four minutes and decrescendos for three minutes.[13]

C. "The Court of Heaven"—The melodic material in this section is based on the five pitches not found in the exotic scale (E, G, C-sharp, B-flat, A-flat), with F included as the common tone between the two pitch sets. The boys' choir sings a free melody on a Latin text from Revelation chapter 9. The Presbyters (male) chorus sings a different Latin text. In between their sung statements they bow strictly in time every five seconds a total of seven times. The two mixed choruses sing a text from Revelation chapter 5 in English. The only instrumental accompaniment is the organ playing both white and black note clusters, the high instruments playing a chromatic cluster, twelve spirit catchers (plastic tubes pitched semitones apart and spun overhead), and, most significantly, two Sanctus Bells. The bell placed at the front of the church strikes at thirty-five-second intervals a total of twelve times. The bell placed at the back strikes at sixty-second intervals a total of seven times. The front bell marks the alternation of the Presbyters chorus with the instrumental groups, the back bell determines the timing of the chanting of the mixed choir.[14] Over all of this musical activity we see the appearance, through lighting, of the Four Living Creatures, who chant text from Revelation chapter 4. The Archangel Michael also makes his first appearance, and John chants a prayer to end the section.

D. "The Seven Seals"—This scene is dominated by the breaking of the seven seals, the appearance of the four horsemen who chase the choirs, and the sealing of the saved by the angels, represented by seven sets of specially made angel wings (constructed of large sheets of aluminum mounted in various parts of the hall). The first four seals are announced by Michael shouting, "Come," which is echoed with shouts from the mixed and speech choruses, accompanied by sung clusters and glissandi by the boys' and women's choruses, thunder sheets, bass drum, and steel drums. Before the fifth seal is broken, the tenors and basses of the mixed chorus intone text on a low F, imitating Tibetan monks. At the breaking of the fifth seal, the horsemen continue to lunge at the chorus of the damned, accompanied by the steel drums, until the breaking of the sixth seal, when Michael interrupts to let the angels seal the elect. At this point the two mixed choruses move to the stage as they are sealed, and the speech chorus flees to the back of the hall in fear of the angels, crying out louder and louder. As the speech choir reaches its climax, the boys' choir re-enters, singing a text in Latin on the same pitch set as in the court of heaven. John speaks of the great host gathering before the throne to praise God.

E. "Psalm"—The two mixed choirs, representing those saved, sing a setting of Psalm 148. At the end of the psalm is an interlude during which the choir exits as smoke billows up, and players with mandala bells (small bells struck then twirled on a string to create a Doppler effect) move through the hall while glass chimes play at intervals of seven seconds. The boys' choir sings an altered reprise of the melody and text they sang at the end of "The Seven Seals," accompanied by a descending improvisation on the organ and low tremolos on the high instruments. The high instruments then switch to ascending semitone trills while the spotlight comes on John, and the women's chorus sings "And I hear angels' wings" on an expanding melody based on the five-note pitch set. Seven angels advance with seven trumpets as John speaks a text of woe from Revelation chapter 13.

F. "The Seven Trumpets"—This scene is also primarily theatrical, and various projections are used throughout this section to depict the natural and man-made disasters referenced by the trumpet blasts. The pitch material is drawn from the exotic scale, first appearing in the brass and organ, which play twelve-second blasts at thirty-six-second intervals.[15] The men's, women's, and mixed choruses sing various "Woe" statements with the same pitches, building complexity in rhythm and texture through the blowing of the fifth trumpet, when red smoke billows up and locust dancers appear. As they dance the choir and percussion play twenty-one short percussive statements, between which the organ plays a repeating motive based on the exotic scale, leading to a fiery passage in the brass leading to the sixth trumpet. Seven strikes on the thunder sheets are accompanied by the men's, women's, and mixed choruses reciting numbers 1 to 7 in various patterns. As this gradually fades away, the boys' choir returns to sing the third statement of its Benediction. Michael hands a scroll to John, who eats it and continues to prophesy.

G. "The Battle between Good and Evil"—The scene begins with the dialogue between Michael and John describing the Woman, the dragon who waits to devour her child, and the war between Michael and his angels and the dragon and his angels. The Chorus of the Lost gradually reassembles, carrying flags of different nations, which they place on a podium. Microphones are installed and six military drummers on stage introduce the Antichrist, punctuating his statements as he speaks to the crowd. After this, in the place where the Woman appeared before now appears the Whore of Babylon, who dances to an accompaniment of Middle Eastern instruments, leading the crowd into "debauched merriment."

H. "Vision of the End"—The lights come up and the seventh angel blows his trumpet on the keynote F, stopping the chorus of the damned in their revelries. The women's chorus, men's chorus, and mixed chorus sing "Woe" three times accompanied by the brass, anvils, high instruments and trumpets, and organ. The boys' choir sings an agitated version of their Beatus, continuing until John's description of the rider on the white horse and the troops that follow him. When John is finished, the tape reenters with a recording of a church bell, and the mixed chorus enters, singing "King of Kings and Lord of Lords" on a melody based on the exotic scale, joined by the Presbyters chorus accompanying themselves on hand drums. As the seven bowls of wrath are poured out, the Chorus of the Lost rush through the church lamenting the fall of Babylon, and the Four Living Creatures chant praise to God. Just before the third bowl is poured, the seven angel wings are activated and the women's chorus sings another text, in Latin, from Revelation chapter 15, again using the exotic scale. The boys' chorus joins after the fourth bowl, the high instruments join after the fifth bowl, the final instruments after the sixth bowl. When the seventh bowl is poured, the texture thins out to a unison trill on F by the high instruments and bass drum. The Chorus of the Lost scream once more and flee the hall as the image of the Cosmic Christ appears.

I. "Lament over Babylon and Transition to the New Kingdom"—At the beginning of the scene, the instruments stop, and over a pedal drone in the Presbyters chorus the boys' chorus sing one more rendition of their text from Revelation chapter 14, gradually fading away. The Old Woman enters, singing a text describing the fall of Babylon, basing her melody on graphic contours provided. As she sings, John speaks a more extended text, taken from Revelation chapter 18. The Chorus of the Saved overlap John's last word, "more," and whisper three extended "Alleluias," underneath which a few men intone the following pitches, with some repetitions: F, G, B-flat, C. After this the singers hum the pitch of six gongs as they are struck at ten-second intervals, dividing as they repeat to overlap pitches. The Four Living Creatures chant a text from Revelation chapter 20, fading out as Michael speaks and the Presbyters chorus sings a simple, repeated, chant-like melody, taking elements from both pitch centers to bring the tonality to F major, slowly joined by the other choruses. The choruses light candles and leave the hall as the sound slowly fades out.

The Children's Crusade was commissioned by Lawrence Cherney, director of Soundstreams Canada, and composed in 2007 for a specific place in mind: an outdoor (but enclosed) quadrangle at University College in Toronto.

> The open quadrangle is surrounded by the tall windows and stone walls of classrooms, with a raised walkway around a grassy centre, giving it something of a medieval quality—or at least the closest thing to the Middle Ages that one might expect to find in Toronto. The walkway suggested a processional work and I immediately thought of the Children's Crusade.[16]

Schafer imagined the performers moving from place to place, accompanied by the audience, who would also participate in the story. Characters such as jongleurs, beggars, and dancers would be mixed into the audience to further place the audience in the action, speaking lines and addressing the crowd. Schafer based the text on a French story about the 1212 Children's Crusade when a young boy named Stephen had a vision about leading a crusade, went to see King Phillip, and although he was laughed at by the court, nevertheless was given free passage to Marseilles when it was pointed out to the king that Stephen's followers were mostly orphans and gutter children so the proposed crusade would result in a social cleanup.

The children walked to Marseilles where they expected the waves of the Mediterranean to part as the Red Sea had parted for Moses. The chroniclers are not very precise on how many children reached Marseilles, but most mention a figure in the thousands. Of course, the waters did not part and the crusade ended in disaster. Many of the children drowned, others were sold into slavery, and others starved to death as they attempted to return home.[17]

Multiple characters are called for in the story, both children and adults, supported by a children's choir that plays the crusaders, a women's choir that plays the Angels and Witches choirs, a men's choir that plays the Judges and Asinorum choirs, and a mixed choir that plays the Audience choir and the Wind and Waves choir. These are accompanied by a medieval consort, Middle Eastern instruments, brass quintet, musical saw, and double bass.

Synopsis

"Prelude"—The piece starts in darkness, with an impression of a storm gathering, while suspended aluminum rods and a musical saw play for about a minute before the notated music emerges. The Angel choir sings a wordless, two-voice melody accompanied.

Scene 1: "The Magus"—The Magus and the Holy Child encounter each other. The Magus gives the boy food and drink, tells the child of his destiny, and gives him a letter to give to the King of France when he meets him. The music is provided by the Wind and Waves Choir accompanied by a wind machine. The Angel Choir sings a newly composed setting of the ancient Latin text "Gaudeat Devotio Fidelium," and the Wind and Waves choir sings a unison "Alleluia" in Dorian mode accompanied by the musical saw.

Scene 2: "Mora"—The Holy Child encounters urchins playing mora (a numbers game) on his way to meet the king. They snatch the letter from him and read it. It says "To His Royal Highness, King of France, The bearer of this letter is the Lamb of God"—As they mock him, an angel appears above with a choir of children and points the child to where he must go, singing a Latin text in D Aeolian, accompanied by crotales and two trumpets that urges the boy to be steadfast to God. The urchins see the angel and choir as the Holy Child begins to sing with the angel and themselves begin to sing, "Holy child, holy child," leading to a joyful three-part chorus in the children's choir, telling the boy not to fear.

Scene 3: "Deo Gracias"—The urchins build a cross of branches that they give to the Holy Child. When he raises it, the church bells begin to ring and the children's choir sings a florid "Alleluia" accompanied by the medieval ensemble. The child moves on, followed by the urchins and then other children. Adults begin to praise them as the children process by, singing a setting of "Deo Gracias" by Schafer based in D major, first in unison then in a three-part canon.

Scene 4: "Ariana"—The Holy Child hears the voice of a Saracen girl, Ariana, accompanied by the qanun. He responds, accompanied by soprano recorder and lute. Their lines begin to overlap more and more as they dialogue, and their accompanying instruments also mix. She calls him to Jerusalem and reminds him that they were in heaven together, a reference to the *Patria* cycle and the relationship between Ariadne and Wolf.

Scene 5: "Entry to the Court"—The children, the Holy Child (now borne on a litter), and the crowd push toward the palace, as the children sing a Benedictus in Aeolian mode. The sergeant stops them and indicates that only the Holy Child can see the king. As the child enters, the children's choir and Audience choir sing a lively hymn in Dorian, accompanied by the hurdy-gurdy. As the audience is seated, lower brass, double bass, and drums play a martial tune in Aeolian.

Scene 6: "The King's Garden Party"—The scene is a private garden party for the king's new mistress. After an opening fanfare by the brass quartet, the first part of the scene is three instrumental dance tunes for the king and his mistress to dance together. The mistress sings a French text found in the Montpellier codex to a new tune in D major and minor, accompanied by organ, alto recorder, and cornet. After a fourth dance the king notices the crowd and instructs his courtiers to throw them some crusts of bread. After one last dance, the rector of Paris University urgently asks for an audience with the king, who grants it but instructs that the rector sing instead of speak. The rector sings a chant with obtuse words, describing how people are abandoning their work and studies to follow the Holy Child, speaking of a new crusade. The king retires to the audience chamber to speak with the Holy Child.

Scene 7: "Audience with the King"—The seneschal asks the audience to rise as the king enters. Twelve judges in black costumes and monkey masks provide mocking sung commentary as the king interrogates the child. After hearing that the child's followers are the "scum of Paris," the king seizes the opportunity to free the streets of these undesirables and gives the child permission to go on the crusade and grants him safe passage to Marseilles.

Scene 8: "La Heaulmière"—As the child leaves he is accosted by an old hag, who sings him a song using music from Ezra Pound's opera *Le Testament*, which sets texts by François Villon. She embraces the boy, says she knows his real mission, and pushes him into a dark room.

Scene 9: "Moloch"—The scene opens with a low-pitched melody in the cello, in G minor, accompanied by contrabass and low-pitched percussion (timpani, gong, tam tam). As Moloch welcomes the child to the Sanctuary and Altar of Love, the hurdy-gurdy joins, and then the rebec, passing a chromatic melody back. A chorus of twelve witches sings a wordless chorus that builds into six-part chord clusters, roughly doubled by the instruments. The chorus takes over the earlier instrumental melody as Moloch takes the child to end of the room where a beautifully dressed woman dances sensually, surrounded by the witches. The witches call upon the boy, first in English, then in Latin, to fornicate with the woman. As the woman draws closer the boy screams and runs from the room.

Scene 10: "Festum Asinorum"—The Holy Child encounters a group of monks, wearing asses' heads, who first sing the Kyrie from the Angelus plainsong mass, braying like donkeys between each statement, then dance to a lively tune played by recorder, bouzouki, kazoo, and jaw harp.

Scene 11: "Damien"—One of monks comes away from the group to kiss the Holy Child as the instruments play a saucy snippet of the tune and asks to join him. They return to the courtyard where the Holy Child's followers are waiting.

Scene 12: "Ariana and David"—The voice of Ariana is heard high above the crowd but they ignore her and move away from the sound. She is with a Jewish boy, David, who dances and plays a pair of sagat (finger cymbals). The Holy Child sees David dance and sings a response. Ariana sings that the three of them will restore Jerusalem and peace will come to the city. David continues his dance as the Holy Child moves on.

Scene 13: "The Departure"—Set in the courtyard, the various extras move through the crowd, all adding to the sound and music of the scene. A group of dancers perform an estampie from a late-thirteenth-century manuscript and a jongleur sings a crusader song by Thibaut de Champagne. The crowd cheers the return of the Holy Child, and the women of the Audience choir begin to sing a plainsong Sanctus (a new setting by Schafer), accompanied by the brass quintet. The men of the Audience choir then sing "Deus lo volt!" again accompanied by the brass quintet. As this fades out the horn, trombone, and tuba introduce the Holy Child's response, in F major, with hints of Mixolydian, which states that they will conquer with love, not force. They prepare for departure as the priests bless them. The children sing a simple duet, then a few with bells sing a lively melody about Jerusalem. As the procession takes form the Audience choir sings a Phrygian tune saying that that they wish they could go and the children respond, singing that their love will win over the Saracens and they will open the walls of Jerusalem to them. After the children are finished singing, the instruments slowly die away as the procession leaves.

Scene 14: "Fatigue"—After a brief intermission when the extras and actors mix with and entertain the audience, the children appear, singing Schafer's setting of "Jesu Dulcis Memoria," a text by the crusader priest St. Bernard of Clairvaux. The singing slowly stops, and the children say they are hungry. Damien and the child speak of the Dark Powers who are now chasing them, and Damien sings that the Holy Child needs to show the other children a miracle.

Scene 15: "The Miracle"—The Holy Child sings words of encouragement to the children with a melody that is based in G minor but is more chromatic, reflecting the troubled feelings of the child. He leads the children in a sung rendition of the Beatitudes, and the Angel choir begins to echo them from a distance. The children begin to hear the angel voices singing, and their hunger vanishes. The children ask which direction they should go, the Holy Child responds that they are going to God, and they all sing a reprise of the crusader's hymn sung by the jongleur in the departure scene, accompanied by a repeated "Alleluia" in the Angel Choir.

Scene 16: "Ariana Returns"—Ariana sings a frantic song, accompanied by the qanun, as well as the riqq and cymbals, asking, "Where are you?" The child responds, and comforts her fears. He says that they are near water, and she answers that Moses will strike the waters and part them so they will reach the Holy Land.

Scene 17: "Marseilles"—The children move on, still led by the Angel choir, which sings a new setting of the text "Beati Mortui Qui in Domino," accompanied by unmeasured notes in the horn and trombone, and a recording of wave sounds. This text is repeated by the Wind and Waves choir in a fuller harmonization, and more instruments are added as the sounds of the waves intensify and the tempo increases. The climax of the ocean music is reached as the procession encounters a wall of soldiers led by William Porcus and Iron Hugh. The two leaders question the group and the Holy Child. Porcus shows them the sea, and cynically waits for the miracle.

Scene 18: "The Drowning"—As the sound of the sea continues to grow, the Holy Child shows the children how to prepare to enter the water, using a simple sung phrase that each child repeats. Iron Hugh and Porcus shout mocking comments as they prepare, and Damien questions what will happen if the waves do not part. As he continues to doubt, instrument and recorded sound continue to grow, reflecting the force of the waves and wind, and the wind machine enters for the first time since the beginning of the piece. The storm briefly dies away as the Holy Child turns to Damien and says, "Are you coming?" Damien's courage leaves him, and he says he must stay behind to record what will happen. The waves and wind rise again as the Holy Child says, "Let the waves part" and the children sing, "Spread your arms like wings." The children walk into the water, and after a lull, during which the organ plays an extended solo, the agitated music returns again. The children realize the water is not parting. Some scream, some continue to sing, and all begin to disappear under the water. The Wind and Waves choir enters, the sea begins to grow calm, the wind machine stops, and the instrumental texture thins. The children from a distance sing, "We are no more" as Porcus cynically tells Iron Hugh to ride and tell the king that the children have been "liquidated." The children continue to sing from a distance, saying that the water and wind have carried away their footsteps and voices. The Angel choir begins to sing to the children that their suffering is over and their joy will be eternal. The Monks choir and the Wind and Waves choir sing a richly voiced "Amen." At the end we are left with the saw, crotales, glockenspiel, and the aluminum rods striking soft, random notes, as the clouds part to reveal the stars.

Chapter Thirteen

The *Patria* Cycle

Schafer's life's passion and crowning opus is his *Patria* cycle, a project that spans thirty years and has grown from its initial triptych to twelve separate segments.

Kirk MacKenzie in his early dissertation on the *Patria* cycle describes the underlying concept as

> the physical, psychological, and spiritual journey of a hero and a heroine towards fulfillment and redemption. The protagonists, who appear in different guises throughout the cycle, derive their main identities from three myths: the ancient Greek legend of Theseus, Ariadne, the Minotaur, and the labyrinth; a myth of Schafer's own making reminiscent of Amerindian legends, "The Princess of the Stars"; and the tale of "Beauty and the Beast."[1]

As the cycle developed, the "Beauty and the Beast" element was not carried through the cycle as extensively as the first two, only appearing explicitly in *Patria 1, 2, 3*, and briefly in *7*. Schafer himself states, "The unifying motif in *Patria* is Wolf's journeys through the many labyrinths of life in search of the spiritual power which can both release and transfigure him."[2] During his travels, Wolf will play many characters, some of them debased, some of them exalted. For him, the Star Princess becomes personified in Ariadne, the mythological Greek woman who helped Theseus escape the labyrinth, and the thread that Ariadne gives Wolf in the cycle is the thread of music as her voice haunts and sustains him.[3] Each part of *Patria* follows the theme of Wolf's wanderings to find the Star Princess and redeem her and him, but the cycle itself is nonlinear. We begin in a prehistoric, mythical past with *Patria Prologue*, move to the twentieth century for *Patria 1, 2,* and *3*, travel back to earlier historical periods in *Patria 4, 5, 6*, and to a certain extent *7*, and return to mythology in *Patria 8*, *9*, and *10* before completing the cycle, and the two protagonists' journey, in *Patria Epilogue*.

Three underlying themes weave their way through the *Patria* cycle. The first is Schafer's desire to draw humanity and the rest of the natural world together through the medium of non–Judeo-Christian religious traditions that emphasize the equality of all living things and treat nature as a sacred mystery. Schafer has often expounded upon this concept in his writings, stating how appropriate forms for this type of approach are "those in which the bifurcation of performer and audience are diminished, namely ritual and participatory celebration."[4]

A second theme flows from Schafer's insistence that works of the "Theatre of Confluence" (his term for this cycle and its related works) must involve all the senses, and the different components (music, libretto, dance, acting) must be developed together with none predominating. He does state that one of the senses may serve as a "keel line" that balances the other elements, so he has chosen to make music the keel line of *Patria*, feeling that the intimacy of music is appropriate for a drama that focuses on connection in contrast to the alienation of modern society.[5]

A final theme is based on the writings of the German psychologist Carl Jung. Waterman posits in her thesis that

> the famous psychologist's ideas are present in the mythological subject matter of the series, in its major themes, and in the use of archetypal protagonists rather than conventional characters.[6]

Jung's concept of the alienation of modern man from the "collective unconscious" is reflected in the alienation of the two primary characters of *Patria*. Wolf is alienated both from society and his subconscious, and the Star Princess has been exiled from her home in the stars. Schafer adopts Jung's belief that humankind needs myths in order to maintain a connection to the divine, and our separation from this divine is the source of our alienation from society and from each other.[7] His belief that these myths transcend the time and location of their creation—are in fact universal—allows him to move his characters freely throughout history and space. The two characters' quest to find wholeness through the integration of their psyche is another important concept in *Patria*, a process that Jung calls "individuation."

> *Individuation* is the term with which C. G. Jung describes the psychological process of inner growth and centralization by which the individual finds its own Self. This does not mean to find one's own ego-identity, as is described by many modern psychological schools. By the term *Self*, Jung understands an ultimately unknowable inner center of the total personality and also the totality itself. This center can only be approached but never integrated. Our destiny and our health depend on it. In the various religions and mythologies it is

symbolized by the image of the "treasure hard to attain," the mandala and all images of the inner psychic manifestation of the godhead.[8]

The two protagonists will ultimately achieve this individuation in *Patria Epilogue* as a symbol of humankind's reconciliation with and reconnection to the natural world. Both MacKenzie and Waterman note that the three major figures in *Patria*—the hero, heroine, and what Waterman calls an "amoral catalyst"—can be matched to Jung's three archetypes of animus, anima, and shadow. Since they are archetypes, they are in one way not characters at all and cannot develop in the same way characters do. Each of the three archetypes takes on two basic forms in *Patria*. The animus (hero) is Wolf and Theseus; the anima (heroine) is the Star Princess and Ariadne; and the shadow (the amoral catalyst) is the Three-Horned Enemy and the Minotaur.[9] The two stories that provide the personifications of each archetype are the newly created myth told in *Patria Prologue* and the ancient Greek myth of Theseus, Ariadne, and the Minotaur.

In *Patria*, Schafer uses the term "editing unit" instead of "scene" and differentiates it in the following way from that more traditional division:

> An editing unit is actually a rehearsal unit. Each editing unit has its own mood or situation, though some flow into one another and some are distinctly separate—like the scenes of a conventional drama.[10]

Each part of the cycle will be discussed as the composer arranged them, which is unrelated to their order of composition. Each section will include a brief discussion of the compositional history and the musical and theatrical approach, and each will include a synopsis.

PATRIA PROLOGUE: THE PRINCESS OF THE STARS

The third part of the *Patria* cycle to be written (completed in 1981), this piece flows directly out of Schafer's engagement with the environment, first revealed in his work with the WSP and developed compositionally in *Music for Wilderness Lake* and *Sun Father, Earth Mother*.

The Princess of the Stars is intended as a ritual, aligning with the first theme of the cycle to draw humanity and the natural world together, and the way the piece is structured and presented reinforces this concept. The performers are hidden by the trees from the audience, and the Presenter at the beginning of the piece turns the audience into trees themselves so that they will not disturb the events they are about to see. The god and animal characters speak a series of unknown languages, which only the Presenter can interpret. Wolf's language incorporates elements of Native American languages, and the texts of the hidden soloists incorporate words from Native

American tribes whose traditional territory was in the woodlands of central and eastern Canada. This technique creates a sense of mythical distance from the audience, suggested by the "real and implied antiquity of the languages its characters speak."[11] Since it is ritual, the prologue can't be produced in a theater or seen on a television set but must be presented in nature, giving the living environment a say in the success or failure of each performance. The performers and audience participate in the ceremony of dawn, to which the prologue has been added as adornment. In the prologue we are introduced to the three archetypes: the animus (Wolf), the anima (the Star Princess), and the shadow (the Three-Horned Enemy), and we learn the cause of Wolf's journey.

The music is written with location in mind, and it also shows the influence of North American chant. Since the music must be heard across water and the singers and instrumentalists need to coordinate across great distances, by necessity the music must be written in such a way to make that possible. The music is simple, often monophonic, with aleatoric sections and flexibility in the notation to allow for performances under different conditions.

Synopsis

Editing Unit 1: The production begins with the unseen Star Princess singing a wordless aria from across the lake. As she sings, the Presenter slowly appears, being paddled across the lake toward the audience.

Editing Units 2–3: As the Princess repeats her aria, the Presenter calls three times across the lake to the audience. After each call, singers around the lake begin to echo the Princess's aria. The Presenter then addresses the audience, telling them what happened with Princess and Wolf before they arrived. (The Princess heard Wolf howling, leaned down from the stars, and fell to earth. Wolf was startled, lashed out, and wounded her. She ran to the lake, where she was captured by the Three-Horned Enemy.) The Presenter then turns the audience into trees so that they can witness the action to come without disturbing it.

Editing Units 4–6: The large figure of Wolf is paddled across the lake, accompanied by percussion groups scattered around the lake. He howls, and sings his aria as he is paddled around the lake. The Presenter goes out to meet Wolf, circling around him in his canoe, as the chorus begins to sing, accompanied by the brass.

Editing Units 7–10: Wolf turns to face back up the lake to invoke the Dawn Birds, so that they can help him seek the Princess. They arrive and move in a slow circle around Wolf. They cannot find the Princess, and Wolf howls. Ariadne's voice is heard again, singing a lament.

Editing Units 11–13: The audience hears the laughter and voice of the Three-Horned Enemy before he appears on the lake, accompanied by music on the brass and percussion instruments. He stops in front of Wolf and speaks to him, then the two creatures surge toward each other, singing their respective war chants.

Editing Units 14–15: The Sun Disk is suddenly revealed on the far side of the lake, with the Dawn Birds on either side of him. He is paddled to the center of the lake, where the Presenter will meet him and serve as interpreter. Wolf and the Three-Horned Enemy face the Sun Disk, who tells the Three-Horned Enemy to return the crown to the sky, declares that Ariadne must remain on earth until her redemption, and says that Wolf must wander the earth looking for her. The Sun Disk then instructs the Dawn Birds to close over the waters of the lake with ice and snow so that Ariadne will not be disturbed.

Editing Units 16–18: As the performers all play the note C, the figures on the lake slowly depart, beginning with the Sun Disk and Dawn Birds, then the Presenter. The Princess's voice is again heard, echoed by the treble voices in the chorus.

PATRIA 1: WOLFMAN

Schafer's underlying concept for a piece he initially called *D. P. (Displaced Person)* but ultimately titled *Patria 1: The Characteristics Man* in 1974[12] was man against the megalopolis, solitude versus the multitude.[13] The mute hero of *Patria 1* is both Theseus and Minotaur, an immigrant in a hostile society, a rescuer turned attacker who threatens Ariadne then saves her by committing suicide.[14] After Wolf is condemned to wander the world in *Patria Prologue*, his first unsuccessful journey is into the modern metropolis of the 1970s. Schafer notes, "The immigrant D. P. arrives in a new country understanding neither the language nor the social customs. He seems to be a sensitive, shy man, lean and ductile, with a Chaplinesque ability to show by limb and eye what he is experiencing."[15] Schafer based the protagonist of *Patria 1* on the subject of a 1996 article in a Vancouver newspaper describing a Yugoslav immigrant who had held a little girl at knifepoint while he listed how Canada had deceived him, then released the girl and stabbed himself.[16] In Schafer's story the Yugoslav immigrant becomes Wolf, and the little girl is a young version of Ariadne, so traumatized by the incident that she will end up in an asylum in *Patria 2*.

Patria 1 is written for a conventional theater space, requiring "a ghetto, walls, inside which the audience huddles and against which the music is hurled,"[17] with a focus on the vertical aspect of the space as the role of the Greek chorus is reinforced by their position high above the action.[18] The plot is often presented in a nonlinear fashion, with use of both flashbacks and flashforwards, but there are structural pillars, both musical and dramatic, that give the piece its shape amid its bewildering array of effects, both aural and visual. The music is characteristic of Schafer's work during this time, with its sophisticated use of electronics, avant-garde notation, and vocal/instrumental demands. All is underpinned by the all-interval row that is the basis of the cycle.

Synopsis

Prelude: The piece starts in darkness, then there are ten seconds of voices on tape.

Editing Units 1–3: After the opening darkness, the first three units are tableaux, accompanied by dissonant noises on the tape. The first tableau ("Miserere") shows D. P.'s suicide; the second ("Requiem") shows Ariadne's suicide from *Patria 2*; and the third ("Service d'accueil aux immigrants") shows present time and an immigration office where D. P. faces an immigration official who shouts through a loudspeaker in a language D. P. cannot understand.

Editing Units 4–5: The first major chorus in the work begins here, a setting from Dante's *Inferno* of the text "Abandon all hope, ye who enter here." Schafer sets other texts in the instruments in Morse code. The pitches for these seven texts are determined by the texts themselves, with each text given to a different group (choir, brass, etc.). The action on stage is happy, with a crowd gathering, but a sign follows D. P. around, labeling him the Victim. After the chorus ends, D. P. is interviewed by various people, including psychiatrist Ovid Klein, a recurring character in the cycle.

Editing Unit 6: This is the first of five "diary" sections in which a voice on tape is mixed with Ariadne's voice. D. P.'s passport is shown, in actuality a photo of Franz Kafka.

Editing Units 7–9: Various scenes show D. P. at work and play. He is marched off to an abattoir where he works, in which one of the carcasses is a woman with a bandaged head. He misunderstands the process for receiving his wages and gets nothing.

Figure 13.1. The *Patria* Cycle All-Interval Row. **R. Murray Schafer**

Editing Units 10–15: The workers drive off in large toy cars, reflecting their prosperity. Ovid Klein analyzes the human condition with a deposed dictator, and two hard-hat characters beat D. P. (sensitivity training). A second diary section occurs in unit 15.

Editing Units 16–20: D. P. tries to help two deaf men but is hustled away by the hard hats to language class. It is a failure and the students assault the teacher (Professor Knicker) and flee, leaving D. P. alone with him. The second major chorus, "An Assyrian Penitential Psalm," begins in unit 19 and will extend as background material until unit 24.

Editing Units 21–26: After the third diary section the stage fills again with the mob, who push D. P. to the side, then the hard hats drag him into the crowd, who listen to various speakers. The crowd vanishes as the police arrive, leaving D. P. alone. They handcuff him to a post, where he does the fourth diary segment, with appearances by the young Ariadne then the mature Ariadne.

Editing Units 27–32: Ariadne is analyzed by Ovid Klein and wins a prize from a disc jockey—a party. At the height of the party Ariadne produces a pistol, and even through D. P. tries to stop her, she shoots herself in the head. The last diary segment appears at this time.

Editing Unit 33: The third chorus, *Gita*, written and premiered in 1967, provides the backdrop for the final scene. The young Ariadne comes through the party aftermath and speaks to D. P. He seizes her as a hostage while the crowd surrounds him. Ariadne escapes and D. P. stabs himself in the stomach.[19]

PATRIA 2: REQUIEMS FOR THE PARTY GIRL

Patria 2 was the first of the cycle to be completed, in 1972, and Schafer notes that it is the most conventional in many ways. The core of the drama is the set of arias that Schafer wrote for Phyllis in 1966, also called *Requiems for the Party Girl*. In 1970, Schafer used the core of the arias and added dialogue to create *Dream Passage*, an hour-long radio drama, and the success of that composition led Schafer to complete the stage work, adding other elements to bring it to its full length but leaving the libretto from *Dream Passage* essentially unchanged.

As in *Patria 1*, the topic of *Requiems for the Party Girl* is alienation, but this time told from the perspective of the female protagonist Ariadne, the Star Princess, who in *Patria Prologue* has been forced by her father the Sun to wander the earth under this assumed name. In *Patria 2* she is a patient in an asylum, having presumably been brought here after her traumatic episode with D. P. in *Patria 1*. As Schafer notes, "Her reign of terror is her own mind and, as we shall see, it can be reached by no medical telescope."[20] Much of the plot and setting are drawn from Schafer's own visits to a medical hospital in Vancouver where he would organize noon-hour concerts. Many of the workers in the institution were from different countries and spoke various levels of English. This inspired Schafer to have all the workers in *Patria 2* speak a foreign language, and much of the other textual material was drawn from the incredible profusion of language, real and indecipherable, that Schafer heard from the inmates. He also studied the writings of J. L. Moreno and Peter Ostwald, who studied the various mannerisms and methods of communication of those suffering from severe mental illness.

Schafer notes that Ariadne in *Patria 2* is three persons. She is a party girl of twenty-five or so, the little girl that Wolf encounters in *Patria 1*, and a dead soul (her all-knowing self). The structure of the play suggests that she is in an unending loop of disillusionment and despair where she will remain until Wolf finds her and restores her to the heavens.[21] She is divine, a castoff from another realm, caught on earth until the final reconciliation with Wolf who appears as another inmate, identified as Nietzsche/Beast, and unable in this guise to help her.

The musical language and style of *Patria 2* is similar to that of *Patria 1*, with the same mix of electronics, avant-garde techniques, and an underpinning of the all-interval row. Several of the segments were written beforehand for inclusion in the production, placing it even more obviously in the style of *Loving* and compositions written in the late 1960s.

Synopsis

Editing Units 1–2: As the show opens, we see Ariadne undergoing a brain operation, to the sound of the Beast's voice and German psychiatrists.

Editing Units 3–4: This sequence uses the first three arias from the earlier *Requiems for the Party Girl*. The other inmates appear, wearing masks suggesting deformity, and Ariadne recounts the day she met D. P. and the day she died.

Editing Unit 5: The earlier piece *From the Tibetan Book of the Dead* is performed with the action on stage darkly lit.

Editing Units 6–9: Ariadne sings the fourth and fifth arias then vomits insects that turn into other inmates and respond to her speech. Eddie le Chasseur, the disc jockey from *Patria 1*, comes to interview her, but she screams while the inmates jerk convulsively.

Editing Units 10–13: Ariadne sings the sixth aria as she is prepared for her bath. Beast's alter ego Nietzsche speaks to her. She calms down but is interrupted by one of the nurses walking by.

Editing Units 14–24: Ariadne sings the seventh aria from her bed then enters a dream sequence. She first meets an Arab alchemist on a seashore who presents her with a stone, representing her self, which she promptly loses. She next recalls the party scene from *Patria 1*. The nurse introduces her to Sigmund Freud, who is dressed as an Indian yogi. The young Ariadne enters with a candle, which she presents to the mature Ariadne. Beast appears, and Ariadne approaches him, but he turns, reveals a formless face, and tries to wound her with a knife. Nietzsche appears again, playing a toy piano, and she approaches him, but he fades back into the party.

Editing Units 25–32: Ariadne sings the eighth aria from *Requiems* then receives a telephone call from a Danish psychiatrist (whom she doesn't understand) who then hangs up on her. The inmates march in, a parody of the mob in *Patria 1*. Nietzsche draws her into the labyrinth, where inmates walk through a series of corridors. A shock treatment machine is drawn in. Ariadne says, "I'm coming, Beast." The choir reappears with the *Tibetan Book* chorus.

Editing Units 33–35: Ariadne sings the final four arias from *Requiems*, narrating her suicide.[22]

PATRIA 3: THE GREATEST SHOW

> In preparation for their later reconstruction, *Patria 1* and *2* are broken in *Patria 3*. They are taken apart, dismantled, pulverized, shaken down scene by scene and action by action until only the siftings remain, then mixed with alien and catalytic elements that will lead the myth-apotheosis to follow in future works.[23]

Schafer first had the concept for a *Patria* segment that he originally called "Pieces" shortly after leaving SFU for rural Ontario. Starting in 1977, several of the smaller commissions he received and other non-commissioned works were written to be included in the first production of *The Greatest Show* in 1986 and its final version in 1987. As a result, several (but not all) of these pieces are based on or at least refer to the cycle's all-interval row.

At the beginning of *Patria 3*, the hero from *Patria 1* (Wolf) vanishes and the heroine from *Patria 2* (Ariadne) is dismembered. With the loss of any protagonist, the plot of *The Greatest Show* crumbles, reduced to small-scale fragments that reference both what has happened already in the cycle and, to a certain extent, what is to come. At the end of the show there is an unsuccessful attempt to resurrect the vanished hero and heroine, which instead brings the return of the Three-Horned Enemy, who had slithered to the bottom of the lake at the end of *Patria Prologue*. The revived monster tears the show to pieces as the performers and the audience members flee.

As Schafer searched for a form that fit his concept for this segment, he thought of the model of a village fair, specifically a North American fair that he experienced in his childhood that had no theme, hero, or message and didn't operate as a traditional work of art. In Schafer's fairground there is one large stage, called the Odditorium, where the show opens and closes, and in between it hosts various cabaret shows. There are three large colored tents called the Rose Theater, the Blue Theater, and the Purple Theater, which have "restricted shows" to which admission can only be had through a ticket won via various game shows or other activities. There are also other smaller centers and tents such as the University Theater, the Gallery of Heroes and Heroines, the Palace of Mythical Beings, and the Minotauromachy Maze. In addition to these traditional theater spaces, there are several elastic spaces throughout the grounds where the performers can move right into the audience. Schafer notes that the "final excitement and satisfaction, is not to be found in the individual attractions, but in the interaction between them, the interstices, the sound spill, the cross-talk—what one hears peripherally as much as directly."[24] In the script for *The Greatest Show*, Schafer meticulously lists all the influences and sources for the various characters within the cycle.

In the main theater (the Odditorium), the following events (Editing Units A1–A14) take place.

Editing Unit A1: Showman Sam Galuppi opens the show, and the Black and White Musicians disappear the hero and dismember the heroine.

Editing Units A2–A13: The Odditorium is filled with various farcical acts in sequence, many including characters from *Patria 1*, *2*, and *4*, including the hard hats and Eddie le Chasseur. Unit A5 uses the earlier composed *Gamelan*; unit A12 uses *Situational Music for Brass Quintet*.

Editing Units A14–18: The performers dance in conga lines leading the audience to the Odditorium. Sam Galuppi welcomes everyone, and the show ends with the reappearance of the hero and heroine, their transfiguration into the Minotaur, and the appearance of the Three-Horned Enemy, who chases everyone away.

The B editing units ("mobile pieces") are intended to be performed intermittently throughout the fair grounds. There are twenty-five of these, some involving music, some not. Several involve previously written pieces, including *Hear Me Out*; *Felix's Girls*; and *Buskers*. As in the Odditorium events, we meet several of the *Patria* characters, including Arturo Schitzlip and H. Stowell Stools (from *Patria 1*), the inmates from *Patria 2*, and Mr. Daedalus from *Patria 5*.

The C editing units ("set pieces") are also out in the fair but are stationary. Many of the events involve the various games that participants can use to win tickets to the theaters, but there are also musical pieces, including the earlier compositions *La Testa d'Adriane* and *Wizard Oil and Indian Sagwa*.

D editing units are found in the Gallery of Heroes and Heroines, many from the *Patria* cycle, and E editing units are unattended display pieces found in various smaller buildings, including a recording of *Dream Passage*, an early study for *Patria 2*.

Beauty and the Beast is the restricted show in the Rose Theater (the F editing units); Dr. Ovid Klein from *Patria 1* and *2* tries to deal with the problems of two characters in the Blue Theater (G editing units); and two pieces from *Patria 5*, *The Crown of Ariadne* and *Theseus*, play in the Purple Theater (H editing units). In the University Theater (the I editing units) there are three events, also discussing various parts of the *Patria* myth (including a reference to Schafer's book *Dicamus et Labyrinthos*). The final set of editing units (J) are the carnival concessions and rides.

PATRIA 4: THE BLACK THEATRE OF HERMES TRISMEGISTOS

After Schafer had decided to expand the *Patria* cycle beyond its original three segments, he paired *Patria 3* and *4* together in his mind since after the failed attempt to revive the hero and heroine at the end of *The Greatest Show*, *The Black Theatre* attempts another revival through alchemy, and in particular a "chymical marriage" as described in the writings of medieval alchemists. The first draft of *Patria 4* was completed in 1982 and took its final form in 1988. Schafer describes the concept of alchemy as

> subjecting the base minerals to various processes of dissolution and coagulation by means of smeltings and burnings in the hope of producing precious metals such as gold and silver . . . the minerals were also viewed symbolically as aspects of the human personality so that the goal of alchemy, regarded philosophically, was nothing less than the attainment of spiritual purification and excellence.[25]

The text that served as the inspiration for *Patria 4* is from the *Tabula Smaragdina* of Hermes Trismegistos, a figure believed to have lived in ancient Egypt and whose grave was supposedly discovered by Alexander the Great. His writings first appear in Arab sources from the eighth century and were later translated into Latin under the title *Corpus Hermeticum*. Schafer uses the following text, along with other magical writings, as the basis of *Patria 4*.

> I come from far to speak the truth. That which is above is like that which is below, and that which is below is like that which is above, to accomplish the same miracle. The moon is the mother. The sun is the father. The wind carries it in its belly. Its nurse is the earth. It is the father of perfection throughout all the earth. Separate the earth from the fire and subtle from the gross, carefully and with great prudence. It rises from earth to heaven and comes down again to earth, and thus acquires the power of the realities below. In this way you will acquire the glory of the whole world, and all darkness will depart. The microcosmos is formed according to the laws of the macrocosmos. For this reason I am called Hermes Trismegistos, for I possess the wisdom of the whole world.[26]

Both Wolf and Ariadne appear in *Patria 4* and contribute to the conjunction of Sol and Luna, bearing witness to the chymical marriage, a symbol of their own future union. Schafer is very specific about the time and location of this production: it must begin at midnight and not be in a conventional theater but a dark space where an oppressive preparation area leads to a more open theater area. *The Black Theatre* is based on the *Patria* all-interval row, but over the course of the work it is transformed into a new row, as shown below. In addition to the written music, the instrumentalists are asked to improvise sounds associated with alchemical signs given as illustrations at the beginning of the score to inspire the improvisations.

Synopsis

Editing Unit 1: After the audience arrives in the preparation area, accompanied by the sounds of musicians playing the signs for the basic elements, the Master Alchemist appears. He tells the audience why they are here, and says that the eight members of the Alchemical Brotherhood will instruct them as they go. He then vanishes to prepare the furnace, and the brothers give the audience the four levels of instruction.

Editing Unit 2: The audience is led into the theater area by the Magister and the Brotherhood, all humming the tone of cosmic unity (B). They surround the "athanor" (a replication of an alchemist's furnace) in the center of the room. The candles are blown out and the Magister sings a magical invocation while the Brotherhood and the Cosmic Choir continue to hum then sing the tone. The light grows as variations of the all-interval row are played.

Editing Units 3–5: Three characters appear. The first is Hermes Trismegistos, who sings a short aria about the various elements and how he holds the secret to the whole world. Melusina then appears from within the athanor and sings an aria in Middle Egyptian. Hermes appears and shouts for Melusina to go back into the dark arteries of the earth until she is called. An old man who calls himself a king enters. The Alchemist asks him if he wishes to regain his crown then instructs him to enter the athanor, warning him that the process will be dreadful.

Editing Units 6–8: The Brothers bring forth the various metals for the ritual. When all are brought forward, the Magister says that something more is required, "Prima Materia." A pair of wolf eyes glow in the dark, and Wolf says that he has brought something that they require. The Brothers describe their impression of the Prima Materia and place it in the athanor.

Editing Unit 9: The athanor reveals Melusina, who sings another aria in Egyptian, proclaiming herself a sorceress. The aria she sings is the earlier piece *Arcana*.

Editing Units 10–15: The Magister lights a candle and speaks to the Brothers, telling an allegory about the rebirth of the king through his sister as the serpent Mercurius. He then instructs them to begin the "Simulacrum." Ariadne is brought forth to serve as sister to the king. She enters the athanor and begins to sing. Mercurius appears, showing three horns out of his brow, and describes himself. Hermes appears above, singing, describing the process and announcing that it is time for the child of silver to come forth. Ariadne reappears singing, dressed in white, with a silver crescent on her gown. While Ariadne recounts her memories (drawn from the story in *Patria Prologue*), Mercurius calls to her, asking to be released. The Magister counsels her on how best to deal with Mercurius, describing his attributes and character. Ariadne describes the scene from *Patria 2* where she met a man who gave her a stone. The Magus Philosophus extends the stone to her, which rises into the air and changes into a crown of eight stars.

Editing Units 16–18: The Magister speaks in praise of Luna, who after lying beside the sun for three days will rise again as the young bride of the chymical marriage. As the choir sings an introit, two figures appear, one a wolf, one a lion, who stalk each other. They each plunge a knife into each other and collapse. One of the Brothers comes and lifts up the lion's head, and it is revealed as the Magister. One of the Brothers assumes the role of the Magister and reads from the book, which says they must wait until the appointed time. The signs of the sun and moon move toward each other very slowly.

Editing Unit 19: The athanor begins to glow, and out of it emerge the king and queen, crowned as Sol and Luna. They embrace and then sing a duet in praise of and longing for each other. The Divine Child emerges from the athanor, advances toward the Brotherhood, and illuminates their candles. The child sings that he is the transformed Mercurius. Hermes appears above, saying that the ritual is now complete. The Brotherhood leads the audience out by candlelight as the orchestra and choir hum the tone of cosmic unity.

PATRIA 5: THE CROWN OF ARIADNE

Schafer traveled to Knossos in 1956, and the impact of that was long lasting, as the concept of the labyrinth and the story around it would underpin the whole *Patria* cycle, and the Cretan and Greek folk tunes he collected would find their way into *Patria 5*. He worked on *Patria 5* for almost two decades before the final revision was completed in 1990.

After our encounters with the myth of Theseus, Ariadne, the Minotaur, and the labyrinth in the first segments of the *Patria* cycle, the myth is told in a straightforward way in *Patria 5*. Schafer follows closely the traditional storyline of the myth but chooses to tell it as a dance drama, preferably on the shore of a calm, warm sea, because he wanted it to be sensed physically, proprioceptively, as if foaming out from inside the body rather than trickling down from the mind as a textbook memory. I wanted everyone to dance, to lift their feet and dance with rose-wreaths on their heads, to dance all day to cymbals and tambourines, sistra and krotala, until they sank exhausted on the seashore as quinqueremes arrived bringing gods and heroes to enact the ancient ritual before the sinking sun and into the torch-lit darkness of the summer night.[27]

In Schafer's drama each character is symbolic. Daedalus represents the civilized aspect of the myth, the rationalist who neither speaks nor dances. Ariadne is a dancer, as well as Theseus, who is an example of pure masculinity: all brawn, no brains. Minos and Pasiphae are actors, with Pasiphae representing a matricentric civilization that, already in decline, is destroyed by the arrival of Theseus, who flees with Ariadne, the heir, and burns the palace. The Minotaur is portrayed as an ambiguous figure of the unconscious, the shadow archetype as found in Jung. Schafer has the soothsayers refer to him both as the Minotaur and as Asterion (Star Creature), implying the divine spark within him as the son of the Moon Queen and half-brother to Ariadne. Minos, Pasiphae, and the chorus speak the most ancient Greek known. The soothsayers act as interpreters, speaking in the profane language of English.

The music of *Patria 5* is less closely tied to the all-interval row. Much of it uses music previously written or commissioned, including the two pillars of the piece: *The Crown of Ariadne* and *Theseus*. The various dances found in *The Crown of Ariadne* are dispersed throughout the drama, similar to how *Requiems for the Party Girl* is used in *Patria 2*. The influence of Greek and Cretan folk music is also evident.

Synopsis

Editing Unit 1: The soothsayer tells the creation story, where Woman was awakened and spoke the world into existence. He then tells of the worship of Gaia, and how it is becoming corrupted through Pasiphae, the embodiment of the goddess.

Editing Units 2–4: Ariadne awakens to the call of her handmaidens. A satyr appears, calling to her with his flute, but he is startled and rushes off. She dances before the handmaidens dress, perfume, and crown her with an eight-star diadem then lead her to the palace, singing to her as the future queen.

Editing Units 5–6: Minos and Pasiphae, surrounded by their court, process to the palace while the soothsayer comments to the audience on the sexual decadence of both the king and queen. Ariadne joins them at the palace, which is built as a huge sound sculpture.

Editing Units 7–10: The soothsayer charges the elders to tell the story of the rule of Pasiphae and Minos and how the double axe of the labyrinth protects the kingdom. Male dancers perform the Dance of the Double Axe, female dancers come forward to perform the Dance of the Sacred Cows. Minos dons the mask of a black bull, and he and Pasiphae dance the Hieros-Gamos, which supposedly serves as a fertility ritual but is too playful and superficial to be convincing.

Editing Units 11–12: Minos pretends to mount the queen then rushes off to exchange his mask for a Golden Pleasure Mask. He grabs a libation vessel of wine and moves toward the beach with the court following with gifts for the sea god. After the gifts are given, a majestic white bull rises to the surface of the water and glides toward the shore. It charges at the crowd as the spectators taunt him and dancers take hold of his horns and somersault over his back. The soothsayer laments that the sacred bull was meant for sacrifice, not games.

Editing Units 13–17: The bull has grown calm, and Pasiphae approaches it, speaking to it with desire. Minos argues with her that what she is considering is unspeakable and she rebukes him, mentioning Minos's own sexual exploits. He rushes off, taking the boys and men with him, while the women mock him. The priestesses enter, helping Pasiphae into a structure resembling a cow. The bull rushes forward then collapses over the cow. As the second part of the drama begins, Pasiphae, now pregnant, approaches the palace from the grove of Gaia, surrounded by the women of Crete.

Editing Units 18–19: Minos returns from the sea on his ship, piled high with riches. Seven prisoners, with Theseus at their head, are escorted in. Pasiphae sees Theseus and draws Ariadne forward to dance. Ariadne dances before Theseus, then they dance together, using music based on the earlier piece *Theseus*. As they dance, Pasiphae suddenly screams in labor.

Editing Units 20–22: Pasiphae dies in labor, and Minos comes forward wearing a tragic mask. The soothsayer laments the death of the moon goddess as mourners exit bearing the body of the queen. The soothsayer has a future vision in which he talks about the two aspects of the creature Asterion, the Star Prince, or the Minotaur, Avenger of Poseidon. He then warns of the danger of Theseus and says to release the Minotaur against him. Ariadne, Theseus, and the Minotaur dance together.

Editing Units 23–24: Minos returns and calls on Daedalus. He demands a thousand workmen to build a labyrinth, enclosing the Minotaur–Asterion at the center. The soothsayer tells Ariadne to watch and memorize the pattern of the building. Minos declares that the Minotaur must be fed with human blood, and Theseus is seized and shackled to the entrance of the labyrinth.

Editing Units 25–26: The night insects dance around Theseus, then a full moon rises (the music is the earlier composition *Epitaph for Moonlight*).

Editing Units 27–30: Ariadne teaches Theseus the movements of the dance that will lead him through the labyrinth. They both enter the labyrinth. Theseus and the Minotaur meet and fight, one of the figures falls while

Ariadne watches, then a bird flies up into the air. Two shadowy figures make their way out of the labyrinth, and one of the figures sets fire to the structure. The two figures leave Crete by boat as the fire spreads to the palace (the music is based on the earlier piece *Fire*), and the soothsayer calls for Ariadne to no avail. The fire dies down to show that the entire set has been turned to ashes as a figure moves to the shore where it calls to the departing boat and is answered by a voice from onboard the boat.

PATRIA 6: RA

Schafer describes *Patria 6* as a hierophany

> a religious drama, based on *The Litany of Re*, "The Book of the Adoration of Re in the West and the Adoration of the One-joined-together in the West (Osiris)," from the New Kingdom period (c. 1550–1070 BC), which invokes the sun-god by his seventy-five names and speaks of the role that the deceased plays in assisting and participating in the descent and reemergence of the solar deity at dawn.[28]

Ra passes the night traveling from west to east over the netherworld, a dangerous time for him, filled with encounters with his enemies. Schafer chose to present the text in the original Pharonic Egyptian, the language of the gods, supplementing it with passages from the *Amduat* and the *Book of the Dead*, and he uses the characters of the Hierophant (the high priest) and his assistants as interpreters for the audience, a group of no more than seventy-five that are initiates being conducted through a mystery ritual that will last from dusk until dawn. Schafer notes that

> these are magic texts, they do not describe or argue; they are certainly not logical. They are hard physical presences and when they are delivered properly they unite themselves with the things of which they speak and literally bring them into existence.[29]

In this *Patria* segment, Wolf becomes Ra and Ariadne is present in many ways but primarily in song, referencing the thread of song that draws Wolf through the cycle and in this segment leads Ra safely through the underworld. The character of Amente Nufe, who directs the soul after death, uses the all-interval row in her aria, the only appearance of the row in *Ra*.

Synopsis

Editing Unit 1: The initiates are robed and met by their three Hierodules (guides and interpreters), who give them individual places from which to observe the setting sun. In the distance a procession bearing the sarcophagus of the dead king is seen, and in the opposite direction a second procession is seen, with Ra in his hawk's head, accompanied by the Sun Barque. The seventy-five names of Ra are chanted.

Editing Unit 2: The sun has set, and the silhouette of the Sun Barque descends below the horizon. The Hierodules approach the initiates and speak to them individually, saying that if they would accompany Ra into the great caverns of the netherworld, they should have no fear but sincerity and a willingness to be initiated into the great mystery. They are met by members of the chorus, who tell of the trials that will await them and lead them to a portal where they are confronted by a masked doorkeeper who questions them to determine their fitness to participate in the ritual.

Editing Units 3–7: The initiates travel down a hallway to a gallery with inscriptions on the walls and the images of Ra and Osiris, accompanied by chanting. As the chanting ends the Hierophant enters then chants dramatically to the images of Ra and Osiris. The initiates are divided into two groups, each of which will learn to chant the names of three of the Egyptian gods, then are led to a terrace where they conjure the six gods. The chorus calls each god into place then calls Ra, who appears and processes into the underworld.

Editing Units 8–9: From behind the initiates the procession bearing the body of the dead king appears. The initiates follow the procession into the alcove, pausing before the Hierophant, who addresses the initiates, asking if they will join the king in his descent into the netherworld.

Editing Units 10–11: The initiates are led inside the temple to the Halls of Preparation, where they must remain silent. They are instructed in the proper way to breathe when they encounter Osiris, given tamarind to purify their mouth, and then instructed on how to recognize different sounds. The initiates are divided into three groups—one group is given some of the names of Ra to remember, one is given incense to inhale and recognize, one is instructed in how to assist in slaying the demon god Apophis. They are taught a chant in praise of Ra, given amulets to wear, and are baptized with balm oil. They then descend to the netherworld in near darkness.

Editing Units 12–14: The Hierophant appears in the guise of Anubis. He tells them to obey his instructions as they enter the corridors of the dead, where they see the seventy-five mummified forms of Ra named by Anubis as they pass. The initiates then enter a chamber where they see victims on the floor attacked by butchers who cut out their ears and put them in giant cauldrons. Ra's Sun Barque crosses safely, and the initiates follow in its wake. They then are given a short rest.

Editing Units 15–17: The god Seker appears and allows them to pass when given the secret names. The initiates pass into a room where the Children of Horus are preparing the body of a king through an extended and elaborate ritual. The king rises and marches off stiffly followed by his procession. The initiates are blindfolded and led on a rope walk, where they encounter various smells and sounds.

Editing Units 18–19: The initiates emerge outside, their blindfolds are removed, and they hear Apophis approaching. Ra arrives suddenly, the two gods battle, and the Hierodules gather the initiates to roar out the names of Apophis to help Ra defeat him. Apophis is defeated, dismembered, and burned. The initiates partake of a celebratory ritual feast of Middle Eastern cuisine in a festive and brightly lit tent.

Editing Unit 20: Hasroet, the goddess of the necropolis, is revealed, lying on a dias. She sings an aria and then presents the Nemes headdress to the king, and he departs triumphantly with his procession. Anubis appears and quickly leads the initiates away, saying that this is a dangerous place for the living.

Editing Units 21–23: Anubis allows the initiates to pause to prepare themselves to meet Osiris, reminding them of their ritual breathing. Anubis then approaches the gods who guard the portal and gains their permission to let the initiates inside. The initiates enter and see the sarcophagus of Osiris. As they sit and breathe the god slowly rises. He enters alone, chanting, bearing his heart in his hands. He kneels before Osiris, who approves his heart. The king exits rejoicing. The initiates are led to a place where they can lie down and rest while Thoth speaks words of comfort to them.

Editing Units 24–26: Incense is lit as Amente-Nufe ("Beautiful West") sings an aria in praise of the west. The dwarf god Bes appears, laughing and dancing before he speaks. He offers to guide the initiates past the Dark Messengers, and the initiates take hold of each other's hands and Bes's tail to safely pass.

Editing Units 27–29: Anubis appears, saying that the initiates have made it to the shore of Nun in the very depths of the netherworld. They must cross the ocean to be reborn as Ra is. The ocean's roar recedes as the initiates pass through, where they are embraced by Mehurt and passed to the Hierodules, who wash their faces and anoint them with perfume. They sit in a circle around Anubis, who speaks to them about the mysteries that they have witnessed and tells them they will now begin their ascent to the living world.

Editing Units 30–31: The Hierodules lead the initiates through a series of corridors where they experience different kinds of incense. The Hierophant appears before the initiates, telling them they are ready to enter the Hall of Judgement, where they will meet Thoth.

Editing Unit 32–34: The initiates kneel in front of the scales of Thoth as the king enters with his heart in his hand. He places it on a scale, where it is weighed against the feather of Maat and is balanced. Thoth inspects the scales and tells Osiris that the king's heart has been found true by trial. The gods murmur their approval. Isis and Nephythys rise and come forward, sing of the king's justification, and attach two cobras to his crown, leading him to

Osiris. Osiris proclaims that the king is now elevated to the status of a God, and he embraces him.

Editing Unit 35–36: "Divine Eyes"—The Sun Barque slowly arrives from the east. Ra descends and comes to the king, and escorts him to the Sun Barque, placing him in the prow. They salute the other gods as the Sun Barque slowly moves away. Osiris and the other gods turn away and depart into the netherworld, leaving only Thoth and the Hierodules with the initiates. Thoth addresses the initiates, telling them that the ceremony is over. The Hierodules step forward and remove Thoth's mask, revealing the Hierophant. He leads them outdoors, telling them that they must go, but he will remain to teach others.

Editing Unit 37: "The Becoming"—The initiates come back to the place where the ritual began. They hear a hymn in praise of Ra and see the Sun Barque high on the wall, ascending to the top of the tower, toward the sun.

PATRIA 7: ASTERION

Asterion in its initial concept is the most intense segment of *Patria* and the most individually experienced since the audience members go one by one through the labyrinth to experience what lies within. As the last to be realized, it includes characters and themes from every segment of the cycle, experienced in a similar format to *Patria 6*, with a linear journey as an initiation into hidden mysteries. Unlike the other segments of *Patria*, which can (even with their somewhat restricted locational needs) be performed in different locations, *Asterion* in its only realized form is tied to a specific location, a hillside on the Schafer property in Indian River. Constructed over multiple summers, *Asterion* was open for two days of performance in August of 2013. The synopsis included here is based on Schafer's original version, drafted in 2002 but not fully realized in the production.

Asterion serves as the middle high-point of the *Patria* cycle and the most thorough exploration of the third of the main Jungian archetypes, the "amoral catalyst," the dark subconscious represented in *Patria* as the Three-Horned Enemy and the Minotaur. *Patria 5* had already revealed Schafer's view of this third character as not simply an evil beast but also the divinely born son of Pasiphae and Poseidon and brother to Ariadne.

Synopsis

A lecture is given at a university on Cretan mythology exploring the ideas of the labyrinth, the Minotaur, Theseus, and the nature of heroism. The lecturer indicates that application forms for the journey from darkness to light have been left on the table. As the lecturer picks up his notes, there is suddenly darkness and a head appears with three small horns protruding from its brow.

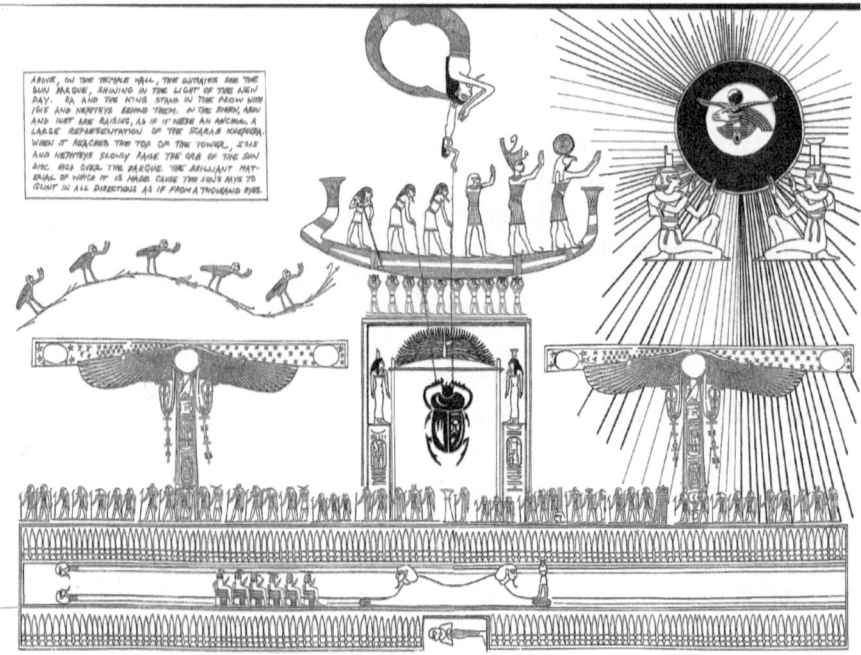

Figure 13.2. Closing Scene—*Patria 6: Ra*. R. Murray Schafer

It speaks to the gathered audience, saying that one of them is a phantom, and that "all your life you have feared facing me."[30] He speaks of the dual nature of light/darkness, Asterion and the Minotaur, then vanishes. Beyond general information, the application has several questions such as "What does fear (or courage, or pain) mean to me?" and "What am I prepared to sacrifice in my life?" Those whose applications have been accepted are informed. They meet at a designated place and are blindfolded and transported to the labyrinth, where each one enters alone. The structure of the labyrinth that the neophytes enter is laid out in eight series, with a finale. Each series is divided into different segments, with different titles depending on the series.

First Series: The Ennead of Encounters—This is the longest and most complex of the series. In addition to the encounters, the neophyte passes through several named passages, each with its own architecture and design. As the neophyte enters they encounter Anubis, who calls down the hallway, announcing that a neophyte is coming who will try to pass the forty-nine stages into the light. The first passage is covered with the Ectocretan tablets from *Dicamus et Labyrinthos*, which Thetis, present in the passage, translated. The next passage is through rising water until Phaedra, Ariadne's sister, calls the neophyte another way, dries their feet, and offers advice about the labyrinth. The neophyte follows a voice through a brick corridor, encountering a dark figure while a voice sings the opening of *Hymn to Night*. A woman's voice identifies itself as the shadowy side of the neophyte and offers the traveler a choice between two doors, one to nightmares, one to bliss. Both doors lead to a room with couches on which many figures from earlier *Patria* segments recline. A sign says to try the ambrosia since there is no way out. Underneath is scrawled a note signed by Icarus: "Press the side of the mirror to escape." After the neophyte presses the mirror, Icarus tells him to replace it and come down the corridor. They encounter a large set of wings, and Icarus tells of how he and his father will escape using them. In the next passage the neophyte hears more of *Hymn to Night*, then a man's voice as Theseus runs by. The final moments of *Hymn to Night* are heard as the neophyte passes through straight passages to a room with whirring machines and useless technology. There they encounter Daedalus, who talks about his great inventions, the climax of which is the labyrinth.

Second Series: The Ogdoad of Trials—This next series is meant to test the neophyte mentally and physically. The neophyte first meets an old man, who talks of how the Minotaur slowly kills those who enter and that there is no escape. To go on, the neophyte must crawl over the old man, who groans under the weight. The neophyte hears a noise like a stone being dragged and encounters the Hierophant, who comes up behind them in the darkness. He warns the neophyte that they are on a tower, above a terrible abyss. They creep forward then stop at the Hierophant's command. The Hierophant instructs the neophyte to kneel, then slashes a sword above their head three times. The neophyte rises and must raise their arms toward what they are told are deadly magnetic currents. The neophyte then turns toward the Hierophant, who is holding two goblets. He commands the neophyte to seize and drink one of the goblets after saying one is poison and one is elixir. The neophyte is locked into a small room for a long time, then a manhole on the floor opens to reveal a narrow hole. A voice commands the neophyte to crawl on their knees to meet the lizard Ophion. Once they encounter him they must whistle and clack like a beetle so that he will let them pass. The neophyte finally reaches a small room, where they are instructed to write down the seven most important things in their life. They then encounter statues, where they are instructed to burn the strips of paper, starting with the least precious of the seven things. They reach Balsides, who asks for the paper with the most precious thing on it and then burns it. He then reveals two curtains, one of which leads to the Heptad of Experiences or the Hexad of Perceptions.

Third Series: The Heptad of Experiences—The neophyte enters a grotto with mythical beings that occasionally move. In the grotto there is a crevice with a stone bench. If it is sat upon, whispering is heard from a small hole in the crevice—a fellow victim in the labyrinth. The Minotaur's voice is heard, then a red eye shines out of the crevice then disappears. The neophyte encounters a headless man in a shabby coat who gestures for him to go down a corridor. It leads past two enormous cloven hooves of a creature, through which the neophyte must pass while a recorded voice praises Baal. After that, lustful images of Melusina, Beast and Beauty, Osiris, and Pasiphae are flashed. At the end the neophyte meets Suchoth, who pulls them along to a room full of ladders that lead nowhere, except for the one exit. This leads to a room with two cups of tea, one labeled "The Water of Forgetfulness" and the other "The Water of Memory." There is also a book where the neophyte can record their experiences and impressions so far.

Fourth Series: The Hexad of Perceptions—These experiences are meant to create awareness of the various senses. The first educates the hands and feet by having the neophyte follow a rope, walking barefoot. The textures of and sensations from the rope and floor change as they neophyte moves forward. The second is a maze of mirrors where at times images are flashed. The third is a forest of brass and steel rods that sound like bells as the neophyte passes through. The fourth is a star-shaped room with eight points, each containing fragrant spices. In the background plays *String Quartet no. 3*. The fifth is a room with seven morsels of food, each with a contrasting accompanying liquid. Each set of pairs is a contrast and are used to cleanse the mouth. In the sixth the neophyte lies down in total darkness to experience the story of Theseus and Ariadne as a series of sensations. At the end a face appears above the neophyte, kisses the neophyte, and withdraws. Afterward Septhura appears, washes the neophyte's hands, and leads them to the next section.

Fifth Series: The Pentad of Contemplations—The first contemplation is a richly colored, slowly-spinning mandala, accompanied by a recording of *You Are Illuminated*. The second is a chamber where one can listen to *Okeanos*. The third is a circle of twelve jewel-stones laid out like a clock in a specific pattern. The neophyte is instructed to contemplate and handle each stone. The fourth contemplation is a garden bathed in moonlight filled with exotic plants, and out of the leaves come whispers. A single flower at the back of the garden moves slowly back and forth. The fifth is an incense clock that also plays monochords every minute. The text from *The Chaldean Inscription* is projected on the wall.

Sixth Series: The Tetrad of Arcana—The neophyte encounters Hermes Trismegistos, who looks like the Shadow encountered in the first series. Hermes speaks of the nature of the number 4 then leads the neophyte down four hallways. The first is lit green and has a fish symbol. Hermes then tells a fable about a traveler and a man, based on a story from the Koran. The second is lit red with a figure whose head is on a pendulum. Hermes speaks of the balance of Yin and Yang. The third is blue and has the wreckage of a boat in sand, and Hermes speaks of Theseus's boat, of what is real and what is replication. The fourth hallway is yellow, with an egg-shaped sculpture, and Hermes speaks of the self, quoting the *Isha-Upanishad*.

Seventh Series: The Trio of Deceptions—Hermes puts on the mask of Anubis and speaks of the labyrinth and how it might end before sending the neophyte along their way. The neophyte sees three horns suspended above and meets Daedalus, who tells of the reason for the three horns: they symbolize creation, destruction, and the hope that progress comes from this cycle. As the neophyte walks on, he hears Ariadne and Theseus discuss how to kill the Minotaur. They approach and each takes one of the neophyte's hands. They move forward and hear a roar, and the neophyte is pushed to the ground. He sees a raised sword, darkness, and hears the flapping of wings.

Eighth Series: The Duet of Divinities—A figure in white approaches. It is the same figure from the lecture hall, revealed as Asterion. He takes the neophyte's hand, leads him to the couch, and ritually prepares his body. He then takes a seat at the side of the couch.

Finale: O Nobly-born—Music plays and colors are projected on the ceiling while Asterion chants texts from the *Bardo Thodol*. Eventually the voice ceases, the colors grow fainter, and the music drifts to silence. The neophyte is now alone. A door is open revealing steps up to ground level, through which streams the light of a new day.

PATRIA 8: THE PALACE OF THE CINNABAR PHOENIX

After the intensity of *Asterion*, Schafer intended the next three segments of the *Patria* cycle to be simpler, set in a series of "fabulous worlds where everything resonates with the miraculous."[31] Schafer early on had a desire to send Wolf to the Orient to seek enlightenment, just as Schafer frequently had done himself, and he coupled this idea with a dream he had had of a multicolored castle rising out of a lake, originally calling it *The Floating Kingdom of Wei Lu*. Schafer continued to work on the concept and text for the piece, settling on the title *Cinnabar Phoenix*, which was also the name of the south-facing gate of the Great Luminous Palace at Ch'ang-an during the T'ang Dynasty, which ruled China A.D. 618–907. Schafer decided to set his original story in that era, and he completed the piece in 2000.

Faced with the task of representing one of the great eras of China, Schafer decided to present the grandeur of the T'ang Dynasty through puppet theater, which would represent the characters in the court. Their voices are represented by solo singers. The lake would become a pond, and the dragons would be real swimmers. The voice of the phoenix would be sung by a children's chorus, and a master of ceremonies would engage the audience in the action, rising each time Wei Lu speaks to respond, "The Son of Heaven has spok-

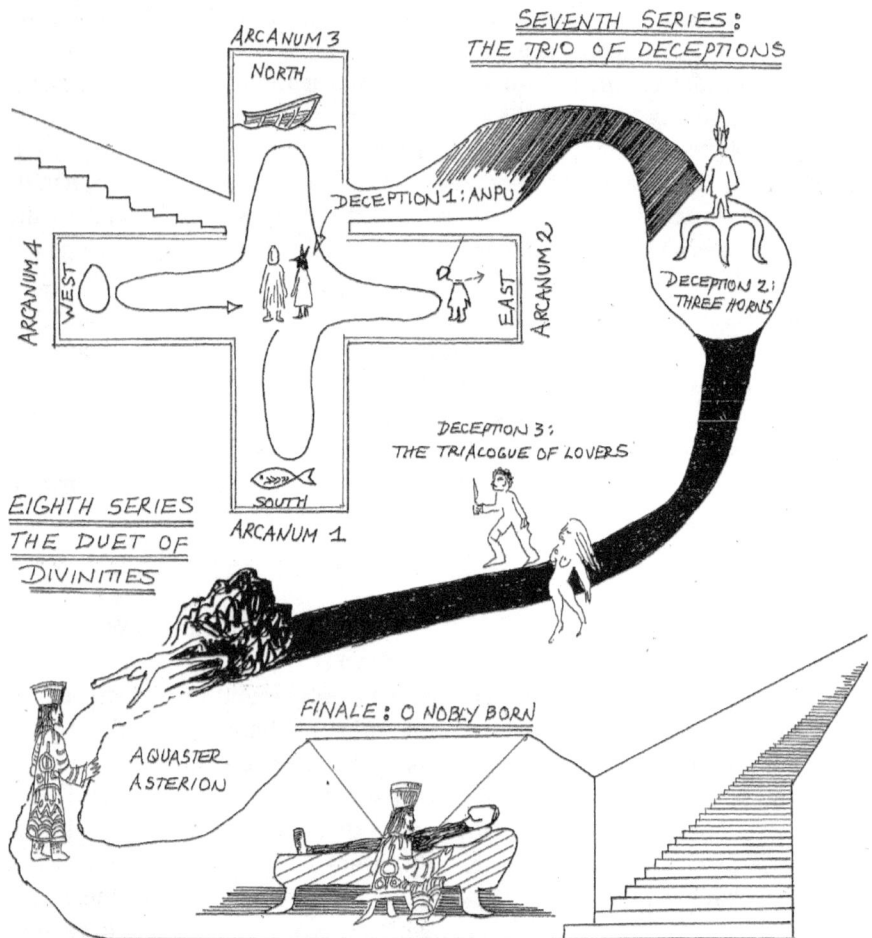

Figure 13.3. Sixth, Seventh, and Eighth Series and Finale—*Patria 7: Asterion*. R. Murray Schafer

en."[32] The audience would also participate in the Feast of Celestial Harmony, accompanied by music.

The background of the story is that long ago, the gods placed on earth a palace as a symbol of celestial harmony and sent down a phoenix to live in it. When the Warring States tried to capture the palace, it and the phoenix vanished and in their place appeared a lake of dragons. Each year Wei Lu, the emperor, comes to the site to mourn the events. The theme of *Palace* is the secret of balance as expressed in Confucian philosophy, reflected most clearly in the speeches of the emperor.

The musical language of *Patria 8*, like that of *Patria 5*, clearly is indebted to the culture that inspired the plot. Schafer includes traditional Chinese instruments in the orchestra, and much of the melodic and harmonic material is also indebted to Chinese traditional music.

Synopsis

Editing Unit 1: After an opening prelude by the orchestra and the Palatial Choir of Yin and Yang (solo soprano, alto, tenor, and bass voices—an SATB choir), Peter Chung King, the host and interpreter, formally welcomes the audience to the production.

Editing Units 2–3: Across the lake the pagoda-boat of the Emperor appears, which carries the Emperor, the Prime Minister, and other court dignitaries. As the boat approaches, the Palatial Choir of Yin and Yang sings a song of praise to the Emperor. The boat docks, and the Court of Heaven reappears on the puppet stage. Peter Chung King instructs the audience to rise and smile at the Emperor. The Prime Minister sings a greeting to the audience, saying the Emperor is pleased to welcome them to the feast. He then tells why the Emperor is here, and the two Guardians (solo tenor and bass) tell the story of the loss of the palace. Their story is commented upon by the Palatial Choir of Yin.

Editing Units 4–6: The Emperor speaks, his words interpreted by the Court Censor, sometimes to the displeasure of the Emperor, who debates with him. The Palatial Choir, Peter Chung King, and the audience respond, "The Son of Heaven has spoken!" The Emperor's son, Wei Li, speaks to the Prime Minister, singing in falsetto, asking him if he has procured a woman for him. The Prime Minister responds that tonight it will be Tuku, the Turquoise Courtesan. She enters and prepares to sing, as the Emperor and the Court Censor debate where music comes from. Tuku enters, bows in the direction of the Emperor. She goes to Wei Li and sings a coloratura aria then dances for him. They disappear into the pavilion as last night's courtesan, Hsi-Shi, exits from the other side. She tells of her meeting with Wei Li and how she has now been cast off. The Prime Minister gives her a piece of jade, and she takes her place among the cast off women, who sing in the Palatial Choir of Yin. The Prime Minister laments how Wei Li is bankrupting the palace with his ways.

Editing Units 7–8: The Philosophers of the Right and Left debate, one lavishly clothed, one naked, according to their philosophical bent, both accompanied by trashy music. One defends Yin, the other Yang. Toward the end they begin to fight, and Peter Chung King interrupts, bemoaning how the visitors are getting a poor impression of what this historical era in China was really like. The Emperor suggests to the philosophers that both music and the movements of T'ai Chi are ways to achieve balance. T'ai Chi performers appear across the lake accompanied first by a live string quartet then a recorded quartet, which plays *String Quartet no. 6* in its entirety while the action continues.

Editing Units 9–10: The Alchemist enters with his daughter and intimates that he has discovered gold. The Prime Minister asks him directly, and when the Alchemist is insolent, they set up a device to pull his ears. Wei Li appears and mocks the Alchemist's daughter for her face, burned in one of her father's experiments. The Emperor appears to see if the Alchemist has made a ring to balance the world, and the Prime Minister offers the daughter enough money to make them comfortable if it is true. The Alchemist agrees, and the ring appears in the air. Wei Lu tries to the use the ring to dry up the Lake of Dragons and restore the palace. When it does not work, the Alchemist says that it also needs its mate, the ring of silver, to accomplish the task. Four dragons appear, mocking the Emperor, and he shakes impotently while archers shoot flaming arrows at the dragons. Eventually the dragons are silent, and the lake grows once again dark.

Editing Units 11–13: The Emperor and Court Censor are alone by the lake, discussing the difficulties of ruling and how to live a life of balance and peace. They see a blue flickering light and hear singing as the Blue Man arrives. As the court gathers to see him, he tells of his journey to the court of T'ang, and how before that he was led by a woman to a cave where he found a silver ring. The ring then drew him forward, leading him on his journey. The Alchemist's daughter confesses that she was the woman, and she tells her story, drawing in much of the mythology of the *Patria* cycle as she tells of her resolve to separate the gold and silver rings. The Emperor gives her the silver ring, and as she approaches the ring the scales fall from her face, revealing her beauty.

Editing Unit 14: "Feast of Celestial Harmony"—The Royal Astronomer announces a fortuitous aligning of the stars, and a feast is declared in which both the performers and audience participate.

Editing Unit 15: As the feast finishes, Wei Lu and the court turn toward the lake. The Palatial Choir is joined by the Choir of the Celestial Numina (two soprano and two alto sections, an SSAA choir) as a pale light is seen from the bottom of the lake. The palace rises, and the phoenix is seen. The Blue Man expresses a desire to return home and tell his own land of the balance of Yin and Yang. Wei Li, singing in his true voice, asks his father if he can take the Alchemist's daughter as his wife. There is no answer, as the Emperor has turned to stone. The water birds come to gather his soul, taking it to the palace.

PATRIA 9: THE ENCHANTED FOREST

The Enchanted Forest, sketched out in 1993, is among the simplest and most tuneful of the *Patria* cycle, with only tangential references to the all-interval row. Similar to *The Princess of the Stars*, the music was intended to work in the natural surroundings in which it is placed, the innovation of the piece not being the musical material but the setting. *The Enchanted Forest* is a logical extension of Schafer's continued environmental advocacy, and Schafer notes, "Its ideal is that the human beings participating in it as performers or audience may discover bonds with the natural environment they had not sensed before or had forgotten."[33] It is presented as an ecological fairy tale, teaching the moral wisdom that contradicts the "arrogance that humans are God's supreme invention. It substitutes the notion that everything is equal, interdependent and in a constant state of transformation."[34] This concept of transformation will be even more present in *Patria 10* and *Patria Epilogue*.

The setting is a forest that is adjacent to a meadow or field and is based on the landscape Schafer saw every day on looking out of the window of his study in Indian River. The musicians and artists are a mix of professionals and amateurs, adults and children. Many of the adult performers in the original production were from the Wolf Project and therefore were familiar with the themes presented in the work. It is the children singers and actors who are at the center of the production. They interact with the audience, who accompany the children on their quest and learn a simple song and other cues to participate in the action.

Synopsis

Editing Units 1–3: The piece begins in a large meadow at sunset outside a forest. Hidden instrumentalists play various birdsongs as Earth Mother comes toward the audience and the sun descends behind the trees. She speaks as the birds grow quiet, telling of how when we sleep we are transported to a different place. A group of children then run up to her, telling how they have lost their friend Ariane. She instructs them to call Ariane's name, and Ariane responds from deep in the forest. Earth Mother calls the Flower Spirits to guide the children to Marsh Hawk, who will know where Ariane is, and she asks the audience to accompany the children on their quest.

Editing Units 4–6: The children walk through the forest singing, reaching another smaller meadow, where they find the White Stag wounded, running around in circles, falling and rising. He sings a song of lament over his death. The Spirits of the Still Earth enter and cover the White Stag with branches. They tell the children to go back, but the children insist they must go on.

Editing Units 7–8: The children find the Marsh Hawk, who confesses to carrying off Ariane on the order of Murdeth the Wizard. He then tells how she escaped his grasp and hid in a birch tree, and he tells the children to give up their quest. As the children turn to go, they discover that their guides, the Flower Spirits, have vanished. They sing a short song to give themselves courage and teach it to the audience before continuing on their way.

Editing Units 9–10: After an encounter with the Tree Screamers—menacing, black, bird-like creatures that appear suddenly—the children encounter Stump, a tree stump out of which a head is growing. He gives them a branch that will lead them to Murdeth the Wizard.

Editing Units 11–12: Creatures called Sleepers appear on either side of the path and say that they have been employed by Murdeth to spy out trespassers. They tell the children to go forward and that Murdeth has been notified that they are coming. The children arrive in front of Murdeth, who is surrounded by drummers. He says that he knows why they have come, and when they question him, he has his two chained hawks, Anvir and Emor, answer them. He then calls upon Mimir, Eye of Night, who tells the children that Ariane is alive and well. The children call to her, and she answers. Murdeth orders the children to leave the forest, and they hear Fenris the wolf howl as they flee.

Editing Units 13–14: The children continue on their journey, coming to a tiny hut, before which sits the old woman Hatempka. After telling the children of Murdeth's plan to use Ariane to draw out Fenris then shoot him with the thunderstone arrow, she agrees to help the children, and she goes into the hut to gather her medicine bundle. They set out to find Shapeshifter, who has the power to stop Murdeth. They arrive at the home of Shapeshifter, and the children sing to bring her out. She appears in the form of a caterpillar and agrees to help the children. She instructs them to roar like the thunder and howl like the wind when the right time comes, gives them all a jewel-stone, then reappears in the form of a butterfly to lead the way to Ariane.

Editing Units 15–16: The party reaches the center of the forest, where they see a small birch tree illuminated with silver lights. Fenris the wolf appears at the edge of the clearing singing a war song. He approaches the birch tree, embraces it, then lies down underneath it. Mimir appears, telling Murdeth that Fenris sleeps. Murdeth loads the thunderstone arrow into his bow, but Shapeshifter flies toward him and swoops about him as the children roar and howl to send the arrow off of its course. Fenris runs off into the forest.

Editing Units 17–18: Shapeshifter tells the children there is no one to harm them now and says that Ariane will stay in the forest as a birch tree to protect it, and will meet Fenris again. The White Stag appears reborn and leads the children back to the meadow where the story began, and where Earth Mother is standing. Ariane and the Earth Mother sing a duet accompanied by hidden instruments and singers as the audience is led out of the forest.

PATRIA 10: THE SPIRIT GARDEN

The original concept of *Patria 10*, like *Patria 8*, came to Schafer in a dream, where he imagined a ritual in which a garden is prepared and planted, with the workers dressed in costume and chanting as they work. Schafer had been looking for a ritual that he could create that would match the tea and incense ceremony he experienced during his travels in Japan. He thought again of his dream while planting his garden in the spring of 1991 and began to further sketch out ideas over the next few years, often in association with the planting of his own garden in Indian River, completing the "Spring" section of the work in 1996 and the "Harvest" section in 1997. Schafer describes the final piece as

> propaganda for nature by putting the audience back into a natural setting, a garden, which they must prepare, plant, care for and harvest over a season, encouraged by two rituals; the first during the planting season, and the second after the harvest.[35]

The stage for the piece is an actual garden, laid out in a specific design. The garden is prepared for planting before the "Spring" section by gardeners, who will also tend the garden after it is planted, then harvest it in preparation for the "Harvest" section in the fall.

The musical language for *The Spirit Garden* parallels that of *The Enchanted Forest* since it is also intended for performance by a combination of adults and children, professionals and amateurs. It requires minimal forces and uses a simplified melodic and harmonic language easily learned by children and adult amateurs.

Synopsis

Part 1: Spring

Editing Units 1–2: The audience gathers at a place close to the garden where they meet the Hierophant, dressed in a yellow robe. He sings an invocation to the gods then tells the crowd that today they will plant the Spirit Garden. The King arrives to a fanfare, gives his blessing to the endeavor, and promises them a banquet if the garden prospers.

Editing Units 3–4: The Hierophant leads everyone to the Tree of Life while the Seed Dancers dance. There they see the Corn Mothers, huddled before the tree, chanting mournfully about giving their seeds for this year's harvest. The Mistress of Planting leads the procession to the garden.

Editing Units 5–7: The Mistress of the Planting goes to the center of the garden while the Hierophant and the King take up places outside. She addresses the tilled earth and then calls the Spring Child, but the King says the child will not come until the Hierophant invokes the sun. He does so with the help of the choir, then announces that the sun has warmed the land and it is ready for raking. The audience then rakes the soil, accompanied by singing.

Editing Units 8–9: Baloom, an enormous puppet on stilts, threatens to squash the raked garden but the gardeners manage to frighten him away with their rakes. Doktor Humus then emerges from the direction of the compost pile and talks about various types of fertilizer until the Mistress of the Planting shoos him away so they can welcome the Spring Child.

Editing Units 10–14: The Spring Children begin to sing, then the Spring Child steps forward to sing, speaking of the gifts his father has given him. After the Spring Bringers dance a ritualistic dance, the Seed Groups step forward, present themselves, and plant the seeds, after which a song is sung. The Spring Child returns with the Corn Mothers to sing a song, then the Mistress of the Planting calls the Thunder Men, who dance to bring the rain. After the dance is over, water is sprinkled over the garden.

Editing Units 15–17: "The Birds"—Birds arrive dancing and singing and begin to peck at the seeds in the garden. The Mistress of the Garden calls for devices to scare away the birds to be placed in the garden, and various scarecrows are paraded in. Two of the scarecrows engage in conversation. The King thanks them for keeping the garden safe, and finally the Mistress of the Planting charges the gardeners to keep the garden while the Hierophant calls upon the gods to bless their endeavors.

Part Two: Harvest

Editing Units 1–4: Everyone processes to the now-harvested garden, led by the Master of the Fires and the Fire Keepers, lighting the path with torches. The Hierophant is present to lead the chorus. They pass trombones that play the *Patria* all-interval row, the only time it appears in this segment. The Fire Keepers mark out the eight points of the garden while the Hierophant chants to encourage them. He then sings a lamentation for Mother Earth, and the Mistress of the Planting speaks of how Mother Earth fed the garden through the summer.

Editing Units 5–8: The Master of the Fires approaches the King while the Fire Keepers line up behind him and ask for permission to start the ritual fire, including the birch log at the center, which is "smeared with wolf blood." The King recounts his experience in *Patria 4*, when he was himself renewed through fire, and gives permission. As the Fire Keepers ignite the fire, the Corn Mothers rush forward to tear the Green Doll of the Spring from the womb of the Corn Goddess. The Hierophant and the Corn Mothers sing in praise of the fire and the ash. The Fire Keepers leap through the flames as the audience beats sticks, after which effigies of devils and evil spirits (representing the sins of the past year) are brought forth and thrown into the fire. The audience and performers dance around the fire.

Editing Unit 9: "Winter"—The dancing is interrupted by the arrival of Winter, accompanied by the Four Winds and the Poorlings, who carry tin cups that they rattle. The Four Winds go to the four corners of the garden, where they throw clods of earth into the fire at the command of Winter, while the Poorlings go through the audience asking for money. The Hierophant acknowledges Winter's authority, and the Mistress of the Planting talks of how next year's seed will sleep until the spring planting. The King announces that all will retreat indoors to banquet on the produce gathered from the garden.

PATRIA EPILOGUE: AND WOLF SHALL INHERIT THE MOON

In the written description of *Patria Epilogue*, Schafer begins by saying,

> In the beginning humans and animals were the same, for humans were also animals. They believed they were descended from the gods, who lived in the heavens as planets and stars. They shared the world together and all spoke the same language. The symbol of their harmony was the Great Wheel of Life which contained all creatures as well as trees, plants and stones in a harmonious cycle. But then humans began to develop the idea that they had ascended from the animals, were therefore their superiors, and began to invent another language which the animals could not understand in order to deceive them. They also took all the best land for themselves, building fences around it and killing all intruders. The animals met together in council to discuss the situation. Each spoke in turn but the last words were given to Wolf and Bear who were the strongest of all the animals and who loved free space the most. Wolf was for declaring war on man but Bear counseled restraint and arbitration. After a full discussion the animals decided to accept Bear's advice. Wolf left the meeting angrily, swearing that henceforth he would live alone in the deepest part of the forest. Each night he could be heard howling and his howls sent shudders of fear through all the animals as well as humans.

Schafer then goes on to describe the wanderings of Wolf and Ariadne through the *Patria* cycle and their unsuccessful attempts to reconcile with each other. He finishes by noting,

> The animals, however, have decided to attempt to restore harmony by a different strategy. They will take some humans into the forest, teach them the ancient myths and incorporate them into a ritual which will bring Wolf and the Princess together at last. The energy of the entire week and the elaborate ceremony of the final day are all directed towards uniting Wolf and the Princess. If this succeeds the great turning point, awaited for centuries, will be

passed, a spirit of sacredness will again possess the earth and gods will illuminate the heavens.[36]

What would become *Patria Epilogue* began with a call in the *Patriotic News Chronicle*, a newspaper published as part of *Patria 3*, to participate in a "free workshop celebrating a new adventure in communal art 'which will be conducted at a remote location.'"[37] Five people replied to that call, and the interested parties held a meeting at Indian River to begin work on a scenario that Schafer was calling *And Wolf Shall Inherit the Moon*, the segment of *Patria* where everything would be made whole and the wanderings of Wolf and Ariadne would end. Sixteen people participated in the initial five-day campout in 1990, and in 1991 they were able to find a permanent home at the Haliburton Forest and Wild Life Reserve. They were then able to develop permanent structures, including a campsite, trails, and encounter sites.

Patria Epilogue is a private event where the performers are also the audience. The songs sung and the stories told are created or borrowed from other sources by the clan members, and some are written by Schafer, but all are tied to the theme of the project itself. The material, both vocal and instrumental, is intended for outdoor performance and reflects that purpose. It is often influenced by Native American music and approaches ritual tone magic, where it is believed that by singing one can influence the natural world.

On the first day of the ritual, the participants are divided into eight clans, each given the name of an animal, and are led to their campsite somewhere in the forest. For the next four days all of the clans are engaged in a prescribed series of activities to prepare themselves for the final ritual, including drumming and creating instruments, learning specific songs and dances, and making special masks. Each night around the campfire, storytellers in each clan narrate legends concerning Wolf's journeys and the origin and history of their clan. During the week each clan will also make several excursions through the forest to encounter sites where they will meet various characters from the *Patria* cycle (including characters unique to the epilogue) to learn about them and how they fit into the drama. Each of the clans is responsible for one of these events, which include dance dramas, nature walks, healing and sweat lodge rituals, and both individual and group pilgrimages. On the sixth day all masks are completed and the clan chants and dances are rehearsed in preparation for the final day.

On the final day the clans join together at the Great Wheel of Life (theoretically near the lake where *Patria* began) and perform a ritual to unite Wolf and the Star Princess. After ceremonial greetings and opening rituals, a shot is heard in the forest, and the Wounded Hunter is brought into the camp. He relates to the clans his encounter in the forest with Wolf and how he accidentally shot himself while hunting, after which he faints from exhaustion and loss of blood. Suddenly there is an explosion in the fire and out steps Shapeshifter, who is a representation of the Three-Horned enemy first encountered in *Patria Prologue*. Through various rituals, Shapeshifter transforms the Wounded Hunter into the White Stag, leads him to the Great Wheel of Life, and tethers him to a post near the center of the wheel as bait to attract Wolf. Hatempka, first encountered in *The Enchanted Forest*, appears out of the forest and instructs the clans to prepare a Temple of Flowers for Ariadne, who emerges from the forest. Ariadne is transformed by Hatempka into the Princess of the Stars and is then led into the Temple of Flowers. Wolf appears out of the forest, recounts his journeys, and then charges at the White Stag. When Wolf sees the princess emerge from the temple, Wolf falls back amazed. He and the Star Princess dance as Shapeshifter sprinkles blood from the White Stag over Hatempka, who is reborn as a young girl. She then opens her medicine bundle and takes the soul of Shalana (the former chief of the human clan) and gives it to Shapeshifter, who places it on the White Stag to transform him into Shalana. The Sun God arrives to announce that the Princess's and Wolf's wanderings are finally over. She will return to the stars, and Wolf will become the moon. During the day they will return to earth "as instinct (Wolf) and love (the Princess) to guide the creatures of earth."[38] Wolf and the Star Princess depart by canoe with the Sun God.

Part IV

The Compositions

Chapter Fourteen

Early and Transitional Compositions

FIRST STEPS

Schafer did write some shorter pieces during his high school years. Most of these exist only in manuscript form, and the composer has made no attempt to publish them even though some of them have been performed. These pieces include a choral piece *If Ye Love Me* from 1950, an early song titled "Sea Shanty" from 1951, and two pieces from 1953—*Nocturne* for piano dedicated to Phyllis and *Festival Te Deum in D* dedicated to John Hodgins, music director at Grace Church on-the-Hill.

During his relatively brief time at the University of Toronto, Schafer had several ideas for compositions, but many of these early works have not survived. He was able to produce the first pieces that he has let stand in his canon of compositions, many of which were not published until over a decade after their creation. By his own admission all of these pieces are musically conservative, even reactionary, showing no influence of the serialism or atonality that his teacher John Weinzweig introduced to him. They reflect his models at the time—the neoclassical pieces of Stravinsky, the compositions of the French group Les Six, and the work of Jean Cocteau.[1] Schafer had discovered Cocteau's 1918 pamphlet *Le Coq et l'Arlequin*, written in support of Les Six's musical aesthetic, and in another pamphlet Cocteau said, "Musical bread is what we want." Schafer attempted to model this simplicity in his early works.[2]

Polytonality for piano solo, written in 1952, is the earliest composition that Schafer has allowed to be published. The composer describes it as a "little exercise in three keys,"[3] and in the manuscript (not the published score), it is described as a didactic piece. The composition is structured over a one-measure ostinato that outlines, in G major, the tonic and supertonic triads. This ostinato appears in 48 of the 54 measures of this simple yet effective composition, only breaking the pattern to play free-relationship triads in measures 37 and 39 and to outline two measures of quartal arpeggios in measures 51 and 52 before a return to the G-major tonic triad in the last two measures of the piece. Over this ostinato the composer places simple melodies in G major, D major, and B-flat major, often layering two of these melodies simultaneously. In the composer's words, it is "an obvious silhouette of Poulenc,"[4] but this miniature shows a fine level of craftsmanship on the part of the composer.

A Music Lesson for voice and piano followed in 1953, written for and performed by Phyllis Mailing with Murray accompanying her at the piano. In this composition we find combined with Cocteau's maxims Stravinsky's thoughts on music as a non-emotional medium. The text of the piece, an explanation and defense of the mysteries of polytonality, is by the composer:

> Polytonality is the simultaneous combination of two or more tonalities.
> Do not condemn it, try to understand it
> Listen to the false relations
> Listen to the tone-colour in these chords:
> It's not exactly dissonant; in fact it's rather pleasing.
> Try to visualize these melodies horizontally in terms of counterpoint
> Instead of vertically in terms of harmony
> Since a thousand years ago we changed from homophony to polyphony
> I see no reason why now we should not change from homotonality to polytonality.

A Music Lesson is almost as brief as *Polytonality* and uses many of the same musical devices. The piano's introduction is a series of superimposed arpeggios a major second apart (D major/E major, D major/C major, etc.). There is more variety in the piano part and greater attempts at development, although Schafer's counterpoint is quite rudimentary. There is much more flexibility in the rhythm and tempo, with one passage superimposing one meter in the voice over another in the piano. The interest in the piece lies in the vocal writing and the original text.

The year 1954 was Schafer's most productive compositional year as a student. In addition to *Concerto for Harpsichord and Eight Wind Instruments*, he also produced *Suite for Clarinet, Cello and Piano* (later renamed *Trio for Clarinet, Cello and Piano*) and the first of the three pieces that would become *Three Contemporaries*.

Schafer initially considered the trio worthy of performance, and it appeared on a 1958 program of music by Schafer and fellow young composers Milton Barnes and Morris Eisenstadt, which also included *Three Contemporaries*. In his review of this program for the *Canadian Music Journal* (the first published review of Schafer's music), John Beckwith was cool toward the trio, which perhaps led to the composer withdrawing it from public use. The composer kept the original score and parts and decided to return to it and publish it in 2016. It is in four movements, where the outer two movements use all three instruments, the second movement clarinet and piano, and the third movement cello and piano. The first movement, marked in the score as *Allegro* but changed in the premiere program to *Moto Perpetuo*, is modeled on the more effervescent flourishes of Les Six but is less successfully executed, with fewer instances of the harmonic color that adds charm to the shorter pieces discussed earlier. The second movement, marked *Allegretto* in the score (*Lyric* in the premiere program) has greater harmonic interest, with often superimposed keys between the clarinet and piano and more effective dialogue between the two instruments. Movement three, marked "Very slowly and deliberately" in the score ("Elegy" in the program) begins with the most interesting passage to this point in the composition, an evocative introduction for solo cello before it is joined by the piano. The fourth movement, marked "Allegro" ("Briskly" in the program), is the first to be written in compound meter, a dance-like movement that has many effective passages (most notably the pianissimo ending), but also many passages of scalar writing that are less inspiring. In the trio we clearly see Schafer coming to grasp with larger forms and continuing to develop the harmonic language he internalized from Les Six.

The first of the three sketches that would become *Three Contemporaries* was originally "Benjamin Butter." The song sets the following dry biographical information about the famous British composer in a neoclassical style:

> Benjamin Britten is a most distinguished composer. Born in nineteen thirteen in Lowestoft he received a scholarship in composition at the Royal College of Music. Among his many works are the operas Peter Grimes and Albert Herring. Benjamin Britten is a most distinguished composer.

Despite the satirical bent of the short, twenty-five-measure character sketch, it shows the young composer's knowledge of Britten's music, which he parodies throughout the work and on two occasions deftly quotes. In this and in the other two later sketches that make up the set, Schafer shows his emerging ability to catch the listener's attention through novel approaches to both text and music.

The most significant work to come from Schafer's study with Weinzweig was *Concerto for Harpsichord and Eight Wind Instruments*. Schafer wrote this extended composition with his harpsichord teacher Greta Kraus in mind and hoped that she would play it, but her love was Baroque music, not contemporary music, and she graciously declined to give the premiere performance. From his studies of Quantz and C. P. E. Bach, Schafer learned much about embellishments and rhythm and incorporated these into the writing for harpsichord, which, although in a twentieth-century harmonic language, is effective and surprisingly idiomatic.[5] Winds were chosen to accompany the concerto because of their incisive attack and clarity, and generally the young composer uses the winds effectively, although he does not explore the full potential range of the ensemble, particularly the bassoons. It was Schafer's first piece to receive multiple performances, due in part to the support of Weinzweig.[6]

Schafer describes the piece as follows:

> My aim was to compose a two-dimensional study. Depth was not so much a concern as surface etching. I had developed an enthusiasm for the early etchings of Paul Klee at the time, and dedicated the second movement to his memory.[7]

Along with the obvious influence of Les Six and the neoclassicism of Stravinsky, this piece also clearly models itself on de Falla's *Concerto for Harpsichord and Five Instruments*, with borrowings from Poulenc's harpsichord concerto. Like the de Falla concerto, it is in three movements, with the first movement in sonata form with toccata characteristics, the second procession-like, and the third a dance-like finale. The concerto is a culmination of Schafer's student compositions, and it is still a student composition in many ways. Looking back at the piece, the composer says,

> The concerto was my first attempt to write a long piece and, of course, suffers from the same deficiencies as countless other attempts by young composers. The principal problem in extending music into larger forms is in the bridging of ideas. This is particularly conspicuous in the first movement, where the toccata is interrupted without warning by the march and then the chorale, neither of which bear relationship to the opening material and merely detract from the momentum of the movement. Some years after it was written I abbreviated the first movement, which was too long, though the faults I mentioned are still evident.[8]

It is true that in the piece Schafer repeats and juxtaposes ideas rather than developing them. The first movement very loosely follows the outline of sonata form, but to the ear it resembles more a rondo form, using the techniques and character of a toccata. The first thematic material certainly resembles toccata techniques, particularly in the harpsichord part, and the two main contrasting sections are a march and a chorale that becomes the thematic basis of the second movement. The second movement is marked "Zur Erinnerung an Paul Klee." The composer had no specific work by Klee in mind, but the loose variation structure creates a canvas reflecting Klee's "rather austere lyricism, represented by bare, sustained lines in the winds, and his angry streak of sarcasm, figured mainly in the highly ornamented harpsichord writing."[9] The structure of this second movement can be divided into an opening statement of the chorale theme, more fleshed out than in its appearance in the first movement; seven variations (each with variations within itself); and a concluding coda. Schafer manages to add a wide variety of textures and character within this slow movement, and he uses the wind ensemble more imaginatively than in the first movement.

In the composer's own words, the third movement "is bright and transparent, a sort of Mediterranean Baroque, in which snatches of Scarlatti sonatas are woven into a lively polytonal and polyrhythmic counterpoint."[10] It is the shortest and in many ways the most effective movement of the concerto. It also falls roughly into sonata form, with two main themes, and outlines of an exposition and development, with truncated recapitulation and an extended coda that almost takes on the character of another development section, recalling material from the first development. This false second development does not lead back to another recapitulation but ultimately serves as a coda.

FIRST INDEPENDENT EFFORTS—VIENNA AND TORONTO

During Schafer's first sojourn in Europe and subsequent brief return to Canada, he continued to hone his compositional craft. Two distinct streams can be seen in his compositions from this time. The first is the continued polishing of the musical language he had adapted from Les Six and Stravinsky, as reflected in *Sonatina*; *Partita for Twelve Instruments*; *Petit Divertissement Angevin*; and *Three Ideograms*. The second stream shows an expansion of his musical language and the influence of the German composers Mahler, Schoenberg, and Weil. *Minnelieder* and *Kinderlieder* clearly show this influence, and in *In Memoriam Alberto Guerrero* we see an effort to incorporate on a very basic level more avant-garde techniques. The most forward looking during this time is the withdrawn *Sonata da camera*.

The ultimately withdrawn *Partita for Twelve Instruments* (fl, ob, cl, sax, hn, bsn, strings, continuo) was begun in 1955 while Schafer was still in Toronto and was intended as a 1955 Christmas present for Phyllis. It ended up being a belated Christmas present as Schafer did not complete the piece until July of 1956, when he was already living in Vienna. It is in six movements (Sinfonia, Lyric, Pastoral, Gavotte, Passacaglia, and Finale) and is clearly in the same style as Schafer's other polytonal music of this time.

Murray considered his *Minnelieder* (original version) for mezzo-soprano and wind quintet his first truly finished composition, and part of the success of this music might be attributed to his love of the beauty and simplicity of the texts he chose to set.[11] The composer says in his program notes, "This cycle of thirteen songs was written in 1956 while I was in Vienna. I was trying hard to learn German, mostly by reading novels and poetry, and this led me back to the Minnesinger (German minstrels) of the eleventh, twelfth and thirteenth centuries."[12] Schafer's quest for simplicity in his writing is

Figure 14.1. First Movement—*Concerto for Harpsichord*. R. Murray Schafer

reflected most clearly in the writing for the woodwind quintet, which is much more effective and transparent than in the earlier *Concerto*. Many commentators have remarked the apparent influence of Mahler in this set of thirteen songs, which Schafer acknowledges as a possibility, given the nature of some of the texts and his sense of isolation during his first year in Vienna.[13] This composition, along with *Three Contemporaries* and the later *Kinderlieder*, were written with Phyllis Mailing's voice in mind, and the highlight of the pieces is the vocal writing, which already shows Schafer's affinity for and ability to write for the voice. The melodic development in these miniatures far outstrips that of *A Music Lesson* and *Three Contemporaries* and has a very different approach to the motivic repetition and fragmentation found in *Concerto*.

Schafer for the most part sets the entirety of the poems he has selected, some of which are quite brief. Stylistic consistency is the hallmark of the music; all movements are through-composed, in either sectional, binary, or ternary forms. The texture is predominantly homophonic, and ostinato patterns are often used, following the example of *A Music Lesson* and *Polytonality*. Although they are firmly tonal, with modal inflections and the occasional bitonal or bimodal passages, this set does mark Schafer's first venture into serialism. The series appears in the introduction of the first song and becomes the basis for thematic material and chromatic motifs that appear throughout the songs. He does not treat the series as a unifying element as in some of his later works, but it does show the composer attempting to move beyond the influence of the neoclassicism that dominates his early pieces.

The first of *Three Contemporaries* was the earlier "Benjamin Britten," (originally titled "Benjamin Butter") with text by Schafer. The text for the second song, "Paul Klee," comes from that artist's diaries, which Schafer read (in German) while in Vienna. The texts Schafer chose to combine in the song reflect Klee's fondness for simplicity, which Schafer tries to reflect in his music, although he describes the musical language as "expressionistic, reminiscent of the young Schoenberg but much less dense."[14] The third song, "Ezra Pound," is the most dramatic of the three settings. This sketch satirically describes Pound's incarceration in St. Elizabeth's hospital, a federal institution for the criminally insane. Despite the gap in composition between the first song and the final two, the three sketches together form a cohesive set, well worthy of the praise given to it by John Beckwith in his review of the 1958 Toronto concert where they were premiered.

Composed in 1958 during the composer's brief return to Toronto, *Kinderlieder* for voice and piano clearly shows the influence of folk song on Schafer's increasing sensitivity to text setting. Although the songs, most of which set texts by Bertolt Brecht, were written with Phyllis in mind, they are indicated for soprano voice, and the tessitura certainly sits higher than *Minnelieder*. The piano accompaniment, which is richly varied from piece to piece, helps create the mood of each movement without wasted notes. The songs are similar in harmonic language to those of *Minnelieder*, although they are more firmly tonal rather than modal and reflect Schafer's comfort in the harmonic language he had developed up to this point. In this set Schafer crafted a fine setting of the Brecht texts that match those of Eisler or Weil without imitating either.

Sonatina for flute and harpsichord or piano is a kindred composition to *Kinderlieder*. Its title is reflective of the genteel character of this brief, three-movement piece that sits firmly within the neoclassical, pandiatonic/polytonal language found in *Concerto*. The first movement is in a tripartite structure, firmly in the sonatina genre, in various permutations of compound meter. The first part introduces two themes, the second derived from the first. The middle section briefly develops a motive introduced in the piano's accompaniment to the second theme, and the third section includes an abbreviated return of both themes, with only one brief statement of the second theme before the movement ends. The second movement is similar to a fantasia. The keyboard has extensive arpeggiated chords similar to what a continuo instrument would do in secco recitative, over which the flute plays extended phrases. This texture is twice interrupted by a chorale-like passage in the harpsichord, the second time joined by the flute. The flute also has two unaccompanied cadenzas in this movement. The third movement is the most substantial of the three and develops its material most thoroughly within the sonatina form. After a brief introduction, two main themes are introduced, separated by a transitional theme. In the middle section new material is derived from a motivic figure in the keyboard part, this time from the accompaniment to the first section's transitional theme. This motivic figure creates a cross rhythm to the compound meter, and as the development section continues, this rhythmic aspect becomes more and more prominent. The final section brings back the primary, transitional, and secondary themes. It ends with a coda that includes a repeat of the introductory material.

Five Greek Folk Dances for violin and piano set folk tunes that Schafer heard and wrote down when he traveled to Greece and Crete in 1957. The first tune comes from the region of Ioannina, the second through fourth tunes come from Cyprus, and the last tune is from the Dodecanese region. The set was never published or performed in this original version, but in 2012 Schafer returned to it, revising the original piano part and joining the pieces so that each of these effective and charming arrangements flow together without break.

The character of each of the five movements in *Petit Divertissement Angevin*, a withdrawn suite for flute, oboe, clarinet, and cello, is either lyrical or playful, living up to the sense given by the title. Although based on piano pieces written before Schafer traveled to Europe and visited Angers (movement 4 is an only slightly altered transcription of *Polytonality*), the suite works remarkably well as a "French suite," reflecting the composer's continuing interest in the early 1950s of the music of Les Six. It is a charming piece, but being an arrangement of the composer's juvenile works, it is a look back stylistically and not reflective of his other pieces during this time.

Sonata da Camera (for two cellos alone) has a very different character than the other pieces written by the composer during his brief return to Toronto. It is energetic to the point of violence and poses significant challenges to the players. It is in three movements in a typical fast/slow/fast progression, and in each movement Schafer explores (and at times perhaps surpasses) the technical limits of the instruments. In addition to exploring the entire range of the cello, Schafer incorporates various types of techniques, including pizzicato; double, triple, and quadruple stops; and sul ponticello. The first movement, "Energetic but always free, as a fantasia," falls into a late-romantic harmonic and musical style, with the free rhythm one expects from the marking. The second movement, "Very slowly and expressively," is the most interesting and musically compact of the three. It is notable for an extensive use of glissandi in the writing, sometimes associated with trills, which would become one of the hallmarks of Schafer's writings for strings going forward. It also makes interesting use of unison or octave melodies, a nice contrast to the thickness of the counterpoint in the first movement. Movement 3, "Fast—energetic," has the same interplay between the instruments as the first movement, with melodies being passed back and forth but not developed, merely transposed. Although there is interesting writing in the work, it is clear that Schafer's primary focus was experimenting with various techniques to see what was possible. It does not reflect any structural, rhythmic, or harmonic development.

The unpublished piano suite *Three Ideograms* is effective and quite idiomatic. "The Dwelling Place" is a charming waltz with a recurring melody ornamented by Baroque rolled chords and roulades and a gentle polytonality reflective of Schafer's other works during this time. It is effective in its use of materials, with clarity of texture and simplicity of means. "The Bull" includes programmatic notes, with two characters, a bull and a man, interacting through the piece, the man dodging the bull until the bull triumphs. As a result, it has a variety of tempi, character, and textures. "The Whip" is a moto-perpetuo movement, marked "As fast as possible." Schafer includes a program note at the beginning: "The old Shaikh whips his camel across the desert to escape occidental infiltrators."[15] Although this set does not add any new compositional techniques, it is of the same quality as *Polytonality* and *Sonatina* and is much more successful as a piece than *Sonata da camera*.

In Memoriam Alberto Guerrero, Schafer's solo composition from 1959, is forward-looking in some of its techniques while still being firmly rooted in the musical language Schafer had developed up to this point. It does reach a deeper level of emotion due to the circumstances of its composition, written shortly after Schafer's learning of the death of his teacher and mentor, and we see some of the techniques that will characterize Schafer's writing for strings, including dissonant clusters, multiple solo instrumental combinations contrasted to the full string orchestra, slow deliberate glissandi, and various pizzicato effects.

SHIFTS AND EXPERIMENTATION — LONDON

Schafer took advantage of his time living and studying in London, which at that time was a hotbed of contemporary styles, to radically change his compositional approach. In particular, his studies with Peter Racine Fricker, who introduced him not only to serial techniques but also the isorhythmic and formalist techniques of Machaut and his Ars Nova contemporaries, opened up new worlds to the young composer. The pieces Schafer wrote during this time show his first attempts to grapple with these new techniques, with varying levels of success. In reviewing his changing style over these two years in London, Schafer cites his intense study of species counterpoint and the serial compositions of his contemporaries as the main causes of the radical changes in his compositional style. Although he has kept elements of serialism in his music, in particular the all-interval row that is one of the core concepts of *Patria*, the main benefit of his time studying and writing serial music was his discovery that, in his words, twelve-tone music was too verbose.[16] As a result of this time of experimentation, there were several pieces that he later chose to withdraw from the public eye, but there were several works of quality that he has chosen to keep in his official opus.

The first significant work Schafer wrote during this time was *Protest and Incarceration*, completed in 1960 and inspired by his 1959 travels to Eastern Europe. He came back from that trip disillusioned about communism as it was being practiced in that time and place, and this piece is his response to the oppression of the people and those regimes. The two texts that Schafer sets in this piece were selected from a collection of several poems written by anonymous or incarcerated poets, given to him and translated for him by Corina, his first interpreter while in Romania. He was able to smuggle the poems out of Romania and turned to them when back in London. *Protest* is Schafer's first attempt to write an extended serial composition and is his first piece for full orchestra. The two songs use variants of the same row, which is crafted to favor chromatic semitones, adjacent whole tones, perfect fourths, and tritones. No thirds appear in the row, which helps the avoidance of triadic harmonies, while the stepwise tones either allow for stepwise melodic figures or dramatic leaps in the vocal part. Schafer uses the row in all four forms and with several transpositions, and there are only a few instances of changes of sequence within the row or additional tones in the supporting parts. Both movements open with direct statements of the row followed by parallel statements in inversion. The vocal line and the leading instrumental lines tend to have the intact version of the row.[17] It is clearly Schafer's first attempt to write a serial composition and remains his most strict use of dodecaphonic techniques.

Brébeuf, based on the life of Jesuit missionary and martyr Jean de Brébeuf, was Schafer's first attempt to tackle a uniquely Canadian theme. For his text Schafer turned directly to Brébeuf's own account of his first Canadian winter in 1625 and added texts from other sources that describe many of the saint's visions and premonitions of his own martyrdom, creating a narrative drawn from various primary sources. The result is "a descriptive narrative of a spring canoe trip up the Great Lakes, interrupted by a series of hallucinatory outbursts."[18] Schafer divides the libretto and his composition into three unequal parts. The first brief part is titled "Winter near Kébec," followed by an orchestral interlude that leads to "The Journey," the longest section of the three, followed by another orchestral bridge to the final section, "The Arrival." Within each part Schafer weaves together a series of isolated vignettes, linked seamlessly together without structural repetition through the careful management of transitions.[19] The piece is also unified through a single cell of six notes, from which the musical material is derived. This hexachord is used as a direct source of melodic and harmonic material with extensive use of different transpositions, sometimes appearing simultaneously, and the occasional use of inversion. The hexachord provides a sense of harmonic stability, with its implications of a C-major triad with added D, F-sharp, and G-sharp. Melodically, the hexachord can be arranged to create a seven-note scale with four adjacent whole tones followed by two adjacent semitones, yielding additional material for the piece, including triads that strongly emphasize whole tones. The vocal writing calls for a few special effects and extended vocal techniques, and otherwise it falls into a melodic declamation of the text, closely bound to its rhythm.[20]

The Judgement of Jael (ultimately withdrawn) was written immediately after *Brébeuf* and completed late in 1961. Drawn from chapters 4 and 5 of the Old Testament Book of Judges, the text is altered by the librettist (Schafer's close friend Bob Walshe) to change the story of Jael from a song of triumph into an anti-war protest.[21] Titled *Cantata for Soprano, Mezzo-soprano and Orchestra*, it looks ahead to many of the composer's later works in his treatment of the large orchestra, and in particular the vocal writing. The singers are called upon to speak, whisper, change vocal color, approach Sprechstimme, and sing wide leaps and difficult intervals. One of the most stunning examples of this occurs in the final part, where the two singers pass notes and words back and forth, reminiscent of the hocket writing of Machaut.[22]

The first part, "Deborah," uses the judge Deborah's speech to the Israelites before they attack the enemy forces. Deborah's text is accompanied only by percussion, requiring four players, and the vocal writing is free, sometimes coordinating with the percussion parts, sometimes independent of it. With the beginning of the second part, "Jael's Song," the orchestral texture increases as Jael waits for Sisera to return from battle and then kills him. Different solo instruments, predominantly woodwinds, weave in and out of the texture so that by the transition to the third part the full woodwind orchestra, including horns, has entered. After a short pause the third part, "The Mother of Us All," begins with the full orchestra entering on a twelve-note chord that then dies away to a single held note in the saxophone, swelling again before the entrance of the two voices, that continue the story in Judges, speaking of the destruction of Jabin and his army after the death of Sisera. At the end of this section the strings usher in an addition to the story, a commentary on war written by Bob Walshe.

> Before you struck his life did you not listen to the warm instinctive rhythm of his heart.
> You killed to deliver peace but soon Sisera's kicking grandsons will prance before your highest gates howling for blood in a half-remembered cause. Pride claimed the right to kill. Pride and Deborah's panting dream of power. Know you not that the hammer and nail are for building. Before me you stand bold exulting destroyer. But I weep for you my daughter, weep forever more. For in that collapsing hour you killed both another and yourself and the guilt thereof shall lie entombed in your blood forever.

At the end both singers speak: "Peace was not known among the Children of Israel, and as it was not known then, neither it is understood unto this day."

Dithyramb is one of two serial pieces for string orchestra from 1961. The composer did not consider it successful and withdrew it. Conceived for a large orchestra (12, 10, 8, 8, 6), it is divided into four movements ("With much vigor"; "Slightly slower"; "Very slowly"; "Fast and vigorous"). This extended work included complex and challenging writing for the ensemble—showing the influence of Schafer's counterpoint studies—as well as a profusion of special effects for the players.

Partita, a companion to *Dithyramb*, is a much more concise piece, restrained in its use of special effects and austere in the use of its tone row. It uses only the original and the inversion of the row, with no transposition, and the focus seems to be on making the series audible to the listener. It is in four movements, and each movement is twice as long as the previous movement (thirty seconds, one minute, two minutes, and four minutes). Schafer also instructs the ensemble to pause for ten seconds between each movement, giving the composition a total length of eight minutes. The rhythm for the most part follows the ethos of transparency and simplicity, and the recurrence of rhythmic patterns helps provide unity to the piece. This composition, along with the later *Untitled Composition for Orchestra no. 1*, closely approaches the music of Webern.

TOWARD A NEW STYLE—CANADA

Upon his return to Canada, Schafer continued his absorption of serial and canonic techniques and also began initial experiments with electro-acoustic music, incorporating prerecorded sounds into some of his compositions.

Figure 14.2. Second Movement—*Partita for Strings.* R. Murray Schafer

One of several pieces begun in London and completed in Canada, *Canzoni for Prisoners* is written for prisoners of conscience—that is, non-violent objectors in any land who are imprisoned merely for their beliefs. I had become a founding member of Amnesty International, the organization devoted to ridding the world of this intolerance. The issue had been brought close to me, having visited several communist countries, though no country is free of this injustice since rulers everywhere would like to mute the opposition.[23]

Canzoni is in five sections performed without a break. In constructing this piece, Schafer chose a row of seventy-six notes, which forms the material for each of the five sections. Schafer manages such an unwieldy row by using primarily the original form, with a few transpositions in the second section. Along with this extension of serial techniques, the influence of Machaut is clearly seen, whose techniques were, in Schafer's words "rigorous and mathematical, but his music is daring and at times ecstatic, more so because of the constraints out of which it seems to burst."[24] Influences of the *Ars nova* composer are reflected in *Canzoni* through the use of isorhythmic and prolation techniques. As Schafer notes, each movement of the piece is an outgrowth and a variation of the material that precedes it.[25]

The piece's five continuous sections are all in tempos proportionally related to the opening bars. Section 1 is a prolation canon on the original row. Section 2 uses the retrograde and transpositions of the row, opening with three simultaneous transpositions (plus the original) of the series. Each layer of the series is interrupted by rests, but each layer has a different length of rest so that the first to enter finishes the series last, the last to enter finishes the series first. Section 3 is for strings alone and treats the material the most freely, using motives from the first two sections. Section 4 is the most rhythmically complex as different sections of instruments play chords derived from the series, adding rests at different, changing parts of the repetition to create uncertainty. Section 5 is a series of crescendos and accelerandos to intense climaxes. The seventy-six-note row is stated only once in each crescendo, with notes repeated freely, and different groups of instruments play the tones of the row in different note values. The piece then closes with a quiet epilogue.

Five Studies on Texts of Prudentius only totals about ten minutes in length and shows most clearly the influence of the formalism Schafer had gleaned from his studies with Fricker. The texts are from Prudentius's *Tituli Historarium*, a collection of poems by the fourth-century Christian poet meant to accompany paintings of important biblical events. Schafer chose to set texts that accompany the paintings *Adam and Eve*; *Moses Has Received the Law*; *The City of Bethlehem*; *The Passion of St. John*; and *The Revelation of St. John*. The composition is intended for spatial performance with the singer on stage and the flutes in the four corners of the room. The spatial movement of the music is centrifugal in "Adam and Eve," diagonal in "Moses Has Received the Law," and circular in the crab canon "The City of Bethlehem."[26] Although this is the strictest of his pieces written during this time, Schafer's underlying romanticism speaks in the sensitive setting of the text, which matches that of *Minnelieder*, although in a very different style.

"Adam and Eve" is a five-part canon, with the melody using only the intervals of the minor second, minor third, and perfect fourth. Two of the parts state the melody in inversion, and the melody in each voice is stated in a basic rhythmic arrangement but the parts enter at different tempi and are meant to progress independently of each other. "Moses Has Received the Law" uses both a rhythmic canon and a melodic canon. The melodic canon is at the unison, using the intervals of the minor second, major third, and perfect fourth. The three-part rhythmic canon is at the distance of one bar, with two of the rhythmic lines distributed between two pairs of flutes in alternate corners of the room. "The City of Bethlehem" is a large palindrome marked with a rest at its center. It has only two lines, one in the voice and the other divided between the four flutes, which use the intervals of the minor second, major third, and perfect fourth. The flutes enter in reverse order from the first song, indicating the incarnation's reversal of the fall. "The Passion of St. John" discusses Salome's dance before Herod. The texture thins out, using only two flutes with the voice in a three-part canon, with one of the parts inverted. It uses the intervals of the major second, minor second, and minor third. "The Revelation of St. John" again has the flutes enter in reverse order, with the Second Coming as the second reversal of the fall. The melodic intervals in this movement are the major second, major third, and perfect and augmented fourths, which are used to create a six-note "series" or motive that is repeated twelve times, each time a semitone higher.

Opus One for Mixed Chorus (ultimately withdrawn) also uses a palindrome form. The choir sings the following text:

> Opus One for mixed chorus is a composition experiment with special vocal techniques which the composer hopes will be useful in a larger future composition. The composition is a study in the invertibility of material. You are hearing the forward and the retrograde of the material simultaneously. The retrograde form is prerecorded. The composer is not concerned with the intelligibility of the text but rather with its elasticity with textures, depths, protractions and inversions. You will now hear vowel sounds in combination with the retrogradation of the foregoing text on tape. Opus One for mixed chorus was composed in September 1962 by Murray Schafer in Toronto, Canada.[27]

As indicated in this text, the second "choir" is a recording of the same material the first choir sings but played backward as the first choir sings. Although tongue-in-cheek, this composition shows some of the techniques that will become the hallmark of Schafer's choral compositions during this time, in particular the use of text in non-intelligible ways, including splitting the text between parts and even splitting the phonemes of words between voices. The focus on language as a series of sounds is further reinforced by the addition of the second choir, whose text becomes a series of random sounds when played backward. The piece is an early experimentation with prerecorded sounds and Schafer's first attempt to write for chorus in his new harmonic idiom.

Divisions for Baroque Trio, also withdrawn, uses prerecorded sounds in a similar way to *Opus One*, where the live performers play against lines they have prerecorded. It was premiered by the Baroque Trio of Montreal as part of a residency Schafer was serving at McGill University. It is in one continuous movement, chromatic and unmeasured, and according to Adams, "the resulting six-part texture is muddy, and Schafer is strangely insensitive to antiphonal and mirroring possibilities."[28]

Schafer's second attempt at choral composition is also his first attempt to set the texts of Rabindranath Tagore. Although *Four Songs on Texts of Tagore* for SSAA chorus are still serial compositions, they are not as strictly structured as some of Schafer's other pieces during this time. The rows are of variable length, ranging from nine notes to fourteen notes. The texture is clear enough that the row is discernible, although repeated notes occur freely throughout as the text and character demand it. All of the rows, and the movements, begin either on G-flat or its enharmonic equivalent F-sharp. The ranges are extreme, and the melodies wide ranging, but there is a consistent technique and language in this set. Schafer approaches the text in different ways in each movement, one of the most notable examples being in the first song, when the word "endless" is broken up into the phonemes *e*, *n*, *d*, *l*, *e*, and *s* and spread out over the different parts of the choir. Textual phrases are also divided between the voices, which often overlap syllables and pass the same note back and forth. There are extensive solos in each song, of various combinations, contrasting and interacting with the full chorus. Glissandi appear throughout, and often inflected speaking or whispered lines are matched with sung lines, roughly following the contour of the sung line. These pieces, demanding enough that they were not performed, are a more effective, though not perfect, venture into choral writing for Schafer and are indicative of the impressive contribution he would soon make in this genre.

Untitled Composition for Orchestra no. 1 from 1963, has a strong connection to the beginning of *Canzoni*.[29] The piece is a clearly audible prolation canon at the interval of the unison for small orchestra, lasting only four minutes. The chamber orchestra is used judiciously and the full orchestra doesn't ever play together. A strict approach coupled with pointillistic orchestration allows the canonic underpinning to be heard clearly.

Untitled Composition for Orchestra no. 2 is also from 1963. It is shorter than its predecessor but uses a much larger orchestra. Instead of using the linear approach to composition found in the first orchestra piece, Schafer treats orchestral sound masses in a contrapuntal fashion. Adams states, "The strings in long note values state the material, here not linear but a sequence of timbres and note clusters which the wind groups twice imitate in succession, using shorter note values."[30]

TOWARD A NEW STYLE—EDUCATIONAL COMPOSITIONS

It was through his work with school children that Schafer began to incorporate graphic notation and aleatoric passages into his compositions. He used these techniques for pedagogical purposes, using his skills as a visual artist in these graphic scores. Aleatory and graphic notation would become a large part of his compositional technique, and these early educational pieces allowed him to become comfortable with these techniques.

Schafer's first piece for youth orchestra, *Invertible Material for Orchestra no. 1*, dates from 1962 but was ultimately withdrawn. It is in three movements and in its orchestration breaks up the orchestra into distinct groups. The first movement has two main motives that are passed between the three groups of the orchestra (winds, horns, strings). The second movement, for a smaller chamber ensemble drawn out of the orchestra (winds, strings, and triangle) is a series of repeated notes that overlap. The third movement uses the full orchestra in a similar structure to the first movement.

Invertible Material for Orchestra no. 2 was written in 1963 as a commission from Keith Bissell, head of music for the Scarborough Board of Education. It is designated a "practice piece" and was well received at its premiere, played by high school students at Cedarbrae Collegiate although Schafer later chose to withdraw it.[31] The piece is laid out on a single page divided into five sections and has individual cards for each instrument. Each player is given a note on which to improvise, within rhythmic and dynamic guidelines. The parts are combined at will by the conductor before moving on to the next section.

Statement in Blue is the first educational piece that Schafer has let stand. It is a result of Schafer's work as part of the Adaskin Project in 1963, written for eighth-grade students who had been playing their instruments for about a year.[32] The score is one continuous page, implying a free-flowing form. The composer gives several notes to the performers and conductor at the beginning of the score covering how the orchestra should be seated and how some of the sections could be realized. Pitch and duration are free throughout the composition, although relative ranges are given. He cautions the players,

> Don't just doodle through the piece; try always to find arresting and beautiful effects as a group. If a section sounds dull or turgid, point it out to your teacher and change it. And don't forget to listen to your neighbours. . . . Sometimes during rehearsals I clap my hands and ask different people what note the flute

or the trumpet has just played.... *Statement in Blue* is not a piece calculated to train you how to play your instrument better technically; it aims to train your ears, your feeling for expressive ensemble playing, and above all to help release whatever creative abilities you might have to make music of your own. In fact, it would be interesting after you have performed *Statement in Blue* if you tried to compose a piece of your own for your class to perform.[33]

Statement in Red is a withdrawn companion piece to *Statement in Blue*, this time for only brass, winds, and percussion. More like *Invertible Material for Orchestra no. 2*, it is a single page, this time divided into six sections. Each of the first five sections has a specific musical gesture that contrasts with the others. As in *Invertible Material*, the sections are combined, the players moving freely between them at the conductor's (or their own) discretion. The sixth and final section brings all of the players together, the brass and wind players realizing certain gestures, the percussion section realizing others, all controlled by the conductor.

FINAL STEPS TOWARD A MATURE STYLE

As Schafer finished his residency at Memorial University in St. John's, Newfoundland, he was on the verge of reaching his mature compositional language. He had absorbed atonal and serial techniques, developed aleatoric techniques, grown comfortable with graphic notation, and begun his first forays into electronic music. The final elements of what we now recognize as his unique compositional language would be developed through his work on his first piece for theater, *Loving*.

Chapter Fifteen

The Compositions for Choir

Schafer's choral compositions comprise a significant part of his output, ranging from educational compositions for children, youth, and adult choirs to more challenging pieces for advanced ensembles and monumental works like *The Fall Into Light*, written for six professional choirs and children's choir. He has written for many of the top choirs in Canada and the world, and his choral compositions have been especially well received in Asia and South and Central America. There are several pieces of choral juvenilia found in his sketchbook, but the first two choral compositions that he allowed to let stand, at least temporarily, are *Opus One for Mixed Chorus* and *Four Songs on Texts of Tagore* from 1962 (see chapter 14).

COMPOSITIONS ASSOCIATED WITH THE *PATRIA* CYCLE

Gita was written in 1967, and the premiere occurred at the Tanglewood Festival in August of that year. Schafer describes the genesis of the piece in this way:

> The inspiration to choose the Bhagavad-Gita for a text came to me one crystalline January morning during a walk in the cold air of Isle Bézard, near Montréal. I was visiting a friend and had been reading the Gita the night before. The passage on serenity and the forces ranged against it (II 55–64) had left a deep impression. That morning I imagined a choir, as serene as newly-fallen snow, being hectored by a group of brass instruments. The choir would sing in the original Sanskrit, aloof and victorious.[1]

Schafer conceived of the piece as an editing unit of *Patria 1*, and he composed *Gita* with that cycle's all-interval row. The row becomes the basis for the choral writing and also the writing for the brass ensemble, but in very different ways. The choir and the tape reflect the philosophy of the ten verses that Schafer sets, where Krishna counsels a mortal prince in the midst of war to achieve spiritual detachment. The brass ensemble mostly reflects worldly conflict and multiplicity, recalling the context of war that underlies the philosophical dialogue between Krishna and the prince.[2]

From the Tibetan Book of the Dead, written in 1968, is in many ways a companion piece to the earlier *Gita*, this time setting texts (in the original Tibetan) from the *Bardo Thodol*, a set of instructions to a dying person preparing them for their stay in the after-death state. Like *Gita*, it was also written to be used as an editing unit for *Patria*, in this case *Patria 2*, and so is based on the all-interval row, which makes both explicit and implicit appearances and is supplemented by such effects as semi-tone and whole-tone descending clusters. In this through-composed piece, the row is used melodically in two-part counterpoint and even as a twelve-note cluster. In addition to the chorus, the piece calls for a soprano solo (who represents the character of Ariadne in *Patria 2*), flute, clarinet, and tape.

Gamelan was written in 1979 for the inaugural concert of the Maynooth Community Choir but also as an editing unit for *Patria 3*. It was written for a small group of singers from within the Maynooth Community Choir, which used to gather in various homes to sing madrigals, and it reflects the composer's continued interest in non-Western music. As the title suggests, the piece is based on the Balinese pentatonic scale (C D F G B-flat), and Schafer uses the Balinese names for the tones (dong, deng, dung, dang, ding) for the text of the piece. Schafer's desire was to suggest the rhythms and sounds of a gamelan orchestra without any claim to have created an authentic example of Balinese music.

Hear Me Out was also written in 1979 and performed by four solo voices in the same concert as *Gamelan*. The text consists entirely of well-known aural figures of speech, juxtaposed in ridiculous and often humorous ways. Lying somewhere between music and theater, *Hear Me Out* invites a wide range of interpretations and is also an editing unit of *Patria 3*.

Felix's Girls was the third choral piece that Schafer wrote in 1979 that was intended for inclusion in *The Greatest Show*. For the piece he turned to a collection of poems he had been given twenty-five years earlier by the Polish-Jewish immigrant poet Henry Felix. These poems each describe a different feminine type (or stereotype), and Schafer chose to set nine of these satirical poems, turning to musical quotation and collage to set the texts. "Gretchen" quotes a Lutheran hymn, "Mary-Lou" quotes jazz, and "Hermine" a Viennese waltz, for example, and Schafer treats his musical sources in the same satirical and ironic way that Felix treats his subjects.

In 1983 Schafer received a commission from the Mendelssohn Choir of Toronto for a piece to sing at the opening of Roy Thompson Hall. At that time Schafer had just come off the first successful production of *Patria*

Prologue: The Princess of the Stars, and he decided for the commission to rework editing unit 14 (*Arrival of the Sun-Disk*) from that piece, creating a piece that he simply called *Sun*. As in the original aria, the text of *Sun* consists of words for the sun in forty different languages, beginning in Japan and traveling west across Asia, Africa, and Europe to South and North America. Since the piece is based on an aria from a *Patria* segment, the underpinning of the all-interval row is seen, although it is altered to be almost unrecognizable. What the ear hears more clearly is the Native American monody that was the basis of *Princess* and Schafer's nod to the music of the various regions of the world from where the text is drawn.

Schafer wrote *The Star Princess and the Waterlilies* in August of 1984 when he was in the midst of preparation for a second production of *Patria Prologue*, to be held in Banff the following summer. When he received a commission from the Toronto Children's Chorus, he turned to the character of the Princess as the source of the piece. This miniature drama uses text by the composer and tells the story of the Star Princess visiting the world to ask children if the stars might come to live on earth. The children help her find the right place for the stars, which in their earthly form become water lilies. An adult alto soloist plays the character of the Star Princess, a child plays the role of the Narrator, and the chorus plays the role of the Children. The piece asks for simple percussion to be played by the singers. Although the piece is based on one of the *Patria* characters, the composer clearly intends it as a concert piece, and the harmonic language is tonal, with no references to the all-interval row that is the basis of the cycle. Even with the simplified harmonic language, Schafer follows his pattern of including some aleatoric passages, aided by the use of graphic notation, to further engage the singers.

Fire was composed in 1986. It was commissioned by the Vancouver Chamber Choir for their performances in Vancouver at Expo '86 and clearly falls into the cycle of environmental pieces begun by *Epitaph for Moonlight*. Like *Epitaph*, this piece focuses on realizing sonically what is primarily a visual event: the burning of a fire. It is a challenging piece in this genre, written for a professional chorus, and the singers are required to repeat short asymmetrical patterns while playing different patterns on hand-held wooden or metal clackers. The text is made up of various vowels only, which often do not line up between the individual voices. It was included, with additional instruments, in *Patria 5* as editing unit 29.

Magic Songs was written in 1988 for the Swedish male chorus Orphei Dränger. Schafer drew on source material from *Patria Epilogue: And Wolf Shall Inherit the Moon* for this set of chants that hearken back to

> the era of "tone magic," when the purpose of singing was not merely to give pleasure but was intended to bring about a desired effect in the physical world.

In spirit culture, everything has its voice, and the aim of the singer is to unify himself with this voice.[3]

Of the nine chants in the revised cycle ("Chant to Bring Back the Wolf"; "Chant to Make Fences Fall Down"; "Chant to Make Fireflies Glow"; "Chant for Clear Water"; "Chant for the Spirits of Hunted Animals"; "Chant to Keep Bees Warm in Winter"; "Chant to Make Bears Dance"; "Chant to Make the Stones Sing"; and "Chant to Make the Magic Work") five are adaptations of *Epilogue* chants. Schafer notes,

> The aim of these songs, with magic texts in a language spoken by no human, is to restore aspects of nature which have been destroyed or neglected by humanity. To the extent that the performers and the audience believe in them, they will be successful.
>
> The modern belief that the purpose of singing is merely to provide pleasure for the ears inhibits the grander theme of Magic Songs. If choirs were to sing them in the dancing light of campfires in the wilderness, they would get closer to the magic power these songs can release.[4]

Schafer decided to excerpt some of the chants from *Magic Songs* and simplify them for use more "for classroom or campfire singing than concert performance, but they could serve as warm-up songs for a choir,"[5] giving the set the title *Six Magic Songs*. "Wolf Song" is based on "Chant to Bring Back the Wolf"; "Hunted Animals" is based on "Chant for the Spirit of Hunted Animals"; "Dancing Bears" is based on "Chant to Make Bears Dance"; and "Mosquito Song" is based on "Chant to Keep Bees Warm in Winter." To these chants Schafer adds "Rain Song," which is based on a *Patria Epilogue* chant that he would later use as the source of *Rain Chant*, and a newly composed piece called "Flower Song," which uses a Cree word for "princess" and an Iroquois word for "star" as the basis of its text.

In 1996 Schafer excerpted two sets of songs from *Patria* segments for separate publication. The first set, *Three Songs from the Enchanted Forest*, was from *Patria 9*, which was first produced in 1993. These short excerpts are pulled essentially unchanged from the original score. Intended for children's chorus, they are conventionally melodic in their approach. The first song, "Sweet Clover," is drawn from editing unit 3 and is sung by the Earth Mother and the children's choir. The second song, "Ariane's Lament," is drawn from editing unit 17, with its beginning altered somewhat to make it a stand-alone piece. It is sung by the girls' choir and Ariane after she has been transformed into a birch tree. The third song, "Lu-li-lo-la," predates *The Enchanted Forest*, being originally written for Erkki Pohiola, director of the Tapiola Children's Choir of Helsinki, on the occasion of his retirement. Schafer used it in *Patria 9* to accompany the long walk out of the forest at the end of the production.

Patria 10: The Spirit Garden was completed in 1996, and Schafer the same year drew out two songs from the work for separate publication. The first, "Raking Song," is drawn from editing unit 7 and is a simple chorus for two voices. "Spring Child" comes from editing unit 10 and is slightly more complex, with the choir divided into three parts. Both choruses and excerpts are unchanged from the original score.

Rain Chant, written for the Taipei Philharmonic Choir for the 2002 World Symposium on Choral Music Conference in Minnesota, is based on one of the songs from *Patria Epilogue*. In that context it is a simple unison chant sung on rainy days, both to celebrate the rain and encourage it to stop. Pressed for time, Schafer turned to the original to create a choral piece, extending and arranging the original.

The Death of Shalana was commissioned by Patria Music Theatre Productions with funds provided by the Laidlaw Foundation for performance in Metropolitan United Church in Toronto by Soundstreams Canada in June 2005, and Schafer wrote the piece in January of that year. Although the piece was written for performance in a traditional concert hall, the source and conception of the piece would ideally be suited for performance in nature, with the required four choirs on different shores of a lake. The text is by the composer, and the character Shalana is the leader of one of the clans (the Human Clan) in *Patria Epilogue*. Shalana leaves the Human Clan and goes to live in the forest with the other animals. When he dies in the forest, his voice lives on and can heard in the sounds of nature. The text of *The Death of Shalana* describes how the voice of Shalana can be heard in water, wind, fire, trees, and animals, and it takes the form of question and answer. Schafer uses the four choirs antiphonally, anticipating the separation of the choruses in a performance in nature, and keeps both the rhythm and harmonic motion fairly simple. A close examination of the first few pages of the score reveals homage to the all-interval row of the *Patria* cycle but altered in such a way as to mask it in traditional harmonic motion.

COMPOSITIONS FOR YOUTH CHORUS

Schafer had been thinking for several years about creating an anti-war piece titled *Threnody* that would deal with the nuclear bombing of Nagasaki. A reason to write the piece came when he received a commission from the Vancouver Junior Youth Symphony Orchestra in 1967. His approach to the subject required youth performers, so the commission provided the opportunity to explore what at that time, at the height of the cold war, was still a controversial topic. The young narrators speak eyewitness accounts of children of the bombing of Nagasaki, supported by the chorus and orchestra who musically depict the horrors of that act. Schafer incorporates into the score opportunities for the performers to thoughtfully create their own music to accompany certain of the texts, further engaging the performers in this serious subject. Schafer has called *Threnody* "a religious piece for our time," and he states in the preface, "Of all my works I hope it will travel the most, the farthest and the deepest. I literally want it to be performed to death. I want it to be performed until it is no longer necessary. Then I will burn the score."[6]

Over the course of a few days in March 1968, Schafer sketched out what unquestionably has remained his most popular choral composition, *Epitaph for Moonlight*. The unusual text for this piece dates back to 1966 when Schafer asked a class of eleven-year-olds, who disagreed with his assertion that the sound of the word "moonlight" was suggestive of its meaning, to create more suggestive words in a private language. He took some of the words ("sloofulp," "neshmoor," "shalowa," "nu-u-yul," "noorwahm," "maunklinde," "shiverglowa," "sheelesk," "malooma," "shimonoell") and set them to music. The piece's close ties to Schafer's educational theories are clearly indicated by its inclusion at the end of his third education pamphlet, *When Words Sing*. *Epitaph* is written using graphic notation, which allows musicians who have not mastered traditional notation to execute and easily follow along with the piece. It is also an ear-training exercise where the singers must pitch their notes by interval from the preceding notes.

Schafer gives the following note in the preface of the score:

> Why did I call it Epitaph for Moonlight? In 1969 American astronauts landed on the moon to the excitement of the whole world. But something died then. No longer would the moon be a numinous and mythogenic symbol; it threatened to become a piece of property covered with neon. That hasn't happened yet, but in today's polluted cities with their twenty-four-hour glare, no one even notices the moon anymore. The moon is dead. I saw her die.[7]

Miniwanka or The Moments of Water was written quickly, on a whim, at a time when Schafer was working on several large commissions, including *Beyond the Great Gate of Light*, *Enchantress*, and *Zoroaster*. It is unrelated to any of these large compositions but is a direct outgrowth of his soundscape work and is a companion piece to *Epitaph for Moonlight*. It is a graphic notation piece for youth choir, the text consisting of words for "rain," "stream," "waterfall," "lake," "river," and "ocean" in several North American Indian languages, including the word that he used for the title. Although there are moments of more traditional notation and even some specified pitches, it is largely graphic and is clearly intended for young performers, either children's choir or mixed choir. Schafer would revise and recopy the piece in 1995.

Schafer initially wrote an SATB piece called *Snowforms* for mixed chorus, which the Vancouver Chamber Choir performed in 1981. He considered it a failure and in 1983 decided to completely rewrite the piece, doing so over

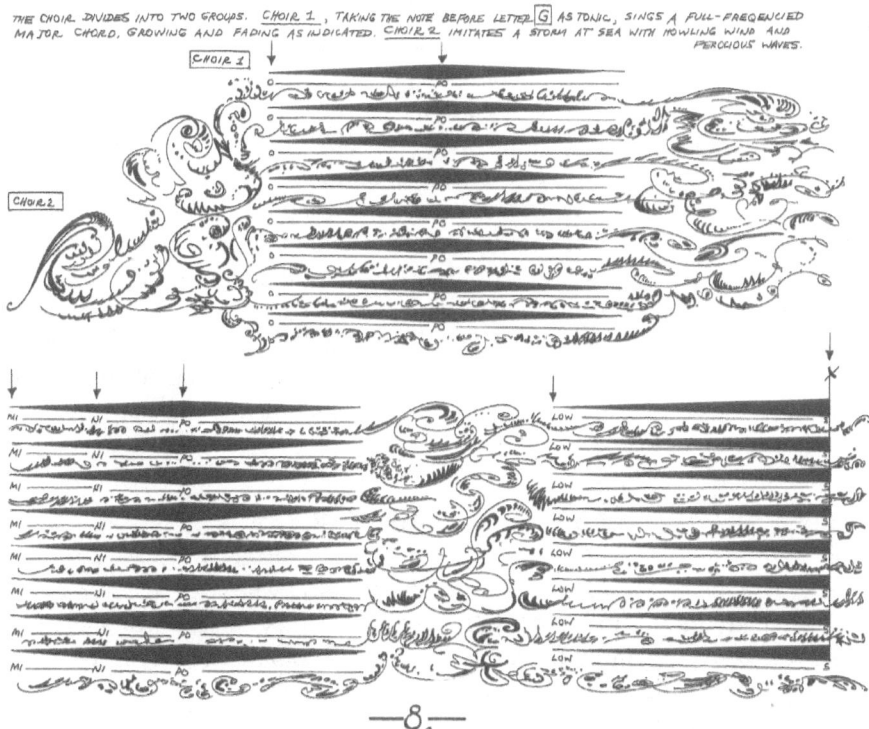

Figure 15.1. *Miniwanka.* R. Murray Schafer

the course of about six days in October. He describes the new, simple piece this way:

> Sometimes I have given children "sight-singing" exercises in which they are asked to "sing" drawings or the shapes of the distant horizon. Snowforms began as a series of sketches of snowdrifts, seen out the window of my Monteagle Valley farmhouse. I took these sketches and traced a pentagram over them. The notes of the piece emerged wherever the lines of the sketch and the stave crossed. Of course I modified the drawings as necessary since the work is primarily a piece of music and only secondarily a set of sketches. I printed the work so that the shapes of the snow were in white over a pale blue background.

The text consists of Inuit words for various kinds of snow: *apingaut*, meaning "first snowfall"; *mauyak*, "soft snow"; *akelrorak*, "drifting snow"; *pokaktok*, "snow like salt"; etc.[8]

Snowforms is clearly related to the earlier pieces *Epitaph for Moonlight*, *Miniwanka*, and *Sun* in its musical depiction of a natural phenomenon. Like the first two, it also uses graphic notation and a free approach to time and tempo, although in this case all notes are predetermined.

You Are Illuminated was written first as a stand-alone piece before being incorporated into the large choral work *The Fall Into Light*. It was written without any commission or performance in mind in 1999 but was spurred by Schafer's reflection on a text he had set many years ago in the piece *Gita*. The text speaks of the attainment of serenity, and after originally setting the Sanskrit, Schafer decided to return to the text and this time set it in English for children's choir. As the composer notes on this unusual choice: "Of course it is above a child's level of comprehension (but then so are many portions of the Mass that boy sopranos—and I was one—used to sing every Sunday). I wanted 'pure' voices to explain the illumination to be obtained by putting aside all desires."[9]

CONCERT COMPOSITIONS

Schafer composed *Yeow and Pax* in the fall of 1969 when he had returned to SFU after his travels in the Middle East and Turkey. These two short anthems for choir, organ, and electronics were a commission from the First Congregational Church in Old Greenwich, Connecticut, and they set two passages from Isaiah for organ, choir, and electronics. The title combines the Hebrew word for "howl" with the Latin word for "peace." Since they were written for a church choir, the harmonic language is simpler, particularly in the last anthem, but Schafer still uses many of the same compositional approaches found in his other choral pieces of this time. There is extensive use of graphic notation and several aleatoric passages as well, but in general the approach is closer to a piece like *Epitaph* rather than *Gita*. Schafer would later use the opening passage of the first anthem in the large-scale work *Apocalypsis*.

Along with the triptych *Lustro*, the extended piece *Zoroaster* (originally *In Search of Zoroaster*) was a direct outgrowth of Schafer's trip in the spring of 1969 to Turkey and Iran. While in Iran he visited some of the holy sites associated with Zoroastrianism and studied the writings of that Persian religious figure. When he received a commission in 1971 from the Dartmouth College Glee Club, he decided to base it on Zoroastrian thought, noting,

> Like many of my works from this period, Zoroaster is a setting of religious texts of mystical character, this time from the Zend-Avesta of Zoroaster and other works inspired by his teaching. The arrangement suggests a history of Zoroastrianism, originally a proud monotheism, which later broke into a confused polytheism full of magic formulas and practices. In the composition the

pantheon of the gods is united again at the close under the supreme authority of Ahura Mazda.[10]

Schafer's original concept was for the piece to be performed without an audience, for the experience of the singers alone, and this extended work moves beyond simple choral writing to a ritualistic event with costuming, movement, and spatial separation, anticipating the later and much larger *Apocalypsis*. The choir, which should not be less than 150 singers, is divided into six separate choirs, each representing a different subsidiary deity within the Zoroastrian cosmology. *In Search of Zoroaster* was revived for a performance in Toronto in 2001 by Soundstreams Canada. In preparation for the performance, Schafer renamed the piece *Zoroaster* and inserted the earlier vocal piece *Tantrika* into the larger composition.

The piece can be divided into three parts, with a prologue where each part is announced by twelve strikes on a wood block. The prologue begins in total darkness with all voices humming a single pitch, the "cosmic sound," and individual voices chant invocations to the various deities to whom their choir belongs. The first section suggests creation from nothing as candles are gradually lit and a chord builds. The second section deals with the coming of Ahura Mazda's son, accompanied by emerging melodic fragments and outbursts that represent the fall of the religion from its first pure form. The third section depicts the journey from this fragmentation of religion back to its ultimate resolution. The singers return to cosmic sound and leave as the candles are extinguished and darkness returns.[11]

The original title of the composition *Psalm* was *Tehillim*, and it was written in 1972. A setting of Psalm 148, it was a commission from the Anglican Cathedral Church of the Redeemer in Calgary in honor of their ninetieth anniversary. Schafer revised the piece in 1976, renamed it *Psalm*, and decided both to publish it separately and to incorporate it in *Apocalypsis*. Schafer describes the piece as "a joyful, almost militant song of praise to the Lord in which the singers clap, snap their fingers, stamp and even play a variety of percussion instruments."[12] It calls for a large choir, divided into three groups at the opening and closing of the anthem. Along with percussion and movement, *Psalm* includes more traditionally notated passages and more conventional harmonies and chords, reflecting its intended use for a parish choir.[13]

Schafer worked on both parts of *Apocalypsis* simultaneously in 1975 and 1976, finishing *Part Two: Credo* first in early 1976. *Part One: John's Vision* sets the story of the Book of Revelation up to the founding of the new heavenly Jerusalem, but Schafer was unsatisfied with the description of heaven as contained in that book and decided that he needed to turn to another text for *Part Two*. He chose a text by Giordano Bruno, a sixteenth-century Italian philosopher and astronomer (and heretic) who described the universe in a way more in accord with Schafer's own beliefs, and he decided to call the work *Credo*.

The musical inspiration was Thomas Tallis's forty-part motet *Spem in Alium*, which Schafer referenced throughout the process of composing. Although written for the same forces as the Tallis work (twelve four-part choruses), *Credo* is much longer, consisting of twelve invocations proclaiming "Lord God is universe" together with twelve responses. The twelve invocations, twelve responses, and twelve choirs correspond to the twelve gates of the heavenly Jerusalem, each inlaid with a different precious stone. Schafer notes,

> In fact, I gave the twelve choirs the names of these stones and planned to have them totally surround the audience so that the sound could be passed around or across the hall from one choir to another. I once had a dream in which I was standing on a stepladder putting the final touches on a choral piece that seemed to reach to the heavens. Credo was that work.[14]

The scope of the piece required Schafer to first work out the mathematical plan for the piece on graph paper and then fill in the notes. Each of the twelve sections begins softly and gradually crescendos to the end of the section, and each syllable of the text has a predetermined dynamic shading, whether it be vowel, consonant-vowel, vowel-consonant, or consonant-vowel-consonant. The melodic and harmonic material is derived from a six-note scale that is altered five times throughout the piece and transposed to match the key center of each invocation and response, as charted on the score. Sometimes additional chromatic notes are added, but not enough to obscure the underlying scale. The invocation uses the material in a descending melodic line, which is then balanced by its following ascending response.

A Garden of Bells was written in 1983 in response to a commission from the Vancouver Chamber Choir through funds from the Canada Council. Schafer decided to engage members of the choir to help him generate the text, which he wished to be onomatopoeic words for bells and bell sounds. To these created words he also added existing words in different languages, including Sinhalese, Spanish, Serbo-Croatian, Hungarian, Indonesian, and Swahili. The music and notation are quite traditional throughout, with specified pitches and rhythms. As with his other choral pieces during this time, Schafer's harmonic language is simplified and often triadic. The focus on the piece is to create a scene that Schafer describes in the following way:

> In A Garden of Bells I had in mind a scene which does not really exist; a soniferous garden filled with bells of all shapes and sizes, through which the traveller might wander at leisure, and be entertained by a tintinnabulation of sounds, not loud but beckoning, sometimes near, but more often far, like the voices of distant friends, which soft breezes barely bring to the ears.[15]

Schafer wrote another important choral piece in 1988, *The Death of the Buddha*, commissioned by the BBC for the BBC Singers, who were scheduled to perform at the 1989 International Choral Festival in Toronto. For this piece Schafer turned back to Buddhist writings to find a suitable text, the first time he had done so for a choral piece since *Gita* and *From the Tibetan Book of the Dead* twenty years before. He chose a text from the earliest canon of Buddhist sacred writing, the *Digha Nikaya*, choosing a litany that describes the Buddha's achieving Nirvana, noting,

> I wanted the music to illustrate the passive quality of the text. The sopranos and altos repeat a series of eleven notes, consisting of an identical number of upward and downward intervals, which undergoes continual modification by semi-tone augmentation or diminution.
>
> Beneath this line the basses sing eighteen evenly-spaced Oms and hums. Om represents the ascent towards universality and hum is the descent of universality into the depth of the human heart; 18 is the number of dhatas or elements in the Buddhistic canon.
>
> The tenors sing the text, rising and falling by semitone degrees. The basses are accompanied by two pitched gongs that sound each time they pronounce an Om or a hum. During the performance a bell tree is sounded three times, once at the beginning, once in the middle, and once at the end of the composition.
>
> In conception The Death of the Buddha is related to Credo, which is also rigorously structured according to numerical symbolism, but it has nothing of the emotional power of the earlier work.[16]

In 1992, Schafer received a commission from The King's Singers for an upcoming performance in Toronto. He became inspired by Andrew Lang's nineteenth-century English translation of Gottfried von Strasbourg's medieval German poem *Tristan*. He thought setting the Lang translation would be appropriate for the ensemble and more accessible to the audience, and he chose the passage describing the scene where Tristan and Iseult mistakenly drink the love potion. Schafer describes his approach to *Tristan und Iseult* in this way:

> Lang's phrases rise and fall here in a manner that suggests both the motion of the waves and the swelling of passion, so that as I read the text aloud I felt each phrase as a physiological unit, held together under a single breath; and after two or three readings I found that I had composed the entire story—or rather it had composed itself—into a work for six interweaving voices, where rhythms, swellings and contractions of the syllable or phrase were shaped into a kind of triple counterpoint between breath, heart and waves.[17]

In 1993 Schafer was invited through UNESCO to give a week-long workshop for music educators in Costa Rica, which was successful enough that he was asked to do another session in January 1994. At that time he was artist-in-residence at Brandon University in Manitoba, and he was able to bring several students from that institution with him for the workshop. As part of the workshop he had asked the English students from Canada to create a list of what they considered the most beautiful sounding words in English, with no concern as to the meaning of the words. The Costa Rican students improvised on those words, without knowing their meaning. He then asked the Costa Rican students to create a similar list of beautiful sounding words in Spanish. When he arrived home he used those words as the basis for a piece called *Beautiful Spanish Song*, reacting to the words as pure sounds since he himself wasn't fluent in Spanish.

Once on a Windy Night was written at the end of 1995 for performance the next year by the Vancouver Chamber Choir, a commission for their twenty-fifth anniversary. This was the fourth piece Schafer had written for the choir (the earlier ones being the initial version of *Snowforms*; *A Garden of Bells*; and *Fire*), and similar to those earlier pieces, *Once on a Windy Night* is a choral evocation of nature, this time of air in the form in which we can best experience it—wind. As Schafer began to work on the piece, he recalled a passage by the French author Victor Hugo from *Les Travailleurs de la Mer*. The rich vocabulary Hugo uses in this passage inspired Schafer, and the composer decided to include some of the words or word fragments in the piece, including *rafale* ("gust"), *bourrasque* ("squall"), *orage* ("storm"), *tourmente* ("gale"), *tempête* ("tempest"), *trombe* ("waterspout"), and a few verbs: *courent, volent, s'abattent, sifflent, mugissant*. The composer notes, "These words just contribute to the texture of Windy Night and are not intended to be comprehensible in themselves."[18] The composer calls this piece a "tone poem for choir," and the music and notation of this extended piece reflects this approach.

A Medieval Bestiary, written in 1996, sets text from an English translation of a twelfth-century Latin bestiary from Lincolnshire, England. Schafer notes,

> In the Middle Ages bestiaries were serious works of natural history. They were anonymous compilations of what was known or presumed about the characteristics and habits of animals, both real and mythological. Because they were compiled by churchmen, the behavior of animals frequently seemed to point up an instructive moral for humans. A modern audience may find these connections strange or humorous; but at the time they were intended in all seriousness.[19]

Similar to the earlier *Felix's Girls*, Schafer uses musical collage and parody to set these texts, drawing on various musical styles from different eras, cultures, and composers of the world, including Tibetan Chant, Notre Dame–style organum, Mendelssohn, and Machaut. Originally a commission by the Uxbridge Chamber Choir, which gave the first performance, it has become one of Schafer's more popular works, perhaps due to its lighthearted nature.

During Schafer's visit to Japan in 1995, he had the opportunity to meet conductors of top Japanese choirs. The connections that he made during that visit would lead over the next few years to several commissions from Japanese choirs and choirs in other parts of Asia, including Taiwan. The first commission he received was in 1996 when the director of the Tokyo Philharmonic Chorus, Chifuru Matsubara, asked for a piece on the theme of nature. This was a natural fit for Schafer, and Matsubara also asked that the piece set a Latin text since that was easier for the Japanese singers to learn, given a similarity in vowel sounds between the two languages.

When Schafer received this commission, he thought of the extended poem *De Rerum Natura* [On the Nature of Things] by Lucretius, the first-century BCE Epicurean philosopher, and he gave the piece the title *Vox Naturae*. Schafer chose to set lines 549–95 of book 4 of this extensive poem, where Lucretius extends beyond a scientific explanation of sound to vivid poetry, describing echoes as the voices of nymphs, satyrs, and fauns led by the god Pan and mocking the world of humans from hidden places. Schafer chose to use three choirs to set this text.

> For this purpose three choirs are used: the stage choir which states the scientific theories; a choir in the hall, reflecting or distorting the statements of the stage choir in illustration of the theory being described; and a backstage choir of satyrs and nymphs. For this reason I call the work Vox Naturae, literally "the voices of nature."[20]

The following year Schafer received another commission from another Japanese ensemble, Choir Utaoni, and their conductor Nobuyuki Koshiba. This group was familiar with Schafer's work, having previously won an all-Japan choral contest singing *Magic Songs*. With no specified text, Schafer thought that he would set a Japanese text for the first time and began reading the haiku poetry of such authors as Basho and Issa. As he began to assemble some possible poems for *Seventeen Haiku*, he thought he would ask the Utaoni choir members to help find additional poems and even to write some contributions. He chose several from the twenty-nine poems he received and added them to the traditional poems to form a selection of poems "that takes us from sunrise to sunset and a festival after dark, closing with the stillness of night."[21] Schafer matches these miniature texts with similarly finely crafted musical settings. He uses all of his mature techniques, including advanced (but non-serial) harmonic language, aleatory passages, and a wide variety of choral textures.

Alleluia was written around the same time as *You Are Illuminated* and was also not written in response to a commission. In the case of *Alleluia*,

Schafer wrote the piece almost in one sitting for acquaintance and fellow composer Susan Frykberg. He had received a letter from her in which she informed him that she had decided to enter a convent. In response to her revelation of finding God, he crafted a simple yet joyful setting of the single word "Alleluia."

Imagining Incense was commissioned by the 2002 Toronto International Choral Festival for performance by the Tokyo Philharmonic Choir, which had earlier commissioned and performed *Vox Naturae*. For this commission Schafer turned to the Japanese ceremony known as "Listen to the Incense" (*Ko wo kiku*), dating from the fourteenth century. The six movements of the piece are based on the characteristics of six types of wood incense as found in a sixteenth-century description:

> *manaka*—light and enticing—a woman of changing moods
> *manaban*—sweet, coarse, unrefined—a rather vulgar person
> *kyara*—gentle, elegant, dignified—an aristocrat
> *sumotara*—similar to kyara but rather sour—a servant disguised as an aristocrat
> *sasora*—cool and sour—a monk
> *rakoku*—sharp and pungent—a warrior

Winter Solstice was commissioned by Diane Loomer and the Vancouver-based male chorus Chor Leoni and was written in 2001. Schafer had originally called this piece *Chant to Bring Back the Light* but he changed the title two years later to avoid confusion with the large-scale work *The Fall Into Light*. Schafer talks about the source of the text, which follows his pattern of mixing onomatopoeic words from real languages with newly created words.

> The words are suggestive of darkness and light. Some come from real languages. Tatqiniqqaq is the Inuit word for the moon of the shortest days. Noche oscura is Spanish for dark night; duister and mörker are Dutch and Swedish words for darkness. Shadion is suggestive of shadow. As for light, lustro and lumina are from Latin, while alo amar is the opening, in Bengali, of Tagore's poem "Light, My Light" from Gitanjali.[22]

The Fall Into Light is Schafer's largest choral work, commissioned for the 2003 celebration of Schafer's seventieth birthday and the fiftieth anniversary of professional choral singing in Canada in 2003. Schafer only agreed to write the piece after a personal request from Soundstreams Canada director Lawrence Cherney since he had not been completely pleased with how that organization had produced some of his other pieces. *The Fall Into Light* was written for six of Canada's professional choirs (Pro Coro Canada, the Vancouver Chamber Choir, the Elora Festival Singers, the Elmer Iseler Singers, the Tafelmusik Chamber Choir, and Studio de Musique Anciene de Montreal), the Canadian Children's Opera Chorus, and six percussionists. Each of the choirs was led by their own conductor, all under the direction of the Estonian conductor Tõnu Kaljuste. The premiere was in the atrium of the Canadian Broadcasting Center in Toronto, where the six choirs were spaced around the building. Schafer describes the piece in this way:

> The Fall into Light is a syncretic work based on texts from a wide variety of sources, gnostic, hermetic and mystical for the most part, but also with texts by Rilke, Nietzsche and some personal reflections. The basic theme is Manichean, the fall of the soul from its heavenly home of light to the darkness of the earth and its attempt to escape from the archons who rule there and to pass through the aeons of space back into the pleroma of light. The direction of this passage may be up or down since the earth is surrounded by starry light, hence the title. Since the soul in Manichean thinking is also a drop of light, the whole work is a study of light within darkness as well as darkness within light.[23]

The work is divided into several parts, and in this, perhaps Schafer's crowning achievement in the choral field, the composer draws upon all of his techniques crafted over the past several decades. He would later excerpt sections 8, 11, and 14 from *The Fall Into Light*, simplify them somewhat, and publish them as *Three Hymns from* The Fall Into Light.

Section 1: "The Fall" sets a paraphrase of an ancient Greek Orphic text, from the theosophical mystery cult that later influenced Gnosticism. Schafer represents the falling soul with some of his most chaotic and frightening music.

Section 2: "The Exile" sets text by Mani, the founder of Manicheism, a religion that incorporated Gnostic ideals. This brief passage includes a soprano solo, and the choral texture thins out to only a few voices.

Sections 3–5: "Dispond" sets a text paraphrased from Job; "Noche Oscura" is based on a text by St. John of the Cross; and "Dark Night" sets a short text by the composer. The despair of the texts and the darkness the soul has fallen into is reflected in the use of the men's voices.

Section 6: "Requiem" sets a text by Rilke from *Requiem für Wolf Graf von Kalckreuth*. This section is given to the alto voices, who in three-part canon sing simultaneously the original German text and its English translation.

Section 7: "The First Archon: Jeo" is an incantation created by the composer to overcome the first Archon, a creature of darkness. The writing is reminiscent of the approach that Schafer takes whenever he writes "tone magic," as in the earlier *Magic Songs* and *Rain Chant*.

Section 8: "First Hymn" sets a paraphrase of a text from the *Poimandres* of Hermes Trismegistos and is in a more traditional tonal idiom.

Section 9: "Night Song" sets the first two lines of "Nachtlied" from Nietzche's *Also Sprach Zarathustra*. It is given to the treble voices of choir 1 only, and the voices sing pointillistic music to depict the fountains spoken of in the poem.

Sections 10–11: "The Second Archon: El Shaddai" and "Second Hymn" are similar in style to the "First Archon" and "First Hymn" sections.

Section 12: "The Eye of the Sun" is a poem from the *Keno-Upanishad*. It is one measure long with a simple statement by all choirs together.

Section 13: "Flame of God" uses a Chaldean text adapted from the *Oracles of Porphyry*. Much as he did in his approach to "Night Song," Schafer resorts to word-painting to depict the text.

Sections 14-15: "The Third Archon: Astophiaos" and "Third Hymn" follow the style of the earlier Archon/Hymn pairings.

Section 16: "Corpus Hermeticum" takes additional texts from the book but adds material from Montaigne. Schafer has parts of the choir declaim these texts over hummed chords.

Section 17: "The Fourth Archon: Imhulu" follows the pattern of the previous Archon sections.

Section 18: "Sophia" draws from various sources in the Gnostic tradition. Schafer also borrows the music for this section, basing it on extrapolations from an ancient Greek papyrus. With this musical material Schafer creates one of the most complex sections of the work, where each choir moves independently, led by its own conductor, creating a vast, ever-shifting canon.

Section 19: "O Nobly Born" is drawn from an English translation of the *Bardo Thodol*, the *Tibetan Book of the Dead*.

Section 20: "You Are Illuminated" is an earlier piece for children's chorus that sets a text from the *Bhagavad Gita*.

Section 21: "O Luce Eterna" sets lines from the closing of Dante's *Paradiso* simultaneously in the original Italian and in English translation. The full choral texture is used in this expansive setting, characterized by slowly shifting harmonies.

Section 22: "Eternity" sets the famous text by the English poet Henry Vaughan. The children's choir declaims the text over sustained chords in the SATB choruses.

The short unpublished piece for choir and alphorn *Roland of Roncesvalles* was written in 2004. For the text for such an unusual combination of musicians, Schafer turned to the *Chanson de Roland*, a French chanson de geste written around 1100. In the poem, Roland signals to Charlemagne on Oliphant, his horn made of an elephant's tusk, and the sound carries thirty leagues ahead to the emperor, who turns back but only to find Roland and all of his knights dead. Schafer adapted a handful of lines from an English translation of the text that focus on Roland's horn, which Charlemagne honors by filling it with gold and placing it on the altar of Saint Severin. In addition to mixed choir and alphorn, the piece calls for bass drum and chimes, and the musical language is simple and straightforward.

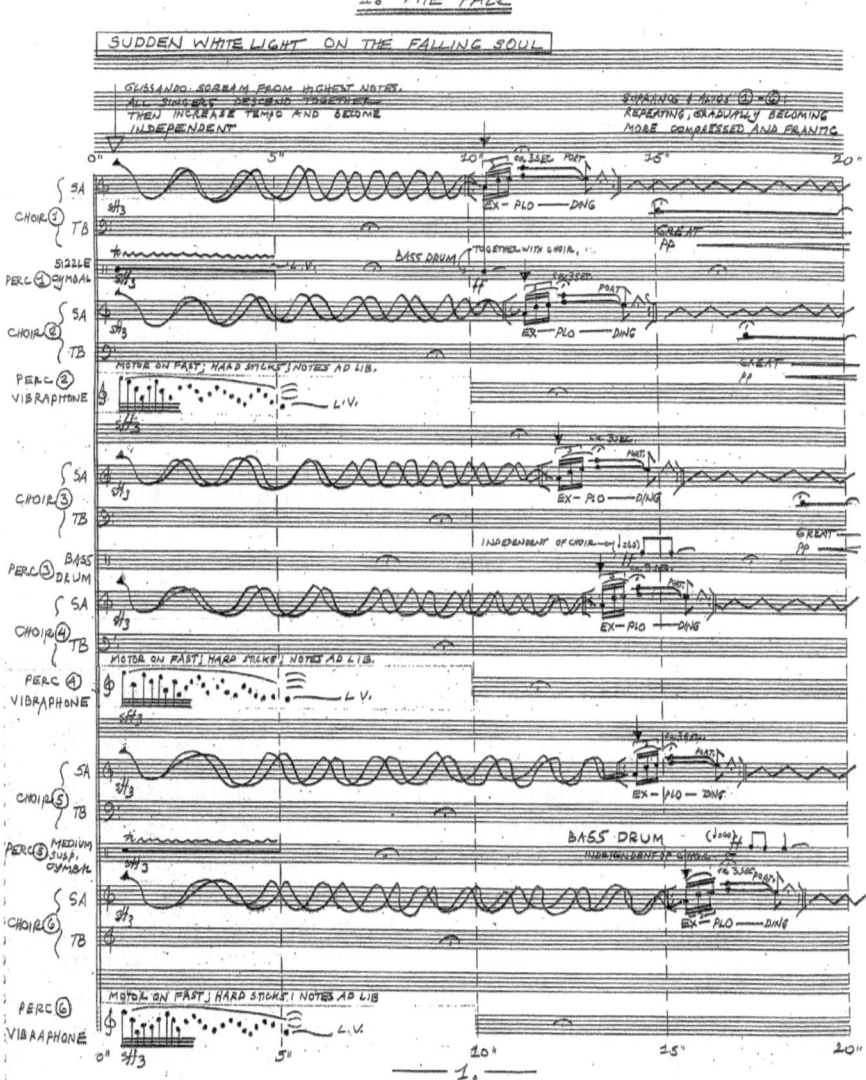

Figure 15.2. Section 1: "The Fall"—*The Fall Into Light.* R. Murray Schafer

The text for *The Searching Sings*, completed in June of 2008, was written by Rae Crossman, a close friend of Schafer who also supplied the text for the solo piece *From the Bow*. By 2008 Crossman had been involved in the Wolf Project for over twenty years, and the poem reflects his and Schafer's joint experience in that project. The music effectively paints the text of Crossman's poem, which joyfully describes various aspects of the wilderness. Schafer uses both traditional techniques and graphic and aleatoric gestures to show the meaning of the poem.

In 2008 the Tokyo Philharmonic Choir asked Schafer for a second choral piece in Latin since *Vox Naturae* had been such a great success. It was also suggested that Schafer follow a similar process as for that earlier piece, where he divided the choir into different locations and even had them move about. Schafer eventually decided to turn to another ancient poet and philosopher, Ovid, selecting the story of Narcissus and Echo from that author's *Metamorphosis* as the text for his own *Narcissus and Echo*. Schafer's initial concept was to have the character of Narcissus be played by a dancer and Echo be sung by several different women's voices from different parts in the hall. To create the final form of the text, Schafer worked with a Latin scholar, Will Pemberton, who functioned in many ways as a librettist. The piece takes the shape of a mini drama, using not only the concert space but also the foyer, beginning the piece while the audience is still gathering as the blind narrator, Tiresias, brings the audience into the hall where the story will unfold. Schafer takes advantage of the large choir, breaking it into several smaller groups, many of which play simple percussion. Many different choral textures are explored, in addition to the treble soloists who realize Echo's voice.

Make Room for God was written in 2008 for performance by the College-Conservatory of Music Chorale and their director Dr. Brett Scott. Schafer was asked to select a sacred text for the commission, and he decided to create his own. Schafer writes, "I imagined the choir inviting God to come and join them in their singing—a whimsical idea perhaps, but one that must surely be in the mind of all singers the moment they open their mouths."[24] Many of Schafer's past themes appear in this piece, including calling upon various aspects of the natural world to praise God, with the expected musical depictions of those natural phenomena. It is a simple and lovely piece, with a mix of traditional and graphic notation.

The Love That Moves the Universe was commissioned by the Vancouver Chamber Choir in celebration of the ensemble's fortieth anniversary in the 2009–2010 season. It was completed in 2009 and premiered in March 2010. The texts Schafer chose to set were the first and last cantos from the "Paradiso" section of Dante's *La Divina Commedia*, setting the opening canto in an English translation, and the last canto in the original Italian. For the orchestration of the piece, Schafer turned to a bit of numerical symbolism, scoring the piece for twenty singers and twenty string players who are intermingled and placed in a circle to visually represent Dante's description of the stars and spheres of light in paradise. *The Love That Moves the Universe* takes full advantage of the forty possible lines, hearkening back to other large-scale works such as *Credo* and *The Fall Into Light*. At times the strings accompany the singers, and at other times the two groups have parts so independent that two conductors are required, one for the voices, one for the strings. Schafer also makes use of space, moving sound across and around the circle throughout the piece.

Landscapes and Soundscapes was completed in February 2010 but started several years before with the opening movement, *Water, Lilies, Carp*, being sketched out as early as 2006. To this initial movement Schafer added over the course of the next few years five other movements. The entire set is for unaccompanied mixed chorus, with two of the movements for treble voices only. The piece is a continuation of the long cycle of pieces written by Schafer that depict things in the environment. We see the same techniques as in other pieces, with subtle choral textures, aleatoric and extended vocal techniques, and graphic notation.

The second-to-last choral composition Schafer wrote was for Soundstreams Canada, premiered in 2010. *The Soul of God* is for four choirs, similar to the earlier *Death of Shalana*, but for this piece Schafer chose to combine texts from the *Isha Upanishad*, a key text in the Hindi religious tradition, with writings of the thirteenth-century Italian philosopher and theologian Saint Bonaventure and some of the composer's own reflections. These texts are meant to suggest the omnipresent revelation of the divine, and Schafer indicates that the four choirs should be spaced around the room to reflect this sense. Similar to *The Fall Into Light*, each choir has its own conductor, and all are led by a central conductor. There are percussion instruments associated with each choir, which can be played by the conductor or by designated players. In its harmonic language and use of choral texture, the piece is reminiscent of some of the more lyrical and meditative parts of *The Fall Into Light*.

Here the Sounds Go Round was written in 2012 and performed in February 2014 as part of the Soundstreams Canada celebration of sixty years of professional choral singing in Canada. (Schafer had written *The Fall Into Light* for the fiftieth anniversary celebrations.) The premiere was sung by three of Canada's professional choirs—Pro Coro Canada, the Vancouver Chamber Choir, and the Elmer Iseler Singers. This was the last choral composition that Schafer would write, and for it he turned back to a text that he first created in 1983 for a traveling exhibition of some of his scores and sound sculptures. The curator had the idea to introduce the exhibit with a record instead of a printed invitation. The poem "Here the Sounds Go Round" was on one side of that disc. Schafer pulled excerpts from this poem, rearranging many of the passages, to create the text for this piece for three choirs. This last piece incorporates many of the techniques we see throughout his career. The choir is asked to do some simple staging to help declaim the text. The harmonic language is simple and various devices are used (including canonic, given the title) to spin out the music.

Chapter Sixteen

The Compositions for Voice

The compositions in this chapter have solo voice as the primary focus of the piece. The accompaniments vary, from no accompaniment at all through chamber ensembles and electronics to large orchestra. The vocal compositions from Schafer's student days (*A Music Lesson* and *Three Contemporaries*), his time in Germany (*Minnelieder* and *Kinderlieder*), and his time in London (*Protest and Incarceration*; *The Judgement of Jael*; and *Brébeuf*) are discussed in chapter 14. Many of Schafer's compositions were written specifically for Phyllis Mailing, his first wife, or Eleanor James, his third wife. Besides those pieces written for his wives, most of the other vocal works were commissions, and often for a specific singer, notably Mary Morrison, Donna Brown, or Maureen Forrester. The works Schafer created for inclusion in larger pieces, including the *Patria* cycle, will be discussed first, followed by those works conceived as stand-alone compositions.

COMPOSITIONS INTENDED FOR *PATRIA* OR OTHER EXTENDED WORKS

The Geography of Eros was the first completed segment of *Loving*, Schafer's first theatrical work. It was premiered as a stand-alone piece in 1964, and in its free form and sophisticated use of electronics we see the emergence of the last elements of Schafer's mature compositional style taking their place alongside the polished atonal, serial, and formalist techniques he had explored in such pieces as *Five Studies on Texts by Prudentius* and *Untitled Composition for Orchestra no. 1*. In contrast to these strictly organized pieces, Schafer calls *Geography* "completely free and almost contrivedly athematic," and he states, "Spiritually and musically *Geography* was a necessary reaction to the rigorousness of Prudentius."[1]

Schafer's described approach to creating this aria is consistent with his assertion that it was not based on a pre-established formula or method. The composer first created a haphazard collection of words and phrases from adolescent love poems, which he cut out and put randomly on a page. From there he created a decorative pen drawing, taking the resulting graphic shapes to suggest the musical contours of the piece. His goal for the piece was to "create an aura in half-lights, allusions, confused vibrations and nocturnal thoughts, to decorate the experience of physical love with a net of sounds and word-sensations."[2] The vocal line shows the influence of jazz and pop music (Mary Morrison, for whom the piece was written, was comfortable in those idioms) as well as the folk music of the Balkans, which was still fresh in Schafer's mind from his trip there several years earlier.

When Schafer received a commission from the CBC to write an extended work for his wife Phyllis, he used the opportunity to begin to create a new extended theatrical work, with the commission being the first material. Initially called *Requiems*, it was performed and published as *Requiems for the Party Girl*, and it would become one of the core elements of *Patria 2*.[3] Written for voice and chamber ensemble, *Requiems for the Party Girl* sets thirteen brief text fragments of contrasting character, including multiple languages and nonsense syllables (all written by Schafer), divided into ten short arias.[4] As Stephen Adams notes, "The sequence presents fragmented spots of time, iridescent glimpses into the party-girl's world, separated and objectified by breathing spaces of silence."[5] Schafer had completed this major commission by the end of 1966, and the premiere occurred in February 1967 at SFU.

The character played by the singer is a young woman, very disturbed, describing various states of her existence, including, at the end, her own suicide. It marks the first appearance of the all-interval row that is one of the foundations of the entire *Patria* cycle in its original form: C, B, C-sharp, B-flat, D, A, D-sharp, A-flat, E, G, F, F-sharp. To this underpinning are added the avant-garde techniques that Schafer had mastered in his previous works, including the extended vocal and instrumental techniques and approaches he had polished in *Loving*. Examples of these techniques are the use of Morse code in the percussion section (and later the other instruments) in Aria 6 and the whispered conversations given by the players to the singer in Aria 5.

Music for the Morning of the World was a commission from the Société Contemporaine for Phyllis, and Schafer began to work on it in June 1970. It was written for inclusion in *Lustro*, the large composition inspired by Schafer's trip to the Middle East, where he had encountered the writings of the thirteenth-century Islamic mystic Jalal-al-Din Rumi. Schafer drew his texts from multiple Rumi collections in English translation, including *Discourses*; *Divan i Shams i Tabriz*; and *Masnavi*. The texts speak of the fusion of divine and human love from the perspective of the individual.[6]

In contrast to the large forces required for the first and third parts of *Lustro*, this extended second part is only for solo voice and quadraphonic electronics. In the program notes Schafer indicates his desire that

> at the beginning of the performance the lights are slowly extinguished to total darkness. The soloist lights a single candle, the only illumination for the aria, and extinguishes it at the conclusion, invoking a mood of spiritual transcendence, appropriate to the Rumi text.[7]

The vocal line shows the influence of dervish flute melodies (a dervish flute appears in the electronics), which center around an individual note. The use of the accompanying electronics is among the most sophisticated Schafer has produced. The original four-track tape depicts the four points of the compass, and all of the spatial possibilities of this arrangement are explored. Concrete and synthesized sounds are freely mixed, and even some conventional musical sounds, including a quote from Bruckner, appear.[8]

Arcana was composed in 1972 in response to a commission for voice and chamber ensemble for the 1973 Montreal International Competition. He was asked to not set a contemporary language since singers from all over the world would compete and any particular living language might give an unfair advantage to individual singers. He was also asked to write the voice part in a medium range to suit all of the competing voices. The composition would later be included as an editing unit in *Patria 4*.

Schafer describes the piece as follows:

> In the program notes Arcana derives its name from its text, which is in Middle Egyptian hieroglyphs, and was discovered near Memphis by the Arabian explorer Al Mamun at the beginning of the ninth century. The fragmentary text is remarkable because it bears little relationship to any other surviving Egyptian hieroglyphs of the period; but it seems to possess a religious significance and perhaps relates to the secret initiation ceremonies conducted in the labyrinth by the Egyptian priests. It was translated for the composer by Professor D. B. Redford of the Department of Near Eastern Studies, University of Toronto.
>
> The compositional method was as follows: each phoneme of the text was given two notes within a range of two octaves, including a few quarter tones. Thus each phonemic element always has the same note or notes associated with it. Often the singer sings one of these notes while the instruments play the other. The frequency with which each phoneme recurs in the text gives the melodic line its character, even a sense of tonality.[9]

This formulaic approach to creating this piece, with strict assignations of musical material in both the vocal line and accompanying instrumental writing, hearkens back to some of his earlier pieces for voice and is in marked contrast to the freedom of *The Geography of Eros*. While his description of the genesis of the vocal line and its accompaniment is accurate, his assertions about the discovery and subsequent translation of the text are not. Schafer had himself created the fourteen short statements that make up the text, then asked Professor Redford to translate it from English into ancient Egyptian and to give an International Phonetic Alphabet guide to the texts.

Hymn to Night was commissioned by Paul Robinson through funds from the Canada Council, and it is a vocal tour de force intended for the noted soprano Riki Turofsky, who sang the premiere in 1978. Schafer turned to a famous set of poems by the German Romantic-era poet Novalis, *Hymnen an die Nacht*, as the inspiration for the piece. He was reading Novalis late one night and was instantly inspired to begin setting the text, sketching out the whole form of that work in one sitting before creating both a chamber orchestra and a full orchestra version. To each version Schafer added two more layers of sound. The first was a recording of an Aeolian harp, which Schafer describes as follows:

> Many are the descriptions and wild imaginings suggested by this instrument in the writings of Romanticists such as E.T.A. Hoffmann, Novalis and Berlioz. Placed outdoors and set in motion by the wind, it sighed like a mysterious stranger in a breeze but wailed painfully in a storm. It was precisely the right instrument to accompany the nocturnal voyage of the soul depicted by Novalis.[10]

The second addition was a method of using recorded delays of the voice in certain passages, often with only the voice and its two recorded delays singing. The approximate delay is four or six seconds, with some flexibility to allow for such considerations as hall resonance.

Although there are recurring motives, the piece is essentially through composed and focuses primarily on evoking the mood of the poem. Schafer calls it one of his most "romantic" pieces, although the harmonic language is clearly in a contemporary idiom. This romanticism is most clearly reflected in the vocal line, which is often ecstatic and always challenging; the ever shifting moods and tempi; and the surprisingly lush orchestration, given the small size of the orchestra. This piece was later incorporated into several portions of *Patria 7*.

Schafer began work on *La Testa d'Adriane* at the same time as *Hymn to Night* but did not finish it until 1977. Schafer notes,

> For some time my friend Joe Macerollo had been after me to write a piece for accordion. Simultaneously Mary Morrison wanted a new piece for voice. But her voice was past its prime and I resisted until it struck me that I could put these two "misfits" together in a kind of carnival attraction. What resulted was the first piece of what was eventually to grow into *Patria 3: The Greatest Show*.[11]

Since Schafer's concept was based on a circus side-show, the choice of a piece for free-bass accordion was a logical one, given the associations of that instrument. At the end of *Patria 2*, Ariadne kills herself. In *La Testa* she reappears as a permutation of that character: a preserved head with an altered name, animated by a side-show barker and his accordion.[12]

> The accordionist, dressed in a tattered tuxedo and top hat, opens with a happy tune to attract an audience. Behind a curtain he claims to have the bodyless head of a woman, saved at the instant before death and preserved by the fantastic art of *leger demain*. When he pulls the curtain of his little booth, we do indeed see a woman's head on a table without a body. She appears to be sleeping, but the barker awakens her with music and she sings a strange aria of gurgles, trills, whispers and pops, finally ending in laughter that descends into weeping before she subsides again into her comatose state. In vain the showman tries to revive her with his accordion. Finally he pulls the curtain shut. The show is over.[13]

The preface to the piece gives extensive directions as to how the piece should be staged, including how to create the illusion of the disembodied head. The music, since it was intended as a *Patria* editing unit, is clearly based on the all-interval row, which is fully expressed in the opening measure's three accordion chords.

Schafer sketched out *Beauty and the Beast* in November of 1979 as a commission for Maureen Forrester and the Orford String Quartet. Since the piece was to be performed in Montreal, Schafer chose to set Madame Leprince de Beaumont's story "Beauty and the Beast," and he created the score with both a French and English text, with Gabriel Charpentier helping to prepare the French version. Like *La Testa d'Adriane*, this piece was also written for inclusion in *Patria 3*. Schafer conceived of it as a mini, one-half-hour-long opera suitable for performance for children and adults. Although it is not explicitly stated in the libretto or in the program notes, Schafer indicates that under the surface of this children's tale he sees a deeper psychological significance through the interaction between the masculine and feminine mystique that is also often found in traditional folk stories.

The singer is instructed to use hand-held masks to help tell the story and differentiate the various characters: Narrator, Father, Beast, Youth, Queen, and Beauty. The vocal line moves between speech and simple, largely stepwise melody in the through-composed form. Each character receives his or her own tonal center, and unique set of notes, while the string quartet helps paint the narrative through repeated motives and coloristic effects. The harmonic language is much more traditional than such pieces as *Arcana* or *Hymn to Night* and clearly shows the influence of French impressionism (which is appropriate given the source of the tale) in its use of nonfunctional

Figure 16.1. *La Testa d'Adriane*. R. Murray Schafer

chord progressions and whole tone melodies and intervals while still showing evidence of the all-interval row that characterizes the *Patria* cycle.

Finished in September of 1980, *Wizard Oil and Indian Sagwa* is one of two pieces that Schafer wrote for speaker with an obligato instrument. Like *La Testa* and *Beauty and the Beast*, it was also written with the intent to incorporate it into *Patria 3*, in this instance as one of the wandering entertainments. As Schafer describes it,

> this humorous work recreates an old-time medicine show in which the speaker, alias Johnny Mailloux, endeavours to sell a cure-all called Wizard Oil, while the clarinetist, alias Chief Sam Padoopi, dressed in Indian costume, endorses the product with his playing and occasional dancing.[14]

The piece was written for bpNichol, a Canadian poet who was also a sound poet and performer. This composition is clearly written for someone of Nichol's talents since no singing is required but high demands are placed on the speaker's acting skills. The clarinetist is also required to move and act, and the demanding clarinet writing explores the limits of the instrument in various, always humorous ways. The connection to the *Patria* cycle is evident in the introductory clarinet line, which outlines the *Patria* row based on the pitch G, although obscured by octave transposition and repeated notes.

Sun Father, Sky Mother (originally titled *Sun Father, Earth Mother*) was the first piece Schafer wrote after he had gone to stay with Eleanor James in St. Gallen, Switzerland, sketching it out in December of that year. The piece is inspired by the mountains, those of the Canadian Rockies, where he had spent some time in the summer of 1984, as well as the Swiss Alps of St. Gallen. As part of his preparations for the *Patria Prologue: The Princess of the Stars* production in Banff, Murray had been researching the sonic properties of a variety of lakes and had decided to further explore the sonic properties of an unaccompanied voice in nature. Although written with a mountain landscape in mind, the piece could also be presented in other wilderness settings, such as near a lake, or in a forest.

The text consists of ten short invocations (nine in the original composition) to Sun Father, Sky Mother, Moon Lover, Stars Brothers, Mountains Protectors, Birds Daughters, Fish Ancestors, Forests Providers, Animals Song, and finally Spirits of the World. Each invocation has its own character, and a pause between each invocation allow the singer (or singers) to move to various locations in order to explore the landscape. Schafer insists that this composition must be performed in an outdoor location so that

> when the singer sings the final lines, "I come to you, I am one with you," the song echoing back would blur the distinction between soundmaker and the soundscape, as if the mountains and the forest were addressing the singer as much as the other way around.[15]

The original version of this aria, *Sun Father: Earth Mother* is sung as part of the yearly performance of *Patria Epilogue*.

Tantrika was the third piece that Murray wrote specifically for Eleanor James, beginning it in 1984 but not completing the piece until 1986, when it was performed by Eleanor at the St. John's Sound Symposium. It was originally scored for singer and one percussionist, intended, as so many other pieces during this time, for inclusion as an editing unit of *Patria 3*. It was revised in 2001 for voice and two percussionists for inclusion in a revival of *In Search of Zoroaster*, where the singer represented the temptress Jahi. In both versions the singer is also asked to play hand-held percussion instruments.

Schafer talks about the source of the text this way:

> Tantra is a cult of ecstasy, focused on a vision of cosmic sexuality. A tantrika is an adept in the arts of Tantra, one who successfully attains sadhana, the ultimate knowledge through meditation combined with sexual rites. The text for Tantrika consists of words associated with the Tantric arts.[16]

The text includes such words as *ram* ("fire mantra"), *nada* ("sound"), *devadasi* ("dancing girl"—dedicated to the worship and service of a god), and *vidya* ("insight"), among others. Since the piece was intended for inclusion in *Patria 3*, we again see the appearance of the all-interval row based on B-flat, although the first note to appear is A. The row is again treated freely, with many repeated notes and motives as the row unfolds. It is a virtuosic piece for both the singer and the players, who play multiple instruments, and the influence of music from Eastern cultures, long a source of inspiration for the composer, is evident.

The four short pieces, *Aubade for Two Voices (or Trumpet and Voice)*; *Aubade*; *Nocturne*; and *Ariadne's Aria*, were written between 1992 and 1995 as music for the annual performance of *Patria Epilogue: And Wolf Shall Inherit the Moon*. Given the wilderness setting of the epilogue, all of these pieces were written to be performed outdoors, and in addition, the two aubades and the nocturne were intended to either begin or end specific days in the epilogue week. The text consists of only vowels, and the pieces are similar in character to *Sun Father: Earth Mother*.

STAND-ALONE COMPOSITIONS

Sappho was written in 1970 through a commission for the Coolidge foundation, and was premiered at the Coolidge Festival in Washington, DC, that year. It was written for Phyllis to perform, accompanied by harp, piano, guitar, and percussion. His first setting of texts of Sappho, he considered it a failure, withdrew it, and later used the same text for *Enchantress*.

Enchantress was begun at the same time as *Music for the Morning of the World* and was also a commission, this time for Mary Morrison with funds from the CBC. Schafer struggled with the piece on and off before finishing it in 1971, finally deciding to reuse the text he had originally set in *Sappho*. The original texts were from the collection *Lyra Graeca*, and Schafer set the original Greek using the unusual combination of voice, flute, and eight cellos, where the flautist is given the choice to use a variety of exotic flutes. The role of the flute is primarily to accompany and add color to the vocal line, although it does have some independent passages. The role of the cellos is largely to provide harmonic support and coloristic effects to the writing. This is a remarkably evocative and sparsely textured piece, showing Schafer's attempt to reflect the meaning and source of the text.

Adieu, Robert Schumann was composed for Maureen Forrester through a commission from John Roberts, who was then director of music at the CBC. It would be the first of several pieces that Schafer would write for the noted Canadian contralto. As indicated by the title, the composition is based on the German Romantic composer Robert Schumann's growing madness, incarceration, and final death in the Endenich asylum in Bonn, Germany. Schafer elected to tell this story from Clara Schumann's perspective, and freely adapted (and translated himself) selections from her diary.

Schafer incorporates several fragments of Schumann's own music taken from several of the lieder (*Dein Angesicht* being the most striking) and portions of *Carnival*, *Kreisleriana*, and *Kinderszenen* in order to "suggest the conflicts in his [Schumann's] mind during the days of his final collapse."[17] He also uses Schumann's own device of hiding musical motives (C-A for Clara and B-flat–E for Robert) in the piece. In the orchestra Schafer calls for an onstage piano to accompany the singer and also either a prerecorded or backstage piano that plays the melody Schumann wrote down during his first hallucination, which he claimed was dictated to him by angels. As the piece progresses, Schafer increasingly stresses the note A in the orchestra, representing Schumann's torment during his illness, when that note kept ringing in his ears. At the end of the piece only that note remains.[18]

The Garden of the Heart was written in 1980. The text is based on a description of a garden that appears in *One Thousand and One Nights*, and to this Schafer added a story, using figures of speech found elsewhere in the book. The summary of the story is as follows.

> A woman has returned to the garden where she and her lover used to meet, knowing she will die there, and beseeching her lover to return one last time to listen to her voice in the dancing water of the fountain.[19]

This was not the first time that Schafer used this text since he had included a calligraphic rendering of it in the earlier graphic novel *Ariadne*, which was first issued under the title *Smoke* in 1976. He would later again use the text, the story behind it, and this composition to create a quasi-fictional novella also called *The Garden of the Heart*.

Schafer wrote this composition for voice and orchestra for Maureen Forrester and had clearly in his mind her (by this time) aging voice, which he considered well suited to portray the woman in the story. He chose a different approach to composing the piece, his first vocal piece in several years that was not associated with any portion of *Patria*, by first writing out the complete vocal line. The orchestral accompaniment is drawn entirely from the vocal line "so that the entire work is, in a sense, imbued with speech, the instruments anticipating and recollecting the thoughts and descriptions of the singer's narrative."[20] The orchestra is in many ways an aural representation of the visual arabesques that accompanied this same text in *Ariadne*, which was itself a representation of the delicate and sensual lines of Persian art.

Schafer wrote *Letters from Mignon* at the end of 1984. He and Eleanor had been writing letters back and forth from the time she left for St. Gallen until he joined her there, and he turned to the text of some of the letters she had written to him for his next piece for voice and orchestra, dedicating it to her but not, in the original score or performances of the piece, indicating where the texts for the songs had come from. "Mignon" was Schafer's pet name for Eleanor, based on the character in Goethe's novel *Wilhelm Meister*, and in the program notes for the first performance Schafer writes,

> There is little doubt that she (Mignon) loved Wilhelm Meister though the exact nature of their relationship is never fully revealed. In these letters we imagine Mignon in all her girlish womanhood pouring out her affection for the man she loves.[21]

The texts themselves mix passages of Italian and German with English. Schafer compares the musical language to that of Wagner's *Wesendonck Lieder*, which was also inspired by poems of the composer's beloved.

In 1986 Schafer returned to *Minnelieder* to create another vocal-orchestral composition for Eleanor for a performance with the Quebec Symphony Orchestra. He left the original songs essentially unchanged in their form and musical material, simply expanding the instrumentation from the original woodwind quintet texture to that of full orchestra. To these he added one new song, "Unter den Linden," to a text by Walther von der Vogelweide, which although written three decades later than the others fits well into the harmonic and melodic mood set by the earlier songs. The orchestration is imaginative, and it is an effective second version of one of his earlier works.

Schafer began *Gitanjali* in 1990, finishing the first draft by the end of the year but not completing it until the beginning of 1991 for performance by soprano Donna Brown and the National Arts Center Orchestra. The text for

Gitanjali is five poems from a collection of the same name by poet Rabindranath Tagore, in an English version the poet created and published in 1913. Schafer had long been a student of Tagore's poetry, even owning a recording of Tagore himself singing several of the songs from his collection. He had first set Tagore's poetry in the early choral piece *Four Songs on Texts of Tagore* and had also included "Light, My Light" in *Beyond the Great Gate of Light,* the third movement of his triptych *Lustro.* Schafer characterizes the work this way: "Of all my works for solo voice, Gitanjali is undoubtedly the most ecstatic. The influence of Richard Strauss is perhaps more felt than actually present in the tonalities of the songs."[22]

After a decade-long break from writing any stand-alone vocal pieces, Schafer began composing *Thunder: Perfect Mind* in 2002 for Eleanor while she was still living in Europe and they were apart. When she decided to move permanently back to the farm in 2003, he worked diligently to finish it and presented it to her as a welcome-home present in July of that year. Eventually he would receive a commission from the CBC to use the piece to finish out a proposed recording, featuring Eleanor singing two earlier works for voice and orchestra also written for her: *Letters from Mignon* and the orchestral version of *Minnelieder.* The CBC would later pull their funding from the project, but it did go forward, and the disc was released in 2007. Schafer notes,

> The text of Thunder: Perfect Mind comes from a papyrus discovered at Nag Hammadi, Egypt, in 1945. It is a revelation discourse delivered in the first person by a female theurgist. The tone is forceful throughout and full of deliberate antitheses and paradoxes, viz.: "I am the whore and the holy one, I am the wife and the virgin." The text also contains exhortations to hear and reflect on these antitheses, revealing that the narrator believes herself to be, and wants us to believe her to be, a seer intimate with all the incomprehensible forces of the cosmos.[23]

From the Bow was the second piece that Schafer wrote for narrator and obligato instrument. Like *Wizard Oil and Indian Sagwa,* this piece was also written for a poet/sound-poet friend, in this case Rae Crossman. This piece was written for performance by Rae with obligato clarinet, completed in July of 2003, and premiered as part of the festivities surrounding the 2003 production of *The Enchanted Forest.* The text describes a journey by canoe made by Rae and one of his children, and it was performed by Rae at the premiere. It has not been published, and the complete score is in the possession of the composer.

The second piece that Schafer wrote for Eleanor James in 2003 was *Tanzlied.* The harpist Judy Loman, for whom he had written several pieces, had asked him to compose an extended work for harp and voice, and he immediately approached Eleanor and asked her what text she would like to sing. The next day she returned with a text from *Also Sprach Zarathustra* by Friedrich Nietzsche. Eleanor and Judy premiered the piece in 2004 as part of the Ottawa Chamber Music Festival. The text is from the third part of *Zarathustra*, with some alterations and omissions of text for the sake of the musical setting. Schafer summarizes the story found within the text this way:

> In it Nietzsche (Zarathustra) confronts and struggles with Life. Throughout the poem the narrator dances with Life, sometimes advancing, sometimes retreating, as Life surges ahead down unknown paths both ecstatic and mysterious. The singer stumbles, gets up and rushes on, sometimes whipping Life mercilessly until Life cries out: "O Zarathustra, don't crack your whip so terribly. You know: Noise kills thought!" At the end Zarathustra and Life embrace one another and weep.[24]

The singer represents both Zarathustra and Life and also plays handheld percussion. At the end of the piece Schafer incorporates two phrases of Nietzsche's own music, which was itself inspired by Wagner. The first is from a song, *Gebet an das Leben*, and the second from an early piano composition, *Heldenklage*, written when the philosopher was eighteen years old.

Six Songs from Rilke's "Book of Hours" was commissioned by the soprano Stacie Dunlop, who had sung in previous *Patria* productions. Schafer turned his attention to the set of songs late in 2006, writing them quickly, almost one a day, so that he had finished the piece by the beginning of December. They were premiered by Dunlop and the Land's End Ensemble in Calgary in May of the next year. Schafer had been first introduced to the poetry of Rilke in their original language during his residency in Vienna in the mid 1950s.

> My interest in Rilke goes back a long time, to the days I spent in Vienna (1955–57). One winter, in an attempt to escape the cold (coal was very scarce at the time), I decided to go to Trieste. There I stayed for a few months with an elderly Austrian woman who was well-connected with the Austrian aristocracy, since titled guests frequently descended to spend a few days with her. (At one time I shared a bathroom with Prince Windischgrätz.) Another guest was the Princess of Thurn und Taxis, whom I recognized immediately since Rilke's Duino Elegies were dedicated to a woman of that name. That was her mother. Rilke had stayed alone one winter in the castle at Duino, a few kilometres from Trieste, and it was there that he began the Elegies. The Princess invited me to visit her in the castle—an offer I regret I never took up.[25]

When he received the commission, he thought of Rilke, in particular the poet's collection *The Book of Hours*, and he decided to set selections in the original German and provide the translations himself for the program.

The last vocal composition Schafer completed was *Four Songs for Harp and Mezzo Soprano*, which had its genesis as a wedding present for his niece.

Schafer asked her and her Iranian fiancé for texts, and she chose the William Butler Yeats poem "Had I the Heavens' Embroidered Cloths" while her fiancé requested a text from Jalal-al-din Rumi, to which Schafer responded by setting "The Lamp." These two compositions and a third song were premiered during the 2010 wedding ceremony in a version for harp, flute, and voice. The third song in the set was too closely linked to the couple to be performed in concert so Schafer withdrew it from the set and inserted as the opening song an aria called *Sophia*, which set texts from the Wisdom of Solomon in the Hebrew scriptures and had originally been written for a collaborative sacred drama called *Job*. Schafer revised the three songs, removing the flute part, and decided that he wanted to add a final song. He turned one last time to Tagore's *Gitanjali* and created the song *The Day Is No More* in 2011. This choice proved to be prophetic, as Schafer remarks in his commentary on his final piece for voice.

> As I face a diagnosis of Alzheimer's, I find myself looking into the shadows of my unknown future. Sometimes, I hear beautiful music from another world singing to me. I try to capture it, but it mostly eludes me. The poem closes with these enigmatic words, "I do not know whether I will come back home/I do not know who I may chance to meet. . . . There at the fording, the unknown man plays upon his harp."[26]

Chapter Seventeen

The Concerti and Other Orchestral Works

Schafer's compositions for orchestra span from his first European trip until his last orchestral piece, *Wolf Returns*, written in 2012. His mature symphonic works have stretched the boundaries of the concert hall, often working to undermine its conventions. It is common for these pieces to play with space, move the orchestra, or add nontraditional instruments. Of particular note is the large-scale triptych *Lustro* and the concerti (see chapter 14 for early and transitional pieces for orchestra).

COMPOSITIONS FOR ORCHESTRA AND CONCERT BAND

Son of Heldenleben was Schafer's first orchestral commission, received shortly after he had moved to Vancouver to begin teaching at SFU. He notes,

> One day in 1967 I received a telegram from the Montreal Symphony Orchestra. It read: "Congratulations! Have been awarded commission by the MSO. Wire acceptance immediately." I wrote back that, flattered as I was by their surprising offer, no discussion had yet taken place concerning the length of the piece, the deadline date, and of course, the fee they were offering.[1]

He and the symphony management were able to work out the details, and Schafer began to think of how he would structure the piece. After listening with a fellow composer to Strauss's tone poem *Don Juan*, Schafer woke the next morning thinking that he wanted to rewrite one of the German composer's tone poems. He chose *Ein Heldenleben*, and imagined that his piece would be a send-up of Strauss's ideas. The Ariadne's thread of Son of Heldenleben is the opening sixteen-bar melody of the Strauss tone poem, rhythmically augmented (almost exactly) at the rate a half note per sixteenth note in the original score. Around this cantus firmus groups of instruments dance and pulse atonally. There are occasional references to other Strauss melodies from Heldenleben and a final swelling up of the main theme at the end, before it is cut short by an electronic chord.[2]

The embedded Strauss theme is from the first sixteen bars of *Ein Heldenleben* and is supplemented by quotes of other themes from that piece, which all attempt to establish the key of E-flat major, against which the other orchestral material fights.[3] Schafer explores all the color possibilities in the large orchestra, uses extended techniques for all instruments, and employs a mix of traditional and graphic notation as well as several aleatoric passages. Toward the end Schafer has those musicians who are not playing say in Greek, "Concerning the labyrinth," further tying the piece to the myth of Ariadne. The musical materials can be divided into three types. The first is material borrowed from Strauss, the second is material derived from two tone rows based on Strauss's theme, the third is material that has been freely composed.[4]

Soon after the successful premiere of *Son of Heldenleben*, Schafer received a commission from the TSO with the following description: "It is agreed that the work shall have a minimum duration of approximately seven (7) minutes and no longer than ten (10) minutes," the piece being clearly intended by the TSO to serve as the beginning of a concert program so that symphony patrons could avoid the piece and come in late if they wished. Schafer responded by creating a unique concert piece, *No Longer Than Ten (10) Minutes*, that defies the conventions and expectations of the concert hall.

No Longer Than Ten (10) Minutes begins out of the tune-up. The conductor enters and begins beating time, but nothing much changes; only gradually does the work gain definition. The climax is reached after a long crescendo precisely at ten minutes. Then the conductor signals the orchestra to cut and turns to leave the stage. But the orchestra continues to hold the last chord, only gradually fading down. Now the instructions are to go back to the beginning of the crescendo if there is applause from the audience and to continue repeating the crescendo to the climax for as long as the applause continues. When the applause finally subsides, the last desk of each string section is instructed to sustain very softly a dominant-seventh chord in the key of the following piece until the conductor returns and gives the down beat.[5]

In addition to the inspiration received from the wording of the commission, other influences are found in this piece. One of these was Schafer's research into noise pollution. As he composed the piece, he had in front of him a spectrum analysis of the sound of traffic noise on a busy street in

Vancouver, and he used those graphs as the basis of some of his sound masses. The middle section with its extended horn solo was inspired by the principal horn player of the TSO at that time, Eugene Rittich, who had developed and shown Schafer a fingering method for achieving quarter tones on his instrument.[6] The piece grows out of the tuning and blurs the end, but it does fall into a ternary form, with the opening and closing sections set in opposition to each other, the first growing from chaos toward clarity, the last going from clarity to chaos.

Divan i Shams i Tabriz was the first outworking of the influences that Schafer came under during his trip to Iran and Turkey in the spring of 1969. While there he visited holy sites associated with the thirteenth-century founder of Sufism, Jalal al-Din Rumi, and Schafer studied carefully his writings. Upon his return he first had a teaching engagement at the University of Chicago, where he met a young Persian scholar who found out about his interest in Rumi and gave him the original Persian texts and additional information about the Sufi tradition. Schafer sketched out *Divan* in the summer of 1969, finishing the initial sketch over the course of a few weeks then revising and finishing the composition in early 1970. The title of the piece is also the title of a collection of mystical poems by Rumi, which speak about the fusing of divine and human love. Schafer quotes these texts in the score, but the texts that the singers perform in the original Persian are from a different Rumi poem, *Masnavi*. The beginning of *Masnavi* is "The Song of the Reed Flute," a text held in special reverence by the dervishes of the Mevlevi order of Sufism.[7]

In *Divan* Schafer breaks the long-held convention of the orchestra being on the stage, separated from the audience. In addition to the stage performers, which consist of four percussionists, organ, contrabassoon, and strings, Schafer asks for thirteen other small ensembles, each with five musicians, which he calls "auditorium groups," to be spread throughout the hall. The seven vocal soloists are each given hand-held percussion instruments to play, and Schafer also includes a quadraphonic tape, with instructions that the speakers be placed at the four corners of the auditorium.

Schafer describes the effect of the piece in this way:

> The Divan opens with a great blaze of electronic sound through which groups of instruments struggle to be heard. Over the first page of this very graphic score I wrote a line from Rumi: "A face like fire . . . the soul was wailing, 'Where shall I flee?'"
>
> After this fiery surge subsides, various groups of instruments and voices begin to be heard from around the hall, at first quietly, then gradually becoming stronger and more connected. After several dramatic eruptions a long unison line binds all performers together. The melody rises to a climax and sustains over a repeated percussion motif, gradually fading away, and the work ends with a tape-recorded nei (Persian flute) sounding as if from nowhere.[8]

The piece's effect is based on stereophony, reflecting a movement from splintered existence to unity. This approach required Schafer to

> make complete aural sense on a great number of levels. Each sound source must make independent sense and be interesting by itself as well as make a coherent addition to any number of separate sound sources around it. Clearly a new form of counterpoint has emerged—a space counterpoint.[9]

The musical underpinning of this endeavor is a series of 180 notes arranged in twenty groups of nine. Each segment uses two intervals (such as M2-m2 in the first group) in a pattern of descending-ascending-ascending-descending-descending-ascending-ascending-descending, which causes the first, middle, and last note of each segment to be identical. To this material and the spatial counterpoint Schafer also adds moments of indeterminacy.[10]

Beyond the Great Gate of Light was commissioned by the CBC in 1971, although Schafer had already begun work on it in the fall of 1970 in response to the death that year of Phyllis's young nephew Steven. When he began the piece he had already conceived of adding it to *Divan i Shams i Tabriz* and *Music for the Morning of the World* to create the triptych *Lustro*. He used the same orchestration as *Divan*, including the thirteen auditorium groups in the same configuration, and only added the mezzo-soprano soloist from *Music for the Morning of the World* to the stage ensemble. *Beyond the Great Gate of Light* sets a text from the original Bengali version of *Gitanjali* by Rabindranath Tagore. The poem Schafer chose is "*Alo amar aloo go bhubon-bhora* [Light, My Light, the World-Filling Light]." The seven singers in the hall join the stage soloist to sing this opening line of text, and after a lengthy introduction the tonality settles into a shifting G-major triad in both the electronic tape and the orchestra while the singers sing the complete Tagore poem.

The row in *Divan* is also the underpinning of *Beyond the Great Gate*, and the auditorium groups use motives from that piece. The first four notes of the row (G, F, F-sharp, G-sharp) become a unifying motive through the movement's four crescendos, and at the peak of the fourth crescendo the tape begins a G-major chord, which continues to the end of the piece. The orchestra and even the tape bring in other harmonies and melodic fragments that conflict with the sonority and try to overwhelm it, but the sonority remains as the conductor slowly cuts off each of the fourteen ensembles, leaving the sound of bells played by the percussionists and singers.[11]

The first complete performance of *Lustro* (*Divan i Shams i Tabriz*; *Music for the Morning of the World*; and *Beyond the Great Gate of Light*) was given in 1973.

East, written for the National Arts Center Orchestra in 1973, was inspired by and based on a text from the *Isha-Upanishad*, translated as follows:

> The self is one. Unmoving it moves faster than the mind. The senses lag but self runs ahead. Unmoving it outruns pursuit. The self is everywhere, without body, without shape, whole, pure, wise, all-knowing, far-seeing, self-depending, all-transcending. Unmoving it moves far away, yet near, within all, outside all.[12]

There are twenty-four letters that appear in the text, and to each of these letters Schafer assigned a pitch according to its frequency of use in the text, using a quarter-tone scale that begins on C and ascends to B. In this technique, recurring groups of letters will have similarly recurring short motives. There are forty-eight words in the text, which are represented by forty-eight gong strikes played alternately by five different pitched gongs and tam-tam. The strikes occur approximately every ten seconds, and orchestral musicians hum the pitch just played in a quiet meditation. Schafer created a diagram on which he further based the melodic sounds, harmonic structure, and the use of the flutes, trumpets, and horns, which punctuate the score freely. The melodic foreground is based on the first two sentences of the text so each word appears several times. In each motif, the pitches are spaced evenly across the measure.[13]

Schafer also asked for three solo instruments to be placed backstage (which he calls "Group A") in the score, and three to be placed at the back of the auditorium ("Group B"), and he asks them to slowly pivot while they play, mimicking the meditative practice of the dervishes.

North/White was commissioned by the CBC for the National Youth Orchestra of Canada. In the original program note, Schafer says the following about the piece:

> I call this piece North/White because, like white light, which is composed of all visible frequencies, it combines all the producible notes of the symphony orchestra from the deepest to the highest instruments.
>
> The North is not described by the adjective "pretty" and neither is this piece. North/White is inspired by the rape of the Canadian North. This rape is being carried out by the nation's government in conspiracy with business and industry. The instruments of destruction are pipelines and airstrips, highways and snowmobiles.
>
> But more than the environment is being destroyed by these actions, for, just as the moon excursions destroyed the mythogenic power of the moon (it ceased to be poetry and became property), Canadians are about to be deprived of the "idea of North," which is at the core of the Canadian identity. The North is a place of austerity, of spaciousness and loneliness; the North is pure; the North is temptationless. These qualities are forged into the mind of the Northerner; his temperament is synonymous with them.
>
> The idea of North is a Canadian myth. Without a myth a nation dies. This piece is dedicated to the splendid and indestructible idea of North.[14]

Schafer decided to add an unusual instrument to the percussion section—a snowmobile—symbolizing the invasion of the North by technology, with all of its noise and pollution. In addition to the snowmobile, Schafer adds several other unusual instruments to the percussion section to represent the harsh climate and landscape of the North. These include two suspended metal sheets of tin and steel, three metal blocks (or anvils), a large chain, four suspended metal pipes, a corrugated metal surface, three Masonite boards, and two or three lengths of rubber hose that can be agitated to evoke the harsh arctic wind.[15] Schafer also places emphasis on the sounds of the large wind section, shifting the overall color of the piece to bright, brittle sounds, and he uses the large string section to create effects, often adding players gradually, from back to front, giving the impression of sound rushing across the stage.

The inspiration for this piece came from a flight from Europe to Vancouver where the flight path took the airplane over Greenland and the Canadian Arctic, including Baffin Island. The tints of green and blue in the ice caps suggested to Schafer the idea of certain orchestral colors emerging from a full spectrum of white sound. Schafer's response to this concept was to create what he calls "textures or densities of sound."[16] There are few independent lines, and the use of quarter tones to create even denser clusters creates the effect of the white noise that the composer discusses. This approach negates any sense of tonal center, although the outer ranges of the clusters tend to center from B-flat to F, with a particular focus on E.

Cortège, written in 1977, was Schafer's second commission from the National Arts Center Orchestra. As the title indicates, Schafer had ideas for what the orchestra would do in realizing this piece. He says in the program notes,

> With *Cortège* I decided that the entire orchestra would be in motion. The work would begin out of darkness with only the conductor and timpanist on stage, the latter giving a slow ceremonial beat for the entry of the string players, moving in slow precision, one step to each timpani stroke. I thought the image of the players in black suits would be enhanced if they all wore white face masks, so I requested this. And after the violinists had slowly raised their instruments to play, they would suddenly begin to spin like dervishes. Other instruments, clarinets and oboes, would emerge from the wings and come down the aisles from the back of the hall passing phrases across to one another. Later the brass would enter doing a quickstep march and the bassoon players would perform a little jig together. After it was all over, the orchestra would slowly leave the stage as if it had all been a dream, and the lights would fade to darkness.[17]

Schafer directed the staging of the first production, and for those performances where he was not present, he gave extensive instructions for the conductor, who was called upon, in his words, to also be "a magician and a choreographer."[18] Along the top of the score Schafer indicates to the conductor what type of gestures he should employ, and in the score itself he gives visual aids as to how the various musicians should enter, walk, and hold their instruments, including diagrams throughout the score that show the direction and positioning of the musicians at various parts in the piece. The orchestral musicians are called upon to hum certain pitches throughout the piece, and several of them play simple percussion instruments when they are stationary. The players are asked to memorize the music that they play as they move from station to station or slowly turn, imitating the meditative practices of the dervishes. Given the extensive motion, the music falls into repeated motives and ostinato patterns, and the whole piece is one of the most diatonic pieces from this time in Schafer's output (essentially C major with added F-sharp and B-flat and rare occurrences of A-flat). It is in the juxtaposition of the often sharply contrasting ideas that the impact of the piece is felt.

Ko wo kiku (Listen to the Incense) was commissioned by the Kyoto Community Bank for performance by the Kyoto Symphony Orchestra in 1985 for the 1,000th anniversary of the founding of Kyoto, the ancient capital of Japan. Schafer visited Japan in 1984 as preparation for the commission, and while there experienced the ancient ceremony known as *Ko wo kiku*. In this ceremony, small jars of burning incense (*Ko*) are passed about, each bearing a different name and odor. The incense can be smelled and also listened to by placing it near the left ear. Schafer decided to write a piece that suggested these various types of incense and that would incorporate elements of the ceremony in the performance. The percussion battery is asked to play unusual instruments, including bamboo or nose flutes in the first movement and various temple bells in the second movement, and they must bounce a variety of balls of different sizes and materials, including rubber balls, marbles, and golf balls.

In the first movement, "Sagano," the conductor turns to the audience, raises his incense jar three times and inhales the incense. He then turns toward the orchestra, where in front of him stand six players, including the principals of the strings (excluding double bass) and the principal flute and clarinet. They raise their jars and inhale as the percussionists begin to play the nose flutes. The leaders carry their jars to their sections, where the jars are passed ceremoniously to their section, then to the other sections of the orchestra. While the jars are being passed, the conductor begins the first movement, which is a long unison melody. All the players have the entire melody in their parts but are instructed to play only the portions of the melody that the incense they have smelled inspires them to play. Certain circled notes in the melody are sustained by the players indicated. Toward the end of the first movement, the different sections begin to split apart, building chords, before the texture thins to solo flute accompanied by the nose flutes.

Movement two, "Nonomiya," expands upon the motives introduced in the first movement, both in the unison melody and in particular the slowly stacked orchestral chords and the short rapid motives in the final flute melody. In addition to slowly combining and morphing these motives, the orchestra players are asked to hum along with the notes they play, to be equally balanced and blended. Movement three, "Shigure," asks the orchestra to imitate the effect of the bouncing balls through random rhythms, including pizzicato, and repeated melodic fragments that are constantly accelerating or decelerating. Movement four, "Higashiyama," opens with slow chords in the strings (supported by four to six mouth organs), over which the brass play slow, quarter-note motives. This alternates with the flutes and clarinets, who play quarter-tone melodies. These disparate elements combine then hearken back to the quick scale fragments from the middle two movements before dying away to just the strings and mouth organs.

Dream Rainbow Dream Thunder was completed in 1986 as a fantasy for orchestra, based on an evening of improvisation at the piano. It was ultimately completed as a commission for the National Youth Orchestra of Canada and dedicated to Schafer's friend and fellow composer Toru Takemitsu. The evening that Schafer improvised the basic material for *Dream Rainbow Dream Thunder* occurred after a visit to Neuschwanstein, King Ludwig's castle in Bavaria.

> Rain and mist shrouded the mountain as we hiked up to pay our respects to this strange edifice, conceived out of love for the music of Wagner. Wagner is detectable in my improvisation, but so are a lot of other influences. I don't think it matters much. Dream Rainbow Dream Thunder joins yesterday with days of long ago and tomorrow with days that will never be.[19]

A fantasy is a good description of this piece, which is improvisatory in nature, having no discernable form other than being through composed. The focus is more on short motives and the subtle orchestration, especially in the use of the large wind section.

Scorpius was commissioned in 1990 by Alex Pauk for the Esprit Orchestra of Toronto. The theme of the concert for which it was commissioned was "Outer Space," so Alex and Murray decided to title the piece, which was already in process, *Scorpius*.

> I have no idea why the present piece is entitled Scorpius, or what its relationship might be to the constellation of stars which barely rises above the southern horizon on summer evenings. With Antares at its head, it appears vigorous and resilient, shaped like a fish hook. Is that why "my" Scorpius is barbed and unsettled? The Greeks said Scorpius stung Orion to death, since he sets as

The Concerti and Other Orchestral Works 301

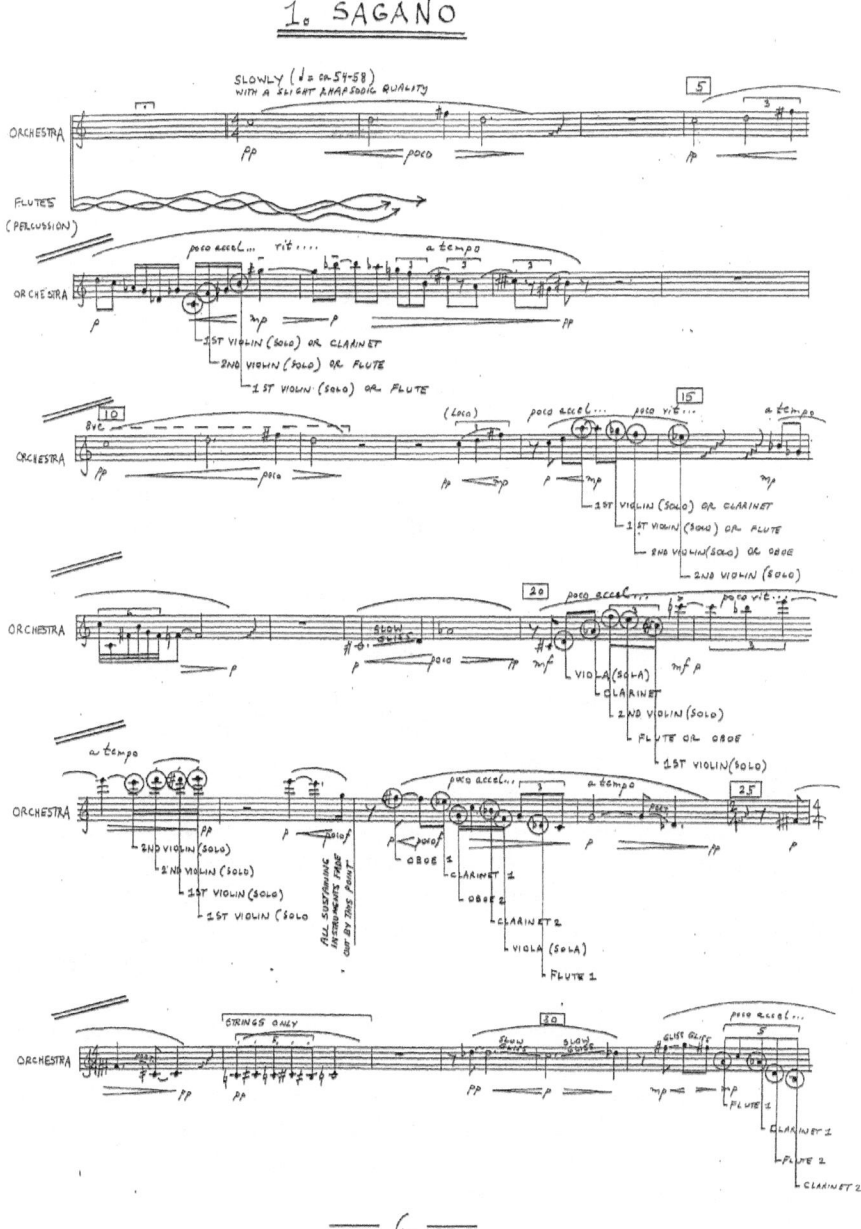

Figure 17.1. Movement 1—*Ko wo kiku*. R. Murray Schafer

Scorpius rises. Am I trying to sting someone with "my" Scorpius? I'll let the listener decide.[20]

The piece is written for a small orchestra, with paired winds and standard brass numbers (including tuba), and a smaller percussion section including piano. Schafer chooses to let the woodwind section drive the piece forward with repeated and syncopated rhythms, while the strings seem to play a secondary or accompanying role.

In the winter of 1991 Claude Schreyer asked Schafer to write a piece for four brass bands as part of a 1992 festival of new music and sound sculptures planned at Le parc Lafontaine in Montreal. Although Schafer had played in a Boy Scout brass band as a boy, he was not very fond of that medium, having only written one or two pieces for brass quintet up to that point. He visited the park with Schreyer, and once he remembered that the park, which was about six blocks square, had once been a military drill ground, he imagined a piece, *Musique pour le parc Lafontaine*, where the bands would break into groups and move about the park while they played. Schafer spent some time researching the history of the park and of the city of Montreal and decided to include quotes from music associated with either. The piece opens with military drumming, which recalls the initial use of the property. Schafer also quotes Native American melodies as notated by Marc Lescarbot in his *Histoire de la Nouvelle France* (Paris, 1609); references the Canadian National Anthem, the tune of which was written by Montreal native Calixa Lavallée; and refers to a Sanctus written by Montreal's first classical composer, Charles Ecuyer, in the early 1800s.

The nature of this piece, which uses motion and space among the players to a greater extent than any other of Schafer's compositions, necessitated a certain style of both composition and notation. Stopwatches are needed for each group, and a timeline is kept throughout the score. Each section, including the opening military drumming, is accompanied by flag signals, which serve more as a visual comment on the event than an effort to coordinate the players.

The commission for *Manitou*, composed in 1994, had been secured by Murray's friend and fellow composer Toru Takemitsu for the International Program for Contemporary Music Composition at Suntory Hall, Tokyo. In the winter months of late 1993 and early 1994, Schafer was an artist in residence at Brandon University in Manitoba, which takes its name from Manitou, the mysterious being who

> for the woodland Indians of North America, represents the unknown power of life and the universe. Sometimes Manitou is associated with the sun to suggest omnipotence, though, like the Christian God, he is unseen. When I discussed native spirituality with a Manitoba Indian he kept using the word "monster" to

describe Manitou and mentioned that his people used to believe that lightning was a serpent vomited up by him.[21]

In the middle of the cold winter months, Schafer sketched out *Manitou*, which clearly shows the influence of the geography and climate of the northern prairies.

Schafer received a commission from long-time patrons Michael and Sonja Koerner to write a piece for the dedication concert of the new Koerner Concert Hall of the Royal Conservatory of Music in Toronto. He completed the piece in 2008 and the premiere took place in September 2009. Although Schafer had not attended the Royal Conservatory (his piano certificate was with the Royal Schools of London) he was familiar with the conservatory building. For the commission he decided to write what he describes as a "quodlibet—a musical form consisting of snatches of various pieces strung together in a loose formation so that each piece rises momentarily, only to be submerged again in a texture of new sounds."[22] He gave the piece the title *Spirits of the House*, referring in this case to the spirits of the music that had been performed over the years in the Royal Conservatory, which would still be lingering in the building. He decided to include music by past teachers, many of whom were composers, performed by various groups scattered throughout and even outside the hall. These quotes are the final chorus from *The Wreck of the Hesperus*, a cantata based on Longfellow's poem by Arthur E. Fisher (1848–1912); *Sonata for Cello and Piano* by Leo Smith (1881–1952); *Butterfly Waltz*, a work by the pianist Ernest Seitz (1892–1978); *Prelude for John Weinzweig* by Samuel Dolin (1917–2002); *The King Shall Rejoice in Thy Strength, O Lord* by Sir Ernest MacMillan (1893–1973); *Rise Up, My Love, My Fair One* by Healey Willan (1880–1968); and *Tribal Dance* from John Weinzweig's ballet *The Red Ear of Corn*.

Schafer's introduction invokes the spirits of the composers he is to reference then suggests the storm of Longfellow's poem, the subject of Fisher's cantata. The following short interlude recalls the storm motive, last played by the cello section, and introduces the solo cello in *Sonata*, which is at one point interrupted by the orchestra playing the storm motive. After the second passage of *Sonata* another bridge passage leads to *Butterfly Waltz*, which is quickly disrupted by Dolin's *Prelude*. The fiery character of the prelude is taken up by the orchestra, which provides a satirical introduction to *The King Shall Rejoice*, given a send-up by the inclusion of saxophone quartet and the orchestral musicians singing the bombastic refrain of the anthem. From there the orchestra plays an evocative, intentionally vague lead-in to *Rise Up My Love*, which is accompanied by strings, harp, and crotales. After this the orchestra abruptly changes character, leading into *Tribal Dance*. Schafer notes,

> My quodlibet ends abruptly in the middle of The Red Ear of Corn's "Tribal Dance," vanishing into a peaceful slumber, which is my last memory of John in the nursing home shortly before his death. We had eaten a light lunch together with his wife, Helen, and I had accompanied them upstairs and helped John into bed where he soon drifted off to sleep.[23]

The composition *Dream(e)scape* was written

> in a streak of twenty-six days in 2009, scarcely without looking back or trying to remember what had been written the day before. I wanted to try to capture the dream experience of incoherence in which everything is shifting and blurred together.[24]

Schafer refers to the piece as both *Dreamscape* and *Dream(e)scape*, noting that both titles fit the character of the piece. He worked by sketching out the full orchestra without making an initial sketch or returning to it for any significant revisions. Despite this process, there is some unity in the piece both tonally and through a phrase that keeps recurring like a leitmotif. In addition to the full orchestra, he asks for an optional soprano voice, which can be prerecorded. Other than these unifying factors, the piece does not seem to unfold with any coherency, moving from a slow opening to a short scherzo-like section, then slowing again before a passage marked "Furiously," followed by aleatoric passages for the winds, a passage marked "Very vigorously," then additional slow and furious passages alternating before the piece ends quietly.

Schafer says the following in the preface to the score of *Symphony no. 1 in C minor*:

> One makes music to get out of this world. No other art form rejects physical existence so insistently, seeking unearthly heights where the soul floats on cosmic rays and sings with the angels. Any rejection of this idea is to cancel the real purpose of music, to ground it, make it corporal, debase it with the rasping noises of the world, the pulsations of the body, the shrieks of the voice. Yet, given the materials of expression we possess, the realization of the infinite is often futile, for the moment we are made aware that the instruments we have for reaching the infinite are quite ordinary violins, drums or voices, the transcendental disappears and we hear only the agony of our terrestrial existence. Still, it can be achieved at times, and when it is, even if only for an instant, a revelation of cosmic consciousness occurs and the Divinity allows us to touch the mists of its unknown Being.[25]

This symphony, written for the TSO, was premiered in 2010. The title for the piece is a little tongue-in-cheek, given in response to a call from the TSO asking for a title for publicity purposes, but it is appropriate since the composition lacks the explicitly theatrical elements of several of his other pieces for orchestra and falls into a traditional three-movement structure of fast-slow-fast. There is no discernable program and only two main effects that take it beyond a very traditional orchestra piece. The first appears in the first movement, when Schafer asks the strings to phantom bow notes that are played by other instruments. The other is in the second movement, when the string players whistle a melody that alternates with the slow chorale of the wind players at the beginning of the movement.

The first movement is primarily based on the opening motive, made up of a descending half step and then perfect fourth, first appearing in the strings as D, C-sharp, G-sharp. This motive is extended and transformed in several ways—through expanding the intervals by half step, through inversion, and through stacking multiple motives to make a disjointed melody that can then be harmonized. In addition to this fundamental motive, Schafer uses two other sets of material. The first is extensive use of chromatic, whole tone, and octatonic scales. The second is a series of repeated chords that serve at first as a disruptive element but eventually pull the tonal center toward C minor.

The second movement starts in C minor with a slow glissandi in the string section (the first one extends over ten seconds), starting with the lowest strings and working up through each section, interrupted first by strikes on the bass drum then by the tam-tam. An extended chorale, with non-tonal harmonizations reminiscent of Stravinsky, follows, alternating with a whistled C-major melody by the string players. After this extended introduction the rest of the movement is primarily an alternation between two different sets of material. The first is solo wind melodies written to give a sense of improvisation and supported by sustained chords in the string section. The other set of materials is a series of slow, soft, chord progressions in the strings.

The third movement is a playful alternation between C minor and C major. The main short theme, which appears several times in the trumpet, is firmly in C major and serves a similar role to the main theme of a rondo form. The repeated C-minor–based chords found in the first and second movement return and at the end of the movement shift to C major. There are two other primary sources of material, which alternate with each other. The first is a series of rapid scalar passages in a variety of scales and keys answered by martelé responses by the strings. The second is a melody that references the second movement but is actually on the opening motive of the first movement.

Figures in the Night . . . Passing was written for the Victoria Symphony in 2012 and revised in 2015. The piece is episodic in nature with some repeated material but similar to *Dream(e)scape* in its through-composed nature and often seemingly unrelated material. It is a series of changing moods and tempi, with the focus being more on orchestral color than melody or motivic development.

Wolf Returns was written as a commission for the Esprit Orchestra in 2012, and in this, his last orchestral work, Schafer decided to incorporate some of the chants from *Patria Epilogue*. Four of the five chants that Schafer incorporates had been used before in other pieces. "Wolf Chant," "Chant for the Spirits of Hunted Animals," and "Mosquito Chant" had been used in the choral composition *Magic Songs*, and "Rain Chant" had been expanded into a choral piece for the Taipei Philharmonic Choir. The remaining song, "Healing Chant," had not previously appeared outside *Patria Epilogue*, where it is sung when someone falls ill during the week. Schafer incorporates these five chants at various points in the piece. At the points where the first three chants occur, the orchestra dies away so that the chant is clearly heard. "Healing Chant" is doubled by the strings, and "Rain Chant" overlays the orchestra writing, first gradually growing louder then fading away under the orchestra. The chanting voices are the composer's way of reminding us of the different role of music in the natural environment, where it can dialogue with natural sounds. He notes,

> You can dialogue with nature, but you can only listen to an orchestra. In the forest, you can exchange sounds with other creatures, while in the urban concert hall, you are not expected to participate in the creation of music. You are a listener to music that has been prepared by others.[26]

The orchestra in this piece represents the noise of urban life, which fades away occasionally to reveal the distant singers, who represent this possible relationship between music and nature. This alternation between the urban orchestra (which includes a police whistle and the obvious influence of jazz) and the chants continues throughout the piece, and at times the orchestra tries to imitate the chants performed by the singers, whether a wolf howl, the buzz of a mosquito, or the sound of falling rain. The singers do have the last say, with the final sound being the howling of the wolves.

THE CONCERTI

Schafer has made a significant contribution to the twentieth-century concerto genre, which is ironic, since he has always been conflicted about the very nature of the concerto form. Many of the following compositions are called "concerti," but just as many are not labeled as such, reflective of Schafer's efforts, as with many of his orchestral pieces, to redefine the genre and defy many of the long-held conventions of the concert hall.

Schafer's first concerto, *Concerto for Flute and Orchestra*, was written for his close friend Robert Aitken, who gave the first performance of the piece with the Montreal Symphony Orchestra. The piece was written when Murray had left his second wife Jean to pursue a relationship with Eleanor

James and was spending the summer in Stratford as part of a residency. Eleanor came to visit him in Stratford, and his agitation over the unsettled nature of his personal life is reflected in the piece, in particular the opening movement. It has become one of the more regularly performed of Schafer's concerti.

The first movement most clearly reflects the personal turmoil Schafer was experiencing while writing the concerto. The movement is titled "Fast and frenzied," and Schafer indicates to the flautist that the rushed frenzy must not abate until the end of the movement, with all breath marks not being actual pauses. The focus of the first movement is almost exclusively on the flute, while the orchestra only provides bursts of color or accompanying lines by such unusual instruments as marimba or a piano/harp combination. It is not until the end that the orchestra builds up, over which the flute plays a line that will become the main theme of the second movement. The second movement begins with the orchestra taking up the final flute theme of the first movement and slowly transforming it into a more lyrical theme. In this movement Schafer asks for the flautist to employ extended techniques such as using microtones and humming while playing to create harmonies with themselves. The third movement returns us to the character of the first movement, but this time in 5/8, with a return in the middle of this movement to the material of the second movement.

Schafer wrote *Concerto for Harp and Orchestra* in 1987 in response to a commission by the TSO for performance by Judy Loman, for whom he had written *The Crown of Ariadne*. He struggled with the piece, being uncomfortable with the concept of a piece that had "as its sole purpose the inflation of a soloist's vanity."[27] During the final moments of the third movement he chose to amplify the harp (with strict instructions not to amplify before that time), allowing the full orchestra to play along without covering this naturally quiet instrument.

The concerto is in three distinct movements. The first movement, marked "Very relaxed" is rhapsodic in nature, with rapidly changing tempo and moods. Schafer is sparing in the use of the orchestra as it accompanies the harp, only using the full forces for the orchestral interludes in between the solo passages. The movement is essentially through composed, with recurring motives but no full return to the opening material. The second movement is titled "Spirited" and is the dance movement of the concerto, featuring the percussion and wind sections. The final movement is marked "Energetically" and opens with an extended solo harp passage. Material from the first two movements is referenced at various points in this final movement, and toward the end of the movement the harp is gradually amplified in order to overpower the full orchestra.

Concerto for Guitar and Orchestra, written in 1989 for Norbert Kraft, for whom Schafer also wrote *Le Cri de Merlin*, consists of six short movements

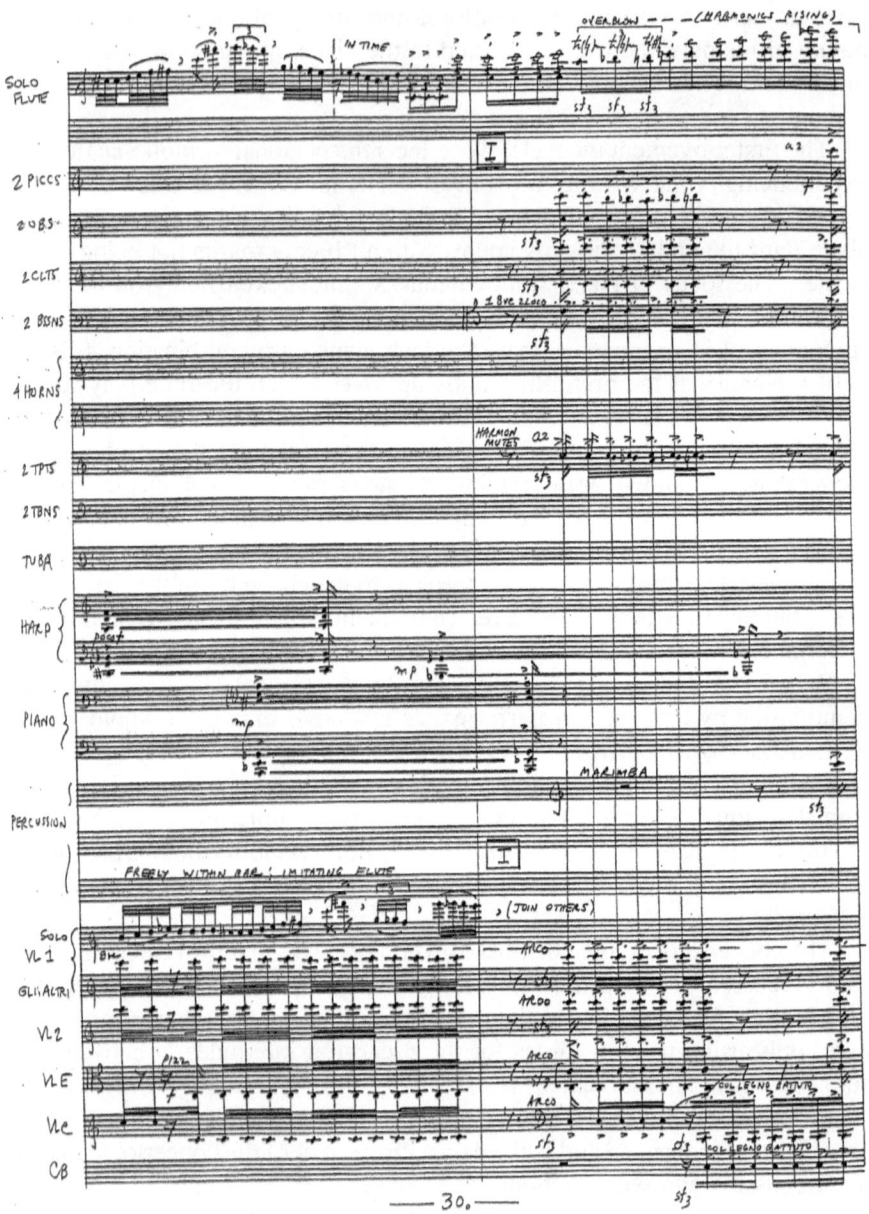

Figure 17.2. Movement 1—*Concerto for Flute and Orchestra*. R. Murray Schafer

played without a break. A Fibonacci number sequence, in which each number is the sum of the two previous numbers, affects the shaping of the piece and forms the basis of the guitar line in the opening section. Schafer had to overcome, as with the harp concerto, the clash between the intimacy of the solo instrument and the full force of a symphony orchestra. He worked hard to balance the two opposing forces and to not have them speak completely different languages since he wanted to combine the two forces more than what he had seen in other contemporary concerti, where the guitar would play a statement, then the orchestra would have an interlude. He also used several extended techniques for the guitar part, including quarter tones and the use of a spoon to create a blues guitar effect.

The first movement, "Very fast and energetic," is a perpetual motion movement, with the guitar playing almost without pause, accompanied by a thin orchestral texture that highlights solo strings and the upper woodwinds that have longer note values. The second movement, "Slowly and expressively," alternates two main ideas: a slow, rhapsodic guitar line over held chords, and complex rhythmic dialogues between the guitar and solo instruments. Toward the end of the movement the guitar returns to the arpeggiated motive of the first movement then gives way to the first true orchestral interlude, which continues the rapid rhythmic figures. The third movement, "Molto Latina," for a while continues the rhythmic patterns of the previous movement but more freely and with sparse orchestral accompaniment. A cadenza-like passage leads to an orchestral interlude and a second cadenza that then leads to the fourth movement. "Night music; Very delicate and mysterious" begins with a guitar passage using various extended techniques over independent lines in the violins. An orchestral interlude, highlighting the musical saw, follows, giving way to a sparser texture over which the guitar returns to the fast rhythmic passages of the first movement. Another cadenza leads to a slow orchestral build-up to the final movement. The fifth movement, "Very rhythmic and nervous," is the most energetic and frantic of the five movements. It again features the opening rhythmic motive of the concerto but this time with a fuller orchestral texture. The rhythm quickens even more than in the first movement, the guitar has several short flourishes that are answered by the orchestra, and the piece rushes to the end.

The Darkly Splendid Earth: The Lonely Traveller was written in 1990 for the violinist Jacques Israelievitch, who had in mind not so much a concerto as a rhapsody. This allowed Schafer to take a different approach to this concerto. In this one-movement piece, he chose to overturn the traditional approach of highlighting the solo instrument and giving the orchestra a subservient role. Taking Israelievitch's suggestion, Schafer chose to write a type of double rhapsody where the soloist and orchestra each went their own way, with their own distinct materials. The orchestra became the "darkly splendid earth," and the violin soloist became the "lonely traveler" passing along its surface. Underpinning the mood of this rather subdued piece is the idea of the fluctuation of consciousness and the "experience of the individual, who does not control the environment, but reacts to it, sometimes contrarily or indifferently."[28] Schafer notes,

> I wanted the soloist to live a life of isolation without reinforcement from the multitude, without the idiotic imitations and repetitions found in all conventional music. If there are friends in this music, they are remote. Only at the close does a solo horn distantly echo a few phrases pronounced earlier by the violinist. A friend? . . . Too late. The soloist moves off into the twilight.[29]

Concerto for Accordion and Orchestra was written in 1992, commissioned by the TSO for performance by Schafer's friend the accordionist Joseph Macerollo to coincide with an international accordion convention to be held in Toronto in 1993. Given the unusual solo instrument, Schafer decided that the orchestra might feature instruments "normally neglected in the concert repertoire (contra bassoon, bass trombone, and English horn)."[30]

The first movement often places the solo instrument at odds with the orchestra, with the accordion playing in different meters than the other players and having the freedom to fit its passages into the general texture of the orchestra. The slower passages in this first movement highlight the unusual instruments used, and the influence of tango is clearly heard in the faster passages. Several solo cadenzas are included, the last leading directly to the slow second movement. The first part of the second movement continues the free solo writing of the accordion, with light accompaniment from the orchestra, again focusing on unusual colors. In the second half of the concerto, the motion, dynamics, and orchestration intensify, leading to the final fast movement. Unlike the first two movements, which focus on the instrument's ability to play melody, this movement focuses on the harmonic possibilities of the instrument, which plays a series of rapid chords for the majority of the movement, showing the virtuosity of the accordion.

The Falcon's Trumpet was written in 1995 for Stuart Laughton, who had participated in *Patria Epilogue* for several years and shared Schafer's love for the wilderness. Schafer was in the middle of residency at the University of Strasbourg in France, and he notes,

> I have no doubt that my nostalgia for the Canadian lakes and forests strongly influenced the conception of this piece, in particular its unusual layout, with groups of instruments spread on stage in the wings and in the auditorium behind the audience.[31]

Schafer's intention with this special separation (a stage group of instrumentalists, which includes the conductor and the solo trumpet; three small groups out in the auditorium; and two groups behind the stage, one stage left, one stage right) was to reflect the sonic impact of a trumpet playing an aubade or nocturne across the lake as part of *Patria Epilogue*, and he added a soprano voice at the end of the work to further take us into that experience. Into the texture of the piece are woven sounds of nature, including birdsong. The concerto is in one movement, with the trumpet "falcon" being the focus of the piece, but as in the wilderness, other creatures comment on the falcon's song, either echoing what the trumpeter plays, or sending their own music back and forth. The textures of the movement vary, with antiphonal writing between the various groups; moments where the orchestra plays aleatoric passages underneath the trumpet's melody; moments when one of the orchestra trumpets echoes the solo trumpet; and an ending duet between the solo trumpet and solo soprano voice.

Concerto for Viola and Orchestra was written in 1997 for renowned soloist Rivka Golani. Schafer struggled for several months to complete the piece, going through several initial drafts and finally deciding he needed to push on without looking back at the material he had composed previously. The only unifying motive is an ascending and descending six-note scale, first presented with the pitches (C, B-flat, A-flat, G, E-flat, D-flat). Other than that one motive, the piece is episodic—"chaotic" is Schafer's word—and characterized by a general lack of moments of relaxation.[32] The approach parallels that in both *Dream(e)scape* and *Figures in the Night . . . Passing* in its constant shifting between different moods, with passages marked "Very quiet and sustained" and "Lyrical" contrasting with passages marked "With savage energy" and "Furiously."

Four-Forty was written in 1999 as a commission for the St. Lawrence Quartet to perform at the Vancouver Festival in August 2000. The title comes from both the tuning note for the orchestra (A = 440) and the total number of instrumentalists (a chamber orchestra of forty plus four soloists). Schafer struggled initially with how to differentiate the solo quartet from the string section surrounding them and decided to use movement in a similar way as in his *String Quartet no. 3*, deciding that theatricality in the first movement would give the solo ensemble "the personality necessary to survive the next two movements seated normally without being too submerged by the orchestra."[33] Schafer uses the pitch A as the anchor note for the composition, returning to it frequently throughout the piece until it dissolves into harmonics at the end.

The first movement begins in an extended passage with the orchestra accompanying the solo cellist, who is alone on stage. The first violin rises from a seat in the middle of the audience and begins a solo passage with the cellist while walking toward the stage. This extended, largely unaccompanied initial duet, which strives to the note A, is eventually supported by the orchestra with a gesture taken from the opening of the piece. The violin reaches the stage then turns and leaves the hall while the orchestra plays an extended interlude. This is interrupted by the second violinist, who has been seated at the back of the first violin section, playing with them. The second violinist stands up, tunes up, then plays a vigorous dance-like solo, while stomping his or her foot. After an extended passage, the soloist moves to the front of the stage and takes a seat with the cellist as the orchestra begins to play a slow, somber interlude. This interlude is interrupted by the bass drum player, who plays a crazy cadenza, striking other instruments, then throws the stick away and grabs a viola, revealing the player as one of the quartet members. The scratching and sawing slowly morphs into a vigorous cadenza, and the violist moves through the orchestra, coming near to and dialoguing with the trombone, then the bassoon, then other instrumentalists before moving toward the seated cellist and second violinist and finally sitting down, exhausted. The orchestra finishes the movement with an energetic flourish but is interrupted by the first violinist, who again appears, slowly crosses the stage, and takes a seat with the other players.

The second movement begins with the quartet all seated. They tune up then slowly play an A-major scale together, focusing on their intonation. As they finish the scale, they are joined by the orchestra. A vigorous section, where the quartet plays largely pizzicato, leads to another tuning passage. Solo and orchestral passages continue to alternate, occasionally disrupted by additional tuning passages. The climax is a series of grand chords in the orchestra alternating with similar chords in the quartet before the texture thins to the quartet alone, leading attacca to the third movement.

The third movement begins with a slow, expressive melody in the orchestra—using quarter tones—that turns into short chords and dies away. The quartet begins to play, accompanied only by clarinets and vibraphone then the flute. This sparse texture grows into a dialogue with additional instruments, and at this point the first violin plays a melody with interjections from the orchestra. The other members of the string quartet join this melody while the full orchestra plays underneath them. The movement dies away with fragmented melodies from the quartet while the orchestral writing becomes ever more amorphous, leading to harmonics in both the quartet and the string section, with the cellos tuned a quarter-tone flat.

Shadowman was written in 2000 for the Nexus percussion ensemble and the University of Toronto Symphony Orchestra. Schafer had long thought about percussion sounds, the effect of striking metal, or how church bells can be melted down and cast into cannons in times of war then cast back into bells in times of peace. He had also thought long about the use of percussion in military settings, and as he began to work on the piece for Nexus, he wanted to highlight both the terror and beauty of percussion instruments.

> The piece celebrates soldiery, or rather the futility of soldiery. The five percussionists are divided: two players impersonate the Forces of Darkness; two the

Forces of Light; while one, dressed in a tattered military uniform, impersonates the individual soldier as he drums his way through victory and defeat on the battlefield. The orchestra accompanies this crusade of courage and folly with a number of tunes from military musical history. In the end, the soldier, mentally deranged, plays a variety of toy instruments and even tries to teach a teddy bear to play a toy drum. The valour and pathos of soldiery is exemplified in the piece, but the anti-war theme is unmistakable throughout the work. To my regret, the work has not achieved the popularity I had hoped for. We need more anti-war demonstrations in music.[34]

Shadowman is an actor as well as a drummer and is always center stage. The Messengers of Darkness are set at the back of the stage, and they enter from the side of the stage. The Messengers of Light are set at the two front corners of the stage and enter from the back, moving fluidly in their white robes as if performing a ritual they know by heart. The piece is divided into several programmatic sections.

Part 1: "Arrival of the Dark Messengers"—Two percussionists enter from backstage, dressed in black, playing wooden bells. On arrival, they play a vicious duet accompanied by the orchestra.

Part 2: "Quick Step 'Seely Simpkins'"—Shadowman is in the middle of the stage with a nineteenth-century field drum, playing military tunes popular in that century, accompanied by fife players and the orchestra.

Part 3: "Retreat"; Part 4: "Surrender"—The orchestra plays a British army bugle call while Shadowman plays a cadenza. As the Messengers of Darkness growl, the field drum falters and Shadowman collapses.

Part 5: "Arrival of the Messengers of Light"; Part 6: "Dance of Light"—The Messengers of Light arrive from the back of the hall, each playing two Japanese ring bells. Once they take their places, they play a dance accompanied by the orchestra.

Part 7: "Zion"; Part 8: "Cloud of Fire"—The tune "Zion" by American composer Lowell Mason is played by the orchestra, who is joined by Shadowman on Jew's harp or harmonica, but the orchestra eventually morphs the tune into a Haydn melody used by the Nazi Party before and during World War II.

Part 9: "Pierced Soul"—Shadowman plays the cuica, a friction drum, as a reminder of the mutilation of flesh, blending the skin of the drum head with the arrow that pierced it.

Part 10: "Tower of Bones"—The Messengers of Darkness play in Morse code a passage from Dante's *Inferno* that Schafer first used in *Patria 1*. Shadowman plays along on the field drum then interrupts this by playing a ratchet.

Part 11: "Redemption"; Part 12: "Living Waters"; Part 13: "Final Riff"—The battlefield is abandoned to the sounds of percussion played by the Messengers of Light. A short passage is then played by the Messengers of Darkness, symbolizing purification and baptism. Restored to life, Shadowman plays a riff on wooden spoons then begins to improvise on various instruments.

Part 14: "Alzheimer's"—Shadowman's rhythms become more erratic as he begins to play children's toy instruments, reflecting the mental and physical deterioration of Alzheimer's, while the orchestra hums Lowell Mason's "Zion" and the trumpet begins to play "Last Post."

Part 15: "Obiit"—Shadowman plays a paper whistle as "Last Post" sounds; the Messengers of Light play bells while the Messengers of Darkness play funeral music. The movement begins to slowly morph into held notes as the thai gongs again play.

Part 16: "Reincarnation"—The other percussionists play instruments shaped like frogs, suggesting the birth of spring and the rebirth of Shadowman in nature. Shadowman plays a bird whistle as the orchestra fades away.

Chapter Eighteen

The Chamber, Solo, and Electronic Compositions

THE STRING QUARTETS

Schafer's string quartets are a significant late-twentieth and early twenty-first century contribution to the genre. Ranging from 1970 to 2015, they explore the possibilities of the medium far beyond traditional parameters, including the incorporation of other instrumentalists and vocalists, movement, staging, and costuming.

String Quartet no. 1 is in one continuous movement but falls into three clearly defined sections (fast-slow-fast) with a coda. Schafer incorporates all the extended string techniques he had been refining in his pieces during this time, including glissandi of various types, clusters, and microtonality, but he does not often vary the texture as all four players play together the majority of the time.

Each of the three sections begins with a single gesture, which is expanded throughout that section. The first section grows out of a descending chromatic gesture outlining a perfect fifth from C to F. Schafer notes, "The players are locked together, trying frantically to break free. Finally freedom is achieved by the second violin, introducing the second section."[1] This descending seven-note chromatic scale is treated serially, appearing in all three sections, although additional motifs not explicitly derived from this material appear.[2] The second section is a series of solo lines based on the opening gesture and supported by slowly shifting chords and accompanying patterns.[3] In this section Schafer employs both microtonal shifts away from and back to unison and a gradual phasing of rhythm away from and back to uniformity. The third section begins with the four players locked together in a unison melody that gradually increases in both tempo and intensity until it returns to the opening chromatic gesture, interrupted along the way by four cadenzas, one for each instrument in the quartet. The return of the chromatic gesture ushers in the coda, which Schafer calls a "recapitulation": a series of snapshots of material from the previous section, signaled by snap pizzicato on the cello, and "at the end, the cello snaps are followed by periods of silence, as if the 'camera' goes on clicking even though the 'film' has run out."[4]

Schafer composed his *String Quartet no. 2 (Waves)* in 1976 and says the following about the genesis of the piece:

> In the course of the World Soundscape Project we recorded and analyzed ocean waves on both the Atlantic and Pacific coasts of Canada. The recurrent pattern of waves is always asymmetrical but we noted that the duration from crest to crest usually falls between 6 and 11 seconds ninety percent of the time. Only ten percent of the time are they of longer or shorter duration. It is this wave motion that gives the quartet its rhythm and structure. The listener will readily hear the dynamic undulations of waves in this piece, and as the piece develops several types of wave motion are combined. Aside from this, I have sought to give the quartet a liquid quality in which everything is constantly dissolving and flowing into everything else.[5]

To highlight the focus on fluid rhythmic complexity, Schafer simplifies the melodic and harmonic material in this single-movement quartet. He uses two primary pitch sets, the first a seven-note scale, the second a string of fourths, both perfect and augmented, built from the remaining five pitches. Schafer notes that a third motive in this piece, a repeating E-A created by extending the five-note pitch set up another perfect fourth, imitates the call of the white-throated sparrow, a regular visitor to Schafer's farmyard while he was composing the piece. The structure of the scale emphasizes the pitch D, in particular through the neighboring E-flat, creating a tonic note that is never wholly obscured. The complexity of the rhythmic patterns "is analogous to the Indian ragas, which sound monotonous to Western ears because of their static pitch arrangements but compensate with a rhythmic intricacy rare in Western music."[6] The piece ends with a return of the opening material, including the E-A fourth, and Schafer also indicates that the two violins and viola should one by one leave the stage, continuing to play when they get offstage.

When Schafer returned to the medium of the quartet in 1981, he decided to connect his *String Quartet no. 3* to the second quartet. Unlike the first two quartets, this quartet is in three discrete movements. *String Quartet no. 2* ended with the cello alone on stage, and *String Quartet no. 3* begins with the cello alone on stage, playing an extended solo that lasts almost half of the first movement. This solo begins with an opening gesture (moving from unison gradually through glissando to one-half step and back) that recalls the techniques used in *String Quartet no. 1*. It also references the closing material of the second quartet, including a largo rendition of the white-throated sparrow motive. The other three quartet members respond to this gesture by beginning to play from other places in the hall, gradually moving to join the cellist on the stage as the writing grows more frantic. In the second movement, Schafer includes

> vocalizations reminiscent of oriental gymnastic exercises. I have always been amazed at the physical energy required by string players during vigorous playing and decided to allow them to release this energy by making vocal sounds similar to those in karate.[7]

This is technically demanding for the players, who must play vigorous and at times challenging passages while simultaneously vocalizing in shouts, moans, and hisses, taking moments to stop playing and audibly pant. After the sometimes frantic energy of the second movement, the final movement brings the texture down to what Schafer calls "a long, quiet meditation in unison." After this extended melody, the first violin splits off both musically and physically, first playing a separate melody while the other instruments hum a simple motive. The first violin then takes this motive, departing backstage, "carrying the phrase into the distance so that in the end we don't know whether we are still hearing it or if it is only lingering in our memory."[8]

While Schafer was working on *String Quartet no. 4* in 1989, he received a phone call from his friend Paul Dutton, who informed him that their mutual friend bpNichol had died quite suddenly. Schafer was living alone on his farm at that time and his sense of isolation coupled with the news of bp's passing caused this quartet to have its lonely mood. Schafer notes,

> Curiously, I had begun playing with a theme from The Princess of the Stars, thinking to incorporate it in the new work when I suddenly realized that it was part of the chant bp had delivered in his performance of that piece at Banff three years before. Aside from this, there is probably little in the work to remind anyone of one of Canada's greatest poets, but the work is dedicated to his memory with the hope that, wherever he is, it may give him some pleasure.[9]

At the beginning of the quartet, the first violin begins offstage, dialoguing with the other three players who are onstage. This continues for a substantial part of the opening of the quartet until the first violin slowly moves toward the stage but remains unseen. Even when the first violin appears on stage, it continues its lonely melody, slowly advancing toward the other players during the many pauses in its music. Once the first violin has joined the other players, it ushers in a more energetic passage that slowly breaks down into an extended passage of long held chords and slow glissandi, which create "a lingering and somewhat directionless quality."[10] The first violin begins a melody reminiscent of the opening as the quartet again picks up tempo and energy only to finally die down one more time. At the very end of the piece, another offstage violin is heard, at the same place where the first violinist was originally heard. This is doubled by a woman's voice from the same direction but even farther away.

String Quartet no. 5 (Rosalind) was commissioned for the Orford String Quartet in 1989 by Toronto businessman Stan Witkin for the fiftieth birthday of his wife, Rosalind. Schafer continues his pattern of tying this quartet to the previous quartets by using the fourth quartet's closing phrase as the opening gesture for this quartet. The other two themes in the quartet are a transcription of a wolf's howl and a theme drawn from *The Crown of Ariadne*. The quartet is in one continuous movement, and Schafer notes,

> My intention was to write a work that expressed the normal existential shifts of mood we all experience every day. One moment I am happy, the next reflective, then I am hungry or I get a headache. And yet we are usually incapable of detecting the exact instant when the change occurs. That is the kind of music I wanted to write, music that moves the listener from one state to another without the listener detecting when or how the changes take place.[11]

After the opening violin line, which is followed by a similar rhapsodic line in the cello, the moods alternate rapidly, with widely differing tempi and motives. At the end of the quartet, crotales are added to the texture, played by members of the quartet.

Schafer's *String Quartet no. 6 (Parting Wild Horse's Mane)*, written in 1993, was commissioned by Michael Koerner for his wife, Sonja. The quartet was inspired by Schafer's second wife Jean's regular practice of T'ai Chi. Schafer chose a T'ai Chi set with 108 moves as the model for his quartet. He chose to use material from his previous quartets in this one-movement work, noting,

> Each move is accompanied by a motif or cluster of motifs drawn from the previous five quartets. In fact, there is scarcely an extraneous note in the work that does not come directly from one of the previous scores—the only real exception being the motif for the move entitled "Ward Off Monkey," which will appear in the seventh quartet. Though these fragments of material have been connected differently, much will sound familiar to those who know the other works. Several methods for binding the quartets together have already been employed, and this is merely one of the more meticulous.[12]

Schafer indicates that the quartet could be performed with or without the T'ai Chi movements, and throughout the score he indicates the placement of each movement in the T'ai Chi set, corresponding with its musical motive.

As Schafer was working on the sixth quartet he was also sketching out *String Quartet no. 7* but would not complete it until 1998 when he received a commission from the Molinari Quartet, who had decided to perform the first six quartets. For this next quartet he decided to write a work in which the members of the quartet would be in motion, an extension of the concept he first explored in the second, third, and fourth quartets. Since the commission specified the addition of a soprano voice, Schafer decided to incorporate a text by an anonymous schizophrenic patient and have the soprano soloist also move throughout the piece. Schafer notes,

> The texts would give the singer a strong, if confused, identity, providing a context for her irrational appearances and disappearances during the work. I set these texts with only a few slight changes and transposition of lines.[13]

Schafer also wished to have each player (and singer) dress in a particular color (red, blue, yellow, green, or white), each color representing a different energy. The musical material quotes from the earlier quartets, and each player is given a different scale (or other musical material) representing their unique color. Schafer instructs the players (and the singer) to interact in various ways, creating a miniature visual drama as well as a musical one.

String Quartet no. 8 was completed in 2001 for the Molinari Quartet to fulfill a commission by Ellen Karp and Bill Johnston to celebrate the fiftieth wedding anniversary of Ellen's parents, Fred and May Karp. Thinking of the achievement of sustaining a marriage for fifty years, Schafer planned a two-movement work that would begin with the closing motive of the seventh quartet and in which both movements would be based on the same material. The first movement would be energetic, reflective of young passion. The second would be gentler, but still with moments of passion.

> For the second movement I decided to double the quartet with pre-recorded material, both to add to the richness of the texture, but also to suggest memories of the past. As the playback of the recorded quartet is behind the live group, and therefore a little fainter, I hoped the distance would give something of the sentimental experience of looking through an album of old photographs.[14]

In the second movement the recorded quartet's sound comes from behind the live quartet, which interacts with it in various ways, including the live quartet miming the notes played by the recorded quartet.

String Quartet no. 9 was written in 2004, commissioned by Bill and Shirley Loeven for performance at the Winnipeg New Music Festival in February 2005. Schafer turned to several sources of inspiration for this quartet, which is in one movement. The first was a recording of the laughing and screaming voices of children recorded on a playground. A second is the theme from *The Crown of Ariadne* which appeared in previous quartets, and a third is one of the principal themes of *Quartet no. 8* sung by a prerecorded boy soprano and supported by a motive unique to *Quartet no. 9*: half note–two quarter notes–whole note. Schafer notes that

> the moods that follow are directly stimulated by the children's voices, and when they are not present the elegiac character predominates, although the last appearance of the boy soprano at the close stimulates a happy ending in a sped up version of the half–two quarter–whole note motif that introduced the work.[15]

The boy soprano voice and its accompanying motive appear early on in the quartet, followed by a passage for the quartet alone, which hearkens back to the *Ariadne* theme. This is followed by a section where the recorded sound of children playing slowly grows louder, fades, grows, and eventually disappears before the boy soprano voice returns.

String Quartet no. 10 (Winter Birds) was written in 2005 through a commission by Radio France for the Molinari Quartet, who had recorded the first eight quartets. The one-movement quartet was written in January and February of 2005, and in those winter months Schafer was inspired by the stillness outside the farmhouse. Unlike summer, there were fewer birds at the feeders outside his window, and the texture and approach of the quartet reflects this stillness. Schafer tries to imply various winter events (swirling snow, a glistening sunrise, the sound of wings) and also incorporates a loose transcription of a wolf howl, a main theme of *String Quartet no. 5*.

Schafer was fortunate to be teaching in Montreal in the fall of 2005 and was able to work with the Molinari Quartet to closely approximate the bird sounds on the stringed instruments, using many different techniques to represent the calls and movements, including fingernail pizzicato, harmonics and glissandi, and tapping on the instruments. Some of the piece is measured, much of it is not, and it moves between calm and sudden flurries of motion, reflecting the changing soundscape the composer is trying to represent. As a guide Schafer notes in the score the aural or visual event he is trying to represent, and toward the end of the piece Schafer asks the viola to play a melody, the rhythm of which matches a spoken (or prerecorded text) by Schafer describing the weather that inspired the quartet.

String Quartet no. 11 was commissioned by the Calgary-based Lafayette Quartet to celebrate their twentieth anniversary and was premiered by them in the summer of 2007. Schafer had started to sketch out this quartet in early 2005, even before receiving the commission, as he finished the tenth quartet. The quartet falls in multiple movements, and Schafer specifies the exact duration he wishes to have between each movement (6, 2, 8, and 10 seconds), hoping that this would create a greater sense of continuity. All five movements of the quartet are based on a theme of eleven notes (its first statement is G, B-flat, D, G, D, E-flat, D, G, B-flat, E-flat, G-flat), which functions as a passacaglia. Schafer mentions that the theme came to him in a dream, but he cannot determine if it is original or a remembered theme from another Baroque or Renaissance composer.

The first movement begins with a passionate melody in the first violin, then the second violin takes up the melody while the first violin moves on to countersubjects. Both players move on to other materials, joined by the viola, and ultimately all the players join in a fast, almost frantic unison melody that the upper three strings continue as the cello plays the first complete statement of the passacaglia theme. In the second movement the viola plays a rapid, energetic statement of the passacaglia, gradually slowing to an elegiac, obligato melody, supported by a three-part canon based on the theme in the other instruments. The third movement is marked "Like the blazing sun," and in the composer's words it is a "musical description of a sunset, from the sun's blazing descent into deep shadows as it passes below the horizon."[16] This movement ties the eleventh quartet to the tenth quartet, which also depicts birds and a sunrise. The fourth movement begins with a cello solo that is reminiscent of the opening of the third quartet. The first violin and viola then play accompanying material while the second violin and cello duet, interrupted by passages where all the players come together and play in unison or pass motives back and forth. The passacaglia theme next appears in the cello. The fifth movement is an extended imitation of an Aeolian harp, completely unmeasured and with approximate durations indicated by a timeline.

Commissioned by Phyllis Lambert for performance by the Molinari Quartet, *String Quartet no. 12* is in one continuous movement, with constantly shifting moods and an energy that the composer remarks may be "unusual for a composer approaching eighty years old."[17] As in the previous quartets, Schafer quotes from the earlier quartets, the most striking being the "snapshot" segment from *String Quartet no. 1* where the quartet is instructed to turn in a different direction and freeze after each snap pizzicato. The main melody of the quartet is initially presented in the first violin, following three measures of continuous descending glissandi—another motive that recurs throughout the piece. This melody descends in an angular fashion, with a descending leap followed by an ascending leap incorporating glissandi. Around this main melody is fashioned material from other quartets, all familiar to those who have heard these other compositions. This is a romantic, lyrical piece and surprisingly traditional with few extended techniques, little movement by the players, and very little of the violence that characterized some of the earlier quartets.

The last string piece Schafer composed, *Alzheimer's Masterpiece (String Quartet no. 13)*, was premiered in 2016 (the composition date is unclear). It is a short, one-movement piece for string quartet (although the divisi at times suggests multiple players) and violin solo. It changes mood and tempo often and is based on three main ideas. The first is introduced in the first violin, a repeated melodic fragment in 3/8. The second is an almost unison ascending melody in the two violins. The third is a melodic fragment outlining the interval of a third, which is repeated and inverted. A fourth motive is introduced in the middle of the piece, based on rapid repeating notes that alternate with ascending arpeggios. The closing coda introduces the solo violin, which plays a rhapsodic melody over slow moving, repeated chords in the lower three strings. In the final chord, the violin solo is replaced by a voice that sings "O-AH" in unison with the first violin note. The quartet ends much like *String Quartet no. 12* with slow repeated chords.

CHAMBER AND SOLO MUSIC FOR HARP

Schafer's first solo piece for harp, *The Crown of Ariadne*, was written for Judy Loman, principal harpist for the TSO. Schafer thought for some time on how to structure the piece and was finally inspired when his composer friend Toru Takemitsu suggested that Schafer should include bells, which would be placed on the harpist's arms to add an improvisational element to the piece. Schafer liked this idea and decided to bring other percussion instruments that could be incorporated into the work. The percussion battery is extensive, requiring two tables placed around the harpist. Schafer also indicates special tunings for the first and last movements, and in "Labyrinth Dance" the player dialogues with a prerecorded harp.

In 1978 when Schafer wrote the work, he was thinking of a *Patria* segment based on the story of Theseus, Ariadne, the Minotaur, and the labyrinth, which would become the dance drama *Patria 5: The Crown of Ariadne*. The solo harp would represent Ariadne, and Schafer structured the commission for Judy as a set of discrete movements, many of which would be dances. The various titles of the movements would indicate Ariadne's involvement in the story. Although this set was intended for inclusion in *Patria 5*, Schafer did not use the all-interval row as the foundation of this piece. Instead, he chose to use different seven-note scales for each movement, with the same scale for the first and last movements, as indicated in the movement description.

"Ariadne Awakens"—Ariadne rises and stretches her limbs to the music while thinking of how she can save Theseus (C, D-flat, E-flat, F, G, A, B).

"Ariadne's Dance"—Ariadne has memorized the twists and turns of the labyrinth into a dance. She goes through the dance to refresh her memory (C, D-sharp, E, F, G-sharp, A, B).

"Dance of the Bull"—In the labyrinth the Minotaur waits for the victims from Greece, who will provide him with his dinner (C-flat, D, E, F-flat, G, A-flat, B-flat).

Figure 18.1. *Alzheimer's Masterpiece. R. Murray Schafer*

"Dance of the Night Insects"—Ariadne visits Theseus in prison late at night, having bribed the guards. She gives him a ball of thread to find his way out of the labyrinth. Theseus promises to take Ariadne back with him to Athens (C-flat, D, E, F, G, A-flat, B).

"Ariadne Dreams" (this movement was added in 1995 at Judy's request)—Ariadne returns to her room and falls into a restless sleep with disturbing dreams (no discernable scale).

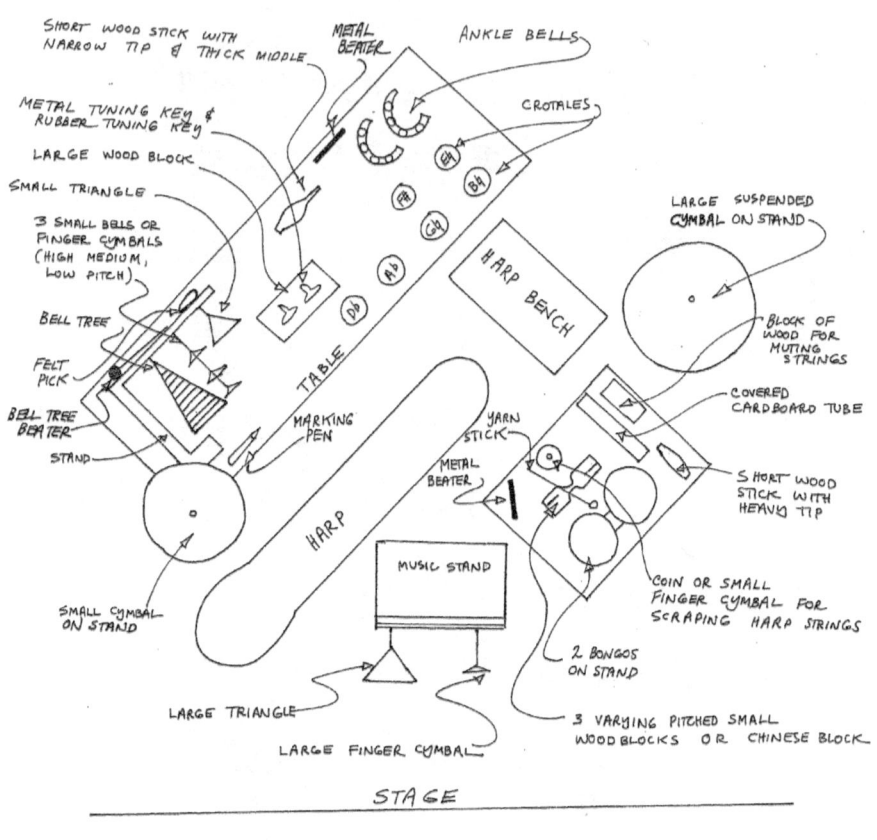

Figure 18.2. Setup Diagram—*The Crown of Ariadne.* R. Murray Schafer

"Sun Dance"—At sunrise Theseus is led to the labyrinth (C, D, E, F, G, A-flat, B-flat).

"Labyrinth Dance"—Theseus comes upon the Minotaur, kills him, and dances victoriously out of the labyrinth (C, D-flat, E-flat, F, G, A, B).

Theseus was a second commission for Judy Loman, written in the summer of 1983. For this next commission he decided to write a companion piece to *The Crown of Ariadne*, one that would also become a segment of *Patria 5*. Unlike the first piece, which was a series of dances, *Theseus* is one continuous movement, and it refers to the male protagonist of the myth, who uses Ariadne's thread to navigate the labyrinth, kill the Minotaur, and return safely. Ariadne's thread appears in *Theseus* in the form of music from the earlier piece, but *Theseus* also includes a new motive, "a descending series of notes, S (E-flat) C H (B natural) A F E, as a kind of signature, a device Shostakovich was also fond of; and, in fact, the Shostakovich influence is easily detectable in Theseus."[18] This motive links Schafer to the character of Theseus, one of the manifestations of the male protagonist in the *Patria* cycle. Within the one movement of the piece there are many contrasting sections, ranging from "quiet, expressive rhapsodical interludes to the shatteringly powerful writing of the dramatic climax which comes roughly halfway through the work."[19] The episodes reflect on the journey of Theseus into and out of the labyrinth, and at the end of the piece the character of Ariadne appears as an off-stage voice that sings with the instrumentalists during the last five measures.

Wild Bird was written in 1997 for Jacques Israelievitch, for whom Schafer had composed *The Darkly Splendid Earth: The Lonely Traveller*. It was commissioned by Jacques's wife, Gabriella, for his fiftieth birthday, and the piece is based on five primary motives, three of which are presented in order at the beginning. This first is a double-dotted rhythm circling an octave leap, the second is a thirty-second and sixteenth note rising-and-falling gesture, the third a series of descending seconds. The fourth motive is presented in compound meter, a descending augmented fourth. The fifth motive is a series of parallel sixth double stops in the violin. The writing is firmly in a tonal language with quite traditional (for Schafer) notation.

Trio (for Flute, Viola, and Harp) was a joint commission in 2010 by Trio Verlaine, for whom it was written, in conjunction with Michael Koerner (a long-time patron of Schafer), the Ottawa Chamber Festival, and the Vancouver concert series Music on Main. The combination of flute, viola, and harp is the instrumentation of Debussy's *Sonata*, and the influences of the impressionistic composer can be heard, particularly in the first movement, which is marked "Freely flowing." The main musical material is based on the opening flute motive (which also appears in the second movement) and is transformed into different characters throughout the movement. The second movement is marked "Slowly, calmly," and Schafer notes the "hymn-like" nature of the opening, which alternates with more rhapsodic passages, creating a struggle between the two elements of the movement. The third movement begins with a driving ostinato in the viola over which is an energetic dance melody that uses the syncopated rhythms and mixed meter of folk music alternating with rhapsodic lyrical lines.

CHAMBER MUSIC ASSOCIATED WITH *PATRIA*

Situational Music for Brass Quintet, originally conceived to be included in *The Greatest Show*, was commissioned in 1981 for the Canadian Brass by Stratford Summer Music for a performance in and around Stratford's city hall. In the cover of the score Schafer provides a map of the area around Stratford's city hall indicating where each of the five players should start and where they should move to. All sections of the piece are based on the *Patria* all-interval row.

Section 1: "Assembling Music"—"In which the Canadian Brass enter the square from all points of the compass." This first section uses short phrases based on 3- or 4-note fragments from the row.

Section 2: "Ascending Music"—"In which the Canadian Brass mount into the air." Once the players reach the base of their assigned building (a different one for each player), they ascend to the roof, playing the original form of the row.

Sections 3–5: "Theme Music"—"In which each player announces his theme"; "Echoes"—"In which the themes are echoed across the rooftops"; and "Talking Music"—"In which the players talk to each other by means of a special code." When all the players are on their respective rooftops, they each announce their unique theme and dialogue with each other.

Sections 6–7: "Pointing Music"—"In which the players point at one another"; "Exciting Music"—"In which the Canadian Brass become very excited." One player points at another player, who plays the first note of a version of the series in the score, then all the players take up a rapid motive.

Section 8: "Descending Music"—"In which the Canadian Brass descend to earth." Each player leaves his or her roof and begins to descend to the ground, playing a retrograde version of the series.

Section 9: "Walking Music"—"In which the players round up the audience and lead them to City Hall." Each player has a marching motive, and they begin to synchronize with each other.

Sections 10–11: "Welcoming Music"—"In which the Canadian Brass welcomes the audience from the steps of City Hall"; "Entrance Music"—"In which the Canadian Brass accompany the audience into the hall." Each player begins by playing a version of the row then they begin to enter the hall, beginning a rapid chromatic buzzing leading to the finale.

Section 12: "Finally"—"In which the Canadian Brass stops playing." The quintet plays a unison line based on the retrograde of the series. This is broken up by pauses in which each player speaks, leading to a closing allegro.

Buskers was completed in October of 1985, the result of a commission from Schafer's friend Robert Aitken, for whom he also wrote *Flute Concerto* and *Flew Toots for Two Flutes*. Since the main compositional focus for Schafer that year was *Patria 3: The Greatest Show*, Schafer decided to write a piece that would become a mobile editing unit for that work. The title implies the practice of musicians playing in public spaces and asking for donations in return for their performance, and the three buskers in this piece are a man (the violin), Life (the flute), and Death (the viola), with each player costumed to reflect their character. Man is dressed in a tattered tuxedo and a top hat, which he takes off and places upside down on the floor in order to encourage tips. Life wears a spring-like costume, green in color. Death wears tails and a skull mask. As the piece is intended to be a miniature show with all three players moving apart and together, they are required to memorize their music and work with a stage director since Schafer includes stage directions in the score. Each of the three characters also has his or her own musical material that is not based on the *Patria* row but on variations of the major and minor scale. The piece is solidly diatonic with no extended techniques, and the primary interest is in how the material of each character circulates to the others as the players themselves come together and go apart on the stage.

Wolf Music is a collection of pieces Schafer wrote for voice and various instruments for *Patria Epilogue: And Wolf Shall Inherit the Moon* starting in 1991. One of the rituals of the week-long project is that each day is framed with an aubade and a nocturne. The aubade is the first thing heard during the day (people wake up in silence) and the nocturne ushers in silence so that it is the last thing heard in the day. They are not intended for concert performance, although some of them have been performed this way. The three *Aubade/Nocturne* sets, one for solo trumpet, one for solo clarinet, and one for solo flute serve this function. *Tapio* for alphorn or French horn is played in the forest with echoing instruments, which can be left to the discretion of the performers. *Departure* for trumpet is performed in the same way but around a lake. *Sunset* for natural trumpet is to be played as the sun descends below the horizon. Given the intent of the pieces, the harmonic language is simple, and there is no appearance of the all-interval row.

CONCERT CHAMBER MUSIC

Minimusic, given its final form in 1972, was Schafer's furthest venture into chance music, a piece for a variable number of voices or instruments of any type. It is made up of thirty-six boxes with instructions and graphic notation. Each player starts with box 1 but can go many different ways. One notable part is box 18, where the person is instructed to play Paul Klee's painting *The Twittering Machine*.[20] Some simple traditional notation is involved, but the focus is on improvisation and the creation of music through listening to the other players and responding to them.

In discussing his composition *Music for Wilderness Lake*, Schafer describes it as

> the first of my environmental compositions. The two sections are called Dusk and Dawn, and my idea was that we would play Dusk as the sun was setting,

then camp at the lake and play Dawn as the sun rose the next morning. I had arranged for the work to be broadcast on CBC Radio and recorded on film.

The lake was not far from my farm, and the time was mid-September. After a rehearsal in my barn, we drove to the lake in the late afternoon and performed Dusk in the evening. I conducted it with coloured flags from a raft in the centre of the lake, from where the CBC was also recording it. The flags were necessary because of the distances separating the players (500 metres [a little less than one-third of a mile] or more), but actually the score is written in such a way that the players take cues from each other aurally most of the time.[21]

The piece was written in 1979 for a commission from Sonaré, a Canadian trombone ensemble. Schafer was heavily immersed in his soundscape research and wanted to compose a piece that drew the music he wrote into a relationship with the soundscape of rural Ontario, where he had been living since leaving SFU. He came up with the idea for this piece after visiting one of the many undeveloped lakes close to him and decided to place the players all around the lake, which was roughly one-half mile long, and have them play to each other across the water. Dusk and dawn were chosen because at those times the wind was at its lowest and the sound reflection off the water would therefore be greatest. Schafer worked with some of the players as he wrote the piece so he could listen to the effect of the sound delay and calculate the entrances for each player depending on their distance from the audience and each other. To help with the coordination, he had all the players play from a full score, and he used flags (as referenced in his program notes for the piece). Players were often required to listen for the sound of the music preceding them as a cue to begin playing, and the music was made up of small motives passed around the lake, sometimes slowly, sometimes more rapidly. Simple canons appeared along with additional material, and the players were sometimes asked to turn in a circle while playing.

One of the most unusual chamber pieces that Schafer wrote, *Harbour Symphony*, was composed in 1983 for performance by ten ships playing their foghorns in the harbor at St. John's, Newfoundland.

In the program notes for *Flew Toots for Two Flutes* from 2004, Schafer writes,

> This little piece for two flutes was written for my friend Bob Aitken for performance on a celebration concert to mark his retirement from the music department at the University of Freiburg, Germany.[22]

This duet is lyrical throughout and shows the composer's comfort in writing for the instrument. The harmonic language is tonally based, with hints of whole tone and other alternate scales. It is a brief piece, sunny and celebratory.

In 2006 Schafer received a commission from Soundstreams Canada to provide a piece for a concert of brass music to be held at St. Anne's Church in Toronto. When Schafer toured the church, which is modeled after the Hagia Sophia in Istanbul, he was reminded of his travels in Turkey and Iran in 1969, where he was able to see the Shah Abbas Mosque in Isfahan. Completed in 1629, the mosque is known for its visual beauty and acoustic effect: "Standing directly under the main cupola a hand clap will return precisely seven echoes. Move a step away in any direction and a hand clap will return no echoes at all."[23] Schafer decided to name his piece *Isfahan*, after that famous mosque, and to base the composition on the number 7. This number underpins the melodic and harmonic material, derived from a seven-note scale: C, D-flat, E, F, G-sharp, A, B. The scale includes two augmented seconds, which are highlighted in various ways throughout the piece. The conductor plays a seven-stroke motif seven times throughout the piece, and at the end also plays a temple bell—pitched to C (the tonic of the scale Schafer uses)—seven times to close the piece. In addition to this internal organization, Schafer designed the piece to use the entire space where it was performed. The three quintets start at different places at the beginning of the piece and move to other positions during the performance, at one point walking toward each other and exchanging notes as they pass. The coordination of these groups is facilitated by the conductor, who gives cues as necessary in those parts where all three quintets play precisely together. In addition to the three brass quintets, there is also an optional soprano voice who can join toward the end of the piece, repeating three short phrases, with pauses in between each.

Duo for Violin and Piano was a joint commission by the Ottawa Chamber Music Festival, the Tuckamore Festival, and the CBC for performance by Nancy Dahn and Tim Steeves in 2008. Schafer notes that it is a conventional piece and one of his most traditional chamber pieces, written in three movements. The first movement is based on a series of arpeggiated triads. Schafer manages to spin out a six-minute movement based on this material, sometimes leaving out the middle note of the triad to create a series of descending fifths and sometimes filling in the triads to create more scalar passages. The second movement takes the tertian motive and creates a descending sequence as the opening melody. This material returns in various guises throughout the movement, often underpinned by a chord sequence borrowed from *Symphony no. 4* of Johannes Brahms. Schafer notes, "The third movement employs aksak rhythms found in Balkan music and ends with an actual Romanian dance tune which I accidentally heard on the radio, supporting a news event from somewhere between Bucharest and Sofia."[24] This is reflected in the time signatures, which alternate between various forms of 16 (such as 8/16 and 9/16). The parallel thirds appear again in the violin and piano part, and toward the end the piano brings back the triadic arpeggios that began the piece.

Schafer wrote *Trio for Violin, Viola and Cello*, his only string trio, in response to a commission from the Arizona Friends of Chamber Music. He began to work on the piece in late 2008 and finished it in 2009. Schafer notes, "There is something unsettling about a trio, like a marriage plus one— a triad of tensions—or at least that is the way I found myself thinking about it when I began to write the piece."[25] This tension is the hallmark of the one-movement work. The beginning is calm, with a Lydian-mode melody in the violin simply accompanied by the other two strings, but after a few bars the tension grows, and it continues with only a few quiet moments. The climax includes a quote on Schafer's name, a descending scale in the cello on the pitches E-flat (S) C H (B natural) A F E. This is followed by a closing adagio that references Gustav Mahler, followed by a reprise of the opening theme.

Quintet for Piano and Strings was commissioned by the ARC Ensemble (Associates of the Royal Conservatory) and was completed in 2010. It is in three movements, simply titled "I, II, III." The first movement is marked "Presto" and is quick and energetic, based on a rapid, circling, scalar passage of sextuplets. This flurry of notes is the main characteristic of this movement, where few melodies or even melodic fragments are found. The second movement, marked "Slowly," begins with a brief duet between the second violin and piano, where the violin plays a melody marked by an ascending fifth and fourth in much longer notes (half and quarters). This melody breaks down into smaller rhythmic groups as the other instruments enter, including a quote from the original sextuplet motive and tempo from the first movement. These two moods alternate throughout the rest of the movement. The third movement has no tempo indication but a fast metronome marking (160). It begins in C major with pizzicato octaves in the strings and scalar passages in the piano. The movement's playful character continues throughout, reinforced by syncopated rhythms and string effects such as rapid glissandi.

Trio for Violin, Cello, and Piano, completed in 2015 and therefore one of Schafer's last pieces, was a commission from the Gryphon Trio with support from several private donors and the Canada Council for the Arts. He began working with the trio in May 2013, after his official diagnosis of Alzheimer's, and this is apparent in the composition. The single movement was initially conceived as the first movement of a multi-movement piece, and the harmonic language and writing for the instruments is tonal and quite conservative. The melodies and melodic fragments are well crafted and idiomatic, and the discrete sections give the listener a sense of a rondo form.

WORKS FOR SOLO INSTRUMENTS

In 1979 the Ontario Arts Council on behalf of Jack Behrens commissioned five Ontario-born composers to compose variations for piano on a one-minute theme of Behrens. Of these five, four completed the task, one of whom was Schafer. His short (under two minutes) response to the theme is his only piece for solo piano between *Polytonality* and *Deluxe Suite*.

Schafer finished *Le Cri de Merlin* in 1987 for the guitarist Norbert Kraft, who would later premiere Schafer's *Guitar Concerto*. Schafer talks about the genesis of the piece this way:

> Le Cri de Merlin was written for Norbert Kraft. I recall visiting him at his cottage in Muskoka to discuss the piece, and sitting outside enjoying the caroling of the birds as the sun set. I thought of the distant cries of Merlin in the darkening forest. That would have been the right place to perform the work, but Norbert wanted to tour with it and record it. We then decided to make a tape of the birds and play it back with the guitar during the final moments of the piece. My hope is that every performer of Le Cri de Merlin will record the birds of his or her native land and play them at the end as a testament to the strange and wonderful voices of nature everywhere.[26]

In Schafer's mind, the cries of Merlin in the forest recall the legend that Merlin, after serving King Arthur, returned to the forest and was not seen again. Schafer also recalls Karl Jung's sentiment that people can still hear the cries of Merlin but the cries can no longer be understood since society has exchanged magic for technology. The part was edited for performance by Norbert Kraft and Douglas Hensley, both accomplished guitarists, so the writing is idiomatic but extends the technique of the instrument. Schafer, in addition to calling for standard techniques including both natural and artificial harmonics, also calls for several nontraditional techniques. These include tuning strings up and down during the performance, crossing strings, using different (and quite specific) strumming techniques, and striking the instrument and strings in various ways. *Le Cri de Merlin* is written as one continuous movement. The writing is episodic but held together by recurring motives, such as major- and minor-second–based repeated notes, passages of parallel thirds and fourths, and a descending arpeggio using harmonics. These alternate with several passages of large, at times violent chords and more complex, two-voice contrapuntal passages.

Schafer began working on *Deluxe Suite for Piano* in 1995 as a response to a commission by the CBC for concert pianist Janina Fialkowska. Schafer didn't particularly like composing for the piano but felt that he had to accept this commission, which he completed in 1996. Schafer had heard Janina Fialkowska play on different occasions, and her technique led him to include the word "deluxe" in the title for this composition. He called it a suite because he included the multiple contrasting movements found in a traditional suite but connected the movements, giving it the character of a rhapsody. The basic pitch material is first heard in the slow introduction, and throughout the influence of jazz, Prokofiev, and Schafer's own habit of improvising at the piano are heard. Hints of the traditional dances in a suite, including a gigue and a march, also appear throughout the piece.

ELECTRONIC WORKS

Kaleidoscope, a 12-foot multi-track tape created for the Pavilion of Chemical Industries for Expo '67 held in Montreal was a joint project between filmmaker Morley Markson and Schafer. They worked together on the piece from the beginning so that in some places the film was completed first and in some places the soundtrack was completed first. A review of the piece described it as "abstract images on a screen, mirrored in four sides to create an endless pattern, are mirrored again in a complex panorama of synthesized sound; the musical impulses seem to take on a visual shape, and abstract color patterns become a kind of lyrical outpouring."[27]

Schafer notes in his description of *Okeanos*, created in 1971,

> Okeanos is a study in sound of the symbolism of the sea, using natural and electronic sounds with voices reciting texts by many authors—Homer, Hesiod, Melville, Pound—who have written about the sea. The work was composed by Bruce Davis, Brian Fawcett and myself in the Sonic Research Studio at Simon Fraser University.
>
> The Greeks had two words for ocean: pontos was the navigable sea and okeanos the wild, untamed, stormy ocean. When I first approached the CBC with the idea of creating a portrait of the sea in sound and words, I was asked how long the program would be. I thought twenty-four hours would be suitable. How could we suggest the limitless magnitude of the ocean in a stingy half-hour show? We were eventually given ninety minutes, and the CBC attempted something I believe they had never done before: they broadcast the program quadraphonically by using the stereo systems of both networks.[28]

Okeanos would later be included as a segment of *Patria 7*.

Appendix A

Chronological List of Compositions

1952

Polytonality; pno; Arcana.

1953

A Music Lesson; voice, pno; Arcana.

1954

Trio for Clarinet, Cello, and Piano; Arcana.
    Concerto for Harpsichord and Eight Wind Instruments; hpscd, 2 fl, ob, cl, bass cl, 2 bn, hn; Arcana.

1956

Three Contemporaries; medium voice, pno; Arcana.
    Minnelieder; mezzo-soprano, wind quintet; fl, ob, cl, hn, bsn; Arcana.
    Partita for Twelve Instruments; fl, ob, cl, sax, hn, bsn, vln, vla, vc, db, continuo; withdrawn.

1958

Kinderlieder; soprano, pno; Arcana.
    Sonatina for Flute and Harpsichord (or Pno); Arcana.
    Petit Divertissement Angevin; fl, ob, cl, vc; withdrawn.

Sonata da Camera; 2 vc; withdrawn.
Three Ideograms; pno; withdrawn.

1959

In Memoriam Alberto Guerrero; str orch; Arcana.

1960

Protest and Incarceration; mezzo-soprano, orch; manuscript.

1961

Brébeuf; baritone, 3-3-3-3/4-3-3-1/pno, hp, celesta, perc, str; Arcana.
    Partita for String Orchestra; str orch; Arcana.
    The Judgement of Jael; soprano, mezzo-soprano, orch; withdrawn.
    Dithyramb for String Orchestra; str orch; withdrawn.

1962

Canzoni for Prisoners; 3-3-3-3/4-3-3-1/pno (celesta), hp, perc, str; Arcana.
    Five Studies on Texts by Prudentius; soprano, 4 fl; Arcana.
    Four Songs on Texts of Tagore; chorus (SSAA); withdrawn.
    Opus One for Mixed Chorus; chorus (SATB), tape; withdrawn.
    Invertible Material for Orchestra no. 1; withdrawn.

1963

Divisions for Baroque Trio; fl, ob, hpscd, tape; withdrawn.
    Untitled Composition for Orchestra no. 1; 1-1-1-1/1-1-1-0/cel, str; Arcana.
    Untitled Composition for Orchestra no. 2; 3-3-3-3/4-3-3-1/pno (celesta), hp, perc, str; Arcana.
    The Geography of Eros; soprano, chamb orch; Arcana.
    Invertible Material for Orchestra no. 2; withdrawn.

1964

Statement in Blue; youth orch (strings and winds); Arcana.
    Statement in Red; brass, winds, perc; withdrawn.

1965

Loving; 4 voices, 2 actors, dancers, chamb orch, tape of electronic and prerecorded sounds; Arcana.

1966

Requiems for the Party Girl; mezzo-soprano, chamb orch; Arcana.
Festival Music for Small Orchestra; withdrawn.
Sonorities for Brass Sextet; brass sextet, tape; withdrawn.

1967

Threnody; 5 child narrators, chorus (SATB), 4-3-3-3/4-4-3-1/pno, hp, perc, str, electronic sounds; Arcana.
Gita; chorus (SATB), 3 tr, 3 hn, 3 trmb, tuba, tape; Universal.
Kaleidescope; quadraphonic tape.

1968

Epitaph for Moonlight; chorus (SATB); Berandol.
Son of Heldenleben; full orch, tape; Universal.
From the Tibetan Book of the Dead; soprano, chorus (SATB), fl, cl, tape; Universal.

1969

Dream Passage; mezzo-soprano, choir, actors, chamb orch, tape; CBC radio program.
Minimusic; any small combination of singers or instrumentalists; Universal.
Yeow and Pax; chorus (SATB), organ, tape; Canadian Music Center.

1970

String Quartet no. 1; Universal.
No Longer Than Ten (10) Minutes; 3-3-3-3/4-3-3-1/ perc, str; Arcana.
Sappho; mezzo, harp, pno, guitar, perc; withdrawn.
Divan i Shams i Tabriz; full orch, 7 voices, electronic sounds; Universal.
Music for the Morning of the World; soprano, electronic sounds; Universal.

1971

(In Search of) Zoroaster, 1971; 150-voice chorus (SATB divided); Arcana.
  Enchantress; soprano, exotic flute, 8 vc; Berandol.
  Okeanos; quadraphonic tape; Arcana.
  Miniwanka, or The Moments of Water; chorus (SA or SATB); Arcana.

1972

Beyond the Great Gate of Light; full orch; 8 voices, electronic sounds; Universal.
  Psalm, 1972; large chorus (SATB), perc; Arcana.
  Arcana; 17 min; middle voice, chamb orch (or full orch); Universal.
  Patria 2: Requiems for the Party Girl; mezzo-soprano, chorus (SATB), actors, dancers, chamb orch, electronic and prerecorded sounds.

1973

East, 1973; orch; Universal.
  North/White, 1973; full orch, snowmobile; Universal.

1974

Patria 1: Wolfman; soprano, chorus (SATB), actors, chamb orch, electronic and prerecorded sounds; Arcana.

1976

String Quartet no. 2 (Waves); Arcana.
  Train; youth orch; Arcana.
  Adieu Robert Schumann; contralto, full orch, pno, prerecorded pno; Universal.
  Hymn to Night; soprano and chamb orch (or full orch), tape delay and prerecorded sounds; Universal.
  Apocalypsis Part 2: Credo; chorus (12 SATB), db, filtered bells prerecorded; Arcana.

1977

Cortège; orch; Universal.
  La Testa d'Adriane; soprano, free-bass accordion; Arcana.

Apocalypsis Part 1: John's Vision; solo actors, singers and dancers, chorus (SA, TB, 2 SATB, boys, speech), winds, brass; Arcana.

1978

The Crown of Ariadne; hp, perc; Arcana.

1979

Jonah; chorus (SATB), actors, children, fl, cl, organ, perc; Arcana.
    Gamelan; chorus (SATB or SASA or TBTB); Arcana.
    Hear Me Out; 4 voices; Arcana.
    Felix's Girls; chorus (vocal quartet and/or SATB); Arcana.
    Music for Wilderness Lake; 12 trombones around a lake; Arcana.
    Beauty and the Beast; contralto, str quartet; Arcana.

1980

Wizard Oil and Indian Sagwa; speaker, cl; Arcana.
    The Garden of the Heart; mezzo-soprano, 3-2-2-2/4-2-1-1/ perc (2), str; Arcana.

1981

Patria Prologue: The Princess of the Stars; soprano, 3 actors, 6 dancers, chorus (2 SATB), 12 instrumentalists, canoeists; Arcana.
    String Quartet no. 3; Arcana.
    Situational Music for Brass Quintet; 2 tpt, hn, tmb, tuba; withdrawn.

1982

Sun, 1982; chorus (SATB); Arcana.

1983

Patria 6: Ra, 1983; 25 solo singers, actors and dancers, chorus (TTBB), chamb orch including Middle Eastern instruments; Arcana.
    Theseus; hp, str quartet; Arcana.
    Snowforms; chorus (SSAA); Arcana.
    A Garden of Bells; chorus (SATB); Arcana.

Harbour Symphony; foghorns; unpublished.

1984

Concerto for Flute and Orchestra; fl, 2-2-2-2/4-2-2-1/pno (celesta), hp, perc, str; Arcana.
    Sun Father, Earth Mother; solo voice; Arcana.
    Letters from Mignon; mezzo-soprano, 3-3-2-2-/4-2-2-0/ pno, hp, perc, str; Arcana.
    The Star Princess and the Waterlilies; narrator, contralto, children's chorus (SA), perc; Arcana.

1985

Ko wo kiku (Listen to the Incense); 3-3-3-3/4-3-3-1/pno (celesta), hp, perc, str; Arcana.
    Buskers, 1985; fl, vln, vla; Arcana.

1986

Fire; chorus (SATB); Arcana.
    Tantrika; mezzo-soprano, perc; Arcana.
    Minnelieder; mezzo-soprano, 3-3-3-2/4-2-2-0/ hp, perc, str; Arcana.
    Dream Rainbow Dream Thunder; 3-3-3-3/4-3-3-1/pno (celesta), hp, perc, str; Arcana.

1987

Patria 3: The Greatest Show; about 150 actors, singers, dancers, musicians, and carnival people; Arcana.
    Le Cri de Merlin; guitar; Arcana.
    Concerto for Harp and Orchestra; hp, 3-2-2-2/4-2-2-1/pno (celesta), perc, str; Arcana.

1988

Patria 4: The Black Theatre of Hermes Trismegistos; 7 solo singers, chorus (SATB), 11 actors, chamb orch; Arcana.
    The Death of the Buddha; chorus (SATB); Arcana.
    Magic Songs; chorus (TTBB or SATB); Arcana.

Patria Epilogue: And Wolf Shall Inherit the Moon; 8 days; 64 adult participants; Arcana.

1989

String Quartet no. 4; Arcana.
    String Quartet no. 5 (Rosalind); Arcana.
    Concerto for Guitar and Orchestra; guitar, 2-1-2-1/1-0-0-0/perc, str; Arcana.

1990

Scorpius, 1990; 2-2-2-2/2-2-2-0/pno, perc, str; Arcana.
    The Darkly Splendid Earth: The Lonely Traveller; vln, 3-3-3-3/4-3-3-1/hp, perc, str; Arcana.

1991

Gitanjali, 1991; soprano, 2-2-2-2/2-2-0-0/ perc, str; Arcana.
    Patria 5: The Crown of Ariadne; 8 solo actors and dancers, extras, chorus (SATB), full orch; Arcana.
    Wolf Music; variable instruments; Arcana.

1992

Musique pour le parc Lafontaine; 4 concert bands; Arcana.
    Concerto for Accordion and Orchestra; accordion, 3-2-2-2/2-2-2-0/perc, str; Arcana.
    Tristan and Iseult; 6 voices (AATTBB); Arcana.
    Patria 7: Asterion; prerecorded music, actors, musicians; unpublished.

1993

String Quartet no. 6; Arcana.
    Patria 9: The Enchanted Forest; 15 solo actors and singers, children's choir (SA), girls' choir (SA), chamb orch; Arcana.

1994

Beautiful Spanish Song; choir (SA); Arcana.

Manitou; 3-3-3-3/4-3-3-1/pno (celesta), hp, perc, str; Arcana.

1995

The Falcon's Trumpet; trumpet, soprano (optional), 2-2-2-2/2-2-0-0/perc, str; Arcana.
Once on a Windy Night; chorus (SATB); Arcana.
Deluxe Suite for Piano; Arcana.

1996

Three Songs from The Enchanted Forest; chorus (SA); Arcana.
A Medieval Bestiary; chorus (SATB); Arcana.
Patria 10: The Spirit Garden Part 1: Spring; 11 solo actors and singers, extras, chorus (SATB), children's chorus (SA), gardeners, orch; *Part 2: Harvest*; 45 min. plus banquet; 8 solo actors and singers, extras, chorus (SATB), orch; Arcana.
Two Songs from the Spirit Garden; children's choir (SA); Arcana.
Vox Naturae, 1996; chorus (SATB); Arcana.

1997

Concerto for Viola and Orchestra; vla, 2-2-2-2/2-2-2-0/ hp, perc, str; Arcana.
Wild Bird; vln and hp; Arcana.
Seventeen Haiku; chorus (SATB); Arcana.

1998

String Quartet no. 7; string quartet, soprano; Arcana.

1999

You Are Illuminated; children's chorus (SA); Arcana.
Alleluia; chorus (SATB); Arcana.
Four-Forty; string quartet, 2-2-2-2/2-2-1-0/hp, perc, str; Arcana.

2000

Patria 8: The Palace of the Cinnabar Phoenix; 5 solo singers, actor, puppets, chorus (SA), chamb orch, including Chinese instruments; Arcana.

Shadowman; 5 perc, 2-2-2-2/2-2-2-0/pno, perc, str; Arcana.

2001

String Quartet no. 8; Arcana.
    Imagining Incense; chorus (SATB); Arcana.
    Rain Chant, 2001; chorus (SATB); Arcana.
    Winter Solstice; chorus (TTBB); Arcana.

2002

Remember Susannah; actors, singers, variable instruments; unpublished.

2003

The Fall Into Light, 2003; chorus (6 SATB), children's chorus (SA), 6 perc; Arcana.
    Thunder: Perfect Mind; mezzo-soprano, 2-2-2-2/2-2-2-0/pno, perc, str; Arcana.
    Tanzlied, 2003; mezzo-soprano, hp; Arcana.

2004

String Quartet no. 9; Arcana.
    Flew Toots for Two Flutes; Arcana.

2005

String Quartet no. 10 (Winter Birds); Arcana.
    The Death of Shalana; chorus (4 SATB); Arcana.

2006

Isfahan for Three Brass Quintets; Arcana.
    Six Songs from Rilke's "Book of Hours," soprano, vln, vla, vc, pno; Arcana.
    Trio for Violin, Viola and Cello; Arcana.

2007

String Quartet no. 11; Arcana.
The Children's Crusade; Arcana.

2008

Duo for Violin and Piano; Arcana.
The Searching Sings; chorus (SATB); Arcana.
Make Room for God; chorus (SATB); Arcana.
Spirits of the House; 3-2-2-3/4-2-2-1/pno, perc, str; off-stage instrumentalists and singers; Arcana.
Narcissus and Echo; large chorus (SATB) dancers or mime; Arcana.

2009

Dream(e)scape; 2-2-2-2/2-2-2-1/perc, str; Arcana.
The Love That Moves the Universe; chorus (SATB), str; Arcana.

2010

Landscapes and Soundscapes; chorus (SATB); unpublished.
The Soul of God; chorus (4 SATB); Arcana.
Trio for Flute, Viola, and Harp; Arcana.
Symphony no. 1 in C minor; 3-3-3-3/4-3-3-1/pno, hp, perc, str; Arcana.
Quintet for Piano and Strings; pno, 2 vln, vla, vc; Arcana.

2011

Job; singers, actors, instruments (flexible); unpublished.

2012

Here the Sounds Go Round; chorus (3 SATB); Arcana.
Wolf Returns; voices, 3-3-2-2/2-2-2-1/pno, perc, str; Arcana.
String Quartet no. 12; Arcana.
Four Songs for Mezzo-Soprano and Harp; Arcana.
Figures in the Night . . . Passing; 2-2-2-2/2-2-2-0/perc, str; Arcana.

2013

Trio for Violin, Cello and Piano; Arcana.
   Alzheimer's Masterpiece (String Quartet no. 13); Arcana.

Appendix B

Select Discography

3 Solos: R. Murray Schafer. (Music for the Morning of the World; Le Cri de Merlin; Deluxe Suite for Piano). Centrediscs CD-CMCCD/DVD, 2006, CD.
20th Century Guitar Music. (Le cri de Merlin). Chandos CD-CHAN 8784, 1989, CD.
Ariadne's Legacy. (The Crown of Ariadne; Theseus; Concerto for Harp and Orchestra; Wild Bird; Tanzlied; Trio for Flute, Viola, Harp; Four Songs for Mezzo-Soprano and Harp). Centrediscs CD-CMCCD 23316, 2016, CD.
Canadian Composer Portraits: R. Murray Schafer (Wolf Music). Centrediscs CD-CMCCD 8902, 2002, CD.
Canadian Music for Flute and Piano. (Sonatina). Independent CD-CML CD 101, 2005, CD.
A Canadian Music Sampler: Centrediscs 30 years. (Wild Bird). Centrediscs CD-CMCCD, 2011, CD.
Chimera. (Theseus, The Crown of Ariadne). Centrediscs CMC-CD 4192, 1992, CD.
A Conversation Piece. (Polytonality). Independent CD-SPP 0090, 2014, CD.
Elmer Iseler Conducts Canadian Music. (Sun). Centrediscs SKU: CD-CMCCD, 1999, CD.
The Esprit Orchestra. (Dream Rainbow, Dream Thunder). Centrediscs SMCD5101, 1991.
A Garden of Bells. (A Garden of Bells, Gamelan, Felix's Girls, Miniwanka, Snowforms, Sun, Epitaph for Moonlight, Fire). Grouse Records, 2000, CD.
The Garden of the Heart. (Garden of the Heart; Gitanjali; Adieu, Robert Schuman). CBC Records CD-SMCD 5173, 1997, CD.
Illuminations. (Wild Bird). Marquis Classics CD-ERAD 297, 2003, CD.
Imagining Incense. (Magic Songs, Three Hymns from The Fall Into Light, Rain Chant, Alleluia, Beautiful Spanish Song, Imagining Incense, Chant for the Winter Solstice, Three Songs from the Enchanted Forest). Grouse Records, 2010, CD.
Into Light. (Three Hymns from The Fall Into Light). Atma CD-ACD 22613, 2010, CD.
Iridescence. (Scorpius). CBC Records CD-SMCD 5132, 1993, CD.
Jean Stillwell. (Minnelieder). CBC Records CD-MVCD, 1994, CD.
Love Songs for a Small Planet. Centrediscs CD-CMCCD 4893, 1993, CD.
Loving/Toi. Centrediscs CD-CMCCD 22516, 2016, CD.
Masquerade. (Concerto for Harpsichord). Centrediscs CD-CMCCD 3488, 2012, CD.
Menotti: The Unicorn. (A Medieval Bestiary). Artist(s): Carolina Chamber Chorale; Timothy Koch; Gary Poster; Katy Williams. Label: Albany Catalogue No.: TROY452 Release Date: 2001.
Murray Schafer R.: Twelve String Quartets. ATMA Classique ACD22672, 2013, CD.
My Life in Widening Circles. (Trio for Violin, Viola, Cello; Wild Bird; Duo for Violin and Piano; Six Songs from Rilke's Book of Hours). Centrediscs, CD-CMCCD 17712, 2012, CD.

Once on a Windy Night. (Once on a Windy Night, Seventeen Haiku, Vox Naturae, A Medieval Bestiary). SKU: Grouse Records CD-GR 105, 2000, CD.

Ovation, Volume 2. (Concerto for Harpsichord and Eight Wind Instruments; In Memoriam Alberto Guerrero; Son of Heldenleben; Epitaph for Moonlight; East; Dream Rainbow Dream Thunder). CBC Records CD-PSCD 2027-5, 2002, CD.

Philomela: In Dreams. (Gamelan). Alba NCD9, CD.

R. Murray Schafer. (Flute Concerto, Harp Concerto, The Darkly Splendid Earth). CBC Records CD-SMCD 5114, 1992, CD.

R. Murray Schafer: Apocalypsis. Analekta AN28784-5, 2016, CD.

Reaching From the Rock. (Snowforms). Furiant Records CD-FMDC 4605-2, 1998, CD.

Remembrance. (Departure Music). Marquis Classics CD-ERAD 307, 2003, CD.

Requiems for the Party Girl for Soprano and Orchestra. Composers/CRI 817, 1970, CD.

Schafer: 5. (String Quartets nos. 1–5). Centrediscs CD-CMCCD 39/4090, 1990, CD.

Schafer: Letters from Mignon. (Letters from Mignon, Minnelieder, Thunder: Perfect Mind). ATMA ACD22553, 2007, CD.

Schafer/Molinari. (String Quartets nos. 1–7). ATMA CD-ACD 22188/89, 2003, CD.

Schafer/Molinari 2. (String Quartet no. 8, Theseus, Beauty and the Beast). ATMA CD-ACD 22201, 2003, CD.

Shadowland. (The Searching Sings). Independent CD-DC 002-09, 2009, CD.

Six Departures. (Trio for Flute, Viola, and Harp). Ravello Records RR7895, 2014, CD.

Unsleeping. (Kinderlieder). Blue Griffin CD-BGR 177, 2008, CD.

Vancouver Soundscape. Cambridge Street Records CD-CSR 2CD 9701, 1997, CD.

Wild Bird. (Duo for Violin and Piano; Wild Bird). Centrediscs CD-CMCCD 16110, 2010, CD.

Notes

1. CHILDHOOD AND EARLY ADULTHOOD

1. R. Murray Schafer, baby book.
2. R. Murray Schafer, *My Life on Earth and Elsewhere* (Erin, Ontario: Porcupine's Quill, 2012), 9.
3. Ibid., 11.
4. *Imperial Oil Reporter* 16:5, 1980.
5. R. Murray Schafer, baby book.
6. Stephen Adams, *R. Murray Schafer* (Toronto: University of Toronto Press, 1983), 5.
7. Norma Beecroft, "Documentary: R. Murray Schafer," *Two New Hours*, April 16, 1978, Canadian Broadcasting Corporation.
8. R. Murray Schafer, baby book.
9. Schafer, *My Life on Earth*, 11.
10. Canadian Broadcasting Corporation, "The Musician," February 25, 1979.
11. Schafer, *My Life on Earth*, 14.
12. Beecroft, "Documentary: R. Murray Schafer."
13. Schafer, *My Life on Earth*, 13.
14. Ibid., 14–15.
15. Ibid., 9.
16. Peter Such, "Murray Schafer," in *Soundprints: Contemporary Composers* (Toronto: Clarke Irwin, 1971), 129.
17. Schafer, *My Life on Earth*, 13.
18. Such, "Murray Schafer," 130.
19. Schafer, *My Life on Earth*, 15.
20. Beecroft, "Documentary: R. Murray Schafer."
21. Such, "Murray Schafer," 131–33.
22. Adams, *R. Murray Schafer*, 5.
23. Schafer, *My Life on Earth*, 14.
24. Such, "Murray Schafer," 133.
25. Schafer report card, February 1950.
26. Beecroft, "Documentary: R. Murray Schafer."
27. Such, "Murray Schafer," 133.
28. Ibid., 132.
29. Ibid., 133.
30. Schafer, *My Life on Earth*, 13.

31. Campbell Trowsdale, "Interview with R. Murray Schafer," 1978.
32. Such, "Murray Schafer," 134.
33. Schafer, *My Life on Earth*, 18.
34. Beecroft, "Documentary: R. Murray Schafer."
35. Schafer, *My Life on Earth*, 17–19.
36. Beecroft, "Documentary: R. Murray Schafer."
37. Schafer, *My Life on Earth*, 19.
38. Canadian Broadcasting Corporation, "The Musician."
39. Schafer, *My Life on Earth*, 19.
40. Adams, *R. Murray Schafer*, 9.
41. Schafer, *My Life on Earth*, 26.
42. Such, "Murray Schafer," 135.
43. Canadian Broadcasting Corporation, "The Musician."
44. Ibid.
45. Schafer, *My Life on Earth*, 19.
46. Such, "Murray Schafer," 135.
47. Schafer, *My Life on Earth*, 20.
48. Eitan Cornfield, "R. Murray Schafer Documentary," in *Canadian Composer Portraits: R. Murray Schafer*, Canadian Music Center, 2005.
49. Adams, *R. Murray Schafer*, 7.
50. Such, "Murray Schafer," 135.
51. Schafer, *My Life on Earth*, 20.
52. Adams, *R. Murray Schafer*, 7.
53. Cornfield, "R. Murray Schafer Documentary."
54. Adams, *R. Murray Schafer*, 7.
55. Schafer, *My Life on Earth*, 27.
56. Beecroft, "Documentary: R. Murray Schafer."
57. Schafer, *My Life on Earth*, 21.
58. Adams, *R. Murray Schafer*, 8.
59. Ibid., 9.
60. Schafer, *My Life on Earth*, 21.
61. Adams, *R. Murray Schafer*, 8–9.
62. Such, "Murray Schafer," 147.
63. Schafer, *My Life on Earth*, 27.
64. Ibid., 23.
65. Adams, *R. Murray Schafer*, 10.
66. Such, "Murray Schafer," 137.
67. Hugh Le Caine, letter to Schafer, July 1, 1984.
68. Schafer, *My Life on Earth*, 27.
69. Schafer indicates that Klee's *The Thinking Eye* was the inspiration for his educational pamphlet *The Thinking Ear*.
70. Schafer, *My Life on Earth*, 30.
71. Ibid., 23.
72. Such, "Murray Schafer," 137.
73. Beecroft, "Documentary: R. Murray Schafer."
74. Schafer, *My Life on Earth*, 20.
75. Adams, *R. Murray Schafer*, 10.
76. Schafer, *My Life on Earth*, 23.
77. Ibid., 24.
78. Adams, *R. Murray Schafer*, 10.
79. Schafer, *My Life on Earth*, 25–26.
80. Beecroft, "Documentary: R. Murray Schafer."
81. Schafer, address to the University of Toronto, 2006.
82. Schafer, *My Life on Earth*, 30.

2. UNCERTAINTY, THE TEMPORAL MUSE, AND WANDERLUST

1. R. Murray Schafer, *My Life on Earth and Elsewhere* (Erin, Ontario: Porcupine's Quill, 2012), 31.
2. Stephen Adams, *R. Murray Schafer* (Toronto: University of Toronto Press, 1983), 12.
3. Canadian Broadcasting Corporation, "The Musician," February 25, 1979.
4. R. Murray Schafer, letter to Bob Walshe, July 1956.
5. Schafer, *My Life on Earth*, 35.
6. Schafer, letter to Belle Schafer, March 19, 1956.
7. Ibid., March 31, 1956.
8. Schafer, *My Life on Earth*, 39.
9. Norma Beecroft, "Documentary: R. Murray Schafer," *Two New Hours*, Canadian Broadcasting Corporation, April 16, 1978.
10. Schafer, letter to Belle Schafer, April 28, 1956.
11. Eitan Cornfield, "R. Murray Schafer Documentary," in *Canadian Composer Portraits: R. Murray Schafer*, Canadian Music Center, 2005.
12. Schafer, *My Life on Earth*, 39.
13. Campbell Trowsdale, "Interview with R. Murray Schafer," 1978.
14. Schafer, *My Life on Earth*, 40.
15. Schafer, letter to Bob Walshe, July 17, 1956.
16. Schafer, *My Life on Earth*, 40.
17. Schafer, letter to Belle Schafer, June 27, 1956.
18. Schafer, *My Life on Earth*, 41.
19. Schafer, letter to Bob Walshe, October 31, 1956.
20. Ibid., July 1956.
21. Adams, *R. Murray Schafer*, 12.
22. Schafer, letter to Bob Walshe, December 1956.
23. Ibid., December 2, 1956.
24. Schafer, *My Life on Earth*, 41–43.
25. Beecroft, "Documentary: R. Murray Schafer."
26. Schafer, *My Life on Earth*, 44.
27. Schafer, personal journal, June 27, 1957.
28. Schafer, *My Life on Earth*, 45–48.
29. Schafer, letter to Bob Walshe, June 1957.
30. Ibid., July 2, 1957.
31. Ibid., July 12, 1957.
32. Schafer, personal journal, July 12, 1957.
33. Ibid., July 28, 1957.
34. Schafer, letter to Bob Walshe, August 1957.
35. Schafer, personal journal, August 1957.
36. Ibid., August 14, 1957.
37. Ibid., August 19, 1957.
38. Schafer, *My Life on Earth*, 52.
39. Schafer, personal journal, August 9, 1957.
40. Ibid., September 19, 1957.
41. Schafer, postcard to Bob Walshe, October 13, 1957.
42. Schafer, letter to Bob Walshe, November 11, 1957.
43. Schafer *My Life on Earth*, 55.
44. Adams, *R. Murray Schafer*, 15.
45. Schafer, personal journal, December 4, 1957.
46. Ibid., December 6, 1957.
47. Schafer *My Life on Earth*, 53.
48. Schafer, personal journal, December 11, 1957.
49. Schafer, letter to Bob Walshe, January 13, 1958.

50. Ibid., March 24, 1958.
51. Ibid., March 22, 1958.
52. Ibid., May 10, 1958.
53. Adams, *R. Murray Schafer*, 15.
54. Schafer, letter to Bob Walshe, March 1958.
55. Ibid., January 31, 1958.
56. Ibid., June 23, 1958.
57. Ibid., September 25, 1958.
58. Ibid., October 8, 1958.
59. Schafer, "Statement of Purpose," Canada Council Grant Application, 1959.
60. Schafer, letter to Bob Walshe, 1959.
61. Schafer, *My Life on Earth*, 61.
62. Schafer, personal journal, no date.
63. Schafer, *My Life on Earth*, 64–65.
64. Ibid., 68.
65. Ibid., 69–70.
66. Ibid., 72.
67. Ibid., 75.
68. Ibid., 74.
69. Schafer, personal journal, September 7, 1959.
70. Schafer, *My Life on Earth*, 75.
71. Ibid., 63.
72. Adams, *R. Murray Schafer*, 14.
73. R. Murray Schafer, "Music and the Iron Curtain," *Queens Quarterly* 57 (1960): 407–14.
74. Schafer, letter to Bob Walshe, January 12, 1959.
75. Schafer, "Statement of Purpose."
76. Canadian Broadcasting Corporation, "The Musician."
77. Schafer, *In Memoriam Alberto Guerrero*, preface.
78. Schafer, "Statement of Purpose."
79. Schafer, *My Life on Earth*, 76.
80. Adams, *R. Murray Schafer*, 16.
81. Ron Gillia, "Interview with R. Murray Schafer," May 5, 1987.
82. Adams, *R. Murray Schafer*, 16.
83. Schafer, *My Life on Earth*, 76.
84. Canadian Broadcasting Corporation, "The Musician."
85. Schafer, *My Life on Earth*, 77.
86. Ibid., 78.
87. Adams, *R. Murray Schafer*, 18.
88. Schafer, personal journal, February 1961.
89. R. Murray Schafer, "Ezra Pound and Music," *Canadian Music Journal* 5 (Summer 1961): 15–43.
90. Schafer, personal journal, March 16, 1961.

3. HOMECOMING AND EDUCATION FROM THE OTHER SIDE

1. R. Murray Schafer, letter to Bob Walshe, January 29, 1962.
2. R. Murray Schafer, *My Life on Earth and Elsewhere* (Erin, Ontario: Porcupine's Quill, 2012), 79.
3. Peter Such, "Murray Schafer," in *Soundprints: Contemporary Composers* (Toronto: Clarke Irwin, 1971), 148.
4. R. Murray Schafer, "The Limits of Nationalism in Canadian Music," *Tamarack Review* 18 (1961): 71–78.

Notes

5. R. Murray Schafer, "Choral Conducting: An Interview," *Music Across Canada* 1, no. 5 (June 1963): 10–12.
6. R. Murray Schafer, "The Creative Process in Music," *Music Across Canada* 1, no. 4 (May 1963): 14–17.
7. Schafer, letter to Bob Walshe, Spring 1962.
8. Stephen Adams, *R. Murray Schafer* (Toronto: University of Toronto Press, 1983), 20.
9. Schafer, *My Life on Earth*, 81.
10. Schafer, *My Life on Earth*, 82.
11. Adams, *R. Murray Schafer*, 21.
12. R. Murray Schafer, *Canzoni for Prisoners*, "Program Notes," www.patria.org.
13. Campbell Trowsdale, "Interview with R. Murray Schafer," 1978.
14. Colleen October Orr, "The John Adaskin Project: A History and Evaluation," master's thesis, University of Western Ontario, 1977, 26–27.
15. Adams, *R. Murray Schafer*, 22.
16. Orr, "John Adaskin Project," 31–32.
17. Ibid., 29.
18. Ibid., 32–33.
19. Ron Gillia, "Interview with R. Murray Schafer," May 5, 1987.
20. Orr, "John Adaskin Project," 153.
21. Ibid., 125.
22. Ibid., 64.
23. Norma Beecroft, "Documentary: R. Murray Schafer," *Two New Hours*, April 16, 1978, Canadian Broadcasting Corporation.
24. Schafer, *My Life on Earth*, 83.
25. Schafer, private journal, September 7, 1963.
26. Ibid., October 16, 1963.
27. Schafer, *My Life on Earth*, 83–85.
28. Such, "Murray Schafer," 150.
29. Schafer, private journal, June 11, 1964.
30. Schafer, private journal, July 16, 1964.
31. Schafer, *My Life on Earth*, 83–85.
32. Such, "Murray Schafer," 150.
33. Schafer, private journal, June 11, 1964.
34. Gillia, "Interview with R. Murray Schafer."
35. Such, "Murray Schafer," 151.
36. Spoken comments before broadcast, date unknown, www.musiccentre.ca, October 9, 2014.
37. Schafer, private journal, September 13, 1963.
38. Ibid., September 24, 1963.
39. Ibid., September 19, 1963.
40. Ibid., September 10, 1964.
41. Ibid., June 20, 1964.
42. Ibid., June, 1964.
43. Adams, *R. Murray Schafer*, 11.
44. Schafer, private journal, September 26, 1964.
45. Adams, *R. Murray Schafer*, 22.
46. Schafer, *My Life on Earth*, 247–48.
47. Schafer, private journal, September 27, 1964.
48. Ibid., November 17, 1954.
49. Schafer, *My Life on Earth*, 87.
50. Schafer, private journal, February 24, 1965.
51. Ibid., April 13, 1965.
52. Ibid., March 8, 1965.
53. Ibid., April 23 or 24, 1965.
54. Ibid., May 4, 1964.
55. Ibid., June 8, 1964.

56. Schafer, *My Life on Earth*, 90.

4. ACADEMIA, NOTORIETY, AND NEW ENDEAVORS

1. R. Murray Schafer, personal journal, September 7, 1965.
2. Stephen Adams, *R. Murray Schafer* (Toronto: University of Toronto Press, 1983), 25.
3. R. Murray Schafer, *My Life on Earth and Elsewhere* (Erin, Ontario: Porcupine's Quill, 2012), 94.
4. Adams, *R. Murray Schafer*, 25.
5. Schafer, *My Life on Earth*, 94.
6. R. Murray Schafer, *The Thinking Ear: Complete Writings on Music Education* (Indian River, Ontario: Arcana Editions, 1986), 3. In this book, Schafer indicates that the Adaskin seminar occurred in the summer of 1965. His diaries and the notes from the Adaskin seminar indicate that this was actually 1963.
7. Ibid., 47.
8. Adams, *R. Murray Schafer*, 26.
9. Schafer, personal journal, September 1965.
10. Adams, *R. Murray Schafer*, 26.
11. Schafer, *My Life on Earth*, 94–96.
12. Adams, *R. Murray Schafer*, 26.
13. Schafer, *My Life on Earth*, 94–95.
14. Ibid., 95.
15. Schafer, personal journal, late 1966.
16. *Loving/Toi* would be broadcast in May 1966 on CBC French and English television networks to very mixed reviews.
17. Schafer, personal journal, September 9, 1965.
18. Adams, *R. Murray Schafer*, 138.
19. Schafer, personal journal, October 1967.
20. Schafer, *My Life on Earth*, 100.
21. Schafer, personal journal, June 27, 1968.
22. Ibid., July 17, 1968.
23. Ibid., July 19, 1968.
24. Ibid., August 4, 1968.
25. Ibid., November 24, 1968.
26. Schafer, *My Life on Earth*, 98–99.
27. Schafer, personal journal, December 1968.
28. Ibid., May 23, 1969.
29. Ibid., 202.
30. Schafer, personal journal, June 26, 1969.
31. Ibid., July 17, 1969.
32. Ibid., August 17, 1969.
33. Adams, *R. Murray Schafer*, 27.
34. Keiko Torigoe, "A Study of the World Soundscape Project," master's thesis, York University, 1982, 42–43.
35. Ibid., 43.
36. Ibid., 90.
37. Torigoe, "A Study of the World Soundscape Project," 91.
38. Ibid., 47–48.
39. Schafer, personal journal, March 3, 1970.
40. Schafer, *My Life on Earth*, 114.
41. Schafer, personal journal, April 1970.
42. Schafer, *My Life on Earth*, 115.

43. Ibid., 111.
44. Schafer, personal journal, May 1970.
45. Ibid., June 6, 1970.
46. Schafer, *My Life on Earth*, 112.
47. Ibid., October 10, 1970.
48. Ibid., January 1971.
49. Ibid., February 7, 1971.
50. Ibid., February–March 1971.
51. Schafer, *My Life on Earth*, 113.
52. Ibid., 117.
53. Torigoe, "A Study of the World Soundscape Project," 52.
54. Adams, *R. Murray Schafer*, 28.
55. Schafer, *My Life on Earth*, 115.
56. Schafer, personal journal, June 4, 1971.
57. Schafer, *My Life on Earth*, 115.
58. Schafer, personal journal, October 1971.
59. Ibid., January 15, 1972.
60. Torigoe, "A Study of the World Soundscape Project," 56–59.
61. Ibid., 61.
62. Schafer, personal journal, May 1973.
63. Ibid.
64. Including Howard Broomfield, Bruce Davis, Peter Huse, Colin Miles, Hildegard Westerkamp, Kathleen Swink, Barry Truax, and Betty Anne Wang.
65. Torigoe, "A Study of the World Soundscape Project," 63.
66. Ibid., 67.
67. Schafer, personal journal, September 17, 1974.
68. Schafer, *My Life on Earth*, 128.
69. Ibid., 129.

5. COUNTRY LIFE, RENEWED CREATIVITY, AND CHANGE

1. R. Murray Schafer, personal journal, December 1, 1975.
2. Ibid., December 1975.
3. Stephen Adams, *R. Murray Schafer* (Toronto: University of Toronto Press, 1983), 32.
4. Schafer, personal journal, February 1976.
5. Ibid., spring 1976.
6. Ibid., January 1, 1977.
7. Ibid., April 14, 1977.
8. Ibid., May 1977.
9. Ibid., August 5, 1977.
10. Ibid., August 5, 1977.
11. R. Murray Schafer, *The Thinking Ear: Complete Writings on Music Education* (Indian River, Ontario: Arcana Editions, 1986), 305.
12. Schafer, personal journal, December 1, 1977.
13. Ibid., December 1977.
14. Ibid., January 1978.
15. Ibid., March 1978.
16. Schafer, *The Thinking Ear*, 295–301.
17. Schafer, personal journal, January 1979.
18. Ibid., May 6, 1979.
19. Ibid., May 8, 1979.
20. Ibid., July 9, 1979.

21. Schafer, *The Thinking Ear*, 302–17.
22. Adams, *R. Murray Schafer*, 181.
23. Schafer, personal journal, September 22, 1979.
24. Ibid., November 28, 1979.
25. Ibid., December 5, 1980.
26. Ibid., December 31, 1980.
27. Ibid., February 8 and 10, 1981.
28. Ibid., April 12, 1981.
29. Ibid., May 9–10, 1981.
30. Ibid., May 1981.
31. Ibid., June 16, 1981.
32. Ibid., March 9, 1982.
33. Ibid., March 26, 1982.
34. Ibid., December 1982.
35. Ibid., February 25, 1983.
36. Ibid., 1984.
37. Ibid., November 17, 1983.
38. Interview with Eleanor James, December 28, 2017.
39. Schafer, diary, late 1984.
40. Interview with Eleanor James, July 12, 2017.
41. Schafer, personal journal, 1986.

6. TWO LOVES, FINANCIAL CONCERNS, AND THE *PATRIA* CYCLE

1. R. Murray Schafer, personal journal, January 1987.
2. Ibid., March 27, 1987.
3. Ibid., May 4, 1987.
4. R. Murray Schafer, *My Life on Earth and Elsewhere* (Erin, Ontario: Porcupine's Quill, 2012), 187. Schafer incorrectly dates the purchase of the farmhouse and the first production of *The Greatest Show* as 1986. I have confirmed through other documentation that the purchase of the farmhouse and the first production were 1987, with the second production occurring in the summer of 1988.
5. Schafer, personal journal, October 5, 1987.
6. Ibid., November 29, 1987.
7. Schafer, *My Life on Earth*, 176–77.
8. Schafer, personal journal, May 13, 1988.
9. Ibid., April 23, 1989.
10. Schafer, *My Life on Earth*, 201.
11. Schafer, personal journal, October 18, 1989.
12. Ibid., December 23, 1989.
13. Ibid., December 23, 1990.
14. Ibid., January 1992.
15. Ibid., February 14, 1992.
16. Ibid., April 1992.
17. Ibid., April 28, 1992.
18. Ibid., June 16, 1992.
19. Ibid., August 1, 1992.
20. Ibid., March 12, 1993.
21. Ibid., March 10, 1994.
22. Ibid., March 13, 1994.
23. Ibid., October 29, 1994.
24. Interview with Eleanor James, December 28, 2017.

25. Schafer, personal journal, June 4, 1998.
26. Interview with Eleanor James, December 28, 2017.
27. Schafer, personal journal, December 28, 1999.

7. LONELINESS, RECONCILIATION, HAPPINESS, AND NEW CHALLENGES

1. R. Murray Schafer, personal journal, June 7, 2002.
2. Ibid., June 29, 2002.
3. Ibid., July 24, 2002.
4. Ibid., August 1, 2002.
5. Ibid., December 17, 2002.
6. Ibid., October 18, 2002.
7. Ibid., March 30, 2003.
8. Ibid., April 2003.
9. Ibid., June 6, 2003.
10. Ibid., November 21, 2003.
11. Ibid., May 9, 2004.
12. Ibid., April 7, 2005.
13. Ibid., July 2005.
14. Ibid., August 9, 2005.
15. Ibid., January 14, 2006.
16. Ibid., April 30, 2006.
17. Ibid., July 2, 2006.
18. Ibid., September 7, 2006.
19. Ibid., October 6, 2006.
20. Ibid., December 6, 2006.
21. Ibid., January 9, 2007.
22. Interview with Eleanor James, May 2017.
23. Ibid., October 18, 2007.
24. Ibid., October 28, 2007.
25. Interview with Eleanor James, December 28, 2017.
26. Schafer, personal journal, December 10, 2007.
27. Ibid., January 30, 2008.
28. Ibid., June 8, 2008.
29. Ibid., June 2008.
30. Ibid., October 23 and 25, 2008.
31. Ibid., November 10, 2008.
32. Ibid., December 23, 2008.
33. Ibid., April 22, 2009.
34. Ibid., May 12, 2009.
35. Ibid., July 21, 2009.
36. Ibid., November 3, 2009.
37. Ibid., November 10, 2009.
38. Ibid., March 2010.
39. Ibid., June 2010.
40. Ibid., July 4, 2010.
41. Schafer, *Ariadne's Legacy*, "Program Notes," CD.
42. Schafer, desk calendar, 2011.
43. Schafer, personal journal, May 4, 2011.
44. Ibid., July 25, 2011.
45. Ibid., September 22, 2011.
46. Schafer, desk calendar, 2011.

47. Ibid., December 24, 2011.
48. Interview with Eleanor James, May 2017.
49. Ibid.
50. Interview with Eleanor James, December 28, 2017.
51. Schafer, desk calendar, 2013.
52. Ibid., 2014.
53. Interview with Eleanor James, December 28, 2017.

8. THE EDUCATIONAL WRITINGS

1. Stephen Adams, *R. Murray Schafer* (Toronto: University of Toronto Press, 1983), 50.
2. Ibid., 22.
3. R. Murray Schafer, "The Graphics of Musical Thought," in *Festschrift Kurt Blaukopf* (Vienna: Universal Editions, 1975), 121, 123.
4. Ibid., 133.
5. Ibid.
6. Colleen October Orr, "The John Adaskin Project: A History and Evaluation," master's thesis, University of Western Ontario, 1977, 38.
7. Ron Gillia, "Interview with R. Murray Schafer," May 5, 1987.
8. Orr, "The John Adaskin Project," 153.
9. Adams, *R. Murray* Schafer, 22.
10. R. Murray Schafer, *The Composer in the Classroom* (Toronto: Berandol, 1965), 6.
11. Ibid., 16.
12. Ibid., 27.
13. Ibid., 33.
14. R. Murray Schafer, *Ear Cleaning: Notes for an Experimental Music Course* (Toronto: Berandol, 1967), preface.
15. Ibid.
16. Ibid., "Amplitude."
17. Ibid., "Melody."
18. Ibid., "Transcript II, Music for Paper and Wood."
19. R. Murray Schafer, *The New Soundscape: A Handbook for the Modern Music Teacher* (New York: Associated Music Publishers, 1969).
20. Ibid., 3.
21. Ibid., 4.
22. Ibid., 14.
23. Ibid., 17.
24. Ibid., 49.
25. R. Murray Schafer, *When Words Sing* (Toronto: Berandol Music Limited, 1970), preface.
26. Ibid., 25.
27. R. Murray Schafer, *Epitaph for Moonlight*, preface.
28. R. Murray Schafer, *The Rhinoceros in the Classroom* (Toronto: Berandol Music Limited, 1975), preface.
29. Ibid., "A Statement on Music Education."
30. Ibid., "Another Statement on Music Education."
31. R. Murray Schafer, *Creative Music Education: A Handbook for the Modern Music Teacher* (New York: Schirmer, 1976), ix.
32. R. Murray Schafer, *The Thinking Ear: Complete Writing on Music Education* (Indian River, Ontario: Arcana Editions, 1986), 294.
33. R. Murray Schafer, www.patria.org.
34. R. Murray Schafer, *A Sound Education* (Indian River, Ontario: Arcana Editions, 1992), 12.
35. Ibid., 144.

36. R. Murray Schafer, *HearSing* (Indian River, Ontario: Arcana Editions, 2005), ix.
37. Ibid., xii.

9. SOUNDSCAPE PUBLICATIONS

1. Keiko Torigoe, "A Study of the World Soundscape Project," master's thesis, York University, 1982, 47.
2. Ibid., 90–91.
3. Ibid., 97.
4. R. Murray Schafer, *The Book of Noise*, rev. ed. (Indian River, Canada: Arcana Editions, 1998), 52.
5. Ibid., 42.
6. Torigoe, "A Study of the World Soundscape Project," 54.
7. Ibid., 136.
8. Ibid., 144.
9. Ibid., 121–27.
10. Ibid., 151–54.
11. Ibid., 171–73.
12. Ibid., 168–69.
13. Ibid., 169.
14. Ibid., 170.
15. Ibid., 176–77.
16. Ibid., 189.
17. R. Murray Schafer, *The Soundscape* (Rochester, VT: Destiny Books, 1993), 5.
18. Ibid., 12.
19. Ibid., 43.
20. Ibid., 90.
21. Ibid., 103.
22. Ibid., 132.
23. Ibid., 161.
24. Ibid., 205.
25. R. Murray Schafer, *Voices of Tyranny, Temples of Silence* (Indian River, Canada: Arcana Editions, 1993), 7.
26. Ibid., 10.
27. R. Murray Schafer, "R. Murray Schafer: A Collection," *Open Letter* (Fall 1979): 90.
28. Ibid., 91.
29. Schafer, *Voices of Tyranny,* 43–44.
30. Ibid., 131.
31. Ibid., 135.
32. Ibid., 158.
33. R. Murray Schafer, "Winter Diary Notes," www.swr.de/swr-classic.

10. SCHOLARLY WRITING AND NONFICTION

1. R. Murray Schafer, "Statement of Purpose," Canadian Council Grant Proposal, 1960.
2. R. Murray Schafer, *My Life on Earth and Elsewhere* (Erin, Ontario: Porcupine's Quill, 2012), 36.
3. Stephen Adams, *R. Murray Schafer* (Toronto: University of Toronto Press, 1983), 17.
4. R. Murray Schafer, *British Composers in Interview* (London: Faber, 1963), 13.
5. Ibid., 14.
6. Ron Gillia, "Interview with R. Murray Schafer," May 5, 1987.

7. R. Murray Schafer, *E. T. A. Hoffmann and Music* (Toronto: University of Toronto Press, 1975), preface.
8. Ibid., 3.
9. Ibid., 60.
10. Ibid., 91.
11. Ibid., 118.
12. Ibid., 127.
13. Ibid., 137.
14. Ibid., 143.
15. Ibid., 155.
16. Ibid., 158.
17. R. Murray Schafer, *Ezra Pound and Music* (London: Faber, 1977), 3.
18. Ibid., 3–4.
19. Ibid., 5.
20. Ibid., 57.
21. Ibid., 295.
22. R. Murray Schafer, "R. Murray Schafer: A Collection," *Open Letter* (Fall 1979): 5.
23. Ibid., 6.
24. Ibid., 8.
25. R. Murray Schafer, *On Canadian Music* (Indian River, Canada: Arcana Editions, 1984), preface.
26. Ibid., 3.
27. Ibid., 20.
28. Ibid., 39.
29. Ibid., 63.
30. Ibid., 64.
31. Ibid., 76.
32. Ibid., 92.
33. Ibid., 104.
34. R. Murray Schafer, *Patria: The Complete Cycle* (Toronto: Coach House Books, 2002), 13.
35. Ibid., 26.
36. Ibid., 83.
37. Ibid., 93.
38. Ibid., 171.

11. WORKS OF FICTION

1. R. Murray Schafer, *Music in the Cold* (Indian River, Ontario: Arcana Editions, 1977).
2. Ibid.
3. Schafer, personal journal, May 16, 2008.
4. R. Murray Schafer, *Ariadne* (Indian River, Ontario: Arcana Editions, 1977).
5. R. Murray Schafer, *The Chaldean Inscription* (Indian River, Ontario: Arcana Editions, 1981).
6. R. Murray Schafer, *The Sixteen Scribes* (Indian River, Ontario: Arcana Editions, 1981).
7. R. Murray Schafer, *Shadowgraphs and Legends* (Indian River, Ontario: Arcana Editions, 2004).

12. *LOVING* AND THE NON-*PATRIA* THEATRICAL WORKS

1. R. Murray Schafer, "Program Notes," 58.
2. R. Murray Schafer, *Remember Susanna*, libretto book.
3. Schafer, "Program Notes," 21.
4. Stephen Adams, *R. Murray Schafer* (Toronto: University of Toronto Press, 1983), 98.
5. Ibid.
6. Ibid., 92–93.
7. Ibid., 93–94.
8. Ibid., 95.
9. Ibid., 209–10.
10. Ibid., 213.
11. Ibid., 169–70.
12. R. Murray Schafer, *Apocalypsis Part 1: John's Vision*.
13. Adams, *R. Murray Schafer*, 214.
14. Ibid., 215.
15. Ibid.
16. Schafer, "Program Notes," 113–14.
17. Ibid., 114.

13. THE *PATRIA* CYCLE

1. Kirk Loren MacKenzie, "A Twentieth-Century Musical/Theatrical Cycle: R. Murray Schafer's 'Patria' (1966–)," PhD dissertation, University of Cincinnati, 1992, 2.
2. R. Murray Schafer, *Patria: The Complete Cycle* (Toronto: Coach House Books, 2002), 103.
3. Ibid.
4. Ellen Waterman, "R. Murray Schafer's Environmental Music Theatre: A Documentation and Analysis of *Patria the Epilogue: And Wolf Shall Inherit the Moon*," PhD dissertation, University of San Diego, 1997, 28.
5. Ibid., 40.
6. Ibid., 42.
7. Ibid., 43.
8. Ibid., 45.
9. Ibid., 46–47.
10. R. Murray Schafer, *Patria 1*, iii.
11. Schafer, *Patria, The Complete Cycle*, 110–11.
12. Schafer, personal journal, April 13, 1965.
13. Ibid., May 21, 1964.
14. Adams, *R. Murray Schafer*, 172.
15. Schafer, *Patria, The Complete Cycle*, 46.
16. Ibid., 55.
17. Ibid., 56.
18. Ibid., 57.
19. Adams, *R. Murray Schafer*, 221–24.
20. Schafer, *Patria: The Complete Cycle*, 68.
21. Ibid., 74–75.
22. Stephen Adams, *R. Murray Schafer* (Toronto: University of Toronto Press, 1983), 224–26.
23. Schafer, *Patria: The Complete Cycle*, 117.
24. Ibid., 125.

25. Ibid., 133–34.
26. Schafer's adaptation in *Patria: The Complete Cycle*, 135 of the text, following the translation of Titus Burckhardt in *Alchemy*, rev. ed. (Louisville, KY: Fons Vitae, 1997) with some reference to the translation by John Read in *Prelude to Chemistry* (Cambridge, MA: MIT Press, 1966).
27. Schafer, *Patria: The Complete Cycle*, 154.
28. Ibid., 176–77.
29. Ibid., 188.
30. R. Murray Schafer, *Patria 7: Asterion*, 16.
31. Schafer, *Patria: The Complete Cycle*, 213.
32. Ibid., 218.
33. Ibid., 221.
34. Ibid., 224.
35. Ibid., 236.
36. Waterman, "R. Murray Schafer's Environmental Music," 57–59.
37. Schafer, *Patria: The Complete Cycle*, 248.
38. MacKenzie, "A Twentieth-Century Musical/Theatrical Cycle," 22–24.

14. EARLY AND TRANSITIONAL COMPOSITIONS

1. Campbell Trowsdale, "Interview with R. Murray Schafer," 1978.
2. R. Murray Schafer, *My Life on Earth and Elsewhere* (Erin, Ontario: Porcupine's Quill, 2012), 27.
3. Ibid.
4. R. Murray Schafer, "Program Notes," 7.
5. Schafer, *My Life on Earth*, 27.
6. Ibid., 21.
7. Schafer, "Program Notes," 7–8.
8. Ibid., 8.
9. Stephen Adams, *R. Murray Schafer* (Toronto: University of Toronto Press, 1983), 64.
10. Schafer, "Program Notes," 8.
11. Eitan Cornfield, "R. Murray Schafer Documentary," in *Canadian Composer Portraits: R. Murray Schafer*, Canadian Music Center, 2005.
12. Schafer, "Program Notes," 9.
13. Ibid., 10.
14. Schafer, "Program Notes," 9.
15. R. Murray Schafer, *Three Ideograms*.
16. Trowsdale, "Interview with R. Murray Schafer."
17. Adams, *R. Murray Schafer*, 75.
18. Schafer, "Program Notes," 14.
19. Adams, *R. Murray Schafer*, 76–77.
20. Ibid., 78–79.
21. Ibid., 80.
22. Ibid.
23. Schafer, "Program Notes," 15–16.
24. Ibid.
25. R. Murray Schafer, verbal notes before broadcast of *Canzoni*, Canadian Music Center, www.musiccentre.ca/.
26. Schafer, "Program Notes," 17.
27. R. Murray Schafer, *Opus One*.
28. Adams, *R. Murray Schafer*, 89.
29. Ibid., 85.
30. Ibid.
31. Ibid., 89.

32. Ibid., 89–90.
33. Ibid., 90.

15. THE COMPOSITIONS FOR CHOIR

1. R. Murray Schafer, "Program Notes," www.patria.org/arcana/Programnotes.pdf, 25.
2. Stephen Adams, *R. Murray Schafer* (Toronto: University of Toronto Press, 1983), 145.
3. Schafer, "Program Notes," 76.
4. Ibid.
5. Schafer, *Six Magic Songs* (Indian River, ON: Arcana Editions, 1988), preface.
6. Schafer, *Threnody* (Indian River, ON: Arcana Editions, 1967), preface.
7. Schafer, "Program Notes," 27.
8. Ibid., 64–65.
9. Ibid., 99.
10. Ibid., 31.
11. Adams, 167.
12. Schafer, "Program Notes," 42.
13. Adams, *R. Murray* Schafer, 164.
14. Schafer, "Program Notes," 53.
15. Ibid., 65.
16. Ibid., 63–64.
17. Ibid., 85.
18. Ibid., 90.
19. Ibid., 91.
20. Ibid., 93.
21. Ibid., 96–97.
22. Ibid., 103.
23. Ibid., 103–4.
24. Ibid., 115.

16. THE COMPOSITIONS FOR VOICE

1. R. Murray Schafer, "Program Notes," www.patria.org/arcana/Programnotes.pdf, 18.
2. Ibid.
3. R. Murray Schafer, personal journal, September 9, 1965.
4. Stephen Adams, *R. Murray Schafer* (Toronto: University of Toronto Press, 1983), 138.
5. Ibid.
6. Ibid., 106.
7. Schafer, "Program Notes," 38.
8. Adams, *R. Murray* Schafer, 107.
9. Schafer, *Arcana*, preface.
10. Schafer, "Program Notes," 50.
11. Ibid., 52.
12. Adams, *R. Murray Schafer*, 153.
13. Schafer, "Program Notes," 52.
14. Ibid., 61.
15. Ibid., 66–67.
16. Ibid., 71–72.
17. Ibid., 49.
18. Ibid.
19. Ibid., 62.

20. Schafer, *The Garden of the Heart*, preface.
21. Ibid., 68–69.
22. Ibid., 82–83.
23. Ibid., 105.
24. Ibid., 107–8.
25. Ibid., 111.
26. Schafer, *Ariadne's Legacy*, "Program Notes."

17. THE CONCERTI AND OTHER ORCHESTRAL WORKS

1. R. Murray Schafer, "Program Notes," 26–27.
2. Ibid.
3. Stephen Adams, *R. Murray Schafer* (Toronto: University of Toronto Press, 1983), 113.
4. Ibid., 112.
5. Schafer, "Program Notes," 35.
6. Schafer, *No Longer Than Ten Minutes*, preface.
7. Adams, *R. Murray Schafer*, 101.
8. Schafer, "Program Notes," 37–38.
9. Adams, *R. Murray Schafer*, 103.
10. Ibid., 104–5.
11. Ibid., 107–8.
12. Schafer, "Program Notes," 44–45.
13. Adams, *R. Murray Schafer*, 131.
14. Ibid., 45.
15. Adams, *R. Murray Schafer*, 127–28.
16. Schafer, *North/White*, score instruction.
17. Schafer, "Program Notes," 51.
18. Schafer, *Cortège*, score instruction.
19. Schafer, "Program Notes," 72.
20. Ibid., 81.
21. Ibid., 88.
22. Ibid., 116.
23. Ibid.
24. Ibid., 118.
25. Schafer, *Symphony no. 1*, preface.
26. Schafer, *Wolf Returns*, written notes.
27. Schafer, "Program Notes," 75.
28. Schafer, *The Darkly Splendid Earth*, preface.
29. Schafer, "Program Notes," 82.
30. Ibid., 84–85.
31. Ibid., 89.
32. Ibid., 96.
33. Ibid., 100.
34. Ibid., 101–2.

18. THE CHAMBER, SOLO, AND ELECTRONIC COMPOSITIONS

1. Schafer, "Program Notes," 33.

2. Stephen Adams, *R. Murray Schafer* (Toronto: University of Toronto Press, 1983), 123.
3. Ibid.
4. Schafer, "Program Notes," 34.
5. Ibid., 47.
6. Adams, *R. Murray Schafer* 133.
7. Ibid., 63.
8. Ibid.
9. Ibid., 78.
10. Schafer, *String Quartet no. 4*, 24.
11. Schafer, "Program Notes," 79.
12. Ibid., 86.
13. Ibid., 98–99.
14. Ibid., 102.
15. Ibid., 109.
16. Ibid., 113.
17. Schafer, *12 String Quartets by Quartour Molinari*, "Program Notes."
18. Schafer, "Program Notes," 64–65.
19. Schafer, *Ariadne's Legacy*.
20. Adams, *R. Murray Schafer* 162–63.
21. Schafer, "Program Notes," 59.
22. Ibid., 109.
23. Ibid., 123–24.
24. Ibid., 115.
25. Ibid., 112.
26. Schafer, "Program Notes," 74.
27. *Time*, October 6, 1967.
28. Schafer, "Program Notes," 39–40.

Bibliography

BOOKS BY R. MURRAY SCHAFER

Ariadne. Indian River, Ontario: Arcana Editions, 1977.
The Book of Noise. Vancouver, privately printed, 1970. Revised edition, Indian River, Ontario: Arcana Editions, 1998.
British Composers in Interview. London: Faber, 1963.
The Chaldean Inscription. Indian River, Ontario: Arcana Editions, 1981.
The Composer in the Classroom. Toronto: Berandol, 1965.
Creative Music Education: A Handbook for the Modern Music Teacher. New York: Schirmer 1976.
Dicamus et Labyrinthos. Indian River, Ontario: Arcana Editions, 1985.
Ear Cleaning: Notes for an Experimental Music Course. Toronto: Berandol, 1967.
The Enchanted Forest. Indian River, Ontario: Arcana Editions, 2005.
E. T. A. Hoffmann and Music. Toronto: University of Toronto Press, 1975.
European Sound Diary. Vancouver: ARC Publications, 1977.
Ezra Pound and Music. London: Faber 1977.
Five Village Soundscapes. Vancouver: ARC Publications, 1977.
The Garden of the Heart. Indian River, Ontario: Arcana Editions, 2008.
HearSing. Indian River, Ontario: Arcana Editions, 2005.
Music in the Cold. Indian River, Ontario: Arcana Editions, 1980.
The Music of the Environment. Vienna: Universal Edition, 1973.
My Life on Earth and Elsewhere. Erin, Ontario: The Porcupine's Quill, 2012.
The New Soundscape: A Handbook for the Modern Music Teacher. New York: Associated Music Publishers, 1969.
On Canadian Music. Indian River, Ontario: Arcana Editions, 1984.
Patria: The Complete Cycle. Toronto: Coach House Books, 2002.
R. Murray Schafer: A Collection. Edited by b.p. Nichol and Steve McCaffery. Indian River, Ontario: Arcana, 1980.
The Rhinoceros in the Classroom. Toronto: Berandol Music Limited, 1975.
The Thinking Ear: Complete Writing on Music Education. Indian River, Ontario: Arcana Editions, 1986.
Shadowgraphs and Legends. Indian River, Ontario: Arcana Editions, 2004.
The Sixteen Scribes. Indian River, Ontario: Arcana Editions, 1981.
A Sound Education. Indian River, Ontario: Arcana Editions, 1992.
The Stones. Indian River, Ontario: Arcana Editions.

The Tuning of the World. New York: Knopf 1977. Reissued as *The Soundscape.* Rochester, VT: Destiny Books, 1993.
Voices of Tyranny, Temples of Silence. Indian River, Ontario: Arcana Editions, 1993.
When Words Sing. Toronto: Berandol Music Limited, 1970.
Wolf Tracks. Indian River, Ontario: Arcana Editions, 1997.

SELECTED ARTICLES BY MURRAY SCHAFER

"Bricolage: There's a Twang in Your Trash." *Music Educator's Journal* 66 (March 1980): 32–37.
"The Canadian String Quartet." *Canadian Music Journal* 6 (Spring 1962): 29–30.
"Choral Conducting: An Interview." *Music across Canada* 1 no. 5 (June 1963): 10–12.
"The City as a Sonic Sewer." *Vancouver Sun*, March 11, 1969.
"Exploring the New Soundscape." *Unesco Courier* 29 (November 1976): 4–8.
"The Graphics of Musical Thought." In John Grayson, ed. *Sound Sculpture.* Vancouver: ARC, 1975, 98–125. Reprinted in I. Bontinck and O. Brusatti, eds., *Festschrift Kurt Blaukopf* (Vienna: Universal Edition, 1975), 120–40.
"The Most Pressing Need for the Future in Music Education in the Schools." *Music Education and Canadians of Tomorrow* (Montreal: Proceedings of the Canadian Music Council, April 1968): 57–60.
"Music and the Iron Curtain." *Queens Quarterly* 57 (1960): 407–14.
"The Philosophy of Stereophony." *West Coast Review* 1 (Winter 1967): 4–19.
"Schafer Sees Music Reflecting Country's Characteristics." *Music Scene* 293 (January/February 1977): 6–7.
"Short History of Music in Canada." *Catalogue of Orchestral Music at the Canadian Music Center.* Toronto: Canadian Music Center, 1963, v–x.
"Two Musicians in Fiction." *Canadian Music Journal* 4 (Spring 1960): 23–34.

FILMS ABOUT SCHAFER

Bing Bang Boom. Directed by Joan Henson. Ottawa: National Film Board of Canada, 1969.
Carnival of Shadows. Directed by Barbara Willis Sweete. Toronto: Rhombus Media, 1989.
Listen. Directed by David New. Ottawa: National Film Board of Canada, 2009.
Music for Wilderness Lake. Directed by Niv Fichman and Barbara Sweete. Toronto: Fichman-Sweet Productions, 1979.

SELECTED SECONDARY SOURCES

Adams, Stephen J. *R. Murray Schafer.* Toronto: University of Toronto Press, 1983.
———. "Schafer, R. Murray." Grove Music Online, 2001.
———. "The Musician." Canadian Broadcasting Corporation, February 25, 1979.
Anonymous. "R. Murray Schafer." BMI Canada, 1971.
———. "R. Murray Schafer: A Portrait." *Musicanada* 23 (October 1969): 8–9.
Ball, Suzanne. "Murray Schafer: Composer, Teacher, and Author." *Music Scene* (May/June 1970): 7–8.
Barber, Dulan. "Murray Schafer: A Discussion with Dulan Barber." *Times Educational Supplement*, June 18, 1971, 19–20.
Bates, Duane. "Murray Schafer Interviewed by Duane Bates." *Canadian Music Educator* 22, no. 2 (Winter 1981): 7–13.
Beckwith, John. "Young Composers' Performances in Toronto." *Canadian Music Journal* 2, no. 4 (Summer 1958): 54–55.

Beecroft, Norma. "Documentary: R. Murray Schafer." *Two New Hours*, Canadian Broadcasting Corporation, April 16, 1978.
Breitsameter, Sabine. *McLuhan's Paradigms and Schafer's "Soundscape": Parallels, Influences, Envelopes, Shifts.* London: Pickering and Chatto, 2014.
Colgrass, Ulla. "Murray Schafer." *Music Magazine* 3, no. 1 (January 1, 1980): 16–23.
Cornfield, Eitan. "R. Murray Schafer Documentary." In *Canadian Composer Portraits: R. Murray Schafer*, Canadian Music Center, 2005.
Crossman, Rae. "Notes from the Wild: An Account in Words and Music of R. Murray Schafer's 'And Wolf Shall Inherit the Moon.'" *Intersections: Canadian Journal of Music* 28, no. 2 (2008): 51–71.
Eatock, Colin. "R. Murray Schafer at 75: An Appreciation." *Queen's Quarterly* 116 (Spring 2009): 1.
Edwards, Barry. "Composer of the Month: R. Murray Schafer." *Fugue* 2, no. 2 (October 1977): 32–34, 40–41.
Galloway, Kathleen Anne. "'Sounding Nature, Sounding Place': Alternative Performance Spaces, Participatory Experience, and Ritual Performance in R. Murray Schafer's *Patria Cycle*." PhD dissertation, University of Toronto, 2010.
Gillia, Ron. "Interview with R. Murray Schafer," May 5, 1987.
Grace, Sherrill, and Stefan Haag. "From Landscape to Soundscape: The Northern Arts of Canada." *Mosaic* 31, no. 2 (1998): 101–22.
Haag, Stefan. "Allegories of the Postmodern: The Work of Wilfred Watson and R. Murray Schafer." PhD dissertation, University of British Columbia, 1995.
Kasemets, Udo. "Schafer, R. Murray." In Keith MacMillan and John Beckwith, eds. *Contemporary Canadian Composers*. Toronto: Oxford, 1975, 199–205.
MacKenzie, Kirk. "A Twentieth-Century Musical/Theatrical Cycle: R. Murray Schafer's *Patria* (1966–)." PhD dissertation, University of Cincinnati, 1991.
Mather, Bruce. "Notes sur 'Requiems for the Party-Girl' de Schafer." *Les Cahiers canadiens de musique/Canada Music Book* 5 (Spring 1970): 91–97.
Menuhin, Yehudi, and Curtis W. Davis. *The Music of Man*. New York: Methuen, 1979, 91–97.
Orr, Colleen October. "The John Adaskin Project: A History and Evaluation." Master's thesis, University of Western Ontario, 1977.
Potter, Keith, and John Shepherd. "Interview with Murray Schafer." *Contact: Today's Music* 13 (Spring 1976): 3–10.
Rea, John. "Richard Wagner and R. Murray Schafer: Two Revolutionary and Religious Poets." *Les Cahiers canadiens de musique/Canada Music Book* 8 (Spring 1974): 37–51.
Schafer, R. M., E. James, and S. A. Standing. "Eco-Theatre." *PAJ: A Journal of Performance and Art* 36, no. 1 (2014): 35–44. Project MUSE, muse.jhu.edu/article/533810.
Scott, L. Brett. "When Words Sing: The Choral Music of R. Murray Schafer." D.M.A Document, University of Cincinnati, 2002.
Shand, Patricia. "The Music of the Environment." *Canadian Music Educator* 15 (Winter 1974): 5–12.
Skelton, Robert. "Weinzweig, Gould, Schafer: Three Canadian String Quartets." PhD dissertation, University of Indiana, 1976.
Southcott, Jane, and Harry Burke. "Interpreting Gesture as Motive: A Transformational Perspective on Replication in R. Murray Schafer's Seventh String Quartet." *Canadian Music Educator/Musicien educateur au Canada* 54, no. 2 (Winter 2012): 19–26.
Such, Peter. "Murray Schafer." *Soundprints: Contemporary Composers*. Toronto: Clarke Irwin, 1971.
Torigoe, Keiko. "A Study of the World Soundscape Project." Master's thesis, York University, 1982.
Trowsdale, Campbell. "Interview with R. Murray Schafer," 1978.
Waterman, Ellen. "R. Murray Schafer's Environmental Music Theatre: A Documentation and Analysis of *Patria Epilogue: And Wolf Shall Inherit the Moon*." PhD dissertation, University of California, San Diego, 1997.

———. "R. Murray Schafer's 'And Wolf Shall Inherit the Moon': The Nexus of Ideal and Real Wilderness." *Journal of Canadian Studies/Revue d'études canadiennes* 33, no. 2 (Summer 1998): 139–51.

Index

Adams, Stephen, 16, 121, 166, 280
acoustic design, 143, 146, 149
acoustic ecology, 100, 140, 142, 145, 149
Adaskin, John, 40, 41, 121
Adaskin Project, 44, 45, 50, 121, 122, 257
Aitken, Robert, 13, 28, 39, 40, 68, 77, 80, 87, 96, 108, 306, 326, 328
Amnesty International, 39
Anhalt, Istvan, 51, 55, 152
Apocalypsis, 64, 68, 69, 71, 75, 76, 108, 117, 266, 267; *John's Vision*, 69, 194–199, 267; *Credo*, 69, 267–268, 276. *See also* Schafer, Raymond Murray, compositions
ARC Ensemble, 114, 330
Arcana Editions, 75, 76, 83, 84, 92, 100, 108, 109
Argentina, 89, 91, 94, 96
Arnold, Malcolm, 33, 157
atonal, 20, 258
Australia, 105
avant-garde techniques, 210, 212; aleatoric, 258, 261; extended vocal/instrumental techniques, 251, 307, 315; graphic notation, 122, 130, 258, 261, 266

Bancroft, 67, 83, 114
Banff, 81, 95
Banff Acoustic Conference, 90
Banff Centre for the Arts, 75, 92, 111

Barnes, Milton, 27, 242
Bardo Thodol, 227, 260, 274
BBC. *See* British Broadcasting Corporation
BBC Singers, 86, 88, 269
Beckwith, John, 11, 13, 28, 152, 242, 247
Beecroft, Norma, 13
Beethoven, Ludwig van, 5, 6, 10, 160
Behrens, Jack, 50, 331
Belgium, 23, 25
Berandol, 27, 75
Berg, Alban, 13, 20, 130; *Wozzeck*, 10
Bhagavad-Gita, 259, 266, 274
Bird, C. Laughton, 45, 123
Bloomfield, Howard, 64, 144
BMI Canada. *See* Berandol
Boulez, Pierre, 33, 62
Brahms, Johannes, 6, 329
Brandon, 112, 302
Brandon University, 94, 269, 302
Brazil, 89, 91, 94, 100, 108, 115
Brébeuf, Jean de, 35, 251
Brecht, Bertold, 27, 247
Britten, Benjamin, 9, 23, 24, 32, 157, 243
British Broadcasting Corporation, 34, 35, 38, 269
British Library, 26
British Museum, 23
Brown, Donna, 89, 279, 288
Bruno, Giordano, 267
Brueghel, Pieter, 151

369

Bucharest, 29, 30, 32
Buczynski, Walter, 35
Bulgaria, 31, 32

Cage, John, 50, 127
Canada Council for the Arts, 28, 32, 33, 40, 51, 53, 74, 76, 89, 268, 330
Canadian Brass, 77, 325
Canadian Broadcasting Corporation, 27, 29, 32, 37, 39, 42, 44, 45, 46, 51, 57, 60, 64, 74, 75, 105, 112, 152, 191, 273, 287, 289, 297, 329, 331
Canadian League of Composers, 28, 37, 39
Canadian Music Centre, 37, 40, 41, 51, 59, 105, 116, 117, 121
Canadian Music Journal, 28, 163, 242
Canadian Opera Company, 78, 84, 89, 111, 112
CBC. *See* Canadian Broadcasting Corporation
Charpentier, Gabriel, 45, 51, 191
Chekhov, Anton, 151
Cherney, Lawrence, 105, 199, 272
Chile, 91
choir Utaoni, 99, 100, 271
Chor Leoni, 104, 272
Chorus America, 104
CMC. *See* Canadian Music Centre
Cocteau, Jean, 27, 241, 242
Coimbra, 71, 105, 106
Concordia University (Montréal), 76, 108, 109, 114
Costa Rica, 92, 94, 269
Crete, 25, 217, 248
Crossman, Rae, 275, 289
Czechoslovakia, 22

Dallapiccola, Luigi, 33, 289
Dante Alighieri, 210, 274, 276
Davis, Bruce, 60, 62, 64, 143, 144, 332
De Falla, Manuel, 244
Debussy, Claude, 124, 147, 325
Delamont, Gordon, 38
Dickens, Charles, 8; *Great Expectations*, 10
dodecaphonic. *See* serialism
Dolmetsch, Arnold, 164; *The Interpretation of the Music of the 17th and 18th Centuries*, 163

Donner Foundation, 62
Doon Art School, 14, 17
Dunlop, Stacie, 110, 290
Dutton, Paul, 195, 317

Earth Day, 153
Eastman School of Music, 13
Eisenstadt, Morris, 27, 242
electronic/electroacoustic, 210, 212, 253, 256, 258, 266, 281, 295
Elliot, T. S., 34
Elmer Iseler Singers, 37
Esprit Orchestra, 89, 94, 98, 117, 300, 306

Fawcett, Brian, 60, 332
Festival Singers. *See* Elmer Iseler Singers
Fialkowska, Janina, 331
Finland, 92, 114
Five Village Soundscapes, 144
FLADEM/FLAMA. *See* Foro Latinamericano de Educacion Musical
Fonterrada, Marisa, 91
formalism, 253, 254, 256
Foro Latinoamericano de Educación Musical, 105, 108, 112, 115
Forrester, Maureen, 68, 76, 77, 78, 95, 96, 279, 283, 288
Freedman, Harry, 13, 38, 104
Freud, Sigmund, 212
Fricker, Peter Racine, 32, 34, 157, 250
Friesen, Doug, 116
Fromm Foundation, 53

Garant, Serge, 39, 46, 51, 62
Glenn Gould Prize for Music and Communication, 84
Glick, Srul Irving, 35
Globe and Mail, 29
Goehr, Alexander, 34
Goethe, Johann Wolfgang von, 21, 288
Gould, Glenn, 11, 28
Governor General's Award for Excellence in the Arts, 99
Governor General's Performing Arts Lifetime Achievement Award, 113
Grace Church on-the-Hill, 9, 14, 241
Greece, 24, 25, 26, 111, 115
Group of Seven, 74
Gryphon Trio, 116, 117, 330

Guerrero, Alberto, 11, 33
Gulbenkian Foundation, 71

Haliburton Forest and Wildlife Reserve, 94, 95, 100, 110
Handel, G. F., 9
Heine, Heinrich, 21
Helmholtz, Hermann von, 128
Hindemith, Paul, 20
Hiroshima, 108, 109
Hodgins, John, 9, 14, 241
Hoebig, Gwen, 108
Hoffmann, E. T. A., 39, 44, 158–162, 177, 282
Hoyem, Roger, 86, 101, 104, 106, 108, 110, 114
Hugo, Victor, 151, 270

IFMC. *See* International Folk Music Council
Indian River, 84, 89, 98, 105, 106, 189, 233
International Folk Music Council, 29
International Society for Contemporary Music, 63, 117
Isha-Upanishad, 296
Isrealievitch, Jacques, 89, 99, 309, 325
Ives, Charles, 13, 126, 147

James, Eleanor, 78, 80, 81, 83, 84, 86, 87, 88, 90, 91, 93, 94, 95, 98, 101, 103, 104, 105, 106, 108, 109, 110, 111, 112, 113, 114, 115, 116, 117, 188, 189, 279, 288, 289, 306, 307
Johnston, Dr. Richard, 15
Joyce, James, 14, 26, 129, 164
Jung, Karl, 206, 331

Kafka, Franz, 26, 210
Karp, Barry, 92
King's Singers, 91, 92, 269
Kingston, 114, 189
Klee, Paul, 14, 23, 24, 44, 244, 327
Kodaly, Zoltan, 32
Koerner, Michael and Sonja, 111, 112, 303, 318, 325
Kraft, Norbert, 88, 307, 331
Kraus, Greta, 12, 20, 243
Krenek, Ernst, 56

Kyoto Symphony, 80, 81, 299

La Jeunesse, 92

Lafayette String Quartet, 112, 114, 320
Lambert, Phyllis, 116
Laughton, Stuart, 98, 310
LeCaine, Hugh, 14

Les Six, 8, 10, 13, 164, 241, 242, 244, 245, 248

Lisbon, 71, 99, 108, 134
Loman, Judy, 115, 116, 289, 307, 322, 324
London, 20, 23, 29, 32, 33, 35, 250
Lou Applebaum award, 101
Lucretius, 271
Luminato Festival, 113, 117

Macerollo, Joseph, 92, 282, 310
Machaut, Guillaume de, 33, 250
MacKenzie, Kirk, 205, 207
MacKinnon, Archie, 49
Madrid, 99, 106
Mahler, Gustav, 245, 330
Mailing, Phyllis, 9, 14, 20, 27, 28, 29, 34, 35, 37, 42, 45, 46, 51, 53, 54, 55, 56, 59, 60, 61, 62, 76, 99, 242, 245, 247, 279, 280, 286
Mann, Thomas, 26, 35
Martin, John, 14
Mather, Bruce, 35
Maynooth Community Choir, 74, 134, 187, 260
Maynooth Lutheran Church, 68, 70
McCaffery, Steve, 195
McGill University, 51, 86, 105, 256
McKay, Sir William, 8, 10
McLuhan, Marshall, 14, 49, 75, 151, 163
Menuhin, Yehudi, 72, 134; *The Music of Man*, 72, 84, 134
Memorial University, 40, 42, 45, 46, 190, 258
Mendelssohn Choir of Toronto, 260
Mercure, Pierre, 45, 46, 190, 191
Metropolitan United Church, Toronto, 69, 194, 263
Mexico, 105, 108, 109, 112, 113, 116

Molinari Quartet, 106, 109, 112, 116, 318, 319, 320, 321
Molson Award, 94
Montréal, 45, 46, 51, 106, 109, 116, 302
Montréal Symphony Orchestra, 39, 53, 55, 80, 293, 306
Moreno, J. L., 212
Morrison, Mary, 37, 40, 44, 104, 279, 280, 287
Morse code, 210
Mozart, W. A., 160, 163
Munich, 22, 101, 103, 105, 106
Music and Environmental Workshop, 94
Mussorgsky, Modest, 124

Nagasaki, 263
National Arts Centre, 59, 64, 74, 76, 89, 91; Orchestra, 60, 62, 63, 70, 71, 98, 112, 113, 288, 296, 298
National Ballet of Canada, 89
National Film Board of Canada, 126
National Library of Canada, 104, 111
National Youth Orchestra of Canada, 62, 63, 297, 300
New Music Concert series, 39, 77
New York Philharmonic, 10, 62
New York University, 73
Newfoundland Children's Chorus, 108
Nexus, 103, 310
Nichol, bp, 195, 285, 317
Nietzsche, Friedrich, 8, 212, 273, 290
North York, 41, 45, 122, 123
Novalis, 21, 282

Ontario Arts Council, 4, 57, 133
Ontario School of Art, 11
Ontario Science Centre, 78
Open Letter, 73, 183, 191
Order of Canada, 116
Orford String Quartet, 87, 88, 90, 283, 318
Orphei Dränger, 86
OSM. *See* Montréal Symphony Orchestra
Ottawa, 98, 99, 116
Ottawa Chamber Music Festival, 106, 116
Ozawa, Seiji, 81

Paris, 25, 26, 27, 35, 96, 101
Patria, 62, 69, 72, 73, 76, 88, 89, 96, 97, 98, 100, 111, 171, 176, 178, 180, 187, 262, 279, 288, 322, 325, 326; *Patria Prologue: The Princess of the Stars*, 74, 75, 77, 81, 89, 92, 98, 99, 100, 110, 111, 112, 170, 171, 172, 207–209, 231, 261, 285, 317; *Patria 1: Wolfman*, 46, 64, 67, 68, 84, 104, 172, 176, 178, 209–211, 259, 260; *Patria 2: Requiems for the Party Girl*, 51, 62, 172, 176, 178, 211–213, 260, 280, 283; *Patria 3: The Greatest Show*, 75, 81, 82, 83, 84, 87, 88, 172, 176, 213–215, 236, 260, 282, 283, 285, 286, 325, 326; *Patria 4: The Black Theatre of Hermes Trismegistos*, 80, 86, 87, 91, 172, 176, 215–217, 281; *Patria 5: The Crown of Ariadne*, 73, 77, 88, 89, 90, 111, 172, 176, 178, 180, 183, 217–220, 261, 322, 324; *Patria 6: Ra*, 76, 77, 78, 173, 176, 178, 220–223; *Patria 7: Asterion*, 98, 110, 116, 173, 223–227, 282, 332; *Patria 8: The Palace of the Cinnabar Phoenix*, 97, 100, 104, 110, 173, 176, 227–230; *Patria 9: The Enchanted Forest*, 90, 92, 93, 94, 95, 96, 97, 99, 100, 105, 109, 173, 176, 231–232, 233, 289; *Patria 10: The Spirit Garden*, 88, 97, 98, 99, 103, 104, 106, 173, 176, 231, 233–235, 263; *Patria Epilogue: And Wolf Shall Inherit the Moon*, 88, 89, 90, 92, 93, 95, 96, 97, 98, 99, 100, 101, 103, 108, 110, 111, 113, 117, 173, 176, 231, 235–236, 261, 262, 263, 286, 306, 310, 311, 327. *See also* Schafer, Raymond Murray, compositions
Patria Music Theatre Productions, 104, 110, 111, 263
Paulk, Alex, 300
Peterborough Festival of the Arts, 88
Pilgrim, Neva, 56
Pound, Ezra, 14, 24, 26, 34–35, 54, 55, 163–165, 201, 247, 332; *Antheil and the Treatise on Harmony*, 165; *Cantos*, 34, 164, 165; *Le Testament*, 34, 164, 201
Prudentius, 254
Purcell String Quartet, 60

Queen's University, 77, 88

Reed, Jean, 61, 62, 63, 67, 68, 69, 74, 75, 78, 80, 83, 86, 87, 88, 89, 91, 92, 94, 95, 96, 98, 99, 100, 101, 104, 108, 110, 113, 114, 306, 318
"Results of a Social Survey on Noise—Vancouver 1969", 139–140
Rhombus Media, 74
Rilke, Rainer, 21, 26, 273
Romania, 29, 30, 32, 250
Rose, Belle Anderson, 3, 4
Royal Schools of Music, 8
Royal Conservatory of Music in Toronto, 8, 11, 114, 115, 116, 303; Koerner Hall, 115, 303
Rumi, Jalal-al-din, 55, 57, 140, 280, 291, 295

Sackville, 105, 106
St. Gallen, 81, 83, 106, 285, 288
St. John's, 40, 41, 42, 44, 46, 78, 108, 258, 328
St. Lawrence Quartet, 311
St. Paul's Anglican Church, 70
Sarnia, 3, 4
Scarborough, 41, 122
Schaeffer, Carl, 14
Schafer, Harold, 3, 4
Schafer, David Paul, 4, 9, 56, 95, 99, 117
Schafer, Raymond Murray, compositions: *Adieu, Robert Schumann*, 68, 69, 72, 87, 106, 287; *Alzheimer's Masterpiece*, 117, 321; *Alleluia*, 101, 271; *Amente Nufe*, 77, 78, 222; *Antigone*, 44; *Arcana*, 62, 281, 283; *Ariadne's Aria*, 286; *Aubade*, 286; *Aubade for Two Voices*, 286; *Beautiful Spanish Song*, 94, 270; *Beauty and the Beast*, 74, 76, 106, 283, 285; *Beyond the Great Gate of Light*, 60, 61, 264, 289, 296; *Brébeuf*, 35, 251, 279; *Buskers*, 81, 214, 326; *Canzoni for Prisoners*, 39, 46, 254, 256; *The Children's Crusade*, 111, 112, 113, 199–203; *Composition for Four Players*, 44; *Concerto for Accordion and Orchestra*, 91, 92, 310; *Concerto for Flute and Orchestra*, 80, 87, 96, 306–307, 326; *Concerto for Guitar and Orchestra*, 88, 307–309; *Concerto for Harp and Orchestra*, 84, 307; *Concerto for Harpsichord and Eight Wind Instruments*, 12, 27, 29, 31, 33, 242, 243–245, 248; *Concerto for Viola and Orchestra*, 99, 100, 311; *Cortège*, 71, 298; *The Crown of Ariadne*, 73, 84, 115, 215, 218, 307, 318, 319, 322–324; *The Darkly Splendid Earth: The Lonely Traveller*, 89, 309–310, 325; *The Death of Shalana*, 108; *The Death of the Buddha*, 86, 269; *Deluxe Suite for Piano*, 97, 331; *Dithyramb for String Orchestra*, 54, 252; *Divan I Shams I Tabriz*, 57, 59, 295–296; *Divisions for Baroque Trio*, 40, 54, 256; *Dream Passage*, 55, 56, 62, 211, 214; *Dream Rainbow, Dream Thunder*, 82, 300; *Dream(e)scape*, 113, 304, 305, 311; *Duo for Violin and Piano*, 112, 329; *East*, 60, 62, 63, 296–297; *Enchantress*, 60, 61, 264, 286, 287; *Epitaph for Moonlight*, 53, 54, 122, 130, 219, 264, 266; *The Falcon's Trumpet*, 96, 97, 115, 117, 310; *The Fall Into Light*, 105, 106, 259, 266, 272–274, 276, 277; *Felix's Girls*, 74, 214, 260, 270; *Festival Music for Small Orchestra*, 51, 54; *Figures in the Night, Passing*, 115, 305, 311; *Fire*, 82, 220, 261, 270; *Five Greek Folk Dances*, 28, 248; *Five Studies on Texts of Prudentius*, 37, 39, 40, 191, 254–255, 279; *Flew Toots for Two Flutes*, 108, 326, 328; *Four Songs for Harp and Mezzo-Soprano*, 114, 115, 290–291; *Four Songs on Texts of Tagore*, 40, 54, 256, 259, 289; *Four-Forty*, 100, 101, 103, 311; *From the Bow*, 289; *From the Tibetan Book of the Dead*, 55, 62, 212, 213, 260, 269; *Gamelan*, 74, 214, 260; *A Garden of Bells*, 80, 268–269, 270; *The Garden of the Heart*, 75, 76, 177, 180, 287–288; *The Geography of Eros*, 37, 39, 44, 45, 190, 191, 279–280, 281; *Gita*, 64, 211, 259, 260, 266, 269; *Gitanjali*, 89, 91, 288; *Haddon Hall*, 10; *Harbour Symphony*, 78, 328; *Hear Me Out*, 74, 214, 260; *Here the Sounds Go Round*, 115, 277; *Hymn to Night*, 69, 71, 72, 74, 180, 224, 225, 282, 283; *If Ye Love Me*,

10, 241; *Imagining Incense*, 104, 105, 272; *In Memoriam Alberto Guerrero*, 33, 38, 245, 249; *In Search of Zoroaster*, 61, 63, 105, 170, 264, 266–267, 286; *Invertible Material for Orchestra no. 1*, 257; *Invertible Material for Orchestra (no. 2)*, 41, 54, 257, 258; *Isfahan*, 109, 115, 329; *Job*, 114, 189–190, 291; *Jonah*, 74, 88, 134, 187–188; *The Judgement of Jael*, 35, 54, 251–252, 279; *Kaleidoscope*, 332; *Kinderlieder*, 27, 245, 247, 248; *Ko wo kiku*, 81, 299–300; *La Testa D'Adriane*, 69, 72, 167, 214, 282–283, 285; *Landscapes and Soundscapes*, 110, 114, 277; *Le Cri de Merlin*, 307, 331; *Letters from Mignon*, 81, 84, 110, 112, 288, 289; *The Love That Moves the Universe*, 113, 114, 117, 276; *Loving/ Toi*, 39, 44, 45, 46, 49, 51, 53, 70, 72, 73, 117, 171, 190–194, 212, 258, 280; *Lu-li-lo-la*, 262; *Lustro*, 60, 61, 63, 280, 293, 296; *Magic Songs*, 86, 261–262, 271, 273, 306; *Make Room for God*, 112, 276; *Manitou*, 95, 97, 99, 110, 302–303; *A Medieval Bestiary*, 270; *Minnelieder*, 20, 23, 27, 33, 82, 110, 245–247, 288, 289; *Minimusic*, 57, 122, 327; *Miniwanka*, 61, 264; *Music for the Morning of the World*, 60, 62, 280–281, 287, 296; *Music for Wilderness Lake*, 73, 74, 112, 116, 170, 207, 327–328; *A Music Lesson*, 14, 242, 247, 279; *Musique pour la parc Lafontaine*, 90, 91, 153, 302; *Narcissus and Echo*, 112, 276; no longer than ten (10) minutes, 60, 170, 294; *Nocturne*, 241; *North/White*, 60, 62, 63, 175, 297–298; *Okeanos*, 60, 61, 154, 226, 332; *Once on a Windy Night*, 96, 97, 98, 270; Ontario variations, 331; *Opus One for Mixed Chorus*, 40, 54, 255, 259; *Partita for Twelve Instruments*, 23, 245; *Partita for String Orchestra*, 54, 252; *Petit Divertissement Angevin*, 28, 245, 248; Polytonality, 241, 242, 247, 248, 249, 331; *Protest and Incarceration*, 39, 54, 250, 279; *Psalm*, 62, 195, 267; *Quintet for Piano and Strings*, 114, 330; *Rain Chant*, 104, 263, 273, 306; *Remember Susanna*, 105, 106, 188–189; *Requiems for the Party Girl*, 51, 54, 56, 62, 211, 212, 213, 280; *Roland of Roncesvalles*, 274; *Sappho*, 53, 60, 286, 287; *Sea Shanty*, 241; *The Searching Sings*, 112, 274; *Scorpius*, 89, 116, 300–302; *Seventeen Haiku*, 100, 271; *Shadowman*, 103, 312–314; *Six Songs from Rilke's "Book of Hours"*, 110, 111, 290; *Situational Music for Brass Quintet*, 77, 214, 325–326; *Snowforms* (original SATB version), 75, 264; *Snowforms*, 264–266; *Son of Heldenleben*, 54, 55, 59, 60, 293–294; *Sonata da Camera*, 28, 245, 249; *Sonatina for Flute and Harpsichord (or Piano)*, 28, 33, 245, 248, 249; *Sonorities for Brass Sextet*, 51, 54; *The Soul of God*, 114, 277; *Spirits of the House*, 111, 113, 303–304; *The Star Princess and the Waterlilies*, 81, 92, 261; *Statement in Blue*, 41, 44, 46, 122, 257; *Statement in Red*, 41, 122, 258; *String Quartet no. 1*, 60, 72, 315, 316, 321; *String Quartet no. 2 (Waves)*, 68, 69, 316; *String Quartet no. 3*, 76, 77, 78, 311, 316–317; *String Quartet no. 4*, 87, 317–318; *String Quartet no. 5 (Rosalinde)*, 88, 95, 318, 320; *String Quartet no. 6 (Parting Wild Horse's Mane)*, 92, 112, 230, 318; *String Quartet no. 7*, 100, 101, 318–319; *String Quartet no. 8*, 104, 319; *String Quartet no. 9*, 104, 108, 109, 319–320; *String Quartet no. 10 (Winter Birds)*, 104, 106, 320; *String Quartet no. 11*, 109, 110, 111, 114, 320–321; *String Quartet no. 12*, 116, 321, 322; *Sun*, 76, 261, 266; *Sun Father, Sky Mother*, 81, 207, 285–286; *Symphony no. 1 in C Minor*, 114, 117, 304–305; *Tantrika*, 82, 115, 267, 286; *Tanzlied*, 106, 116, 286, 289–290; *Te Deum*, 13, 241; *Theseus*, 215, 218, 324; *Three Contemporaries*, 24, 28, 54, 242, 243, 247, 279; *Three Hymns from The Fall Into Light*, 273; *Three Ideograms for Walter Ball*, 29, 245, 249; *Three

Songs from the Enchanted Forest, 262; *Threnody*, 44, 53, 54, 60, 109, 112, 133, 263; *Thunder: Perfect Mind*, 104, 106, 110, 289; *Train*, 62, 69; *Trio for Clarinet, Cello and Piano*, 28, 242; *Trio for Flute, Viola, and Harp*, 114, 325; *Trio for Violin, Cello, and Piano*, 116, 117, 330; *Trio for Violin, Viola, and Cello*, 111, 112, 330; *Tristan und Iseult*, 91, 92, 269; *Toccata*, 13; *Two Songs from the Spirit Garden*, 263; *Untitled Composition for Orchestra no. 1*, 44, 252, 256, 279; *Untitled Composition for Orchestra no. 2*, 44, 256; *Untitled Composition for Voices*, 44; *Vox Naturae*, 99, 271, 272; *Wild Bird*, 99, 115, 325; *Winter Solstice*, 104, 272; *Wizard Oil and Indian Sagwa*, 75, 214, 285, 289; *Wolf Music*, 327; *Wolf Returns*, 115, 293, 306; *Yeow and Pax*, 57, 266; *You Are Illuminated*, 101, 226, 266, 271. See also *Apocalypsis*; *Patria*

Schafer, Raymond Murray, writings: Ariadne, 44, 68, 69, 177, 178–180, 182, 183, 287, 288; *Bing Bang Boom* (documentary film), 57, 126; "A Birthday Tribute to John Weinzweig", 169–170; *The Book of Noise*, 58, 100, 140–141, 142, 145, 148; *British Composers in Interview*, 32, 38, 157–158; "Canadian Culture: Colonial Culture", 170; *The Chaldean Inscription*, 73, 180, 226; "Citycycles", 166; *The Composer in the Classroom*, 41, 42, 45, 50, 123–124, 126, 127; *Creative Music Education*, 133; *Dicamus et Labyrinthos*, 70, 73, 167, 176, 180, 183, 215, 224; *E. T. A. Hoffmann and Music*, 42, 68, 158–162; *Ear Cleaning*, 50, 125–126, 136; *The Enchanted Forest*, 178; Ezra Pound and Music (article & book), 35, 70, 163–165; "The Future for Music in Canada", 169; *The Garden of the Heart*, 112, 177, 288; "The Graphics of Musical Thought", 50, 121–122, 132; Harry Somers' *Riel* on Stage and Television, 169; *HearSing*, 136–137; "The Limits of Nationalism in Canadian Music", 38, 168; "The Listening Book", 166; *My Life on Earth and Elsewhere*, 114; *Music for Wilderness Lake*, 170; *Music in the Cold*, 70, 71, 170, 175–176; *Music Media Box* (with Harry Somers), 57, 133; "The Music of the Environment", 61, 141, 145; "My First Stage Work: Loving", 167, 171; *The New Soundscape*, 54, 57, 58, 127–128, 134, 142; *On Canadian Music*, 167–171; *Patria: The Complete Cycle*, 167, 171–173; *Patria Prologue: The Princess of the Stars*, 171; *Radical Radio*, 77; *The Rhinoceros in the Classroom*, 62, 64, 68, 130–133; "Serge Garant and His Music", 169; *Shadowgraphs and Legends*, 94, 104, 182–183; *A Short History of Music in Canada*, 38, 167; *The Sixteen Scribes*, 77, 180, 182; *A Sound Education*, 77, 98, 135–136, 137, 150; *The Soundscape: Our Sonic Environment and the Tuning of the World*, 145; *The Stones*, 178; "Ten Centuries Concerts: A Recollection", 168; "The Theatre of Confluence I", 167; "The Theatre of Confluence II", 172; "The Theatre of Confluence III", 173; "The Thinking Ear: On Music Education, 133–135; *Triangle, Circle, Square*, 178; *The Tuning of the World*, 62, 64, 68, 70, 71, 145–150, 152; "Two Musicians in Fiction", 35; "Ursound", 73, 150, 166, 167; *Voices of Tyranny, Temples of Silence*, 91, 150–154; "What is this Article About", 168; *When Words Sing*, 57, 59, 128–130, 264; *A Winter Diary*, 99, 154; *Wolf Tracks*, 92, 99, 176–177, 178

Schenker, Heinrich, 165
Schoenberg, Arnold, 13, 20, 35, 54, 130, 165, 245, 247; *Pierrot Lunaire*, 39, 54; *A Survivor from Warsaw*, 123
Schreyer, Claude, 99, 154, 302
Schumann, Robert, 287
Scotia Festival, 93, 188
Seiber, Matyas, 33

Selestat, 96, 103
Seminar for Graded Educational Music, 122
serialism, 20, 35, 247, 250, 252, 253, 254, 256, 258, 296, 315; all-interval row, 210, 212, 216, 218, 220, 231, 259, 261, 263, 280, 283, 285, 286, 322, 326
SFU. *See* Simon Fraser University
Shostakovich, Dmitri, 325
Simon Fraser University, 14, 46, 55, 57, 61, 64, 67, 99, 125, 130, 133, 134, 143, 145, 152, 213, 293; Center for the Study of Communications and the Arts, 49, 50; Department of Communications Studies, 57; Sonic Research Studio, 60
Smith, Diane and Jerrard, 112, 113
Somers, Harry, 13, 31, 35, 38, 53; *Louis Riel*, 53, 169
Sonaré, 328
Sophocles, 130
soundscape, 91, 92, 96, 127, 141, 146, 147, 149
Soundstreams Canada, 105, 108, 109, 114, 199, 263, 272, 277, 329
S. S. *Imperial Windsor*, 19, 20
Stockholm, 100, 101
Strasbourg, 96, 97, 98
Strasbourg, Gottfried von, 269
Stratford, 77, 78, 112, 116, 307, 325
Stratford Festival (Ontario), 62
Strauss, Richard, 54, 177, 289; *Ariadne auf Naxos*, 177; *Don Juan*, 54, 293; *Ein Heldenleben*, 54, 293, 294
Stravinsky, Igor, 14, 20, 164, 242, 244, 245, 305
A Survey of Community Noise By-laws in Canada, 142
Swiss Soundscape Association, 98
Symonds, Norm, 38

Tagore, Rabindranath, 40, 256, 272, 289, 291, 296
Taipei Philharmonic Choir, 104, 105, 263, 306
Takemitsu, Toru, 80, 97, 300, 302, 322
Tallis, Thomas, 268
Tanglewood Festival, 53, 259
Tapiola Children's Choir, 262
Ten Centuries Concerts, 38, 39, 40, 44

A Thousand and One Nights, 177
Tippett, Michael, 33, 157
Tokyo, 97, 110, 302
Tokyo Philharmonic Chorus, 99, 105, 112, 272, 276
Tokyo Symphony, 94, 95, 97
Tolstoy, Leo, 26
Torigoe, Keiko, 62
Toronto, 3, 4, 6, 19, 27, 37, 40, 46, 104, 105, 109, 110, 116, 122, 245, 247, 249, 255, 329
Toronto Children's Chorus, 81, 261
Toronto International Choral Festival, 88, 105, 269, 272
Toronto Mendelssohn Choir, 77
Toronto Symphony Orchestra, 10, 46, 55, 59, 60, 96, 113, 114, 116, 294, 304, 307, 310, 322
Toronto Wind Quintet, 27
Trio Verlaine, 325
Trismegistos, Hermes, 215, 273
Truax, Barry, 64, 68, 143, 144, 145
TSO. *See* Toronto Symphony Orchestra
Turkey, 25, 329
twelve tone. *See* serialism

UNESCO, 58, 59, 60, 61, 62, 132, 141, 269; *Journal of World History*, 61, 141; International Music Council, 132, 141
Universal Editions, 59, 60, 75, 142
University of Arizona, 111
University of British Columbia, 98, 114
University of Calgary, 76
University of Cincinnati, 112; College-Conservatory of Music, 276
University of Montreal, 46
University of Ottawa, 94
University of Strasbourg, 98, 99, 310
University of Toronto, 9, 13, 15, 16, 33, 34, 44, 111, 112, 133, 241; Emmanuel College, 111, 115; orchestra, 103, 109, 312
University of Victoria, 98
University of Waterloo, 116, 170
University of Western Ontario, 75, 77
Uruguay, 91

Vancouver, 49, 51, 114

Vancouver Chamber Choir, 80, 82, 92, 98, 113, 117, 268, 270, 276
Vancouver Children's Choir, 88
Vancouver Junior Youth Orchestra, 53, 263
The Vancouver Soundscape, 61, 99, 142–144, 145
Vancouver Symphony Orchestra, 57
Verlaine Trio, 115
Victoria, 112, 115
Victoria Symphony, 305
Vienna, 19, 20, 24, 25, 26, 29, 245, 290
Vienna Academy, 21
Vienna Philharmonic, 96
Villon, Francois, 34

Walshe, Bob, 14, 20, 24, 27, 29, 34, 35, 86, 90, 96, 115, 251
Walter, Arnold, 15, 16
Walton, Sir William, 34, 157
Waterman, Ellen, 206, 207
Webern, Anton, 20, 33, 252
Weil, Kurt, 245, 248
Weinzweig, John, 10, 13, 28, 31, 37, 63, 92, 105, 110, 116, 169, 241, 244, 303, 304
Westerkamp, Hildegard, 64

Wilfrid Laurier University, 104
Willan, Healey, 15, 303
Winnipeg, 3, 103, 106, 108, 112
Winnipeg New Music Festival, 94, 99, 112, 319
Winnipeg Symphony Orchestra, 99, 108, 117
World Exposition, 53
World Forum for Acoustic Ecology, 105, 110, 113, 114, 115
World Harp Congress, 115
World Listening Day, 114
World Soundscape Project, 57, 58, 59, 62, 64, 67, 69, 73, 127, 139–145, 148, 149, 152, 207
World Symposium on Choral Music, 105, 109, 142, 263
WSP. *See* World Soundscape Project
Wyre, John, 78

Yeats, W. B., 164, 291
Yugoslavia, 22, 24, 29, 30
York University, 98

Zoroaster , 56, 61, 266
Zoroastrianism. *See Zoroaster*

About the Author

L. Brett Scott is associate professor of ensembles and conducting at the College-Conservatory of Music, University of Cincinnati. A contributing writer to the Grove Dictionary of American Music, second edition, he has served as editor of the *Research Memorandum Series* and associate editor of *The Choral Scholar*. He has published extensively and lectured in his home country of Canada, in the United States, and in Europe on contemporary Canadian music and musicians. He is currently president of the National Collegiate Choral Organization.

R. Murray Schafer: A Creative Life is the outgrowth of the author's long-lasting friendship with Raymond Murray Schafer and his wife Eleanor.

Brett lives in Cincinnati, Ohio, with his wife, Krista, and four children, Aedhan, Colum, Kenna, and Serrin.

www.ingramcontent.com/pod-product-compliance
Lightning Source LLC
Chambersburg PA
CBHW022008300426
44117CB00005B/77